DETECTIVE I[

The Real Story of Frank Geyer

JD Crighton

RW Publishing House
Murrieta, California
www.rwpublishinghouse.com

Ninety-five (95) historical photos and illustrations

PUBLISHER'S CATALOGING-IN-PUBLICATION DATA:

Names: Crighton, JD, author.
Title: Detective in the White City : the real story of Frank Geyer /
    JD Crighton.
Description: Murrieta, CA : RW Publishing House, 2017. |
    Includes bibliographical references and index.
Identifiers: LCCN 2017961027 | ISBN 978-1-946100-02-3 (pbk.) |
    ISBN 978-1-946100-05-4 (large print pbk.) | ISBN
    978-1-946100-04-7 (hardcover) | ISBN 978-1-946100-03-0
    (ebook)
Subjects: LCSH: Geyer, Frank P. | Mudgett, Herman W.,
    1861-1896. | Detectives--United States--Biography. | Serial
    murderers--Illinois--Chicago. | Chicago (Ill.)--History--1875- |
    BISAC: TRUE CRIME / Murder / Serial Killers. | HISTORY /
    United States / State & Local / Midwest (IA, IL, IN, KS, MI,
    MN, MO, ND, NE, OH, SD, WI) | HISTORY / United States /
    19th Century.
Classification: LCC HV6248.M8 C75 2017 (print) | LCC
    HV6248.M8 (ebook) | DDC 364.152/32--dc23.

In memory of

Mrs. Mary Elizabeth Geyer and
Edna Camilla (Geyer) Strohm

The wife and daughter that lived

Contents

List of Illustrations   *xi*

Prologue: Profound Untruth   1

PART I - HOMETOWN

    Chapter 1 - Franklin Pierce   9

    Chapter 2 - American Civil War   16

    Chapter 3 - Centennial Guard   28

    Chapter 4 - Femur and Horses   33

PART II - BLOODY BAD

    Chapter 5 - Bullitt   41

    Chapter 6 - Bizarre Story of a Cat   48

    Chapter 7 - A Mighty Gruesome Package   53

    Chapter 8 - Modern Borgia   75

    Chapter 9 - White Chapel Row   90

    Chapter 10 - Send Flowers to My Funeral   98

    Chapter 11 - Secret Search   107

    Chapter 12 - Etched in Time   118

    Chapter 13 - Where Are You?   124

PART III - DEVIL IN DISGUISE

    Chapter 14 - Two Enemies   137

    Chapter 15 - Suspicions Intensify   139

    Chapter 16 - Sweet Innocence   143

    Chapter 17 - Little Howard   152

    Chapter 18 - Just Deserts   166

    Chapter 19 - The Devil in Him   205

PART IV -A PLOT, A RIOT, AND LA GRIPPE

    Chapter 20 - He Must Die   210

    Chapter 21 - Regret to Inform You   233

    Chapter 22 - Police Scandal   239

    Chapter 23 - La Grippe   247

SUPPLEMENTAL PHOTOS   255

APPENDIX A: ADDITIONAL GEYER QUOTES 287

Acknowledgements 290

Bibliography 293

Notes 308

Index 377

List of Illustrations

(Illustration sources are listed with each individual image)

Fig. 1. Franklin P. Geyer and Mary Elizabeth Marriage   5

Fig. 2. 1900 United States Census, Geyer Family   5

Fig. 3. Geyer Vacation Home, 110 E. Palm, Wildwood   6

Fig. 4. Portrait of Frank P. Geyer   8

Fig. 5. Ancestry Chart, Franklin Pierce Geyer   13

Fig. 6. Map of Geyer's Neighborhood, 1647 Cadwallader   13

Fig. 7. Samuel L. Clemens (Mark Twain), 15 yrs old   14

Fig. 8. President Pierce's Wife, Jane, and Son, "Benny"   15

Fig. 9. Ruins of the Bank of Chambersburg, 1864   18

Fig. 10. Mower US General Hospital   21

Fig. 11. Volunteer Refreshment Saloon and Hospital   22

Fig. 12. Sergeant Boston Corbett   25

Fig. 13. John Wilkes Booth Deringer   26

Fig. 14. President Lincoln's Hearse in Philadelphia, 1865   26

Fig. 15. Philadelphia Police Officers, *circa* 1876   31

Fig. 16. Liberty Torch at the Centennial Exposition, 1876   32

Fig. 17. Men's Ward of Episcopal Hospital, Philadelphia   36

Fig. 18. Buck's Extension Traction Splint   37

Fig. 19. Annie McCracken Rogue's Gallery Photo   38

Fig. 20. Ellen Callahan Rogue's Gallery Photo   39

Fig. 21. Chief of Detectives Francis R. Kelly   43

Fig. 22. Chief of Police General James Stewart, Jr., 1887   44

Fig. 23. Philadelphia City Hall, 1899   45

Fig. 24. City Hall 5th Floor Detective's Offices, 1890   46

Fig. 25. Dr. Mary "Alice" Bennett, Norristown Hospital   52

Fig. 26. Hannah Mary Tabbs Rogue's Galley Photo, 1887   67

Fig. 27. George H. Wilson Rogue's Gallery Photo, 1887   68

Fig. 28. Philadelphia Detective Bureau Police Badge   74

Fig. 29. Mrs. Sarah Jane Whiteling, 1889   86

Fig. 30. Murdered Whiteling Family   87

Fig. 31. Philadelphia List of Executions, Mrs. Whiteling   88

Fig. 32. Rough on Rats Advertisement   88

Fig. 33. Annie Klaus and Otto Kayser   106

Fig. 34. Gideon Marsh, Ex-President Keystone Bank   114

Fig. 35. Postmaster General John Wanamaker 115
Fig. 36. "Honest" John Bardsley, Philadelphia Treasurer 116
Fig. 37. Rio de Janeiro, *circa* 1909 117
Fig. 38. Captain Joseph Schooley, 1892 122
Fig. 39. Captain Joseph Schooley, Mt Moriah Cemetery 123
Fig. 40. James "Jimmy" C. Logue 131
Fig. 41. Alphonse F. Cutaiar, Jr 132
Fig. 42. Alphonse F. Cutaiar, Jr., looks like H. H. Holmes 133
Fig. 43. Murder Victim Johanna Logue 134
Fig. 44. District Attorney George Scott Graham 135
Fig. 45. Herman Webster Mudgett *alias* H. H. Holmes 142
Fig. 46. Benjamin Pitezel, Alice, Nellie, and Howard 164
Fig. 47. Little Howard Pitezel's Teeth Found in Ashes 165
Fig. 48. Holmes Trial Officials: District Attorney 202
      Graham, Judge Arnold, Defense Attorney Rotan,
      and Defense Attorney Shoemaker
Fig. 49. Holmes' trial officials: Coroner Ashbridge and 203
      Coroner's Physician Mattern
Fig. 50. Kymographion Used on H. H. Holmes 208
Fig. 51. Advertisements for Detective Geyer's Book 213
Fig. 52. Frank P. Geyer's Patent, No. 556,141, 1896 214
Fig. 53. Charles O. Kaiser, Emma P. Kaiser, James A. 231
      Clemmer and Lizzie DeKalb
Fig. 54. Lit Brother's Store, Philadelphia 238
Fig. 55. Frank P. Geyer Detective Agency Business Card 244
Fig. 56. Frank P. Geyer's Patent No. 872,619, 1907 245
Fig. 57. Orrie C. Strohm's Patent No. 1,206,939, 1916 246
Fig. 58. Flu Victim Escorted by Philadelphia Police 252
Fig. 59. Geyer's Cemetery Plot, Hillside Cemetery 253
Fig. 60. James R. Riggins at Geyer's Cemetery Plot 253
Fig. 61. Frank Geyer, Mary, and Edna, *circa* 1887 255
Fig. 62. Frank Geyer, Mary, and Edna, *circa* 1896 256
Fig. 63. Edna Camilla Geyer, *circa* 1900 257
Fig. 64. News, Edna Geyer, John Welsh School, 1901 258
Fig. 65. John Welsh School 258
Fig. 66. Orrie Strohm with Father, John Strohm 259
Fig. 67. Baptism of Elizabeth Alice Strohm, 1909 259
Fig. 68. Baby Elizabeth Alice Strohm, 1909 260

Fig. 69. Geyer's Granddaughter, Elizabeth Alice Strohm   261
Fig. 70. Portrait of Frank P. Geyer, *circa* 1913   262
Fig. 71. Portrait of Mary E. Geyer, *circa* 1913   263
Fig. 72. Detective Geyer in Knights Templar Parade   264
Fig. 73. Frank and Mary Geyer, Edna, Orrie, and Geyer's   265
    granddaughters Elizabeth and Dorothy
Fig. 74. Geyer Grandchildren Elizabeth, Frank, Dorothy   266
Fig. 75. Portrait of Edna Camilla (Geyer) Strohm   267
Fig. 76. Geyer's family, Strohm's and Elliott's,   268
    Thanksgiving 1941
Fig. 77. Geyer's family, Elliott's and Riggins, 2015   269
Fig. 78. Justice of the Peace William Henry Buck   270
Fig. 79. Rogues' Gallery of Criminals, 1887   271
Fig. 80. The Bertillon System   272
Fig. 81. Miss Leona Bland, Actress, Orpheum Theatre   273
Fig. 82. Charles Wilfred Mowbray, Anarchist Arrest   275
Fig. 83. Philadelphia Police Patrol Wagon *circa* 1887   276
Fig. 84. Philadelphia Police in Front of Marsh's Saloon   277
Fig. 85. Philadelphia Police Guarding Car Barns   278
Fig. 86. Philadelphia Police Officers with Police Wagon   278
Fig. 87. Smith & Wesson 1896 Hand Ejector Revolver   279
Fig. 88. Police March Outside Baldwin Locomotive Wks   280
Fig. 89. Police Outside Shibe Park, 1914 World Series   280
Fig. 90. Police Inside Shibe Park, 1914 World Series   281
Fig. 91. Philadelphia Police on Motorcycle with Sidecar   282
Fig. 92. Police Harbor Patrol, *WMS Stokley*   283
Fig. 93. Philadelphia Police, 7th District Station, 1894   284
Fig. 94. Philadelphia Police, 40th District Station, 1913   285
Fig. 95. Philadelphia Police, Fire, 18th District c1912   286

The page divider image used throughout the book is a common bank robber's tool from 1887 called a "sectional jimmy"

Sectional Jimmy Source:
Sprogle, Howard O. *The Philadelphia Police, Past and Present.* Philadelphia, PA: publisher unknown, 1887, p. 283.

Prologue: Profound Untruth

I want you to listen to these statements. They are marvelous productions in the line of fiction; they are wonderful statements, with scarcely an element of truth in them.

-District Attorney George S. Graham,
Commonwealth v. Mudgett, *alias* Holmes[1]

SOMEWHERE IN THE MIDST of a great story was a profound untruth so dark, that if true, would have wiped the direct line of Detective Frank Geyer's future generations of family off the face of the earth. A fabrication told and retold to readers young and old.

No, Detective Geyer did not experience "enormous personal tragedy" in March 1895, before the world knew he investigated H. H. Holmes, the killer known in the twenty-first century as the 'Devil in the White City.' No, a fire did not "consume Geyer's home, killing his beloved wife, Martha, and only child . . . Esther," as an author wrote, and because no loss happened, Geyer was not "infused with even greater zeal for the search." These untruths did not take place. Even so, the story of the deaths perpetuated in the United States, internationally, and online, to the disappointment of Geyer's descendants.[2]

How could nonfiction authors get it so wrong? Was the inaccuracy written to stir up emotions and suck readers deeper into a great story, or an honest, albeit, catastrophic mistake? For, the story of the deaths were not just a few erroneous facts, it was the death of two family members.

Her name was Mary not Martha, and the Irish beauty never died in a house fire. Frank met his beautiful bride while she waited tables at a tavern across from where his longtime police district would soon move to at the corner of Fourth and York. Police frequented taverns to nab criminals while on duty and to unwind after a long, stressful day at work. At the time, Philadelphia had an abundance of taverns and saloons, many doubling as homes with a simple sign placed above the door that read "[last name of resident] Tavern." People could walk next door, or a few blocks to a tavern managed by a neighbor. With 5,444 of them in Philadelphia in 1877, there was practically one on every corner.[3]

Geyer's family wasn't thrilled with the relationship, not only because Mary was a barmaid, but because, like many Irish at the time, her parents had immigrated to the United States in poverty. Most people in Ireland had depended on potatoes for food and when crops failed three years in a row, over 750,000 Irish starved to death. Two million survivors immigrated to the United States. Geyer's German ancestors also immigrated, but most had enough money to settle comfortably. Americans were hostile towards Irish at the time, primarily for religious differences and because they worked for less than people in low-paying jobs. To drive home their point, signs appeared in windows and on doors that read, "No Irish Need Apply"[4]

Geyer's ancestors were prominent, well-educated people traced to the Founding Fathers of America. His ancestors could also be traced to a General of the Revolutionary War, as a reporter wrote in 1895. Geyer, opposed to making more than a few statements during interviews, stood next to Mr. Gary from Fidelity Mutual Life Association, while he told the reporter Geyer was a descendant of a general.[5]

"Mr. Gary pays him the high compliment to say that he would be fully the equal, if not the superior, of his ancestor in case he were called upon for the same service." The reporter wrote that Mr. Gary did most of the talking, while Geyer corrected him as needed to get the facts straight. "Most of the story as given . . . was obtained from Mr. Gary, although occasionally Mr. Geyer would make a remark in the way of correction as to detail," the *Indianapolis Journal* reported.[6]

In contrast to Geyer's family, Mary was penniless, except for the small amount she earned at the tavern.

Although Mary had a fine head for business, she was illiterate, and like many women in the mid-nineteenth century, she could neither read nor write.[7]

But all those things were meaningless to Geyer—hollow and insignificant. For how prominent or wealthy you are, or even how well you read or write, doesn't define you as a person.

Geyer knew if he persisted, his family would come to their senses, and they did. Charmed and fascinated with the Hartford, Connecticut Irish beauty, thirty-one-year-old Geyer proposed, and Reverend W. S. Pugh married the couple on a chilly, partly cloudy Monday, March 9, 1885.[8]

Frank and his real wife, Mary, lived a happy and fulfilling life together, rich with wonderful family memories, traditions, and celebrations. On a wintery-white day in December 1886, the devoted couple had a beautiful part-Irish, part-German baby girl named Edna, not Esther, and she never died in a house fire either. No such thing ever happened. Mr. and Mrs. Geyer celebrated all of Edna Camilla's milestones—first words, first steps, teenage years, graduation, marriage, and children—Frank and Mary's grandchildren.[9]

Indeed, Frank and Mary celebrated thirty-three wedding anniversaries and enjoyed all the usual family traditions. They were a family long endeared to law enforcement, except for a few, brief frustrations over the years. Good at his job, Geyer ranked among the best of the best. He worked hard and earned titles like World Famous Detective, Murder Detective, Murder Geyer, and the silly, Electric Detective.

Mary stood by him during city and department turmoil that happened off and on, especially after elections. She sympathized with well-publicized disciplines—a couple aimed at Geyer—and large-scale terminations and arrests of fellow officers, that, for good reason, bypassed her husband. And Mary mourned right alongside Geyer at heart-wrenching officer suicides and deaths, some while on duty. The law enforcement family life was rough but also rewarding.

Mary was Geyer's biggest supporter when people all around the world commended him for famous cases he worked on, such as the Modern Borgia poisoning committed by Sarah Jane Whiteling; the gruesome torso murder perpetrated by Hannah Mary Tabbs and George Wilson; and the famous cross-country, international, Pitezel murders by the 'Devil in the White City' killer.

Geyer's faithful wife cheered when he received frequent awards and commendations. She encouraged him on new inventions such as the shutter and door fastener or the pocketbook safety lock. And Mary was beyond proud when he authored a book about the H. H. Holmes and Pitezel investigation and it became an instant bestseller. And she couldn't be prouder when he opened his own detective agency with recommendations from top officials in the city and state.

Detective Geyer appreciated Mary's many blessings and support for his service-oriented groups and committees too, especially ones that promoted family, religious beliefs, integrity, honesty, and courage. All traits championed by Freemason organizations he took part in like his father before him, and our founding father, Benjamin Franklin, and fourteen United States presidents. Author Mark Twain, who lived and worked near Geyer, was also a Mason, as were numerous Philadelphia mayors and officials, like District Attorney George S. Graham, who prosecuted the H. H. Holmes case and later became a congressman.[10]

Family, church, community, and law enforcement, altogether, made Detective Geyer into the man he had become. A man who, above all, enjoyed time with his family. He looked forward to vacations in the beautiful resort areas of Wildwood and Cape May on the New Jersey coast. Geyer liked it enough to build the family a vacation home in Wildwood—a home Mary moved to a few years after his death and rented to boarders for income.[11]

No one knows for sure what would motivate authors to write that Geyer's family died, but one thing we know is true, Detective Geyer was an honorable man devoted to his family—Mary not Martha, Edna not Esther.

Who was the famous detective who outsmarted criminals from the Gilded Age and never lost his family in a fire?

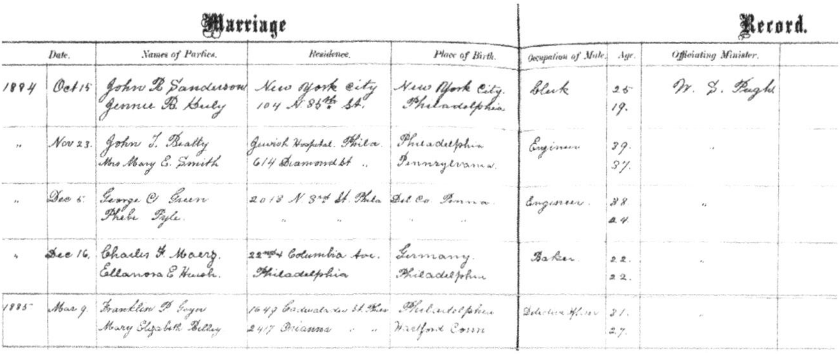

Marriage Record.

	Date.	Names of Parties.	Residence.	Place of Birth.	Occupation of Male.	Age.	Officiating Minister.
1884	Oct 15	John R. Sanderson Jennie B. Guly	New York city 104 N. 35th St.	New York City. Philadelphia	Clerk	25 19.	W. S. Pugh
"	Nov 23.	John T. Beatty Mrs Mary E. Smith	Jewish Hospital. Phila. 614 Diamond St "	Philadelphia Pennsylvania	Engineer	39. 37.	"
"	Dec 6	George C. Green Phebe Pyle	2018 N 3rd St. Phila " "	Del. Co. Penna. " "	Engineer.	38 24	"
"	Dec 16.	Charles F. Maerz. Ellanora E. Hesch.	22nd & Columbia Ave. Philadelphia	Germany. Philadelphia	Baker	22. 22.	"
1885	Mar 9.	Franklin P. Geyer Mary Elizabeth Rilley	1649 Cadwalader St. Phila 2417 Brianna " "	Philadelphia Hartford Conn	Detective Officer	31. 27.	"

Fig. 1. Franklin P. Geyer married Mary Elizabeth Rilley (sometimes spelled Riley and O'Riley) on March 9, 1885. Geyer, thirty-one, and was listed as a detective officer. Mary was twenty-seven. Image source: Pennsylvania Marriage Record, Franklin P. Geyer & Mary Elizabeth Rilley.

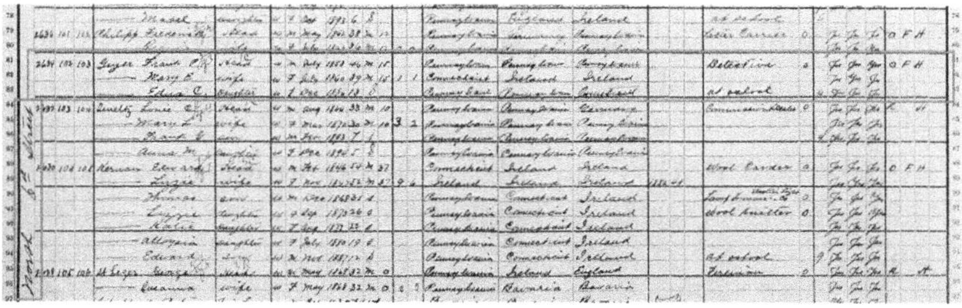

Fig. 2. 1900 United States Census. Frank P. Geyer, Detective with his wife Mary E. Geyer and Edna C. Geyer, living at 2634 North 6th Street, Philadelphia. Image source: United States, Twelfth Census, Schedule No. 1 - Population, Supervisor's District No. 1st PA, Enumeration District No. 400, Sheet No. 56, 19th Ward, Philadelphia, PA, June 6, 1900, Line No. 81-83.

Fig. 3. Frank Geyer built this vacation home in New Jersey at 110 East Palm, Wildwood Crest. After Detective Geyer's death, Mary moved to the New Jersey home and managed a boarding house there. The photo was taken in 1924. Image source: Courtesy of Mr. and Mrs. David Elliott and family, descendants of Detective Frank P. Geyer.

PART I

Hometown

Fig. 4. Detective Frank P. Geyer. Image source: Frank P. Geyer. *The Holmes-Pitezel case.* Philadelphia, PA: Publishers' Union, 1896.

CHAPTER 1

Franklin Pierce

The rights which belong to us as a nation are not alone to be regarded, but those which pertain to every citizen in his individual capacity, at home and abroad, must be sacredly maintained.

-President Franklin Pierce inaugural address[12]

Philadelphia, PA, 1853

A LARGE CROWD CHEERED on the banks of the Delaware River, waiving banners and flags. In a show of American pride, star-striped red, white, and blues covered most of the wharf and boats. Officers saluted and presented ceremonial arms, solemnly firing successive shots into the air.

President Franklin Pierce waived to Philadelphians from the *John L. Stevens* that steamed into the Navy Yard and docked. A procession of government officials escorted the president through Philadelphia streets to Independence Hall. Eager citizens followed on horseback and carriages.

It was more than a show of support for the new president, it was a show of immense compassion, for two months before his inauguration, Franklin Pierce and his wife, Jane, suffered an unthinkable tragedy while returning from the funeral of Jane's uncle January 6, 1853.

The train axle suddenly broke on their car, and it rolled down a steep embankment, cracking and jerking until it came to a rest on a rocky ledge. Pierce held his wife, and son, Benny, as the car rolled down the bank but Benny fell out and slipped into a crack where the floor joined the side of the car. In an instant, the opening closed and crushed his head. Eleven-year-old Benny died a horrific and unforgettable death witnessed by his distraught parents.[13]

Reverend Fuller from New York described the scene:

"I was looking out at the window, when we felt a severe shock, and the car was dragged for a few seconds, the axle of the front wheel being broken . . . In another second, the coupling which joined our car with the other, broke, and our car was whirled violently round, so as to reverse the ends and we were swung down the rocky ledge . . . I shall never forget the breathless horror which came over us during the fall. There was not a shriek nor an exclamation, till the progress of the car, after having turned over twice on the rocks, was arrested and with a violent concussion, having parted in the middle, and being broken into many thousand fragments.

Rev. Fuller continued:

There was another mother, whose agony passes beyond any description[.] She could shed no tears, but, overwhelmed with grief, uttered such affecting words as I never can forget.—It was Mrs. Pierce, the lady of the president-elect; and near her in that ruin of shivered wood and iron, lay a more terrible ruin, her only son, one minute before so beautiful, so full of life and hope.[14]

Little Benjamin Pierce was the only fatality. President Pierce's inauguration took place a few months after Benny's death, but his wife did not attend. No inaugural ball was held either, for the presidential family was in mourning.

President Pierce wholeheartedly thanked the Philadelphians:

"Mr. Mayor, and citizens of Philadelphia—It grieves me that I am physically so unable to respond to this most hearty and touching welcome. Sir, my heart is full of gratitude to you, and full of gratitude to all this [sic] people, who have placed you in the position which you occupy. I did think that I had tried in my day to do some little for the cause of my country; but such a day as this makes a man's heart overrun with gratitude to a people like the inhabitants of the city of Philadelphia. I have been much surprised—awy, sir, filled the profoundest awe—at the manner in which you have received me."[15]

Excitement from the presidents' visit lingered in the air two weeks later when a beautiful mother gave birth to a nineteenth century, world's-famous detective in the making. Camilla Buck, the daughter of a prominent blacksmith and lumber mill family, and Reuben Geyer, a successful and popular carpenter, named their newborn son in honor of the president of the United States. Baby Franklin Pierce Geyer was born on a cloudy Thursday, July 28, 1853, a time when the city bustled with just under a half a million people of all nationalities and religious backgrounds.[16]

Although baby Frank was too little to know it, another soon-to-be world's famous celebrity worked two miles[17] from the Geyer family home just after Frank's birth—eighteen-year-old Samuel L. Clemens (Mark Twain), a substitute typesetter who worked the night shift from seven o'clock in the evening until three o'clock in the morning at *Pennsylvania Inquirer* (later renamed *Philadelphia Inquirer*). At first Mark Twain described Philadelphia as a fantastic place to live when he wrote his brother, Orian:

"Unlike New York, I like this Phila amazingly, and the people in it."

But a month later, a disillusioned Twain wrote:

"I always thought eastern people were patterns of uprightness, but I never saw so many whiskey-swilling, God-despising heathens as I find in this part of the country. I believe that I am the only person in the Inquirer office [who] does not drink."[18]

Somewhat downtrodden about working the night shift, Twain wrote about it to his brother and also complained about the large number of foreigner's in America:

"The printers, as well as other people are endeavoring to raise money to erect a monument to [Benjamin] Franklin, but there are so many abominable foreigners here (and among printers, too,) who hate everything American, that I am very certain as much money for such a purpose could be raised in St Louis, as in Philadelphia. I was in Franklin's old office this morning... and there were at least one foreighner [sic] for every American at work there."[19]

After Mark Twain left Philadelphia for New York in 1854, little Frank and his older sister Anna Elizabeth were joined by two more siblings, William Henry and Katharina (Kate) Geyer. The family of six moved into a small, but cozy home on Cadwallader Street owned by Frank's uncle, Daniel Buck, a few blocks from Daniel Buck and Brothers lumber yard off Oxford. The Cadwallader neighborhood was west of the Delaware River, where swimming contests were held in the summer and Philadelphians skated across the frozen river to New Jersey in winter.

Frank's uncle transferred the Cadwallader property to the Geyer's in 1874, two years before Frank began his law enforcement career at the City of Philadelphia.[20]

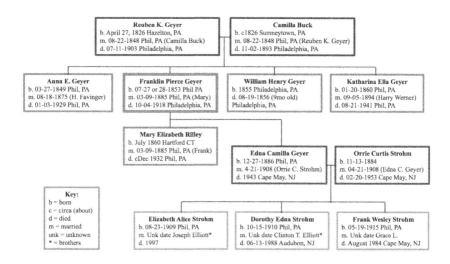

Fig. 5. Ancestry of Franklin Pierce Geyer. Image source: Illustrated by author.[21]

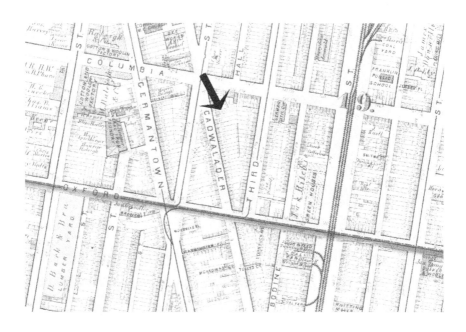

Fig. 6. Frank Geyer's childhood home at 1647 Cadwallader Street (spelled here as Cadwalader), located in Ward 19. Image source: Griffith Morgan Hopkins, Jr. *City Atlas of Philadelphia by Wards.* Philadelphia: G.M. Hopkins, 1875-1876.

Fig. 7. Fifteen-year-old Samuel L. Clemens (Mark Twain),
printer's apprentice, 1850. This is one of the earliest known
images of Mark Twain who is shown here in a printer's cap
and holding a composing stick with 'SAM' spelled in the type.
Image source: Courtesy of the Mark Twain Project, The
Bancroft Library, University of California, Berkeley, Image ID
PH 00001, November 29, 1850.

Fig. 8. President Franklin Pierce's wife, Jane, and son, Benjamin "Benny" Pierce, *circa* 1844 to 1850. Image source: Author of image is unknown; image also appears on the White House Historical Association website at www.whitehousehistory.org.

CHAPTER 2

American Civil War

Fremont Journal
EXTRA.
Saturday Morning, April 13, 1861.
THE WAR COMMENCED!

April 1861 to July 1865

WHILE EIGHT-YEAR-OLD Geyer and his family slept in the pre-dawn hours of April 12, 1861, America's deadliest war began at Fort Sumter in Charleston Bay, some 670 miles south of Geyer's home.

Frictions came to an uncertain head for unions and confederates after President Lincoln's administration refused to recognize the seven southern states that broke away from the union. Though President Lincoln planned to send provisions two days before the attack, tensions bowled over at union-held Fort Sumter causing the bombardment before relief supplies arrived. A series of heated telegraphic correspondence had occurred between Confederate States Secretary of War LeRoy P. Walker, and Brigadier General P. G. T. Beauregard that showed hostility leading up to the attack. Beauregard had demanded the union surrender Fort Sumter and telegrammed the secretary of war to describe the response he received from Major Anderson, who holed up at the fort:

Charleston, April 11th 1861.

To, L. P. Walker, Secretary of War: —Maj. Anderson replies, "I have the honor to acknowledge receipt of your communication

demanding the evacuation of this Fort, and say in reply thereto, it is a demand which I regret that my sense of honor and my obligations to my Government prevent my compliance." He adds, "probably I will await the first shot and if you do not batter us to pieces we will be starved out in a few days."
Signed G. T. Beauregard.[22]

In response, Secretary Walker discouraged bombardment of Fort Sumter and told Beauregard to avoid bloodshed. Offering one more chance for surrender, Walker advised:

"If Maj. Anderson will state the time at which, as indicated by him, he will evacuate and agree that in the meantime he will not use his guns against us unless ours should be employed against Fort Sumter," he continued, "If this, or its equivalent, be refused, reduce the Fort as your judgment decides to be the most practicable."[23]

Fort Sumter's Major Anderson, Brigadier General Beauregard's instructor at West Point, refused to evacuate and Beauregard and his men attacked the fort.

Philadelphians, unsure how the war would impact them, reluctantly prepared themselves to fight.[24]

Thousands of union soldiers dressed in wool uniforms and forage caps with bayonets in scabbards were ready to fight the confederate's, but thirty-five-year-old Reuben Geyer did not yet serve. Men with wives and small children to care for, took advantage of draft brokers and offered $1,000 for substitutes in place of those who received draft notices. Desperate women paid for substitutes in place of husbands and children and congregations paid substitutes for clergymen.[25]

Everything changed two days after Frank Geyer's eleventh birthday, when confederates raided the town of Chambersburg in Pennsylvania, July 30, 1864. General Couch, and about one hundred union soldiers, protected Cumberland Valley with only two small cannons when Brigadier General John McCausland and his men attacked Chambersburg in retaliation for union soldiers burning down six or eight houses in Virginia. Knowing townsfolk wouldn't be able to pay it, McCausland demanded a ransom of $100,000 in gold or $500,000 in northern currency. But, as he suspected, the townsfolk could not afford the ransom and McCausland ordered confederates to burn down the town, leaving more than seventeen hundred people homeless. *The Press* reported upwards of 250 houses burned in addition to public buildings, stores, and hotels. The town was completely devastated.[26]

Fig. 9. Ruins of the Bank of Chambersburg after the burning on July 30, 1864. Image source: Courtesy of Library of Congress.

President Lincoln issued a call upon Pennsylvania for 12,000 volunteers to serve one hundred days after the Chambersburg burning. Philadelphia, slow to respond, received a scathing letter of forceful admonishment from the governor of Pennsylvania July 10, 1864:

> "You are not responding freely . . . The authorities of the United States at Washington are so impressed with the necessity of immediate effort, that they have this morning, by telegraph, authorized men to be mustered in by companies, which they had yesterday peremptorily refused."[27]

Three months after the admonishment, at thirty-nine-years-old, Geyer's dad left the family to fight in the Civil War with a promise of $1,131 for a year's service. Reuben Geyer mustered in at the rank of private to Independent Battery "H" Light Artillery on October 13, 1864, assigned to provost guard duty under General John P. Slough's command in Alexandria.[28]

While Frank's dad fought in the war, Philadelphia bustled with soldiers at nearby camps and hospitals. Those who remained in the city, volunteered to help at area hospitals and refreshment centers. Geyer's mom did her best to fill in as both mother and father and keep family life as normal as possible. Geyer's younger brother, William, died of purpura hemorrhagica as a toddler nine years earlier, which meant Geyer was the only man of the house, albeit a young man. His older sister, Anna, sixteen, helped mom with cooking and household duties. Frank's younger sister, Kate, was only six.[29]

Frank and other boys his age watched with wonder and excitement as squads drilled in vacant lots throughout the city. They fantasized about joining the Army to show support for the cause. If the government let high-schoolers fight alongside fathers, uncles and brothers, why not let fifth and sixth graders join the Army too? The boys often detoured to recruiting stations and begged mustering officers for an exception to allow them to serve, only to be rejected—tears streaming down their faces. Frustrated, the boys watched new soldiers board military trains and ships that sailed from the nearby Navy shipyard. Geyer's mother, was certainly thankful he was not yet in high school. Local officials encouraged boys to join by making special concessions for those in the highest grades who enlisted, allowing them to graduate with their class in absentee.[30]

Philadelphia filled with war activities. Mower General Hospital, and Satterlee General Hospital, the largest Union hospital in the Civil War, overflowed with thousands of injured soldiers. Constant news reports of the war no doubt worried the Geyer family, hoping beyond hope for Reuben's safety. They were very much aware of the number of soldiers injured because the city held a fundraiser before Reuben went to war. Generous residents united with President Lincoln to attend the United States Sanitary Commission's Great Central Fair, held for two weeks in Philadelphia's Logan Square. They raised a whopping $1,046,859 for bandages and medical supplies for wounded soldiers[31].

Fair organizers auctioned rare collector items to raise additional funds too. Citizens snagged autographs from the Duke of Cambridge, Royal Family of England, and other high-profile people. Someone even bought a piece of a shirt from General Barksdale, a rebel killed at Gettysburg.[32]

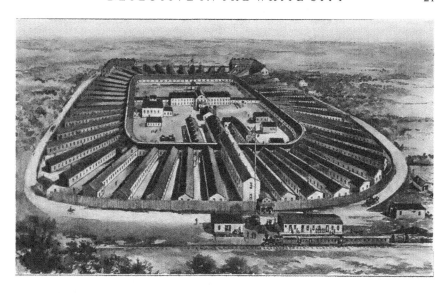

Fig. 10. Mower US General Hospital at Chestnut Hill housed injured soldiers. The hospital opened January 17, 1863 with a 2,820 bed capacity. Image source: Frank Taylor. *Philadelphia in the Civil War 1861-1865*. Philadelphia, PA: Published by the City, 1913.

H. C. Phillips, Photographer.

Fig. 11. Union Volunteer Refreshment Saloon (middle) and Union
Volunteer Hospital (left), Washington Street, Philadelphia, PA.
Image source: Courtesy of Library of Congress.

A few days shy of three months as a soldier, Frank's dad
transferred to the 204th Regiment, Battery C, 5th Heavy Artillery.
The 204th fought in the Bull Run battlefield in spring of 1865,
burying nearly two thousand men.[33] Prior to mustering out,
Reuben transferred again, this time to the 147th Regiment,
Company E.[34]

At home, the Geyer family celebrated with all of Philadelphia,
when on April 3, news of the capture of Richmond, Virginia,
brought about blowing of steam whistles, ringing on bells, and
striking the gong in front of Independence Hall. Jubilant
processions paraded the streets of Philadelphia. All public schools
closed and Frank and his friends marched with the other
schoolchildren through their neighborhoods singing songs and

waving flags. A few days later, General Robert E. Lee surrendered the last confederate army to General Ulysses S. Grant at the Appomattox in Virginia. It was Palm Sunday and the war was unofficially over.[35]

Rejoice! Fathers, husbands, uncles, and sons were coming home.

News of the surrender of Lee's Army brought about another celebration with whistles and bell ringing and the firing of the little historic cannon, one blast for each of the thirty-six states. Celebrations continued throughout the week. Frank Geyer and other school children, with clothes dripping wet from the rain, marched on Chestnut Street Monday morning. At noon, the Union League Battery fired two hundred rounds from Broad and Market Streets.[36]

But celebration turned to grief.

President Lincoln was shot at Ford's Theatre on Good Friday while watching *Our American Cousin.* John Frederick Parker, a Washington cop who guarded Lincoln's private box left his post to watch the show from the front gallery. During intermission, he went to the Star Saloon with Lincoln's footman and coachman. "It was the custom for the guard who accompanied the president to the theatre to remain in the little passageway outside the box," Frederick Hatch later said. Hatch was also one of President Lincoln's guards.[37]

John Wilkes Booth, who once acted and lived in Philadelphia, entered the box, shot President Lincoln in the back of the head, then stabbed Lincoln's guest, Major Henry Rathbone, in the arm with a knife. Booth vaulted over the balcony onto the stage, some twelve feet below, fracturing the fibula on his left leg upon his landing, then stumbled out through the back of the theatre.[38]

President Lincoln, carried to the house across the street from the theatre for treatment, died at seven twenty-two the next morning, April 15, 1865. Twelve days later, soldiers trapped Booth at Garrett's barn near Port Royal, Virginia. Soldiers demanded Booth and his partner, David Herald, surrender. Herald surrendered but Booth refused. Soldiers gave him a deadline to come out or they would set the barn on fire, which they did. Smoke billowed, but before Booth came out, Sergeant Thomas

"Boston" Corbett fired an unexpected shot from his pistol and Booth collapsed on the floor. Soldiers rushed in, grabbed a hold of his jacket and drug him out. Booth, with curly hair crumpled around his eyes and face, lay limp and defeated. The fatal shot rang out at fifteen minutes past three in the morning, April 26. Booth lingered in agony for more than two hours and died as the morning sun lit up the awful scene. His last words, "Tell my mother I died for my country, and I did what I thought was best." Booth asked officers to raise his hands, which they did. As they laid them down, he said, "Useless, useless!"[39]

In Philadelphia, Geyer, and other Philadelphians crowded into Old Town, but this time it was in shock and sadness, not celebration. In a somber show of mourning, 100,000 Philadelphians draped their homes with black cloths.[40]

After a White House funeral in the East Room, staff placed President Lincoln's body in a funeral car for a procession down Pennsylvania Avenue. American's viewed his remains in a rotunda at the eastern entrance of the Capitol. Carefully placed on a funeral train, Lincoln went on a 1,500 mile journey, stopping at Baltimore, Harrisburg, Philadelphia, and New York City. The train also stopped in Albany, Buffalo, Cleveland, Columbus, Indianapolis, and Chicago, and then Lincoln went to his final resting place in Springfield, Illinois.[41]

Philadelphia officials escorted President Lincoln's remains in a formal procession through the city to Independence Hall. He lay in state in the very room where eighty-five years ago the history of our nation began. In an uncanny twist, it was also where President Lincoln stood February 22, 1861, and while referring to liberty and freedom, he said, "But if this country cannot be saved without giving up that principle, I was about to say I would rather be assassinated on this spot than to surrender it." Four years and two months after he made those remarks, he ironically lay close to the old liberty bell.[42]

Thousands of soldiers, ink barely dry on discharge papers, begged in vain to start a new campaign of revenge. Citizens lined up, silent and solemn, and each viewed President Lincoln's peaceful body. America was in mourning.[43]

Fig. 12. Sergeant Boston Corbett, a member of the 16th New York
    Calvary, is shown in this photo taken circa 1860-70. Sgt.
    Corbett disobeyed direct orders and shot President Lincoln's
    assassin, John Wilkes Booth, while Booth was holed up in a
    barn. Afterwards, his lieutenant pronounced Corbett a most
    worthy soldier and offered him one of Booth's pistols as a
    memento, but Corbett declined. A short time later, a man
    offered Corbett one hundred dollars for his own pistol that he
    used to kill Booth, but he declined that also and said, "That is
    not mine—it belongs to the Government and I would not sell it
    for any price." After the war, Corbett wandered all over the
    country, peddling and doing odd jobs. He was appointed
    doorkeeper for the Kansas House of Representatives, but
    during the 1887 session, he caused a ruckus by drawing a
    couple revolvers and waving them around. Panicked House of
    Representatives staff climbed all over each other to get out of
    the building. After the incident, authorities placed Corbett in an
    asylum, but he later escaped, and official records listed him as

dead.[44] Image source: Courtesy of Library of Congress.

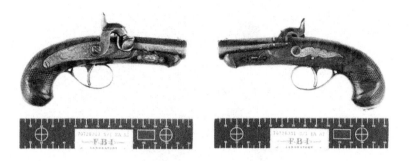

Fig. 13. John Wilkes Booth used this small .44-caliber pocket
pistol produced by Henry Deringer firearms factory in
Philadelphia. Notable features of the pistol included a black
walnut stock with checkering and scrollwork on the sideplates.
The Deringer was stamped on the lockplate and top of the
breech plug with the 'Deringer Philadela' trademark. Image
source: FBI.

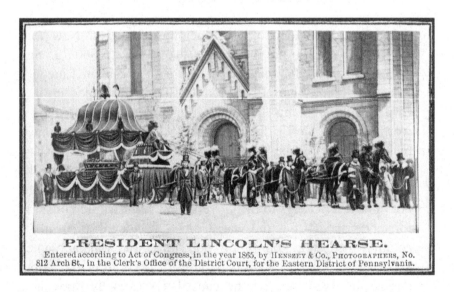

Fig. 14. President Lincoln's Hearse, 1865. Image source: United
States Government.

Three months after Lincoln's assassination, General Order No. 160 directed Bartlett's entire division to muster out at once. Reuben Geyer and his 147th Regiment comrades moved to the vicinity of Washington DC and mustered out July 15, 1865.

A few days later, about half past six o'clock in the evening, July 19, Reuben and the 147th marched up Broad Street to Walnut in Philadelphia. Nine fire companies returning from a fire response, stopped alongside the road, tipped their hats to the soldiers, and rang the bells of their hose carriages.

Reuben Geyer and fellow soldiers marched to Camp Cadwallader on Islington Lane, east of Ridge Road near Odd Fellows' Cemetery. The camp overflowed with soldier's most of the time and had a large group of barracks, cook house, mess hall, hospital, and officer's quarters, along with several other buildings. In the rainy season, soldiers complained the camp turned into a muddy mess. But it was summer, and after processing paperwork and collecting final salaries, Reuben and the 147th Regiment soldiers were once again civilians.[45]

Hallelujah! Reuben was home—just in time for Frank Geyer's twelfth birthday.[46]

CHAPTER 3

Centennial Guard

The majority of the men had been in the armies of the United States or the Confederacy during the War, but scarcely any of them had any knowledge of police duties . . . It must, however, be admitted that the manner in which the men performed their arduous duties and preserved order amongst the unprecedented crowds visiting the Exhibition reflects the highest credit upon the officers who directed this heterogeneous body of men, entirely new and unused to the difficult task they had to perform.

-Mr. Inspector Hagen, London
Metropolitan Police
Report to Her Majesty
Re: Centennial Guard[47]

May 1876 to 1877, Philadelphia

DRESSED IN A NEW uniform, wood baton on his belt, and badge pinned and prominently displayed, Frank Geyer prepared to police the World's Fair and its thirteen-thousand-plus exhibits. The International Centennial Exposition featured marvelous displays like the massive, two hundred ton Corliss Steam Engine, Alexander Graham Bell's telephone invention, and a ginormous bronze statue of an arm and hand holding the torch of liberty. A sight to behold and a historical celebration too, for it was in commemoration of the United States' 100th anniversary of the Declaration of Independence and Frank Geyer couldn't wait to be a part of it.[48]

Mayor Stokley appointed young Geyer, one month shy of his twenty-second birthday, to patrolman, acting on an ordinance authorizing the mayor to appoint five hundred men for the

Centennial Exposition. Geyer's first assignment for the department was to serve on the centennial guard, stood up specifically for the event. The city hired soldiers to supplement the guard and bring an average of eight hundred officers on duty each day. England, Germany, France, and other foreign countries provided their own special police forces besides the centennial guard.[49]

Geyer policed the vast number of exhibits, ensured visitors resisted the temptation to touch, deface, or worse, steal inventions, art, and other valuables. He kept the peace and reunited lost children with parents, and received, recorded, and attempted to return lost items. He and the guards were required to, "...act as telegraphic messengers to thousands who seemed to have lost their wits," one author wrote in 1877.[50]

It was a high-profile job and if he worked hard enough, the city might keep him after the exposition. Geyer set out to work the only way he knew how, give a one hundred percent effort to enforce all rules and regulations of the expo and city, to which he upheld with utmost professionalism. Until then, Geyer had mastered the carpenter trade and helped his dad run their popular family business. But he longed for something more, to make a difference in Philadelphia and in the world. It was an amazing opportunity and his family was proud of him.

Centennial guardsmen kept drunkenness to a minimum. With the exception of a few thefts—some from enterprising guards—not much was stolen. Officers carefully recorded and tracked lost items, which included enough traveling valises to supply a thousand carpet-baggers. Umbrellas, parasols, and hoop-skirts were abundant and pistols, shoes, jewelry, and garments too. Police found people's pocketbooks, front hair pieces, and the most surprising of all, a set of false teeth. As many as fifty-eight or more lost children, teens, and adults were taken charge of in a single day and all reunited with friends and loved ones except a traumatized one-year-old. Unable to find his parents, officers kept the toddler overnight and located the anxious mother the next morning.[51]

Geyer and fellow officers lived at five single-story centennial police stations and one two-story police station at the southwestern extremity of the grounds that had a courtroom and magistrate's office for prisoner hearings.[52]

All guards, including Geyer, remained on site at the centennial grounds but received a pass to visit family and friends once every three days. No officers traveled outside the city, except with special permission to rest and relax at Niagara Falls after the end of the hot summer. He and the centennial guards earned a flat, two dollars per day, with one week's pay retained as a forfeiture in case of dismissal for misbehavior. Though the men reported the food was not fit for hogs, their bosses withheld $3.50 from their pay each week for food and lodging.[53]

Sleeping in cramped quarters posed an unforeseen health problem and typhoid fever and malaria readily spread among the guards, especially during the hot months of June, July, and August. Eight guards died, six from typhoid and typho-malarial fevers, one from organic disease of the heart, with rupture, and one from Variola (smallpox).[54]

The United States Government did not spend a dollar on the exposition, except for an appropriation for their own exhibit. In fact, the Centennial Commission found themselves embarrassed to declare they were out of funds for printing and distribution of books and appealed to the citizens of Philadelphia for aid. To make up for the shortfall, the city appropriated $50,000 (equivalent to $1.1 million in 2017) as a provision for current expenses of the Commission.[55]

After the close of the Exposition, November 10, 1876, Patrolman Geyer and his fellow centennial guards received an engraved certificate from the Centennial Commission. In the 159 days the exposition remained open, almost ten million people from all over the world attended.[56]

Geyer's exceptional work ethics paid off. The City of Philadelphia transferred him to the Third Police Division, Eighteenth District station at Dauphin Street and Trenton Avenue on February 23, 1877. Of the six districts in their division, the Eighteenth had the second highest number of arrests for the year ending 1878, at 2,256. Shortly after his new assignment, Geyer promoted to special officer.[57]

But, he was about to suffer a setback.

Fig. 15. Philadelphia police officers pose for a portrait on 2nd Street above Christian Street in the old Commissioner's Hall, *circa* 1876. Image source: Courtesy of the Special Collections Research Center, Temple University Libraries, Philadelphia, PA. From the George D. McDowell Philadelphia Evening Bulletin Collection.

Fig. 16. Centennial Exposition in 1876. Colossal bronze arm with
hand torch "Liberty." During the later part of the Exposition, a
small house was erected near Machinery Hall to accommodate
the arm, hand, and torch. A railing was installed near the top
with a narrow stairway inside the arm that led to the landing
where people could be seen gazing at the surrounding
scenery.[58] Image source: Courtesy of Library of Congress.

CHAPTER 4

Femur and Horses

The fracture having united, the apparatus was removed at the end of seven weeks, and the patient was permitted to use crutches. A fortnight later he left the hospital.

-Dr. Robert P. Thomas
Surgeon at Episcopal Hospital, Philadelphia[59]

December 1879 to 1886, Philadelphia

CHANCES ARE, IF YOU were drunk in the City of Philadelphia, you could count on officers slapping nippers on your hands and escorting you to the slammer. Of 40,714 total arrests in 1879, fifty-nine percent of those arrests involved some form of intoxication. It certainly kept Geyer and other officers busy. Special Officer Geyer made other arrests that year too, including several larceny arrests and an arrest and conviction of Nathan Levy for highway robbery and John Burns for house robbery. Levy went to prison for eighteen months and Burns went to the house of refuge.[60]

With three years of law enforcement under his belt, Geyer was on his way to becoming proficient at interpreting laws and regulations, and how to best navigate the complicated court system. And he memorized the always changing department policies, too. But as he got into his groove, an unexpected injury sidelined his career.

A few days before Christmas, Geyer and his sister were on their way to the funeral of a relative when they got into an accident.

A steam-powered dummy car approached the corner of Kensington Avenue and E Street and suddenly the horses from a cab they were riding in jerked and twisted, reared up, and bucked. In an instant, Geyer ejected from the cab and landed hard on the ground. Seconds later, it rolled on top of him. Horses, still attached, heaved and pulled, and dragged the cab across the road. But the damage was done. The weight of the cab fractured Geyer's femur, the strongest and longest bone in the human body. The painful injury often required surgery, a traction splint, and several months recovery. Special Officer Geyer was transported to Episcopal Hospital at the corner of Front Street and Lehigh Avenue. Geyer's sister and the cab driver suffered minor injuries.[61]

Geyer spent a few months in recovery at the hospital and at home, then returned to work, assigned to light duty at first. By May 1880, Geyer returned to capturing criminals. His first documented case after the accident was the arrest of a woman familiar to law enforcement, Annie McCracken, a frequent flyer. Rough-looking with determined eyes and a couple aliases, Annie liked to wear fancy hats. Geyer arrested her at the beginning of May for larceny and she spent three months in county prison.[62]

After working several larceny cases and sad abortion, rape, and incest cases, Geyer investigated a couple United States mail fraud incidents in the spring of 1881. By late October, Geyer received an offer from the United States Post Office he couldn't refuse. He had been working on an illegal mail fraud scheme committed by James B. Redmond and Robert Cunningham, and based on his success so far, he was offered a job as a United States postal agent investigating mail fraud. Geyer would now follow through with the case as a postal agent. Besides, though he stayed clear of politics for the rest of his career, Geyer was an election officer for the Fourth Division, Nineteenth Ward and the mayor had recently made an order prohibiting police officers from taking part in politics. So, Geyer resigned from the police force November 2, 1881, and took the job. He immediately continued the investigation into the Redmond and Cunningham case, among others, and secured enough evidence for a conviction May 29, 1882.[63]

But Geyer missed law enforcement. He vowed to put politics aside and two-and-a-half years after he resigned from the force, Geyer returned to work for the City May 20, 1884. Not yet a detective, Geyer was selected for his efficiency and intelligence to work in a dual role as special officer in both the Eighteenth District and the Detective office at Central Station in City Hall.[64]

Officials required Geyer to report to Chief of Detectives Francis R. Kelly and his regular lieutenant from the Eighteenth District.[65]

Chief Kelly summarized Geyer's investigations with the detectives in a report to Mayor Smith. Among others, Geyer arrested James McAvoy (*alias* Reardon) for highway robbery and Albert Hepting for assault and larceny.[66]

Officers encountered numerous nuances at the time. District stations not only had duty officer quarters to sleep in and holding cells for suspects, but they also housed tramps and vagrants, as they called them, for overnight stays. Two years into Geyer's law enforcement career, an 1878 annual mayor's report listed 7,418 homeless who sought lodging at Geyer's Eighteenth District station for the year. The number housed across all stations that year reported at 148,137. In exchange for lodging, vagrants split an eighth of a cord of firewood.[67]

Besides normal policing duties, Geyer and fellow officers provided animal control within the city. And whenever a murder or death occurred, bodies would often lay on the floor or a cot at district police stations, where up to a hundred or more citizens would parade through to identify the body. In Geyer's 1889 murder case of young Annie Klaus, officers transported her body from the hospital where she died, to the Eighteenth District station for identification. *Philadelphia Times* reported, "A thousand people flocked to the station house . . . The girl's dead body was laid out in the corridor." Due to the large response of citizens, twenty-five officers stood in a line to keep the crowd back.[68]

As a part of their duties, Geyer and other officers attended court hearings and inquests, often on their day off. An officer could come off night shift at six in the morning, attend a three hour hearing at ten, then be expected to work their next shift that same day.[69]

Geyer's dual role came to an end May 1886. Still a special officer, he transferred to Central Station at City Hall to work one hundred percent of his time in Detectives to take charge of murder cases.[70]

All nuances and duties aside, Geyer liked being an officer and giving back to his community. Around the same time he permanently moved to City Hall, one such opportunity presented itself. Geyer showed courage and bravery by preventing an accident, like the one he suffered, from escalating into a crash that could have involved deaths. Geyer's determination and presence of mind saved several people from serious injury when a front wheel came off of a crowded vehicle at the corner of LeHigh Avenue and Leamy (later renamed to "B" Street). The accident occurred right in front of the same Episcopal hospital Geyer went to after his own accident. The spooked horse reared up, jerked and pulled, dragged the mangled carriage, and broke into an uncontrolled run. But big, burly Geyer jumped into action and stopped the horse and carriage, saving nine occupants. The crash fractured Mr. Miller's collar bone and crushed his mother's hand. Besides rattled nerves, the rest of the occupants, including three children, suffered bruises.[71]

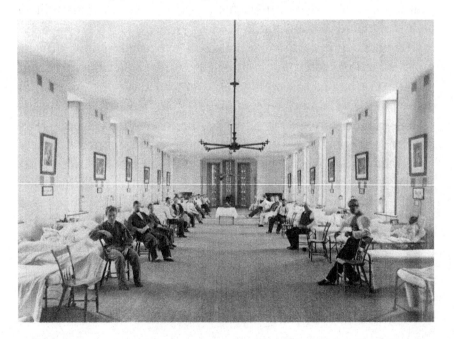

Fig. 17. The men's ward of the Episcopal Hospital on Front Street and Lehigh Avenue, Philadelphia, where Geyer was transported to following his accident. Image source: Courtesy of Library of Congress.

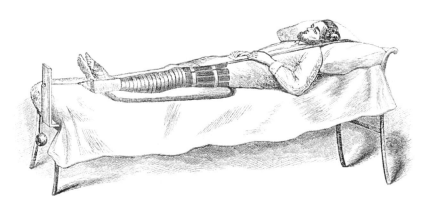

Fig. 18. Buck's extension traction, a weight and pulley apparatus
   invented by Dr. Gurdon Buck that reduces spasms and swelling
   and helps maintain the length of the femur bone following
   fractures. The Buck's extension apparatus was used at hospitals
   all over the world including Episcopal Hospital in Philadelphia
   where Geyer was treated for his femur fracture. The apparatus
   would be applied to the injured leg and patients remained
   immobile for four to eight weeks before being released from
   the hospital on crutches until reaching a full recovery. Image
   source: Gurdon Buck, MD An Improved Method of Treating
   Fractures of the Thigh. Illustrated by Cases and a Drawing,
   1861, a paper included in the New York Academy of Medicine.
   The Transactions of the New York Academy of Medicine, Vol.
   II. New York: Bailliere Brothers, 1863, p. 231.

Fig. 19. Detective Geyer arrested Annie McCracken three times for
larceny. For the first arrest, May 1, 1880, Annie was found
guilty and served three months in the county prison. Her prison
sentence increased to six months for the two remaining arrests,
January 10, 1881 and April 23, 1885.[72] Image source: Courtesy
of Philadelphia City Archives, arrest number 1079.

Fig. 20. Geyer arrested Ellen Callahan, a boarding house thief, August 11, 1881.[73] Image source: Courtesy of Philadelphia City Archives, arrest number 2015.

PART II

Bloody Bad

CHAPTER 5

Bullitt

I was chairman of the committee which reported the original bill. Of course I support it . . . The chief objection to it appears to be on the account of the power that would be vested in the present Mayor. The people should be able to elect a man capable of filling a place so vested with honor and ability. The man who at present holds it is only a sort of Chief of Police.

-S. Davis Page, Chairman of the Joint Committee of Councils, re: Bullitt Bill[74]

Philadelphia, 1887

THREE MONTHS AFTER FRANK married his beautiful wife, major changes brewed at City Hall. Pennsylvania passed an Act for the Better Government known as the "Bullitt Bill" and Mayor William B. Smith approved an ordinance to comply with it that shifted responsibilities and merged departments. Geyer's department merged into the new Department of Public Safety and the Mayor appointed a Public Safety Director with an annual salary of $7,500. There was one major caveat. The director had to provide a $25,000 security deposit as a condition for the faithful discharge of his duty. Former Mayor William S. Stokley readily took on that role and gave his deposit to the city.[75]

The Bullitt Bill provided law enforcement new protections. No more sudden dismissals, unless supervisors requested it in writing or a police court trial composed of equals or superiors was held.

Geyer's new boss was a strict disciplinarian. Known as "Martinet Stokley," he had a habit of not trusting subordinates. He kept Geyer and the other men on their toes by making unannounced visits to station houses, often firing officers on the spot. This was a habit he carried with him into his new role as the public safety director.[76]

But Stokley got himself into hot water when several officers filed against him for wrongful termination. The Supreme Court reviewed the cases and learned Stokley fired officers for not wearing overcoats while on night duty. Stokley admitted the dismissals were without compliance of the Bullitt Bill; however, he felt vindicated because the city solicitor suggested there were serious doubts about the constitutionality of how it applied to dismissals. The Supreme Court disagreed and the mandamus prayed for was issued in the cases.[77]

Despite Stokley's quirks, most of his men loved and respected him—including Frank Geyer, who later served on a committee to honor Stokley's twentieth anniversary of the Centennial Exposition, Geyer's first assignment as an officer. He, and the committee, visited Director Stokley at his home on North Broad Street for a ceremony and gave him floral tributes.[78]

When all changes were implemented, the police department became known as the Bureau of Police and a superintendent position was instituted. But the successful candidate was also required to provide a security deposit, this time $10,000, equivalent to almost $260,000 in 2017.[79]

Fig. 21. Francis R. Kelly, Chief of Detectives. Kelly was Geyer's chief while he was assigned the dual role of reporting to both the supervisor of the Eighteenth District and Chief Kelly in the Detective Department (renamed Detective Bureau) at City Hall. In an April 1887 shake up, officials gave Chief Kelly the ax and replaced him with ex-Fire Marshal Charles W. Wood. This move caused numerous influential businessmen and political allies to demonstrate against his removal. Testimonials in favor of Kelly were reported in newspapers, including one from the United States Treasury Department, Secret Service Division in Washington DC, where Kelly had previously worked. Philadelphia offered Kelly a position within the ranks, but he took that as an insult and abruptly resigned from the force. Kelly went to work as chief of the fire brigade at John Wanamaker's store at Thirteenth and Chestnut Street and then became a bank detective for the financial district of

Philadelphia.[80] Image source: George Washington Walling. *Recollections of a New York Chief of Police.* NY: Caxton Book Concern, Limited, 1887, p. 559.

Fig. 22. Philadelphia Police Chief General James Stewart, Jr. Stewart served in the Civil War, quickly rising in ranks, becoming first lieutenant of Company H, Ninth Regiment, Infantry, in 1861, then captain in spring of 1862, major in December of the same year, and lieutenant-colonel one month after that. Stewart was appointed colonel six months later and then brevet brigadier general on March 13, 1865, for meritorious services during the war. While police chief, Stewart instituted a policy for a daily ten o'clock meeting of all captains and lieutenants at police headquarters, where staff reported every accident, every crime, and any dereliction of duty. Stewart required arrests by officers be reported to the him in writing.[81] Image source: *Recollections of a New York Chief*

of Police. NY: Caxton Book Concern, Limited, 1887, p. 553.

Fig. 23. Philadelphia City Hall in 1899. Work was prepared for the new City Hall August 16, 1871, and the first corner-stone laid with appropriate ceremonies July 4, 1874, two years before Frank Geyer started his employment. In the summer of 1884, Geyer worked a dual role as special officer and reported to both the Eighteenth Police District and to City Hall, Detectives. Geyer promoted to detective January 7, 1888,

formalized by Mayor Fitler January 19, and from then, until his
retirement in 1903, he worked at City Hall.[82] Image source:
Courtesy of Library of Congress.

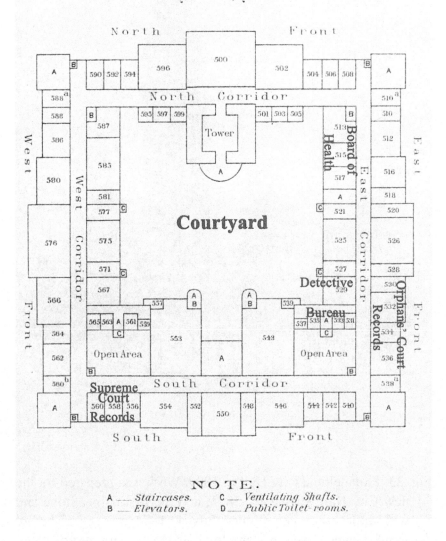

Fig. 24. City Hall floor plan for the fifth floor, 1890. Detectives
were originally located on the second floor, but after the Bullitt
Bill took effect, Director of Public Works Louis Wagner moved

into their offices and detectives were relocated to odd-numbered rooms 529 thru 537 on the fifth floor. The police captains' room, officers' room, and rooms for supervisors of reserves, matrons, turnkey's and other police staff were located on the sixth floor. The police prisoners' cell and court detention rooms were also on the sixth floor. As of 2017, the detectives' rooms are occupied by judges from the First Judicial Court of Common Pleas.[83] Image source: The Commissioners for the Erection of the New Public Buildings. *The New City Hall Philadelphia Directory of Offices Occupied; or Allotted and in Process of Completion, with Diagrams of Various Floors, and Other Miscellaneous Information Appertaining to the Building.* Philadelphia, PA: Printed for the Commissioners, 1890, p. 15.

CHAPTER 6

Bizarre Story of a Cat

From her manner, you wouldn't suppose anything was the matter. She just looked us in the eyes and told us the cat story three or four times as coolly as could be.

-Lieutenant Ferguson, Philadelphia Police[84]

142 West York Street, Philadelphia, December 27, 1885

FAMILY AND FRIENDS GATHERED around holiday tables to savor traditional family recipes like stuffed turkey, mashed potatoes and gravy, and scrumptious pumpkin pie. Sweet memories were told and retold and new ones cherished. But for others, the holidays were filled with sadness. On a cold, winter day, two days after Christmas, thirty-one-year-old Special Officer Frank Geyer met Lieutenant Ferguson and Officer Mason at 142 West York Street to investigate a bizarre story of a vicious tomcat, a mother, and her ten-week-old baby boy.[85]

Mrs. Annie Gaskin had an eerie calmness about her. As if reciting how to sweep the kitchen floor, she told a peculiar story, the first of its kind officers had responded to in Philadelphia.

The night after Christmas, Mrs. Gaskin put her three young children to bed as usual, but this time she locked the neighbors' tomcat in her room to catch mice while she slept. She hoped the cat would kill the little critters so she wouldn't have to hear them crawl and scamper about in her room each night.

At four o'clock the next morning, she heard a loud noise and when she opened her eyes; the cat jumped across the room. Annoyed, Mrs. Gaskin got out of bed, let the cat out of the room, and went back to sleep.

Mrs. Gaskin checked on baby Joseph around seven, but her baby was stiff and covered in blood. Little Joseph lay dead on the bed with several, deep cuts across his throat. All she could think of was the tomcat killed baby Joseph with its claws! She panicked and removed her baby's bloody clothes, filled a bucket with water, washed him, and put his clothing in to soak. She dressed him in a clean white slip and petticoat and laid baby Joseph back on his bed.

She called Mrs. Annie Gillan, who lived in the same house, and told her the cat killed her baby. Mrs. Gaskin then woke her sister, Mrs. Mary Alcorn, who also lived in the house and Mrs. Alcorn immediately called police. When Deputy Coroner Ashbridge arrived on scene, without further investigation, he ordered the tomcat shot.[86]

Geyer and Mason listened to the far fetched story. Why did the mother wait so long to call for help? What made her remove baby Joseph's clothes and clean and redress him? Why was blood on the bed, but not where the baby slept?

While officers investigated her story, Deputy Coroner Ashbridge took Mrs. Gaskin into custody to await a coroner's inquest. Special Officer Geyer and his partner viewed the baby's remains first. Baby Joseph lay motionless on a marble slab with several large gashes to his throat. One wound sliced clear through to the baby's spinal cord. No way a cat could have done that, even with sharp nails.[87]

Geyer and Mason returned to Mrs. Gaskin's house. The men went upstairs to the baby's room and found absolutely no blood on the baby's bedding to support Mrs. Gaskin's claim the cat attacked her baby while he slept. Instead, Geyer found a trail of blood in Mrs. Gaskin's room that led down the stairs to an outhouse. They found the bloody bucket of water with baby Joseph's clothing. Inside the outhouse, blood covered the floor and parts of the walls. Investigators found a large bloodstained butcher knife.[88]

Geyer interviewed Mrs. Gaskin's neighbor, Robert White. He wasn't able to provide valuable information other than after Mrs. Gaskin told him the cat murdered her baby, he went upstairs and found baby Joseph dead. And like other witnesses said, Mrs. Gaskin had already washed and dressed him in fresh clothes.[89]

Officers continued interviews with family, friends, and neighbors, which caused Geyer to theorize Mrs. Gaskin killed her baby because he kept her from working to support the other two children.[90]

Mrs. Gaskin and her children slept crosswise on one bed. The sheets and bed covers were soaked with blood, but not a particle of blood was on the area Gaskin claimed baby Joseph slept, nor on his pillow slip. The carpet and door-knob to her room had blood on it, as did the stairway and closet below.[91]

Coroner Powers held the inquest December 29, 1885. Thirty-year-old Mrs. Gaskin, who wore a gray cotton dress wrapped in a green shawl with a spotted calico apron tied around her waist, admitted to nothing. She stuck to her story and when questioned further, she said, with emphasis on the last word, "I wish to say *nothing.*" Cold-hearted and defiant, the petite, but stout woman, who had buried her husband four weeks earlier and would soon bury her baby boy, was completely without emotion.[92]

Geyer, who one year later would hold a baby of his own, provided details of the investigation, emphasizing the lack of blood on the infant's bedding. Instead, he said they discovered a blood trail from the outhouse to Mrs. Gaskin's room and a ten-inch butcher knife with blood. He testified the cat had blood on its fur, but he believed Mrs. Gaskin put it there to conceal her crime. Geyer testified he found a bloody silver dollar inside Mrs. Gaskin's handbag.[93]

Coroner's Physician Dr. Henry F. Formad, a distinguished pathologist and blood expert that later contracted blood poisoning, then died from cholera morbus during his recovery, confirmed the baby's wounds were from a knife, not a cat's claws. Baby Joseph had a six-inch long, one-inch deep incision across his throat and several other cuts as if the murderer used a dull knife and tried several times to cut the throat.[94]

In an effort to explain Annie Gaskin's odd behavior, Mrs. Alcorn said, "My sister was always of a quiet disposition. She has had wild looking eyes ever since she had the measles."[95]

At the conclusion of the testimony, the verdict was that baby Joseph Gaskin came to his death from a wound to his throat committed by parties unknown. Mrs. Gaskin was held without bail to await trial.

Mrs. Gaskin's February 1886 murder trial, featured all the same testimony as in the earlier inquest, with the addition of five physicians who testified they believed she acted under an uncontrollable impulse when she committed the murder. A sympathetic jury agreed and found her not guilty by reason of insanity. Mrs. Annie Gaskin was ordered confined to the State Lunatic Hospital at Norristown, outside Philadelphia.[96]

A little more than a year after her confinement, Mrs. Annie Gaskin caught a break. While under the care of Dr. Alice Bennett, the doctor rallied for Mrs. Gaskin's release and requested and received a court hearing on behalf of Gaskin. Dr. Bennett testified that although Mrs. Gaskin was of low mental grade, she was able to work and care for her own household. Dr. Bennett said Gaskin regularly suffered headaches and dizziness during her menstrual cycle. At the time of baby Joseph's murder, Mrs. Gaskin was on her period and Dr. Bennett felt that coupled with grief and anxiety from the recent unexpected death of her husband, and afterward facing extreme poverty, Bennett reasoned Mrs. Gaskin took the life of her son without the apparent realization of the act at the time.[97]

"In her year or more of hospital life with us she was uniformly gentle, patient and industrious, never ill-tempered or even irritable. For about two days each month she complained of her head and generally spent time in bed and was quieter than usual; there was never any out-break of violence," Dr. Bennet said.[98]

Dr. Bennett's testimony was a blessing for Mrs. Gaskin. The court released her into the care of her friends.[99]

Fig. 25. Dr. Mary "Alice" Bennett was the first woman
superintendent of the women's section of the State Hospital for
the Insane in Norristown, Pennsylvania. Dr. Bennett
successfully testified for the release of Mrs. Annie Gaskin who
killed her ten-week-old son, Joseph. Later, Dr. Bennett
testified, unsuccessfully, for the acquittal of poisoner, Mrs.
Sarah Jane Whiteling (Detective Geyer's case). Image source:
US National Library of Medicine, National Institutes of
Health.

CHAPTER 7

A Mighty Gruesome Package

First I took the head across the river and hid it along the bank. Then I took the legs and put them with the head, and then I took the arms over and put them all together. This was in the afternoon. Then about 8 or 9 o'clock I went over and tied them all together with a rope, and put a lot of bricks with them and threw them over.

-George Wilson Confession[100]

1642 Richards St, Philadelphia and Colonel Mann's Ice Pond, February 1887

SILAS HIBBS LEFT HOME at seven o'clock Thursday morning to walk to his carpenter job. The married man in his sixties crossed over a small bridge at Colonel Mann's ice pond near Eddington flag station on the Pennsylvania Railroad, but that morning, he stopped at the top of the bridge to check out a blue calico garment that lay in the roadway. He kicked it and noticed blood stains. He walked to the edge of the bridge and looked at an object wrapped with brown paper that floated in the ice-cold water near the edge. Hibbs descended the bank and as he got closer, he saw a bloody package tied with thick strings, lettered, "Handle with care." He reached out, tugged on the package, and drug it up the bank to examine it closer.[101]

Hibbs untied the strings, opened the box, and stared at the gory remains of a mutilated, dismembered torso of a headless, limbless man.[102]

Word of the discovery spread lightening fast among villagers. Curious onlookers gathered to glimpse the horrific site.

Bucks County officials and reporters descended upon the

quaint, Eddington village in Bensalem Township. Just four miles south of Bristol, outside Philadelphia, the village had the usual stores, churches, and businesses that doubled as homes, for about two hundred residents.[103]

Investigators spent the next couple days searching for the victims' head and limbs. Eddington's Constable, Frederick Jackson, directed staff to drain the pond, but heavy rain hampered their efforts. Authorities trudged through the mud in hip-high boots and did their best to search every inch of the area. They found shawl straps that matched the garment Silas Hibbs kicked on the bridge, but no body parts.

Students, accompanied by the school mistress, were interviewed in the two-story, two-room Eddington schoolhouse, near Dunks Ferry where General Cadwallader and his troops crossed the Delaware during the Revolutionary War. Investigators hoped the children would provide important clues, but after the interviews, they were no closer to solving the case.[104]

The coroner held an inquest to assist in their investigation. In an unusual move that would raise red flags today, officials used the private residence of Silas Hibbs, some seventy yards from where he found the mutilated torso. Though their investigation was far from over, authorities had no reason at the time to suspect Hibbs in the crime.[105]

At first authorities thought the bloody torso was from dissecting tables of medical schools, but they rejected that theory after Coroner William S. Silbert, and Coroner's Physician Dr. Evan J. Groom, determined the victim was alive when the head and limbs were removed. Dr. Groom explained that the head was severed at the fourth vertebra, and the left arm, at the shoulder. Part of the left humerus remained attached to the torso with the limbs and lower portion of the abdomen removed above the pelvis, but below the navel, and the victims' bowels protruded from the torso. Dr. Groom said the flow of blood proved the crime was committed as recent as Wednesday afternoon or evening. Based on the wounds, the murderer used a sharp saw, perhaps like one a butcher used in a meat market.

There was talk the torso belonged to a human head found Tuesday on a farm near Burlington, New Jersey. But right away authorities were sure the head came from a medical college because someone sawed off the top of the skull and removed the brain. Investigators later determined it belonged to a student at Philadelphia's Jefferson Medical College.[106]

Dr. Groom described the condition of the Eddington torso. "The trunk was certainly not that of a cadaver used by medical students and the body had not been kept in alcohol... I should say that he was not more than five feet five inches in height and weighed about one hundred and twenty-five pounds." The victim, about thirty-years old, had black, woolly hair on the torso. There was a distinct deformity on the shoulder blades where it appeared the victim carried his head on his shoulders in a hunched manner. Coal dust coated each cut in the flesh, which proved dismemberment took place in a cellar or outhouse. "It is a case of murder beyond a doubt," Dr. Groom said.[107]

Without the head and limbs, it was difficult to determine the victim's nationality. Coroner Silbert thought he was a Chinaman, while other officials thought he was Italian or a 'colored' man, a common term used at the time to describe African Americans. To solve the dilemma, Coroner Silbert brought in a colored woman named Jane to the examination room. He grabbed her wrist and held it up next to the torso to compare colors but Jane shuddered, backed away, and refused to go near the torso again. They asked another colored woman if she thought the body was that of a colored man.

"White folks look so much like colored folks nowadays, hard to tell the difference," she said.[108]

After some debate, officials agreed the torso belonged to a light-skinned colored man, possibly a person of mixed ancestry like a mulatto.

Eager to forward the grisly case to Philadelphia police, Bucks County met with the Philadelphia police chief and Francis R. Kelly, chief of detectives. Chief Kelly was familiar with the case and had followed news reports in the papers. A few days after the torso discovery, a Pennsylvania Railroad train conductor named Frank Swain contacted Chief Kelly about a suspicious woman from the Philadelphia area who rode his train just before Mr. Silas found the bloody torso. Swain told Kelly he thought the woman had something to do with the murder.

He described a tall, colored woman, about forty-years-old, dressed in dark clothes. She carried two bundles, one similar to the package found at the pond. The odd thing was, she bought a return ticket for Cornwall at Broad Street in Philadelphia, but paid extra to get off at Eddington.

The conductor remembered the woman because she opened the train window in the dead of winter to let the cold air in. She also appeared nervous so Conductor Swain attempted to talk to her. The woman told Swain she had just come from Episcopal Hospital because she fell on the ice and was still not feeling well. The conductor told Chief Kelly when it was time for her to get off the train, he offered to help carry the packages but the woman snapped at him and said, "No! No—don't touch them."[109]

Chief Kelly took charge of the case and assigned his best detectives: Special Officer 'Murder Geyer,' Special Officer James Tate, Detective Thomas Crawford, and Detective Peter Miller, who in 1896, became captain of detectives.[110]

Detectives struggled to focus on the torso case in the midst of a rogue colleague who went on a wild shooting spree at Philadelphia's Twenty-third District police station, Saturday night, February 19, 1887.

John MacIntire, a suspended fellow officer, boasted at local saloons he planned to kill his lieutenant, Edward Lyons. No one paid attention to him because he was blowing off steam after his recent suspension.

In 1887, the department provided officers with double-breasted blue coats, a pair of blue trousers, and a black helmet for winter. Summer uniforms were a lighter-weight version of the coat, single-breasted, similar trousers, and a light-gray helmet. Officers were issued a wood baton as a weapon, decorated with a blue cord and tassel, worn on the belt, concealed under their coats.

No guns were issued to officers.

The week before the incident, on a Thursday morning, Chief Stewart gave short notice and ordered all lieutenants require each officer buy a regulation pocket revolver with their own funds by six o'clock that same evening. MacIntire and four other officers showed up for roll call without revolvers and were suspended.[111]

MacIntire had been terminated for drunkenness and neglect of duty in the past and another time for drunkenness and assault with a blackjack of Constable Ackerman during an arrest. After each incident, officials reinstated MacIntire for political reasons, and though arrested for the blackjack assault case, police permitted him to work while he awaited trial.[112]

The short, but powerful police officer left a saloon and went straight for the police station, set out to do exactly what he planned even if no one believed a drunk like him. Lieutenant Lyons had already finished roll call and went home to dinner by the time MacIntire arrived. A desk sergeant sat near a partially open armory door talking with fellow officers, one of which said he heard Officer MacIntire had spouted off at the mouth about a plan to kill the lieutenant.

Officer MacIntire burst into the district station and went straight past the desk sergeant into the armory where officers stored their personal revolvers when off-duty.

"I'm going to show Lyons who's lieutenant here," Officer MacIntire shouted. "I'm the boss of the place, and I'll kill every cuss in the room." He grabbed two pistols, one in each hand. "I was bounced because I had no pistol, but I'll have the best one in the place now," MacIntire said.[113]

The sergeant ordered him to put them down, but MacIntire ignored him and pointed a revolver at his head.

"Get out of here, or I'll blow your brains out; I'll kill you all if you don't get out." Unarmed officers ran out doors, jumped out windows, and hid behind stairways. MacIntire fired guns using both hands. A bullet whizzed close to the sergeant's head and hit the wall. MacIntire meant business and fired shot after shot in all directions. As fast as he emptied one revolver, he threw it away and picked up another from the armory.

"Send Lyons in here. I'll kill him," MacIntire yelled as he noticed men under the stairwell and fired shots in that direction, which sent officers into the cellar. One jumped into the ash bin and the other two officers followed him. All three almost suffocated.

Officer Carpenter stuck his head out to get air and MacIntire saw him and said, "Oh, you're in there are you? Just wait till I get two more pistols and I'll finish you." The men used the opportunity while MacIntire went back to the armory to escape onto the street and Officer Carpenter ran to notify Lieutenant Lyon. When the lieutenant arrived on scene, he ordered several officers inside to capture MacIntire, but they all refused. One officer went to the backyard and fired a shot at MacIntire through a window, but missed.

Lieutenant Lyon borrowed a pistol, went inside, and called out to Officer MacIntire, who responded, "I own this place and I intend to call the roll tonight,"

MacIntire continued, "I'm going to kill you, lieutenant," he yelled then lunged forward, firing both revolvers in the lieutenant's direction, one bullet an inch from Lyon's head. Lieutenant Lyon fired back and struck MacIntire in the arm and he fell to the ground. Officers rushed MacIntire but he struggled and fought back. Six officers held him while one searched for weapons and found eight loaded revolvers in his pockets. Officers locked MacIntire in a cell until an ambulance arrived and when it did, four officers rode with him to subdue him, while he shouted, "I'll do Lyons up if you put him in here with me."[114]

Though MacIntire got drunk and attacked his station on a Saturday, there were concerns that officials encouraged officers to drink because of enforcement of Sunday liquor laws.

Six months after the shooting, a grand jury handed a final presentment to Judge Reed in the Quarter Sessions. They reviewed Sunday Liquor Law cases, the law that prohibited liquor sales on Sunday. While the grand jury approved enforcement of the law, they disapproved of officials requiring officers to go drinking from saloon to saloon, no matter how often, to secure evidence to convict the owners. The judge agreed with their opinion and said he knew of no principle of law nor rule of morality or propriety that required officers to do it, and he could readily see that if it were a necessity, how unfortunate a thing it might prove to be for the police force.[115]

Official's fired John MacIntire—permanently.

The frightening incident and the gruesome torso case were

both the talk of Philadelphia for days to come.

The murder victim was identified as Wakefield Gains. His sister, Mrs. Jennie Cannon, read news reports of the torso and asked to speak to Chief Kelly and detectives right away. She cried hysterically as she told them her brother, twenty-year-old Wakefield Gains, went missing right before the torso was found in Eddington. Her brother always made it a point to stop by her house once a day and let her know anytime he planned to be out of town. Gains came to her home the Tuesday before the discovery of the torso and when he left, he said he would see her again the next day but never showed up.

She described her brother as medium height and build with low, hunched shoulders, like the man she read about in the paper.

Mrs. Cannon told officers a jealous woman named Mary Tabbs was responsible for his death because she threatened to kill him two weeks ago when she walked past Mrs. Cannon's home and found Gains talking to a girl on the street. Mrs. Tabbs became so outraged that she suddenly attacked her brother and he ran inside to seek refuge. Mrs. Cannon heard the commotion and hurried out of her room. Her brother ran toward her for help, blood dripping all over his face from a large cut. Tabbs yelled into the house she would get even and kill him.[116]

Mrs. Cannon said Mrs. Tabbs was possessive of Gains and followed him wherever he moved to. They used to work together, along with Tabbs niece, Annie Richardson. All three were servants for two rich brothers. One day, Waite joked with Annie and Tabbs became livid. Soon after, Annie Richardson mysteriously disappeared and four months later Mrs. Tabbs stopped working for the brothers.[117]

Mrs. Cannon's description of Tabbs fit the one Conductor Swain gave Chief Kelly. At the conclusion of the interview, Chief Kelly, Special Officer Geyer, Crawford, Miller, and Tate made plans to bring Mrs. Hannah Mary Tabbs in for questioning.[118]

She was not home when detectives called on her but they remembered Mrs. Cannon told them Mrs. Tabbs would make a trip to Bristol to see the torso.

Geyer went to Bristol to look for Tabbs while the other detectives staked out train stations in Philadelphia.[119]

But instead of riding the train to Bristol, Tabbs went back to Eddington and reported her niece missing. She slyly mentioned her missing friend, Wakefield Gains, perhaps to see what she could find out about the torso investigation.[120]

Meanwhile, as Tabbs talked with officials in Eddington, Geyer's train whizzed past her on his way to Bristol with instructions to bring her back to Philadelphia. Geyer searched arriving and departing trains there and thought he saw a woman that matched her description, so he followed the lady all around Bristol, but it was not her.[121]

While Geyer followed the Bristol lead, Mrs. Tabbs rode the train from Eddington back to Broad Street in Philadelphia, right into the arms of Miller and Tate who were watching incoming trains for any sign of her. They arrested Tabbs on the spot and brought her in for questioning.[122]

Surprised and agitated, she protested her arrest and claimed they made a huge mistake, but when Chief Kelly and Miller and Tate questioned her, she burst into tears. Every question asked, was met with the same two answers. The reason Conductor Swain noticed her strange behavior was because she was in pain and had just returned from the hospital for her sore hip she injured on the ice. Yes, she knew Wakefield Gaines but that was because she and her missing niece, Annie, worked with him as servants for two rich brothers. Each time they asked her a follow-up question, Mrs. Tabbs contradicted herself or would not give a straight answer. Frustrated, they put her in a holding cell while they continued their investigation.[123]

The next morning, Chief Kelly visited Mrs. Tabbs at the Fifth District station house. An officer brought her into the corridor and Chief Kelly asked about her health and if she rested easy during the night. She said she had a headache and had tied a handkerchief around her head hoping it would help. Chief Kelly got her a good breakfast and asked her if there was anything she wanted to say to him yet, but she shook her head no.

"I will leave you to your own thoughts for the present. I may

call again this afternoon. If you have anything to tell me you can
send for me at any time."[124]

A few hours later, Detective Crawford tried to persuade her to
talk about the murder but she would have none of it. Each time
Crawford asked her a question, Mrs. Tabbs interrupted and said,
"Why don't you get Wilson; why don't you get Wilson?" When
Crawford asked her to explain, Mrs. Tabbs completely shut down
all conversation and demanded to speak to Chief Kelly. Crawford
telegraphed central police at City Hall and fifteen minutes later,
Chief Kelly, accompanied by two detectives and Clerk Moffitt,
arrived at the station. They brought Mrs. Tabbs into the
lieutenant's room and she made a full confession.[125]

Mrs. Tabbs said on Wednesday morning, February 16, between
nine and ten, Wakefield Gains came to her house at 1642 Richards
Street, Philadelphia. While Gains read a newspaper and she ate
breakfast, her friend George Wilson knocked on the door. Gains
opened it, didn't say much, and went back to read the paper. She
said Wilson announced he planned to bring her daughter [niece]
from Jenkintown, north of Philadelphia, and take her riding. Mrs.
Tabbs asked George Wilson what time he would be there on
Sunday and he said twelve o'clock.

Gains looked up from his newspaper.

"Is he going with her now?"

"I don't know, and I don't care as long as I see my little girl,"
Mrs. Tabbs confessed she told Gains. When they all worked
together as servants, Wakefield Gains paid too much attention to
Annie for her liking.

"With that[,] Gains jumped up and struck George Wilson.
Wilson ran backwards as if he was looking for something, and
Gains followed him up; then they clinched and fought all over the
kitchen, and fell up against the sewing machine," Mrs. Tabbs said.

George Wilson grabbed a chair and struck Gains on the head,
knocking him against the stairs.

"He struck him several times more with the chair while
[Gains] lay on the floor," Mrs. Tabbs said.

Wakefield Gains never got up again.

Mrs. Tabbs came down the stairs, stepped over Gains' legs, and
told George Wilson it was awful what he did.

"Well, he shan't get the best of me; he struck me first," George Wilson told her.

"Then Wilson pulled the carpet from under him and I washed it out and hung it on the line. There was some blood on it and some on the steps. Then George Wilson grabbed hold of the body and moved the coal scuttle off the cellar steps and pushed and pulled the body down the cellar," Mrs. Tabbs said.

George Wilson went into the cellar, and she, halfway down the steps. She said, "What are you going to do with him?"

"I'm going to take off his clothes," George Wilson said.

He took off Gains clothes and tied them up into a bundle. Mrs. Tabbs went all the way into the cellar and both George Wilson and her stood there and stared at Gains body. George searched for something to block the cellar window so no one could see inside and came back with a butchers' cleaver in his hand. While George was in the cellar with Gains body, Mrs. Tabbs went upstairs, looked through the window slats, and made sure no one was coming. George Wilson was in the cellar for a while. When he finished, he came up and said, "I have got it fixed now."

Mrs. Tabbs went back into the cellar to see what George Wilson did to Gains. Wilson had cut Wakefield Gains into pieces, wrapped his head in paper, and put the rest of his body against the side of the stairway, with his arms and legs stuffed underneath the steps. Wilson said, "I am going out with this head and will bring something back to wrap up this body, and if you can make away with that I want you [to] take it to Media [Pennsylvania] and I will get away with rest of it." Mrs. Tabbs said she wouldn't be able to lift the body but George explained that it wasn't heavy now that he cut it short to make it easier for her to carry. He also would wrap it up for her so no one could see inside.

"We can get it all out of here tonight if you just help me," Wilson told her. Mrs. Tabbs agreed to take it but said she wouldn't be able to go to Media, Pennsylvania, which was about ten miles west of Philadelphia. Instead, she told George Wilson she would take the body to Bucks County.

Tabbs said Wilson carried the body up from the cellar. She got an old calico shirt and a shawl strap to carry it and waited until dark. While she waited, George Wilson brought up a leg, wrapped in an old bag, and left the house with it. When it came time for Mrs. Tabbs to leave the house, she walked to the train depot at Seventeenth Street, below Spruce and to her surprise, George Wilson showed up. He needed the key to her house, which she gave him. Before he left, George asked when her husband would be home and she told him eight-thirty. George said he would meet her at the depot again later.

"I took the 6:30 train and bought a return ticket for Cornwalls Station," Mrs. Tabbs said. But she didn't get off at Cornwalls. Instead she went on to Eddington and paid the conductor the difference in the fare. When she got to Eddington, she went up the hill and stopped at a house there to ask for directions.

"A white lady came to the door and [I] asked her the way to Bridgeport. I left my two bundles at the gate, for I had a bundle containing Gains' clothes besides the body. A colored man came out with a lantern and showed me the road," Mrs. Tabbs said.

She left the house and picked up her bundles but the colored man followed her for a while. She walked as fast as she could but he still followed. She stopped to let him pass. That worked. The man turned around and went home. Mrs. Tabbs continued to the bridge and set down both bundles. She took off the shawl strap and a piece of calico material holding the torso package.

"I then threw the body over in the water. It went on the side where I threw it, and did not sink, as I expected. I threw the shawl strap over and brought the piece of calico over the bridge and threw it down."

Two men came along in a buggy and she hid in the bushes until they passed. The tall woman grabbed her bundle of clothes, walked to Cornwalls, and took the nine o'clock train back to Philadelphia. George Wilson met her at the Broad Street train station, but to his surprise, she still had the bundle of clothes, which she kept because she thought Gain's name was on them.

Mrs. Tabbs told George she threw the body over the bridge but it didn't sink and George said it was probably because of the brown wrapper. George took the bundle of clothes and said he would see her the next morning around eight-thirty. George Wilson came back to her house on Friday and said someone found the body and it was all over the papers. He warned her not to tell anyone and if she did, it would be just as bad for her as it was for him. Mrs. Tabbs didn't see or hear from George again.[126]

Chief Kelly and detectives listened to her confession, noting her calm and matter-of-fact demeanor. As she spoke of the fight, murder, dismemberment, and disposal of the body, she showed little emotion, almost as if she and George had slaughtered a chicken, and cooked and ate a good meal from it. Listening to her confess, they made up their minds she took a more active role than she admitted, especially since Mrs. Tabbs had a black eye. Chief Kelly asked how she got it and Mrs. Tabbs insisted it was from the recent slip and fall on the ice.[127]

<hr/>

Police searched for George Wilson. Geyer and Crawford staked out his last known address while Miller and Tate were at another location on Lombard Street. After six o'clock in the evening, Wilson approached the Lombard Street home and Miller and Tate arrested him and took him to Central Station at City Hall for questioning. They asked Wilson about his whereabouts on the day of Gains' disappearance, but he said he was no where near Gains that day because he was working at his aunt's furniture factory on Lombard Street. When detectives followed up, they confirmed Wilson wasn't at the factory at all that day. They placed eighteen-year-old George Wilson into a holding cell to await a hearing.[128]

It took time, but George Wilson confessed to Chief Kelly and corroborated most of what Mrs. Tabbs said, except after he hit Gaines with the chair, Wilson said he ran out of the house. When he returned around noon, Mrs. Tabbs had already dismembered Wakefield Gains and gave Wilson a package and told him to throw it in the river. Mrs. Tabbs threatened to kill him if he opened the bundle. Wilson admitted he threw the head and limbs into the Schuylkill River at the Callowhill Bridge and afterwards, did not return home until about eleven o'clock that night. He did not see Mrs. Tabbs again until after her arrest.[129]

Geyer and Crawford bundled up and left early Friday morning, February 25, aboard the *Samuel G. King* police boat with

Lieutenant Francis to dredge the Schuylkill for Wakefield Gains' arms, legs, and head Wilson threw into the river. A curious crowd of onlookers and reporters along the shore watched while they used two yawls launched from the *King* to search. Detective Crawford and Lieutenant Francis on one, and Geyer with another officer on the other. Altogether, they dredged one hundred square yards but found nothing.[130]

An unexpected incident aroused excitement a few days later. Special Officer Tate escorted George Wilson from Moyamensing Prison to a court hearing. To avoid a large menacing crowd on the way back to prison, Tate detoured Wilson through a small thoroughfare on Minor Street above Chestnut. But as soon as they reached Sixth Street, Wilson freed himself from Tate's grip and ran as fast as he could. Special Officer Tate, followed by a crowd of people and reporters, chased him. When Wilson reached Fifth Street, someone from Smith's Brewery ran out and hit Wilson on the head with a heavy tool, knocking him to the ground. It took a great deal of effort, but Tate wrestled a pair of nippers onto Wilson's hands and took him back to Moyamensing Prison. The embarrassing incident hit newspapers the next day.[131]

Detectives interviewed witnesses and prepared for the upcoming inquest and possible trial. Geyer made a trip to Eddington and brought back several witnesses who identified Mrs. Tabbs in the Eddington area. He also brought with him the bloody calico garment found on the bridge and the paper wrapping that the remains were in.[132] The next day, Geyer rode the train, accompanied by Philadelphia's deputy coroner, to Bucks County with a request to exhume the torso authorities had already buried at Potter's Field. Buck's County released the torso to Geyer and the deputy coroner, who traveled back to Philadelphia with it in a pine box.[133]

Special Officer Geyer, Crawford, Miller, and Tate brought Mrs. Tabbs and Wilson from Moyamensing prison and locked them up in cells at City Hall until questioned at the coroner's office, where *Philadelphia Inquirer* reported "several hundred colored men and women" waited.[134]

News of the dismembered torso spread throughout the country and reporters clamored for information, pushing and shoving, and following detectives hoping to get an official statement or sneak a listen to a private conversation.

When the time came for the coroner's inquest, staff moved the torso to a small store room. Clerk Donal and Undertaker Matthews removed the lid and covered the body with a sheet. Officers escorted Mrs. Tabbs to the room and without hesitation, the sheet was thrown off. Not a muscle moved on Mrs. Tabbs face as she gazed at the dismembered torso.

"Do you recognize that body?"

"Yes, that is the body of Wake Gains, and it is the body I took down with me on the train to Eddington and threw down upon the bank of Tothams creek," Mrs. Tabbs said.

Tabbs identified a shawl strap and bloody shirt, and then she was returned to Central Station.[135]

Magistrate Smith held a hearing at City Hall. Mrs. Tabbs and Wilson sat on a bench outside the dock and neither one would look at each other. Smith ordered the two remanded to county jail until action of the coroner's jury.

At the coroner's inquest, Mrs. Tabbs, a slender woman with prominent features, was dressed in all black. George Wilson seemed indifferent, as if he was unaware of how much trouble he was in. Occasionally, he chewed tobacco given to him by a detective. Several witnesses testified, as did Geyer and his colleagues. Afterwards, the coroner's jury returned the following verdict March 2, 1887, "The coroner's jury find that Wakefield Gains came to his death from blows received at the hands of George H. Wilson, and that Mary Hannah Tabbs was accessory to the crime."[136]

Two weeks after the coroner's inquest, the press reported a contractor smelled a strong odor of decaying flesh in the cellar of a colored family Mrs. Tabbs knew. The contractor found two foul-smelling packages wrapped in heavy cord. It was suspicious, not only because Tabbs knew the family, but the day before Wilson confessed, the family suddenly moved. Coroner's Physician Dr. Henry F. Formad, examined the remains and in a formal report to Coroner Ashbridge, stated his examination conclusively proved the flesh was that of a cow or bullock and *not* human flesh.[137]

Fig. 26. Hannah Mary Tabbs, age 38, Rogue's Gallery photo, which included her original signature. Image source: Courtesy of Philadelphia City Archives, Rogue's Gallery Book, 1887.

Fig. 27. George H. Wilson Rogue's Gallery photo, age 18. Image source: Courtesy of Philadelphia City Archives, Rogue's Gallery Book, 1887.

Spectators lined up in front of the new courthouse May 31. District Attorney George S. Graham announced he would try George Wilson first and after jury selection, he opened the case for prosecution. Graham provided a history of the case and concluded his opening statement by describing the horrific nature of the crime:

"We will show by scientific testimony that Wakefield Gains was dismembered while there was yet life in the body."[138]

Graham called Coroner Silbert of Bucks County to testify about the torso and then had Special Officer Geyer verify he was present when Mrs. Tabbs identified the remains. Other witnesses repeated testimony from the earlier coroner's inquest.

The witness of the day was Mrs. Tabbs, dressed in deep mourning clothing. She repeated her written confession and told how Gains and George Wilson quarreled. Gains hit Wilson first, then Wilson hit Gains on the head with a chair. Afterwards, Wilson drug Gains' body downstairs into the cellar, and the next time she saw Gains, Wilson had dismembered him. She told of how she threw the torso in the water and how George Wilson threatened her to keep their secret. Graham displayed Gains' clothing and asked Mrs. Tabbs to identify them, which she did. He also showed the witness a hatchet and asked if she had seen one like it.[139]

"I believe that is the hatchet I saw on the cellar steps one or two step from the top on the first morning . . . I went down in the cellar the second morning and saw the shoes and hatchet, and I put them in the basket," Mrs. Tabbs said.[140]

Tabbs talked about a young colored girl named Hattie Armstrong. She called Miss Armstrong to her house the day of the crime and asked her to take a large bundle to Reuben Cohen's pawn shop at Seventeenth and Bainbridge streets. Miss Armstrong verified Mrs. Tabbs told her to fetch two dollars for the bundle because she was in need of money. She also pawned a pair of shoes, a hatchet, and a blue dress the next day, which Mrs. Tabbs put in a basket along with a pitcher of milk so people would think Hattie was going to the market.[141]

Mrs. Tabbs paid Hattie twenty-five cents for her trouble. Hattie later testified that while she was at Mrs. Tabbs house, she noticed the unusual appearance of the room, with the carpet removed and several tubs standing nearby, everything in a disarray. When officers retrieved the bundle, they found an overcoat, two sack coats, one brown and one bloodstained pair of blue pantaloons, and a blue vest. There was also blood on the paper used to wrap the clothing in. When compared, the paper was similar to the one the dismembered trunk was wrapped in.[142]

Mrs. Tabbs alternated between looking at the floor and scowling during trial.

Over the next four days, witnesses identified George Wilson as the man who came into the pawn shop looking for a cleaver to buy. Mary C. Bailey, Mrs. Tabbs' neighbor, stated she saw Wakefield Gains enter her home at about 9 o'clock A. M., the morning of his murder, and heard loud noises, like they were quarreling, before George Wilson entered the house later. Did Mrs. Tabbs fight with Gains before George Wilson got there? Is that why she injured her hip and got a black eye? Maybe Mrs. Tabbs carried out her death threat she made against Gains when she saw him talking to a girl. She could have hit him and then forced Wilson to help her dismember Gains.[143]

Special Officer Tate was called to the witness stand and described the search for the victims' head and limbs in the Schuylkill. George Wilson was on the boat and showed officers where he threw the dismembered body parts. On cross-examination by Wilson's attorney, Mr. Brown, asked Tate about showing George Wilson Mrs. Tabbs written confession while he was on the boat and if he asked him what he thought about it.[144]

"Do you remember whether there were any comments made at the time in relation to that statement?" Attorney Brown said.

"I asked him what he thought of it, and he said there was a great deal of it true, and a great deal of it that was not true," Tate said.

"Did he tell you what parts of it were true, and what parts not?"

"No, sir. I will say to you he mentioned at that time the striking with the chair."

Trial onlookers raised eyebrows when Wilson's attorney asked Special Officer Tate about giving Wilson alcohol and a cigar while on the boat. But on cross-examination Tate said Wilson asked for it, and others were taking a little stimulant too because it was cold and chilly that day.[145]

Wilson's attorneys called at least nine colored witnesses to verify Wilson worked at Matthias & Lee's chair-caning establishment the day of Wakefield Gains' murder. But prosecution found several flaws in the testimony. On cross-examination, three of the witnesses admitted they told authorities different stories when interviewed by detectives.[146]

Although District Attorney Graham mentioned it in his opening statement, there was a collective surprise when Dr. Henry F. Formad confirmed beyond a doubt that Gaines was alive when dismembered.[147]

At the end of the fifth day of trial, Judge Hare gave his charge to the jury. He summarized the circumstances of the crime and while horrific and shocking, if Gains had died in the fight, it would not have been murder in the first degree under the facts in the case.[148]

"Dr. Formad has said that at the time this man was cut to pieces he was living. It is for the jury to say whether the prisoner had noticed that he was living. If he believed that he was dead and in his ignorance arrived at that conclusion then it would not amount to a case of murder in the first degree, because the prisoner could not intend to take away what he believed was not there. On the other hand, if he had reason to suppose that Gains was still alive and recklessly went on without ascertaining whether he was alive or not, then I think in the eye of morality, common sense or humanity and in the law there is a case in which a verdict of murder in the first degree could probably—I will not say must—be rendered."[149]

Officers returned George Wilson and Mrs. Tabbs to prison while jurors deliberated. When announced the jury reached a verdict, authorities brought Wilson back but not Tabbs, as the district attorney had said at the beginning of trial he would try her separate. Just before nine o'clock, the jury filed back into the courtroom. The foreman of the jury arose and announced they reached a verdict. George H. Wilson was found guilty of murder in the first degree. Amid the silence and shock of the spectators who took a moment to absorb the news, George Wilson was unmoved and unconcerned about his fate.[150]

Wilson's counsel made a motion for a new trial, which Judge Hare granted. On July 1, 1887, Judge Hare accepted a plea of second degree murder and sentenced Wilson to twelve years in Eastern Penitentiary.[151]

The district attorney tried Hannah Mary Tabbs for accessory to murder and Judge Hare sentenced her to two years in prison.[152]

People all over the world were interested in the case not only because it was gruesome, but because it involved domestic violence and adultery and issues of mixed-race relationships. Hannah Mary Tabbs was an older, colored, married woman involved in an adulterous affair with a much younger, mixed-race man, Wakefield Gains, uncommon in the nineteenth century.

The *New York Herald* reported about a week before his murder, Mrs. Tabbs nearly poisoned Gains to death by putting arsenic in his beer. Gains' boarding housekeeper and Annie, Mrs. Tabbs niece, witnessed the attempted murder. After a doctor gave him medicine and he recovered, his boarding housekeeper asked him what happened.

"Oh, it was a woman." He wouldn't say who it was, but said, "She did it."[153]

Mrs. Tabbs' missing niece wasn't missing after all. Turns out, she ran away to escape Tabbs' violent outbursts.

Geyer, Crawford, Miller and Tate never found Gains' head or limbs. Aside from the head discovered early in the investigation, a fifteen-year-old boy found a skull on the shore of Schuylkill at the Bainbridge Street Wharf, early June 1887. But Coroner Ashbridge examined it and determined it was not Gains' head, but was one of the many that medical students threw into the Schuylkill.[154]

Philadelphia's Bureau of Police seemed in a constant state of turmoil, especially during political changes and this time was no different. Philadelphia elected a new mayor, Edwin H. Fitler, who had transitioned into office a month before Wakefield Gains murder. Fitler, like others before him, wasted no time putting his mark on the city. He appointed a new superintendent of police,

John Lamon, then moved Frank Geyer and the detective's out of their offices to make room for Louis Wagner, the new director of public works. Perhaps the biggest surprise of all: Public Safety Director Stokley removed twenty-eight men from the Bureau of Police, including Geyer's boss, Francis R. Kelly, once a United States secret service agent. Stokley replaced Kelly with ex-fire Marshal, Charles W. Wood.[155]

Word of Kelly's removal sent shock waves through the community and local businesses immediately protested. The press pounded on Superintendent Lamon's door late that night, demanding explanation of Kelly's removal. The next day, *Philadelphia Inquirer* printed numerous testimonials Kelly received over the years, which included the letter of his initial appointment to chief of detectives that described him as loyal, zealous and efficient.[156]

To add insult to injury, Director Stokley offered Kelly a demotion to a detective position within the department he once was in charge of, which he promptly declined. Kelly accepted a bank guardianship position that offered him much more than he was making. Kelly returned June 3 to testify for the prosecution in the trial of George Wilson in the torso case for the murder of Wakefield Gains.[157]

The press reported Geyer was a detective for years, but his official job title was special officer, assigned to work with detectives at City Hall. That changed early January 1888 when Geyer promoted and Mayor Fitler formalized it at the January 19, Select Council meeting. Geyer and four other officers promoted to detective at the time, which included E. D. Kurtz, John Murray, and James Tate, Sr.[158]

By the time Geyer promoted, he investigated hundreds of crimes and accumulated a tremendous amount of experience spotting wrongdoings of criminals. His cases involved larceny, highway robbery, aggravated assault and battery, and fraud. Geyer worked on gang-related crimes and broke up a notorious group of thieves that operated among Kensington factories. The gang operation extended over many years and the press reported, since Geyer's arrest of the thieves, there were few complaints in the gang-infested area of the city. His cases also involved incest crimes, cruelty to children, and rape as well and he investigated arson, attempted murder, and the incredible infanticide case of the strange story of a cat that killed a baby and the gruesome torso case. Detective Geyer had good success rates too. Of sixty-two arrests analyzed, eighty percent were convicted.[159]

But there was more to come. Much, much more.

Fig. 28. City of Philadelphia Detective Bureau police badge. Image source: Courtesy of the Special Collections Research Center, Temple University Libraries, Philadelphia, PA. From the George D. McDowell Philadelphia Evening Bulletin Collection, date unknown.

CHAPTER 8

Modern Borgia

Insanity often comes on at a particular period of female life. I examined the prisoner and she told me about her physical condition, and, among other things, that she had for years had fainting spells, and, in one had dropped the child on a stove and in another had fallen down stairs.

-Dr. Charles K. Mills, expert witness testimony for Sarah Jane Whiteling defense[160]

1227 Cadwallader Street, June 1888

THE FIRST MAJOR CASE Detective Geyer investigated after his promotion was another one that grabbed worldwide attention. It involved a woman named Sarah Jane Whiteling, who the press called, "Modern Borgia."

Mrs. Whiteling's house was familiar to Geyer, as it was three-tenths of a mile from his childhood home on Cadwallader Street, where his parents still lived.

The Whiteling investigation earned Detective Geyer a couple firsts. Geyer was inadvertently thrown into the midst of a public rift between his department and the coroner's office, which the press reported in local papers. And like killer H. H. Holmes, the case involved life insurance money. But that wasn't a first. The other first for Geyer, was also a first for the City of Philadelphia.

Mrs. Sarah Jane Brown was a widow with a baby out of wedlock who fell in love with a handsome cigar maker from Philadelphia. The two dated and when Sarah Jane's daughter, 'Birdie' was nine months old, the couple married and later had a little boy named Willie.[161]

For all appearances, John Whiteling and Sarah Jane were a happy couple, and the children content. But soon John looked thinner, his face pale, eyes dark and sunken and visibly dull. He often missed work due to illness, which put pressure on the families' finances. Over time, he became sicker and sicker. To keep the family housed and fed, Mrs. Whiteling washed neighbors clothes for extra income. Birdie did her share to help take care of little Willie, and daddy too, when he was sick. But everything was about to change.

Mrs. Whiteling couldn't do any more to help her husband get well, so she summoned their family physician, Dr. George Smith. He gave John medicine, but his health continued to decline and thirty-eight-year-old John Whiteling died. Dr. Smith said the cause of death was pleurisy and inflammation of the bowels.

Broken hearted Sarah Jane, Birdie, and little Willie coped with their emotional loss as best as they could. John's brother moved in for a few weeks to help take care of Birdie and Willie, but abruptly moved out when Birdie got sick. She too, became sicker and sicker. It seemed she had a bad case of the flu. Mrs. Whiteling wasted no time. She called Dr. Smith right away, hoping this time the doctor could make her well. Dr. Smith gave Mrs. Whiteling an elixir for the nine-year-old, but Birdie died a few days later.

People suspected Mrs. Whiteling. First her husband died, then Birdie one month later. Reluctant neighbors could not decide if they should offer sympathy or call police, so instead, they did their best to avoid her.

But Mrs. Whiteling's hardships were only beginning. Now, little Willie was sick with the same symptoms his daddy and Birdie had. Mrs. Whiteling again sent one of the neighborhood boys to get Dr. Smith, but this time the doctor insisted another physician examine Willie.

Mrs. Whiteling was furious. How could her doctor abandon her like that?

Dr. Smith opened the morning newspaper and read an article that jolted him out of his chair. Little Willie died. He threw the newspaper down and immediately called on Coroner Ashbridge. Each of Whiteling's family members died one month after the other, John, March 20, 1888, Birdie, April 24, then Willie, May 26. Coroner Ashbridge thought it odd too and wondered why Mrs. Whiteling showed no symptoms. He promised to follow up and send Deputy Coroner Powers to Mrs. Whiteling's home to examine the drainage system for defects. Arsenic toxicity can sometimes leach into the water and cause chronic symptoms like Dr. Smith explained the Whiteling's had, so they had to rule that out first. But, as expected, Deputy Coroner Powers found nothing of the sort in their water system.[162]

Detectives Geyer and Crawford went to work on interviewing residents in Geyer's neighborhood. How well did they know the Whiteling's? Was there anything unusual they noticed about the family? Had she or any other family member confided in them? One neighbor described Mrs. Whiteling's odd behavior since her husband and children died. She would laugh uncontrollably, then burst into tears. Another neighbor said she offered to help Mrs. Whiteling care for her husband, John Whiteling, and found it strange that she left his room right as he took his last breath. She didn't even stay to console him. Several neighbors said they suspected she poisoned their children by giving them tainted candy.[163]

That was enough for detectives to get an order of exhumation of the bodies of John, Bertha, and Willie. Officials directed suspects attend exhumations to observe their reaction, and this was no different. Coroner Ashbridge ordered Mrs. Whiteling to the Mechanics' Cemetery. When she arrived, Professor Henry Leffman was busy removing viscera from her loved one's remains, but she gave no reaction. Not one tear flowed from her eyes, not even a sad look—nothing.[164]

Later that night, Mrs. Whiteling went to Dr. Smith and asked if he knew anything about the bodies. "I gave her no satisfaction[,] and she said she would go to the Coroner's the next day," Dr. Smith told the *Philadelphia Inquirer*.[165]

Professor Leffman examined the remains of all three bodies and found they contained arsenic in large quantities. Acute arsenic poisoning caused nausea, vomiting, severe abdominal pain, and diarrhea, all symptoms the three exhibited. Leffman notified Coroner Ashbridge right away.[166]

In an unusual move, the coroner bypassed Detective Geyer and Crawford, and instead requested Special Officers Henry and Kenney arrest Mrs. Whiteling. Geyer found out about the arrest and went to her cell Monday morning and got a confession.

But Coroner Ashbridge wasn't having any of that. *He* was the one that went to her house after Dr. Smith reported his suspicions. *He* sent his employee to test the water. *He* told the special officers to arrest her. So, in an unusual move, Coroner Ashbridge went to Mrs. Whiteling's cell on Tuesday and got a second confession. *Philadelphia Inquirer* reported the public bantering between Chief of Detectives, Wood, and Coroner Ashbridge.

Chief Wood said,[167]

"There is one thing about this case that I don't like. I think the Coroner and his officials have acted very unfairly with this office in connection with this case. When Geyer told me what information he had on Wednesday I wanted the Coroner to allow him to arrest Mrs. Whiteling at once. He was not yet ready to arrest her. Again on Thursday I suggested the same course. He refused, as he also did on Friday and Saturday. On Sunday he called on Special Officers Henry and Kenney, and had the woman arrested and taken to his office. When Geyer learned on Monday morning of Mrs. Whiteling's arrest he visited her in the cell and got a confession from her. This was made known to the Coroner, who dragged the woman before him Tuesday afternoon and got the same confession."

Coroner Ashbridge gave a slightly different version of events to the *Inquirer:*

"Mrs. Whiteling; if you will only tell all you know about this affair your conscience will not trouble you." She looked at me for a minute or so, and said, "So I will, but I must pray to God first to give me strength." She asked me to leave her alone for a few minutes while she prayed, and I retired. Having an engagement out of the city, and being unable to remain any longer, I called on Chief Wood, and at my suggestion Detective Geyer was sent to her cell to get the confession she had promised me she would make. This is how the detectives got into the case.

Regardless of how Sarah Jane's confession came about, the dueling offices agreed on its contents.

Mrs. Whiteling told detectives she bought a box of Rough on Rats poison from George Bille's drugstore to exterminate bugs but John forbid her to use it because it might hurt the children.[168]

John was sick for three or four weeks and one day she heard him tell Birdie to be a good girl and mind her mother. Mrs. Whiteling went into John's room after Birdie left. Her husband called her to his bedside and said he took the poison she bought.

Right away, Mrs. Whiteling asked the neighbor boy to get Dr. Smith and when the doctor got there, neither John nor Sarah Jane told him about the poison. The doctor gave them medicine to treat stomach flu.

"He suffered great agony, vomited and had terrible pains. He died at 7 o'clock on Tuesday evening, March 20. The doctor saw him daily until he died. After taking the poison he only lived three days," Mrs. Whiteling said.

Her husband never told her why he took the poison, but she thought it was because they were poor.

John took out a small life insurance policy with John Hancock Insurance Company. After Mrs. Whiteling paid for the funeral, pawned her husband's watch while he was sick, then bought herself a watch, she used the rest for household expenses.

Birdie was a healthy girl and never got sick. Sarah Jane said she wanted to poison herself the week before Birdie died, but could not figure out what to do with her children.

"Saturday morning, 8 or 9 o'clock, the 21st day of April I gave Bertha poison. I opened the box and with a spoon took out a small quantity, mixed it in water, called her and said: "Birdie, here is some medicine I want you to take; now take it." I gave her a teaspoonful about every half hour," Mrs. Whiteling said.

Charlie Gilbert, the neighborhood boy, went to get Dr. Smith for Mrs. Whiteling. The doctor examined Birdie and left a couple powders to dissolve in water and give her every half hour.

"I did not give her any medicine on Saturday at all; only gave her the poison in water every half hour, the same as the medicine should have been given. On Sunday morning I felt sorry for having given her the poison and stopped. Then gave her the medicine for the first time. The doctor called every day until she died."

Mrs. Whiteling collected twenty-two dollars from life insurance for Birdie and then moved upstairs to a smaller room.

Willie was next. Mrs. Whiteling mixed up the poison and gave it to Willie every half hour and again sent Charlie Gilbert to get the doctor. He left two powders for her to mix and give to Willie, but like she did before with Birdie, she did not give it to him.

"The next morning I received a letter from Dr. Smith saying I should get another doctor in consequence of his losing my husband and Birdie," Mrs. Whiteling said.

She was furious and sent Charlie back to Dr. Smith's house, to demand he come right away, but he refused and said to get another physician. Sarah Jane summoned Dr. Martin, who lived a few doors down on Cadwallader Street.

Little Willie died and she again collected life insurance.

She told detectives she threw the rest of the poison into the water well. She talked to them about terrible thoughts she had after the deaths, and how she moved to Columbia Avenue to get away.

"My only motive for poisoning my children was that Birdie might grown [sic] up to be sinful and wicked, as she had at various times stolen pennies from people and once a pocket book from her teacher, Miss Darby, at the school on Hancock Street, near Thompson. Birdie acknowledged taking the pocket book. She told many bad stories. She was sinful so young that I did not want her to grow up and become a great sinner.

"My little boy was sinless and I poisoned him because he was in the way. I could not go out to work for there was no one to take care of him and he was a burden to me. Without him I could get along.

"Now I know my children are angels in Heaven and I want to meet them there when I die. I don't expect to meet my husband there because he committed suicide, and a suicide cannot go to Heaven," Mrs. Whiteling confessed.

Callus and emotionless, the mother talked about how she heard Rough on Rats was arsenic. She bought the first box for the bugs, and the second box for her children.

"The devil must have possessed me. I did not do it for money. All I cared for was enough to place my children under ground, and I am glad I have not one penny of that money to live on," Mrs. Whiteling said and then told detectives she was sorry and wanted them to pray for her.

"My conscience is now clear, having confessed everything. I could not sleep until I told all and asked the Lord to grant me strength to tell all I have. I can swear before Almighty god that I did not poison my husband. He took the poison himself, but I did poison my children."

The coroner's office and Detective Bureau put their animosity aside and brought Mrs. Whiteling to Ashbridge's office June 15 to see if they could get her to confess to killing John before the coroner's jury trial. Detective Geyer had suspected she killed John too, but could not prove it. Arsenic found in his system did nothing more than help prove Mrs. Whiteling's version he committed suicide by poison.

In the one hour meeting held behind closed doors, Mrs. Whiteling sobbed and told Coroner Ashbridge and Detective Geyer she killed her husband.

"On the way home with this [poison], I thought over what the man had said about it killing people. That was the first I thought, for the devil must have put it in my head for me to give it to my husband. I was tempted by the devil. I mixed for him a glass of egg nogg [sic] and put it in that," Mrs. Whiteling said.

"We were very poor. So poor that we owed everybody—the grocer and everybody else. The insurance money I got on my husband only did a little while and I thought what was placed on Bertha's life."[169]

Ashbridge and Geyer brought Mrs. Whiteling out of the private room to begin the coroner's inquest. Detective Geyer and other officials, a drugstore clerk, and Mrs. Whiteling's neighbors, testified before the jury. Elizabeth Gilbert, of 1219 Cadwallader Street, told jurors that on the day Mr. Whiteling died, he was in a great deal of pain and frequently vomited. She suggested to put hot plates on his stomach and it seemed to relieve the pain. Gilbert rubbed his back and put hot irons to it. He said, "Oh that feels so good!" Mrs. Gilbert testified those were his last words. He turned on his stomach and Mrs. Whiteling went downstairs. Mrs. Gilbert saw he was dying and called for Mrs. Whiteling to come back upstairs. Mrs. Whiteling said, "Oh, I can't look at him die!" John Whiteling died ten minutes later.

Another witness, Mrs. Emma Pomeroy of 943 North Third Street stated she knew Mrs. Whiteling for five years.

"Mrs. Whiteling visited me last Monday week. She came in the back door laughing. She sat down in a rocking-chair and began crying all of a sudden. She rested her elbows on her knees and her face in her hands. I said to her, 'What on earth's the matter?' just that way. She mumbled something about the three bodies being taken up. I could not exactly say what it was. She worked herself all up into a stew, and she says, 'I've done something that I oughtn't have done.' I said, 'My God, what have you done?' She said it was nothing but the Cadwaladar [Cadwallader] street talk," Mrs. Pomeroy testified.

"She said there was some talk about her children having been poisoned by eating candy, and that she had said something she oughtn't have said, and that the next time she would think twice before speaking once. She said they were going to open her children's bodies to see what caused their death, and she was afraid they had really been poisoned by eating candy. I said if they were my children, I would want their bodies opinged [sic] to find out what it was. I told her to keep her spirits up, and if she had a clear conscience she would come out of it all right no matter what the people in Cadwalader [Cadwallader] street said. I told her not to care a snap for them. I sympathized with her because I thought she was in trouble. If I'd 'a known she'd poisoned her children she'd never set a foot inside my door."[170]

Before leaving the witness stand, Mrs. Pomeroy identified Mrs. Whiteling. Sarah Jane raised her black mourning veil and showed Mrs. Pomeroy a half silly smile.[171]

The coroner's jury found Mrs. Sarah Jane Whiteling guilty of all three deaths. With one hand on a handkerchief and the other on a palm-leaf fan, Mrs. Whiteling sat with her face hidden behind her veil while the verdict was read. A grand jury indicted Sarah Jane on September 12, 1888, and her trial began that same year, late November.

Sarah Jane Whiteling's attorney's put up a good insanity defense, and presented a physician as an expert witness; however, a law prohibited a doctor with less than two years' experience from sending a person to an insane asylum, so the judge disqualified him.

Dr. Alice Bennett, who persuaded a judge to release Annie Gaskin in Geyer's bizarre story of a cat case, testified she found the woman had low mental organization and was physically diseased. She found Sarah Jane had a disease of the heart, often associated with insanity, and as a result, felt Sarah Jane was insane.

Dr. Charles K. Mills, a well-known expert on insanity, said, "Insanity often comes on at a particular period of female life. I examined the prisoner and she told me about her physical condition, and, among other things, that she had for years had fainting spells, and in one had dropped the child on a stove and in another had fallen down stairs."

On cross-examination though, Dr. Mills said he believed the woman to be of a weak mind, but she was not insane when he examined her in her cell. The only evidence he could base an insanity diagnoses on was from statements Sarah Jane made about herself and such a condition would only produce insanity in one out of ten thousand cases.[172]

An undertaker testified he thought her behavior was odd. She wanted to wash Willie and would laugh and cry alternatively then talk about getting married. Her brother-in-law said he always believed something was wrong with her but never thought she was insane. After a three day trial, the jury rejected the insanity defense and found her guilty of all three murders. The judge sentenced her to hang.[173]

Governor Beaver gave Mrs. Whiteling two reprieves amidst a public outcry and petitions to commute her sentence, but he signed her death warrant.

On the morning of her execution, several clergy prayed with Mrs. Whiteling. She requested Dr. Alice Bennett, who obliged, and came to her cell to console her. Attorney Reuben O. Moon, who later served as H. H. Holmes' attorney, visited her. That fateful morning, she requested a breakfast of eggs, toast, and chocolate but never touched it.[174]

Detectives Frank Geyer and Thomas Crawford were among twelve jurors selected to witness Sarah Jane Whiteling hang. It was a first for Detective Geyer and a first for the City of Philadelphia. For never in its history, had Philadelphia executed a woman.[175]

Mrs. Whiteling's life came to an end June 25, 1889, at Moyamensing Prison. After doctor's declared her dead, authorities took her body to the Philadelphia School of Anatomy where Drs. Alice Bennett, Francis Dercum, Boenning, and Formad conducted an autopsy. They found no sign of insanity. Afterward, Dr. Alice Bennett took the brain for microscopic examination.[176]

Sarah Jane Whiteling's body lay buried next to her murdered husband and children at United American Mechanic's Cemetery in Philadelphia, but officials moved it to Philadelphia Memorial Park when the cemetery later closed to make way for construction.[177]

In the end, Mrs. Sarah Jane Whiteling was executed for poisoning her husband, daughter and son to benefit from insurance proceeds—$230 for her husband John, $122 for her daughter Bertha and $47 for her son Willie. "For this paltry sum this unwomanly woman sacrificed the lives of husband and children."[178]

Geyer and Crawford never forgot the small-framed sanctimonious memoriam's Sarah Jane Whiteling displayed on the walls of her home for her husband and children. They read:

Epitaph for John Whiteling:

In Loving Remembrance
JOHN WHITELING
Died March 20, 1888.
In the 39th year of his age.

'Tis hard to break the tender cord,
When love has bound the heart;
This hard, so hard, to speak the words:
"We must forever part."

Dearest loved one we have laid thee
In the peaceful grave's embrace,
But thy memory will be cherished
Till we see thy Heavenly face.

Epitaph for Baby Willie:

In Loving Remembrance.
WILLIE C. WHITELING,
Aged two years and two months.
This lovely bud so young and fair,
Called hence by early doom,
Just came to show how sweet a flower
In Paradise could bloom.

Ere sin could harm or sorrow fade,
Death came with friendly care,
The opening bud to Heaven conveyed,
And bade it blossom there.

Epitaph for Bertha "Birdie":

In Loving Remembrance.

BERTHA M. WHITELING,

Died April 24, 1881,

In the 9th year of her age.

[Mrs. Whiteling repeated the same wording at the end of her husband, John's epitaph][179]

Fig. 29. A rare 1889 illustration of Mrs. Sarah Jane Whiteling. Image source: *National Police Gazette*, New York, January 12, 1889, p. 5.

JOHN WHITELING.

BERTHA WHITELING.

LITTLE WILLIE WHITELING.

Fig. 30. Mrs. Sarah Jane Whiteling's family that she poisoned. John Whiteling, age 38 (top), Bertha "Birdie," age 9 (bottom left), Willie, age 2 (bottom right). Image source: "Hanging a Woman," Buffalo Sunday Morning News, June 30, 1889, p. 1.

Fig. 31. Official records documenting the execution of Sarah Jane
   Whiteling. She was the first woman executed in Philadelphia
   and the twenty-eighth person executed between 1839 and 1916
   in Philadelphia. Image source: List of Executions Book, City
   of Philadelphia Archives, 1839 to 1916.

Fig. 32. Rough on Rats ad. According to the president of the State Pharmaceutical Board, Alonzo Robbins, a fifteen-cent box of Rough on Rats, has enough arsenic to kill twenty persons.[180] Image source: *New York Daily Tribune*, April 28, 1901, p. 3.

CHAPTER 9

White Chapel Row

I went to the stable, got my horse and wagon, drove to my house and put the body and the legs in the wagon, and took it to Fairmount Park, and put it in an iron pipe.

-Sworn confession witnessed by
Frank P. Geyer, New Year's Day, 1889[181]

1212 Cadwallader Street, Christmas 1888

IT SEEMED CHRISTMAS WAS a time of year for murders lately, and 1888 was no different. The day after Christmas, while sweet little Edna Geyer played with her new toys and anxiously waited to celebrate her second birthday in a few days, Detective Geyer left their home to investigate the murder of a man that lived on Cadwallader Street near Geyer's parents. The murder was across the street from the Whiteling's house, where Sarah Jane Whiteling murdered her entire family. There was so much crime on the street at that time, police nicknamed Cadwallader Street "White Chapel Row."[182]

John Magg, a farmer near Philadelphia's East Fairmount Park, woke Tuesday night to his dogs barking as if someone were breaking into his home. Mr. Magg picked up his revolver, opened the front door to investigate, and saw a shadowy figure in the park. He yelled out to the man, but he didn't answer. Mr. Magg pointed his revolver in the air and pulled the trigger to scare the man, but it misfired. His cartridges were bad. He ran to the Reservoir Hotel and asked the proprietor for help. Officer Weaver, of the Twenty-third District, was at the hotel and accompanied Mr. Magg to his farm to search the area. After the officer and Mr. Magg left to search the farm, the hotel proprietor noticed a man moving from a swamp area, which was unusual to see someone in that area at night. The proprietor yelled twice at the strange man, who broke into a run and disappeared into the night.[183]

The next day, four teenage boys, Walter Bennett, Thomas Kenny, George Herwood, and Frank McCabe couldn't wait to do a little exploring outside. Though the day was extra cold, winter never stopped them from having fun. They walked to Snyder's Woods at Thirty-third Street and Columbia Avenue, which was a great place for boys to hang out. Except for a stack of water pipes, the empty lot was a marshy-ground filled with scraggly blackjack brush.

The four friends grabbed sticks and banged on a couple thirty-six inch iron water pipes, which made a cool noise that sounded like a drum, but this time it was different—a muffled noise, as if something was stuffed inside.[184]

"Look at the bundles of tramps clothes," Walter Bennett said.[185]

One boy leaned into the pipe, held onto the edge of the stick, and poked the bag.

"It feels pulpy."[186]

Someone reached inside and tugged and pulled until the bag came out. They peeked in a small hole in the bag and one boy cried out, "It's chickens!"

McCabe took out his pocket knife and cut a hole in one of sacks and all at once they realized it wasn't chickens.

"It's a body! It's a dead man!"

The boys panicked and ran as fast as they could until they found workmen at the reservoir to help them.

A couple workers returned to the water pipes with the boys to be sure it was a human body, which it was. The workers telephoned the Twenty-third District station for a patrol wagon. Officers arrived a short time later and removed the bags.[187]

The case was horrific, one that even the most hardened detective would be sickened by, and it was Geyer's first dismemberment case since the Wakefield Gains torso case.[188]

Detectives Geyer and Crawford responded to investigate the discovery of the mutilated murder victim. Geyer and Crawford opened the sacks and found the nude legs of a man in one bag, and his head, covered with clotted blood, and trunk with hands tied across his chest, in the other bag. His head looked as if someone bashed it with an ax or something heavy and sharp. Three knife cuts were on the left side of the victims' face, one under the chin, and two on it. The condition of the remains showed the murder was as recent as twenty-four hours ago. The trunk had three layers of shirts and a strap for the trousers. He was about thirty-five, five feet six inches tall, and had dark brown hair with a thin mustache and light blue eyes. Authorities thought him to be German or Italian but after the coroner examination, they determined he was of German nationality.[189]

At the crime scene, Geyer and Crawford discovered a bloody newspaper dated December 5, 1888, with German words handwritten across the bottom and "Mrs." written over and over several times. They also found carriage and wheelbarrow tracks, and a broken whip. Most likely workers hauling reservoir water made the carriage tracks, but the wheelbarrow tracks were fresh. It wasn't much to go on, but it was a start.[190]

Police Chief Wood's initial theory was that the man was a brewery employee decoyed and slain on his way home from work, with robbery as the motive. He assigned officers from the Ninth and Twenty-third Districts to bring foremen in from each brewery to view the remains in hopes of an identification. One-by-one, they gazed at the disgusting mutilated remains of the man whose mouth was stuck open in terror, eyes locked straight ahead, and cheeks sunken. The horror of what the murdered man must have gone through no doubt etched permanently in their minds. None of the foremen could identify the man.[191]

The next day, Chief Wood told reporters a new theory.

"My idea of the crime is simply this. A fight has taken place in a house near the place where the body was found during which somebody was killed. The murderers—for there must have been two, no one man could carry the trunk and legs unassisted—then cut off the legs for the purpose of making it portable and not with any idea of destroying the identity. They slipped over to the water pipes, deposited their burden and came back by the railroad, where they were seen by the track-walker." Chief Wood said they have nothing to work on at the moment and can do nothing but theorize until they identify the victim.[192]

Like Geyer's earlier Wakefield Gains' torso case, the coroner's physician ruled that someone dismembered the victim while he was alive and he lived for at least a half hour after his skull was crushed.

While Geyer and Crawford continued their investigation, several Philadelphia officials received anonymous letters and telegrams offering to deliver the murderer to justice. One such offer to the police superintendent requested $25,000 and another one to the mayor requested $1,000. Police Chief Wood reported two anonymous letters of "Jack the Ripper" type, which stated police would never capture the murderer and the next victim would be a prominent lawyer in the city.[193]

On New Year's Eve, there was a big break in the case. Special Officer Henry learned a German man named Anton Schilling was missing since Christmas Day. Schilling lived at the same residence as his business partner, Jacob Schoop, on Cadwallader Street. The officer brought a half-dozen neighbors and friends to the morgue where each person identified the remains as that of Anton Schilling,[194]

News of the break came to Chief Wood via a drug store telegram. Wood and Detective Geyer hurried to the station on a carriage, arriving there with horses covered in foam. Schilling's roommate and business partner were placed under arrest until detectives could confirm involvement, while the chief, Detective Geyer, and a captain and lieutenant remained in a conference to determine future action.[195]

Back at the Cadwallader house and business, officials found Jacob's bloody clothes. In the cellar, they found clots of blood, a three-foot long board saturated with blood and pieces of human remains, and an ax that looked like someone wiped it with a cloth.[196]

Detective Geyer interviewed Jacob Schoop in German, and with the overwhelming amount of evidence found in his cellar,

Schoop confessed. He told Geyer he and the victim ran a small grocery store together out of their home at Gillingham and Cadwallader. Schoop woke up about five o'clock Christmas morning and went to the kitchen to get his cancer-stricken wife food, but got angry at Anton because there was no food left. Schoop said he knocked the victim to the floor and beat him with a heavy piece of wood. After the victim was dead, Schoop cut off his legs then threw the body and legs into the cellar. Later, Schoop put the dismembered body in two bags, placed them in his horse-drawn wagon, and drove to East Park reservoir where he stuffed the bags into the pipe.

"In addition to the statement made at the station house, [at] Front and Master streets, I recognize the saw produced by Special Officer Henry as the saw I pawned . . . and the one I used to cut Schilling's legs off," Schoop confessed.[197]

Detective Geyer, Chief Wood, Lieutenant Beale, and Special Officer Henry seated themselves in a carriage. Geyer rode in the front seat with the driver. The officers drove to district headquarters to pick up the prisoner, then Central Station, after which, Jacob Schoop was brought to the morgue to identify his victim. Officials pushed through a large crowd of onlookers and escorted the tall, slender man to where Schilling's mutilated body lay. At first Schoop showed no emotion, but then burst into tears.[198]

"What is the man's name?" Detective Geyer asked him in German.

"Antoine [Anton] Schilling."

"Is this the man you killed?"

"Yes."

"And cut off the his legs?"

"Yes."

"You don't deny, then, in the presence of these witnesses, that this is the man you killed?"

"No," Schoop said between sobs.[199]

The men escorted Schoop while he clung to Detective Geyer in fear of the ensuing mob outside. After the carriage was a safe distance away, Geyer gave him a cigar which he coolly lit and smoked.[200]

Schoop returned to his cell to await arraignment where he spent most of the night crying.[201]

Jacob's daughter made a sworn statement that gave police a different story. Detective Geyer translated it aloud for police officials. In the statement, Susan Schoop described how she came to America to live with her father a few months before he killed Anton Schilling. She said it was her father that sent for her, but she later learned her dad got the money from his business partner.

"I found out it was Anton Schilling that furnished the money for my passage [boat from Switzerland to Philadelphia]," Susan Schoop said.

She arrived in Philadelphia October 2, 1888. Unbeknownst to Susan, her father and stepmother planned for her to help them get Anton's money.

"When I was at my father's house, about four weeks ago, my stepmother suggested I should marry Schilling, as he had some money coming to him from Germany, and that after I was married to him[,] I could get his money and leave him." Susan declined and said, "No, I will not do that."

Her stepmother upped her game. She told Susan to put a spoonful of soap or soda in Schilling's coffee and in his soup until he died. But Susan refused. Her stepmother was livid and cursed at Susan. She said, "He has the constitution of a horse, for I had started to give him wash soda in his soup when we lived in Wilmington. He complained of feeling sick the second day after I had given it to him. I continued giving him the soda[,] and he got worse." Her stepmother stopped the concoction because Anton Schilling said he would buy them a grocery store to run.

Soon after, Susan heard her father say he bought laudanum and put it in a whiskey drink for Anton, but when Anton took a drink[,] he noticed it right away and said, "There is medicine in this."

Later, Susan went upstairs into her stepmother's bedroom and noticed a rope lying in the corner. Susan asked her what it was for and her stepmother told her they planned to put it around Anton's neck when he fell asleep and hang him up in the yard so it would look like he committed suicide.

Susan heard her stepmother ask her father if he did it yet and he said, "No, I can do nothing with him tonight."

It was a crazy situation for Susan and she needed to get away. A nice lady that lived in apartment in the back of their home let her move in with her.

Susan went to her father and stepmother's home and asked where Anton was. Her father told her he went away to work on a farm, but Susan knew they must have killed him.

Detective Geyer finished translating her statement and then officers brought Susan's father from prison. Geyer read Susan's statement to him in her presence. Jacob Schoop listened and then denied everything.

"You know that every word is God's own truth," Susan Schoop said to her father in German.[202]

Chief of Detectives Wood arranged for the arrest of Jacob Schoop's wife. She was in delicate health due to cancer and the arrest of her husband. Special Officer Henry lifted Mrs. Schoop off her bed and carried her to the patrol wagon waiting outside her home. He took her to Philadelphia Hospital where she remained guarded.[203]

Coroner Ashbridge held an inquest and found Jacob Schoop guilty. Detective Geyer described the discovery of the body and read Schoop's confession and witness statements, which included the one from Schoop's daughter. When Geyer read the part where the daughter said her stepmother proposed to hang the victim, the stepmother, Mrs. Schoop, cried out, "Oh, my! No, no," and then Mrs. Schoop grew faint and ill.[204]

A jury found Jacob Schoop guilty of first degree murder February 21, 1889. During trial, defense attorney's objected to introduction of the confession Schoop made to Geyer, but the judge overruled it. Schoop's defense was that he killed the victim in the heat of the moment because there was nothing to eat or drink in the house and he thought the victim would strike him after he accused him of eating everything. The poisoning talks his daughter claimed he and his wife had, were only a joke. Defense said Schoop cut the body up after the victim was dead because he didn't know what to do with the body.[205]

The jury didn't buy Schoop's story and sentenced him to hang. His accomplice, Schoop's wife, was found insane and sent to Norristown Hospital.[206]

Officials executed fifty-five-year-old Jacob Schoop in a double hanging at Moyamensing Prison with convicted murderer, Thomas J. Cole, on February 20, 1890. Three priests comforted Schoop just prior to his execution, one of which, was Father Dailey, the same priest that comforted H. H. Holmes at his hanging in 1896.[207]

CHAPTER 10

Send Flowers to My Funeral

*I am not sorry for him. It is better that he is dead. I am sorry
for the poor girl, for she was innocent . . . I wonder if they
will let me get up tomorrow. I would like to see the devil.*

-Mrs. Kayser's statement[208]

*Hope Street, between Montgomery and Berks Street, February
1889*

"I'LL BE DEAD IN a week, Mr. Hoffman. Are you going to send
flowers to my funeral?" Annie Klaus said, flashing chocolate
brown eyes at Levi Hoffman and Louisa Fania. The three friends
from the mill let out a good laugh, for Annie, the daughter of a
German shoe dealer, was only nineteen and had her whole life
ahead of her.[209]

Did Annie know something no one else did or was she just
having some good old-fashioned fun? Detective Geyer would soon
discover Annie was a bubbly, fun loving teenager—a breath of
fresh air, who refused to let teenage worries get her down.

———

Edward Travis and Lot Moorhouse walked along Montgomery
Avenue about eleven o'clock Saturday evening when they heard a
groan coming from a girl collapsed on the pavement near the
snow-covered bank at Hope Street. Thinking the girl had fainted,
Edward stayed with her, while Lot Moorhouse ran to a nearby
home and asked for a glass of water.[210]

Lot banged on Mrs. Palmer's door and when she opened it, he
explained about the girl who had fainted. Mrs. Palmer shook her
head no and said, "I guess she's shot, for I heard a pistol shot a few
minutes ago followed by the sound of someone running away."

Why didn't she call for police when she heard the gunshot?

Mrs. Palmer gave Lot Moorhouse a cup of water and followed him outside to the injured girl. Edward Travis, who had been comforting the girl, noticed a nasty wound on her left eye and a bloody clump of ice stuck in her hair. The girl was badly injured and her breaths labored. No doubt about it—she was slipping away. Edward placed her head in his lap and when he did, she let out a long gasp and muttered something. They all three looked at each other to see if anyone understood, but no one did. Maybe she had a parched throat. They poured water in her mouth but it rolled right back out. Mrs. Palmer knew it was hopeless and gently stroked her gloved hands.[211]

While the young girl lay dying in the empty lot, twenty-four-year-old Otto Kayser rushed into his father in-laws' home in a state of wild excitement, pacing up and down the once-quiet sitting room.

"Where is pop?" Otto asked his mother-in-law, Mrs. Lare, "I want to tell him of the crime that I have committed."[212]

Pop was not home yet, so Mrs. Lare begged Otto to tell her what was wrong.

"No, I won't tell anybody my secret," Otto Kayser said. He smelled of alcohol and wasn't making much sense. Otto's wife heard the commotion and asked what was the matter.[213]

"I've lost my job on the cars," Otto blurted out just as his father-in-law, Pop, came through the front door. Suddenly, Otto pulled a .32 caliber Defender out of his pocket and waved it over his head.

"I've committed a terrible crime," Otto said in a state of desperation. His voice begged forgiveness. They tried everything they could think of to calm him down, but nothing worked. Was the gun loaded? What was he planning to do? No matter what anyone did or said, Otto continued to stomp back and forth and wave his gun. His wife slipped away and called for police. A short time later, Officer Nace from the Twenty-fourth District arrived and wrestled Otto Kayser's gun away from him. No one bothered to tell the officer about Otto's drunk admission of a terrible crime he committed. The officer gbbed Otto's arm and pushed him towards the door but Otto's wife and her parents begged the officer not to arrest him. Otto was drunk and just needed a good nights sleep in his own bed. Officer Nace relented, but confiscated the gun.[214]

Back at Montgomery and Hope Street, Edward Travis, Lot Moorehouse, and Mrs. Palmer knew there was no hope the young girl would survive. Mr. Moorehouse ran to Second and Columbia and found Officer Robinson, who rang the nearest patrol box to summon a police wagon. The wounded girl was driven by ambulance to St. Mary's Hospital where doctors pronounced her dead. Sergeant McGarvey and Special Officer McKibben arranged to transport the girl to the Eighteenth Police District for identification.

The call woke Detective Geyer just before one o'clock Sunday morning, February 3. Careful not to wake three-year-old, Edna, Geyer slipped away to meet Lieutenant Scott at the Eighteenth District station where the body of a teenage girl lay. She was dressed in a close-fitting brown ulster coat with astrakhan trimming and a knit hood that blanketed her dark brown, bloodstained hair. The black mittens covering her hands would never warm them again. Geyer and Scott leaned over her body and examined the wound on her left eye, blackened with gun powder. Whoever killed the girl must have jammed the pistol into her eye and pushed her eyelid in as the gun went off. She had no other markings on her body. There was no way to identify her.[215]

Detective Geyer inspected a basket filled with bakery cakes found near the girl. The goods were still fresh so the murder must have occurred on her way home from a bakery. If they could find out where she bought them from, maybe someone could identify her. Officers canvased bakeries in the area, and although the bakeries were not open yet, owners were busy making goods for the day.

More than a thousand people showed up at the Eighteenth District police station to have a look at the victim and help identify her. Twenty-five officers stood in a line to protect the girl's body that lay on a stretcher on the corridor floor.[216]

Meanwhile, patrolmen continued to search the area for anyone who knew the victim. Detective Geyer received a dispatch from Central Station that a man named Henry Klaus, and his son-in-law, reported a nineteen-year-old girl missing that matched the dead girl's description and they were on their way to the Eighteenth District station to identify her.

Klaus and his son-in-law arrived at the station house and Detective Geyer and Lieutenant Scott led them past the crowd, back to where the young girl lay lifeless on a stretcher.

"Oh, God! It's Annie," old man Klaus cried out as soon as he saw her body. Tears welled up in his eyes. The two officers let Klaus spend his last moments with his dead daughter, then brought him into a private area to question him.

Mr. Klaus told officers Annie made a weekly trip each Saturday to the bakery owned by both son's-in-laws, but this time, Annie never came home. Klaus' daughter was the youngest of three girls. Mr. Klaus told Geyer and Scott he knew Annie was sneaking around with a man named Tom, a horse car conductor on the Second and Third Street Road. Mr. Klaus didn't like Tom and forbid Annie to see him. He told them he warned Annie that if he caught her, she would suffer severe punishment. He said Annie's friend's would know the man's name. Detective Geyer, Captain Quirk, Lieutenant Scott, and Special Officer McKibbin went to the Second and Third depot looking for a man named Tom but no one by that name worked there. With Mr. Klaus' permission, investigators went to their home and looked through Annie's room and correspondence to see if they could learn anything that might lead them to Tom's identity. There they learned about a friend named Louisa Fania, who might have information on who the conductor was. Louisa gave investigators a description. He was about twenty-five and had light hair and a light-colored mustache. Louisa said the man worked on car No. 210 of the Second and Third Street line. Geyer, Quirk, Scott, and McKibbin returned to the depot and learned a man named Otto Kayser fit the description. He had worked the No. 210, but was recently fired.[217]

Geyer and the investigators determined Otto Kayser lived with his father-in-law at 2738 Kensington Avenue. The four investigators prepared to confront him at the home. Officers banged on the front door at five o'clock in the morning, ready with a ruse to get him out of the house.

Kayser raised the second story window sash and yelled, "Who's there?"

"Get dressed. You are wanted at the depot to take out an extra car," Lieutenant Scott said.. But Kayser knew police were there because of the murder of Annie.[218]

Kayser grabbed a razor and hurried to the bed where his wife and two baby boys slept. Without hesitation, he slashed his wife's throat with a razor, making a four inch gash under her chin. When she screamed, Kayser jerked his arm up and slashed the left side of her neck, making a deep twelve inch cut that reached from ear to ear and down to her right shoulder blade.[219]

Blood spurted out of her wounds. Mrs. Kayser screamed, "Murder!" Then grabbed Richie, her youngest child, and rushed down the stairs. Officers heard the commotion and just as they were about to burst in the door, Mrs. Kayser opened it.

It was a ghastly scene. Mrs. Kayser stood at the front door, clad in a robe, holding her crying baby. She was a bloody mess. Officers couldn't tell if the baby was injured or covered in the mother's blood.

"Who has cut your neck?" Detective Geyer said.

"My husband!" In a gargled voice, she said, "Up stairs."[220]

Lieutenant Scott took Mrs. Kayser and her baby in his arms while Geyer and the others drew their pistols and rushed upstairs. They found Kayser sprawled on the bed. He slashed his own throat from ear to ear and a massive amount of blood flowed out of his jugular vein, which was completely severed. The razor lay on the bloody sheet next to him. Detective Geyer took in the scene around him and found Kayser's second son sound asleep near his dead father, unaware of what he had done.[221]

Officials pronounced Otto Kayser dead at 5:45 Sunday morning.[222]

Detective Geyer and Special McKibbin and one other officer continued their investigation to determine the motive. Otto Kayser had passed himself off to Annie as a single man named Tom Lynn. They theorized Annie Klaus found out he was married and confronted him.[223]

Detective Geyer and Lieutenant Scott interviewed Otto's wife at the Episcopal Hospital a few days later. She told them she didn't suspect her husband was cheating until another conductor's wife told her Otto paid attention to a young girl and was fired from his job. Though terminated, Otto pretended to go to work, leaving the house each day at the time his shift would have started. The day before he murdered Annie, Mrs. Kayser secretly followed him and saw him drinking instead of working. That night when he came home, she scolded him about it. The next day he returned home with a pistol, waving it about. Otto threatened to kill her so she called for an officer who took the pistol away and told her husband to calm down or he would lock him up.[224]

Otto had seemed uneasy when he went to bed that night. When they heard officers banging on their door early the next morning, Otto woke her up and suddenly slashed her with the razor. She felt something but didn't know what happened until blood ran down her neck. That's when she grabbed one of her sons and ran downstairs.[225]

The last curtain fell on the sad story of Annie Klaus and Otto Kayser Wednesday, February 6. It seemed a cruel coincidence that Annie predicted her own death. Maybe she knew if she confronted Otto, he would react the way he did and was willing to accept the consequences.

Annie Klaus and Otto Kayser's funerals were held simultaneously and because of the large crowds, law enforcement assigned over forty men from the Eighteenth District to maintain peace. Annie Klaus' body lay covered with a white shroud in a silver-trimmed coffin in her father's sitting room at the back of his store, which doubled as their home. Beautiful floral wreaths adorned the casket and overflowed into surrounding areas. Two floral pillows, inscribed with the name "Annie" rested at her head and feet. In contrast, Otto Kayser's body was covered in a black shroud, and as if to show profound mental anguish, an indescribable expression was etched on Otto's face. As each mourner passed his body, his mother raised her eyes as if asking for forgiveness for her dead son.[226]

Four or five weeks after the two funerals, Mrs. Kayser recovered from her injuries and could leave the hospital. Her husband had sliced her twice with the razor. One wound was four inches long in front of the neck and down the windpipe with several large veins sliced open. The second one was a twelve inch cut on the left side of the neck, running around to the right ear and down the shoulder. That one severed blood vessels, large veins, and muscles. Dr. Van Pelt would not let Mrs. Kayser attend the funeral and instead ordered her to recover in the hospital several weeks. Mrs. Kayser was glad to be alive. The doctor said he never had such a plucky patient who did not wince once when he put over one hundred stitches in her throat.[227]

Annie Klaus' good friend, Emma Berger, had trouble getting over the tragedy. After the murder, she became insane and attempted suicide twice, once by setting her house on fire, and the second time she threw herself out a window. She later recovered and married a man named Samuel Blanrue of Philadelphia.[228]

Annie's mom, Antone (Anna), died sixteen years after Annie's murder. Her father died February 24, 1909. All three were buried at Greenmount Cemetery in Philadelphia.[229]

A reporter once said Geyer was about as big as John L. Sullivan, the Irish-American boxer recognized as the first heavyweight champion from 1885 to 1892. Geyer was quick-witted, perceptive, and above all, tenacious. "Geyer can hug a fellow like a hungry bear," the reporter said. In the Annie Klaus murder case, Geyer entered Otto Kayser's house and mistook the man standing behind a bloodied and panicked woman, as the person who caused her harm. He wasted no time. Geyer closed in on the man and gave him an awful bear hug. "I didn't do it . . . my brother . . . upstairs," was all the man could say while being squeezed. Geyer drew his revolver, ran upstairs, and found the perpetrator had killed himself with a razor with his young son fast asleep nearby.[230]

No doubt police work for Detective Geyer was stressful at times. It's true for all law enforcement. Police officers often invoke feelings of uneasiness in people. Some become fearful or may panic when an officer approaches even if they did nothing wrong. Unfortunately, there is no easy way to mitigate that. Crimes must be investigated and perpetrators brought to trial to face consequences.

Besides being a 'hungry bear,' Geyer had other nicknames like Murder Detective, Murder Geyer, and World's Famous Detective, for he was persistent and used his keen intuition to solve even the most gruesome murders. But soon, fellow officers and the press would give him another nickname.

One Tuesday night in the spring of 1889, a frantic middle-aged woman rushed into police headquarters.[231]

"Save me from a fiend. He continually sends shocks through me. There it is now!" the woman said to Detective Geyer and his partner Eckstein.

"I am pursued at every turn by this man."

Geyer tried to calm the woman. He gave a glance to Eckstein and instantly thought of a way to calm her.

Geyer offered the distraught woman a chair. "Sit down, madam. You are under a spell and in a few minutes, I will relieve you of your torture."

This peaked her curiosity. The woman forgot about her woes and listened to Geyer.

"Now, madame," Geyer said, "you must have faith in what I do, or I will not be able to help you. When I strike this table with my forefinger, the spell will leave you entirely."

The woman watched Geyer's finger approach the table. He touched it and in an instant, five incandescent lights went out. Geyer, Eckstein, and the woman sat in complete and total darkness. The two officers didn't plan for the lights to go out. It was as if the woman's complaint and Geyer's solution was real.

When the lights came back on a short time later, the woman's demeanor changed as if a demon left and an overwhelming air of calmness overtook her body. She was no longer hysterical.

Detective Geyer, in complete disbelief, sat there in shock for a full minute without speaking.

The grateful woman thanked Geyer profusely and left the station free from the electric fiend.

Geyer and Eckstein looked at each other and immediately burst into laughter. Papers reported Geyer's new nickname as: "Electric Detective."[232]

Fig. 33. Annie Klaus, seventeen (left) and her murderer, Otto Kayser (right). Otto was a married street car conductor with albino features. Annie Klaus was unaware he was married until around the time of her death. Annie's photo was taken shortly before her murder. Image source: "Ten Fateful Hours that Set a Record in Detective Feats," *Philadelphia Inquirer*, August 22, 1937, p. 88.

CHAPTER 11

Secret Search

I thought his absence would be only a matter of a week or two. Now it has passed into months and I have received only a very few letters from him, and the news I get from Mr. Crawford is of the most meagre description. If he should die tomorrow, I would know nothing about it until the department chose to tell me, and even then I would not know where to look for him unless they told me that also.

-Mrs. Mary E. Geyer, statement about
Detective Geyer's sudden absence[233]

South America, April - September 1892

"I NEED YOU IN a meeting right away," Police Superintendent Robert Linden told Detective Geyer. Geyer entered his office and closed the door.

Mayor Stuart was seated in the small room and next to him was a man named William H. Wanamaker, accompanied by his attorney John R. Reed, and Superintendent Benjamin Franklin, from the Pinkerton detective agency Wanamaker employed.

The City of Philadelphia would soon embark on a stealth operation and Superintendent Linden and Mayor Stuart felt Detective Geyer was the best man to do it.

William Wanamaker paid a $20,000 bond for Gideon Marsh, president of the failed Keystone National Bank in Philadelphia, but Marsh skipped town in 1891 and was now a fugitive connected with the Keystone Bank scandal involving William Wanamaker's brother, Postmaster General John Wanamaker. During investigations into the scandal, the Postmaster admitted he received discounts from Keystone Bank for three times more than the law allowed without providing collateral. He denied he knew about Gideon Marsh's illegal activities though and if Marsh was caught, John Wanamaker felt he could clear his good name. When Gideon Marsh was last seen May 27, 1891, he wore a brown derby hat, brown or snuff-colored overcoat, plaid-check pantaloons, patent leather shoes with over-gaiters, and carried a small alligator satchel and umbrella.[234]

Marsh was recently seen in Rio de Janeiro and rather than pay a shady guy $1,000 to turn over Marsh to him, William Wanamaker told Mayor Stuart, Superintendent Linden, and Detective Geyer, he would like to propose the City of Philadelphia send a detective to South America to search for him. William Wanamaker would pay all city expenses for the search. This seemed agreeable as the city had issued a resolution in 1891 offering a $5,000 reward to bring Gideon Marsh to justice. After some discussion, Mayor Stuart ordered Linden to detail Detective Geyer for the job.[235]

"Superintendent Linden told me to get ready to go on a long trip. I thought he wanted me to go to Portland, Ore., where I had located a criminal who was badly wanted . . . I did not care for the trip, as I knew that persons were dying [of yellow fever] at the rate of four hundred-fifty a day," Detective Geyer said.[236]

Geyer had good reason for concern. There was a yellow fever outbreak in Rio de Janeiro and so far, 4,313 people died, and of those, 3,643 were foreign-born victims like Geyer. The supervising surgeon general of the Marine Hospital Service wrote in 1892, "It is a characteristic feature that the foreign-born inhabitants constitute not less than about 85 per cent of the victims of yellow fever. Newcomers are all in great danger during the summer months."[237]

Besides the risk of yellow fever, Detective Geyer had limited knowledge of the country and was not familiar with the fugitive, but he consented to go if they would provide his wife with a $10,000 life insurance policy and a $5,000 accident policy, which William Wanamaker agreed to fund. The problem was that when Geyer had to ship out, the insurance policies were not yet complete. "Mr. Wanamaker then gave my wife a bond for $10,000 to provide for her in case anything should happen to me."[238]

Authorities deemed the mission classified to prevent media from tipping off the fugitive. No one knew the details, not even his wife, Mary, and five-year-old daughter, Edna.

Detective Geyer and Mary celebrated their seventh wedding anniversary and fourteen days later, without a single word to anyone except his supervisor, Geyer sailed on the *Martha* steamship out of Brooklyn on April 23, 1892.

His distraught wife told the *Philadelphia Inquirer* she didn't know her husband left the city until the Philadelphia Detective Bureau told her. Detective Geyer left the house like it was a normal work day and didn't return for five months.

"My husband left the house one morning with the expectation of returning in time for supper. Tea-time came, but Frank did not appear. I waited some little time for him, as he is very often delayed. Late in the evening someone rang the bell, and thinking that it was he I hurried to the door. Instead of Frank, it was his fellow worker, Mr. Crawford. He told me he had come over to let me know that Frank had been sent upon some mission from the office. Frank's work, he said, would take some time to complete and he would not report back until it was finished. In the meantime the department would keep me posted about him as far as it could and would send him any letters that I might write."[239]

The German steamship was not licensed to carry passengers to South America, so Geyer joined them as a member of the crew.

"I shipped as able seaman under the name of Frank P. Roberts," Detective Geyer said. "The first stop that we made was at St. Thomas, in the West Indies. There I made a thorough search for Marsh. Let me say right here that in every place I visited I made a thorough search. I inquired at all the American consulates and hotels and places where an American would be apt to frequent."[240]

He sailed to South America for thirty-two days, arriving in Rio de Janeiro May 25, 1892, but due to yellow fever, the inspection general of Health of Ports for Rio de Janeiro ordered all ships to halt until they followed orders. All ship captains had to employ specific hygiene measures such as washing their ships daily with phenic acid mixed with water and disinfecting their water-closets with chlorate of lime and chloronet of zinc. Captains were instructed not to allow soiled clothing in bunks and to destroy tainted victuals and water. Officials discouraged sailors from coming ashore as they would likely drink to excess and fall easy pray to yellow fever. The inspection general instructed captains to cease labor during the hot hours of the day and hoist the signal of medical visit as soon as the first symptoms of any disease were seen. Despite this, Captain Ahren Kiel issued discharge papers to Detective Geyer and gave him an Indian rupee as a souvenir.[241]

Geyer, under his assumed name, Frank P. Roberts, made headquarters at Hotel Frietas and soon after, he met with the American minister and his staff and was introduced to William H. Lawrence, secretary of the American legation. Geyer negotiated with Lawrence for the return of Marsh if he caught him. Through Lawrence, Geyer secured the services of a member of the Brazilian police but he couldn't speak English. By coincidence, the man was fluent in German.[242]

Detective Geyer searched hotels and other places where he thought Americans might frequent and found sixty-one, but none were the disgraced banker, Gideon Marsh. Some Americans worked in Rio de Janeiro and some were there for medical reasons. The only person Geyer found who knew Marsh was Langford, the man who wanted $1,000 from William Wanamaker to turn Marsh over to him. Geyer investigated Langford and like William Wanamaker suspected, Langford was a schemer. He was unemployed and living on the earnings of his school-teacher wife.[243]

Geyer searched several more locations for Marsh after Rio de Janeiro, but could not find him. "I went to Santos, which is considered the pest hole of the earth. Every morning yellow fever victims, to the number of twenty-five or thirty, are picked up in the street," Detective Geyer said.[244]

Mary thought Frank would be home by the July 4 holiday, but Geyer was in Buenos Ayres in the Argentine Republic searching for Marsh. Mary and Frank's birthdays in July came and went with no sign of Frank Geyer. The only news Mary had to go on with was a few letters and a little news from his longtime partner, Detective Thomas Crawford.

"If he should die tomorrow I would know nothing about it until the department chose to tell me, and even then I would not know where to look for him unless they told me that also," Mary Geyer said.[245]

Mary thought it odd that when the department gave her a letter from her husband from time-to-time, it was in a plain, blank envelope without even a postmark. Also, his handwritten letters never contained a date, and she had no idea when he mailed it.

"I do not receive them in the original envelope; they are given me by Detective Crawford in a blank envelope. In fact I have no means at all of knowing where he is," Mary Geyer said.[246]

By the time Detective Geyer returned to Philadelphia in September 1892, he had searched all ports on the way to Rio de Janeiro, the interior of Brazil, and Montevideo. He also searched towns and villages of the Argentine Republic, Bahia, and Pernambuco and when finished, he took a steamer for St. Vincent, Cape Verde Islands, and Portugal. From Portugal, Geyer went to France and England. After a five month search, Detective Geyer took the *Catalonia* in Liverpool for Boston and returned to Philadelphia empty-handed.[247]

Postmaster General John Wanamaker felt the heat for his involvement in the Keystone Bank scandal, especially since his brother William Wanamaker was Gideon Marsh's bondsman, so he made public speeches he hoped Marsh would read in newspapers.

Kansas City Star printed Postmaster John Wanamaker's statement:

"There is nothing that will please me so much as Marsh's return, and I welcome the opening again of every book and paper of the bank to public gaze even as I did years ago. If my foes will bring this man, doubtless more sinned against than sinning, into court, and he will tell the truth, I will use my utmost endeavor in securing all the leniency possible in his sentence, and after he has finished it I will assist him in re-establishing himself and his family in life. I publish this to the world hoping he will see it wherever he is, and I [unintelligible word] to it that I have friends who will put in the hands of Quay, Penrose and Andrews whatever money is needed to pay the expenses of Marsh's return, as they seem to know where he is. One of them claims to have been in recent correspondence with him. If the poor man, who can yet redeem his life, who must have been crazed when he ran away, will send me word where he is as soon as these words bear him the message of these dastardly assaults upon me I will come to him in person in any part of the world and accompany him back."[248]

The *New York Times* printed the following statement:

"Gideon W. Marsh, if the newspapers print this, and you read it, I appeal to you, as one man to another, who must be met and faced in the day of final reckoning to return immediately to Philadelphia. Even though the books and papers of the bank are conclusive enough in themselves as to the falsity of this accusation against me, it will be some satisfaction to me to have you open your lips upon all the facts to those who probably would not believe the truth even though one arise from the dead."[249]

His idea worked. Gideon Marsh read John Wanamaker's statement in the papers and communicated with an old friend in Philadelphia named E. F. Pooley. They arranged to meet in Philadelphia with Gideon's bondsman, William H. Wanamaker and Gideon's ex-wife, who divorced him while he was on the run. For his part in the bank scandal, after seven years in exile and being chased all over the world by detectives, including Frank Geyer, in 1898, Gideon Marsh agreed to face charges and help clear John Wanamaker. Judge Butler convicted Gideon Marsh on December 13, 1898. Gideon received twelve years, three months in Eastern Penitentiary and was ordered to pay a fine of $500, plus costs of his prosecution. President Theodore Roosevelt later commuted his sentence and the day before Christmas, December 24, 1902, Gideon Marsh became a free man.[250]

The pardon was granted on the condition that Marsh pleaded guilty to three indictments merged into one but instead received three separate sentences. It was also based on the fact that by the time Marsh became president of the bank it was already in bad financial condition and Marsh committed the offenses to keep up the bank's credit. Former District Attorney Beck recommended the commutation and Attorney General Knox approved of the action. Numerous bank presidents signed the pardon petition including presidents of First National, Central National, Bank of North America, Penn National, Consolidated National, and Western National and other prominent people in the banking and financial industry. Arrangements were made for Gideon Marsh to take a clerical position with a large manufacturing company upon his release from prison. Marsh planned to live with one of his sons.[251]

The Philadelphia City Treasurer, ironically nicknamed "Honest" John Bardsley, also played a role in the bank scandal that led Detective Geyer to search for Gideon Marsh. Bardsley admitted loaning between $500,000 and $600,000 of public money to Keystone National Bank, of which he collected between two and three percent interest. In return, the bank discounted notes to Bardsley and paid him up to four percent interest on public money he deposited. Officials indicted Bardsley. He pleaded guilty to seventeen counts in three bills of indictment and was arraigned. He admitted he loaned and invested public money for private gain and agreed to receive interest on deposits of public money. The judge sentenced Bardsley to sixteen years imprisonment in Eastern Penitentiary. After serving several years, Bardsley was also granted a pardon.[252]

Fig. 34. Gideon Wells Marsh, the fugitive ex-president of the Keystone National Bank of Philadelphia. Image source: "The Keystone Bank Wreck." *The Illustrated American*, Volume VII, No. 71, 1891.

Fig. 35. Postmaster General Wanamaker. Image source: "The Keystone Bank Wreck." *The Illustrated American*, Volume VII, No. 71, 1891.

Fig. 36. "Honest" John Bardsley, the City Treasurer of
Philadelphia, pleaded guilty to seventeen counts for
malfeasance in office. Image source: "The Keystone Bank
Wreck." *The Illustrated American*, Volume VII, No. 71, 1891.

Fig. 37. Rio de Janeiro a few years after Detective Geyer's search for Marsh. Image source: Courtesy of Library of Congress, circa 1909.

CHAPTER 12

Etched in Time

He was an old soldier, brave as a lion, and he wouldn't have hesitated a moment once he had decided upon the act.

-Anonymous close friend of Captain Schooley[253]

Philadelphia City Hall, May 11, 1892

WHILE GEYER WAS ON the German steamship to Rio de Janeiro, his co-workers struggled to cope with intense emotions. The day after forty-five miners died in the Roslyn, Washington, explosion, Philadelphia suffered a tragedy of their own—one that would rock City Hall and its police force to its core.

Captain Joseph M. Schooley answered morning roll call on an overcast Wednesday morning, May 1892. The large, broad-shouldered man listened quietly while police lieutenants took turns briefing from each district.

Fifty-five-year-old Schooley, who "always stood up for the boys," excused himself from the briefing to finish a report. He made his way to the empty captain's room on the sixth floor of City Hall. Schooley stood in front of a mirror, pulled out his service pistol, and shot himself in the right temple. Captain Schooley's body slumped over and fell to the floor a little before noon.[254]

No one heard the shot. Captain Brown discovered Schooley's body when he went into the captain's room expecting to find his friend writing reports but instead found him dead. Schooley wasn't suicidal. In fact, the day before, Schooley dropped by the Twentieth District station house in his division. House Sergeant Behrens remembered he and Captain Schooley talked about the recent suicide of Patrolman Rogers from the Eighth District. Schooley told Behrens, "I cannot understand what gets into their heads."[255]

Captain Schooley joined the Philadelphia police force during the Civil War, appointed to patrolman by Mayor Alexander Henry. By 1874, he advanced to lieutenant of the Seventeenth District and later Mayor William S. Stokley promoted him to captain of the First Police Division.[256] He served in that role until Mayor William Burns Smith terminated Schooley November 1885 for reportedly turning a blind eye to illegal gambling. A man with Schooley's experience would be disciplined instead of fired, but it was common for new administrations to find reasons to fire people that do not share the same political views. As soon as Mayor Smith left office in April 1887, former Mayor William S. Stokley (now Public Safety Director) rehired Schooley to his old position and demoted the lieutenant that the old administration had promoted to take Schooley's place.[257]

Schooley wasn't without his own controversy though. He made news headlines October 1889 when he chewed the thumb of Second Ward Common Councilman James P. Park in a bar fight. The two enemies socialized with other council officials at McCuen's Saloon when Schooley and Park got into a heated political discussion. Park accused Schooley of using the police force to defeat him when he ran for office. Their hatred toward one another dated back to when Park and the Committee of One Hundred had Schooley summoned before the mayor for intimidating voters.[258]

Witnesses in the saloon heard Schooley say, "You are a lying cur." Schooley lunged at the councilman and grabbed his throat. Park got away from Schooley's grip, threw him on the floor, and held him down. Schooley struggled to get up but could not loosen Park's grip so he chewed his thumb. Park freed himself. Enraged at Schooley for his bloody thumb, he pounded on Schooley's face. The rest of the group pulled the two off each other. Later, Councilman Park pressed Philadelphia's mayor to investigate Captain Schooley. Mayor Fitler organized a board of inquiry composed of chief of detectives, the superintendent, and a chief clerk. Against common protocol, Park demanded to be represented by an attorney and bring a stenographer to the hearing. Mayor Fitler denied the request so Councilman Park declared he would not appear. Meanwhile, a couple men attacked Councilman Park and later, a suspicious fire damaged his business and his insurance company canceled his policy.[259]

"If Director Stokley knew how I am hounded and how it is dangerous for me and my family to go around our own neighborhood, he would perhaps think it time to call a halt. The men who set upon me on Monday night and attempted to beat me must be protected in high places or they would not dare to assault and insult me so openly. There is apparently no law for me, at least not at police headquarters," Councilman Park said.[260]

Councilman Park, good on his word, was a no-show at the hearing and Mayor Fitler decided the case without him, dismissing charges against Captain Schooley.

A few months after the Schooley-Park feud died down, Mayor Fitler, Chief of Detectives Wood, Superintendent Lamon, Director Stokley, Captain Schooley, a few of the detectives, and several elected officials became ill with the influenza epidemic that took hold of Philadelphia in January 1890. Of the sick Philadelphia officials, Chief Wood and Captain Schooley were most affected by the illness, but returned to their police duties. It was said Captain Schooley suffered lingering effects from his influenza illness, which may have also been a factor in his suicide.[261]

In 1891, Joseph M. Schooley, was appointed acting superintendent of police. Although favored to take the permanent position, for reasons unknown to anyone, according to Philadelphia Times, he declined. Whether he declined or was passed over for the permanent promotion to superintendent, Schooley returned to captain duties early 1892.[262]

No doubt Schooley worried about rumors heard around City Hall. People talked of his potential dismissal from the force. Perhaps that, together with his invalid wife's medical complications, weighed heavily on his mind. Captain Schooley also suffered severe pains in his neck and spinal cord as his friend Captain Brown testified to in an inquest Deputy Coroner Dugan held after his death.[263]

Whatever his reasons, Schooley ended his life symbolically on the sixth floor of City Hall while standing in front of the mirror. Family, friends, and government officials were puzzled as to why he chose his final breath to be permanently etched into what is now known as a National Historic Landmark right in the heart of downtown Philadelphia. Was it an 'in your face' statement to government officials and colleagues? Or did he hear something in the briefing that fateful morning that caused him to breakdown? Perhaps it was a complex emotional build-up over the years and he couldn't bear to live his life one more second.

For Schooley's funeral, officers kept the peace and directed about 6,000 bereaved mourners from the parlor of Schooley's modest two-story home where his body lay, to a side door exit onto Carpenter Street. City officials, members of the police force, and Geyer's colleagues were among those who paid respects. Beautiful floral arrangements were in abundance, adorned with tributes such as, "Patrolman's Friends . . . Our Captain . . . His First Command . . . Our Friend."

Frugal with money, Captain Schooley invested in real estate and left a comfortable sum to his widow, Margaret. This was a wise decision. As a promoter of the police pension fund, he knew the constitution well—it prohibited widows or children from collecting from the fund in the event of a suicide.[264]

Captain Schooley's wife died four years later. In her husband's honor, she left some of her estate to the Philadelphia police pension fund. Together, they were buried at the historic Mount Moriah Cemetery in southwest Philadelphia. In a strange twist, ex-Mayor William Burns Smith, who fired Schooley in 1885, and ex-Common Councilman James P. Park, whom he fought with, were also buried at Mount Moriah.[265]

Geyer returned from his long international search for Gideon Marsh a few months after Captain Schooley's death. By then, the captain's room at City Hall was cleaned up, but the memory of what he had done still lingered.

THE LATE CAPTIAN SCHOOLEY.

Fig. 38. Captain Joseph Schooley. Image source: *Philadelphia Inquirer*, May 12, 1892, p. 1.

Fig. 39. Captain Joseph Schooley headstone at Mount Moriah Cemetery. Image source: Courtesy of Friends of Mount Moriah Cemetery.

CHAPTER 13

Where Are You?

When reviewing all the facts and evidence in the case it was impossible for me to exclude the thought that I had not proved first degree murder beyond a doubt.

-George S. Graham, Philadelphia district attorney
Statement to Board of Pardons for commutation of
Alphonzo F. Cutaiar, Jr.'s death sentence[266]

1250 N. Eleventh St., Philadelphia, October 1893 - 1895

DETECTIVES GEYER AND CRAWFORD began a murder investigation in 1893, after a carpenter found skeletal remains at the old home of a notorious career criminal, Jimmy Logue, on North Eleventh Street in Philadelphia. The carpenter tore up kitchen floor boards when repairing the house and found a woman's skeletal remains.[267]

Right away, authorities believed the remains were of Jimmy's wife, Johanna, who went missing sixteen years ago. Detectives could not find Jimmy so they had her brother, William Gahan, identify her remains. He recognized his sister from her distinct gold fillings and wedding ring engraved with 'J.L. to J.L,' which stood for James Logue to Johanna Logue.

Johanna was the sister of Jimmy's second wife, whom he married without divorcing his first wife, Mary Jane Andrews. Johanna's sister died of alcohol consumption, and a short time afterward, Jimmy married Johanna May 25, 1871, while he sat in the courthouse dock at Philadelphia's Central Station. Right after the marriage ceremony, Jimmy went to Eastern State Penitentiary to serve a seven year, six month sentence. He bought a house on North Eleventh Street after his release and fitted it with a barber shop for his stepson from his earlier marriage to Johanna's sister. He, Johanna, and his stepson, Alphonso Cutaiar, Jr., lived there until she disappeared in 1879.[268]

Geyer and Crawford suspected Jimmy. But during their investigation, they learned that although Jimmy was insanely jealous, he hunted all over the country for his wife after she disappeared, taking out advertisements in the local papers and offering a $500 reward. He traveled to several cities to view remains of unidentified victims, too.

Mrs. Mary Ann Friend, told detectives Johanna came to her house the night before she disappeared, which wasn't unusual because Mary Ann sheltered Johanna when she fled the house in terror from Jimmy. On the night Johanna went missing, Jimmy called Mary Ann and offered her money to tell him where she was.

"He was desperate and excited," Mary Ann said.[269]

Officers were at a loss. On one hand, Jimmy was the obvious suspect. But what perpetrator would offer a reward and travel the country to view bodies in hopes of finding his wife either dead or alive? There wasn't enough evidence to arrest Jimmy Logue and the case went cold. That is, until Jimmy unexpectedly showed up a few years later about midnight, March 5, 1895, at Coroner Ashbridge's home.

"I am Logue—James Logue—and I want to give myself up, as I understand there is a warrant for me," Jimmy said. Coroner Ashbridge knew nothing about a warrant, so he locked Jimmy up for the night at the station house at Tenth and Thomson Streets, under the alias, William Casey. Coroner Ashbridge intended to keep it a secret until he could investigate further but somehow news of the capture showed up in the next day's papers.[270]

That same night, Coroner Ashbridge asked Public Safety Director Beitler if he could assign Detective Frank Geyer to the case and Beitler agreed. Detective Geyer reported to Coroner Ashbridge for the next several weeks. Jimmy was brought to City Hall on the sixth floor and kept there as the 'mysterious prisoner' while Ashbridge and Geyer investigated his story.

Jimmy told them he arranged for his stepson, Alphonso Cutaiar, to run a barber shop business at his home, and Alphonso, Jimmy, and his wife Johanna, all lived together. While Jimmy was away on nefarious, so-called business, his wife went missing. He immediately telegraphed his stepson to ask where she was but didn't receive an answer so Jimmy took a train to Philadelphia to confront Alphonso, who said he didn't know where Johanna was. Alphonso told Jimmy she came home on Friday. On Saturday, she drank heavily, then stuck her head in the hall door and said, "I'm off." She left for New York and that was the last time Alphonso ever saw her.[271]

Jimmy told Coroner Ashbridge and Detective Geyer about his long search for his wife that turned up nothing and his suspicions she ran away with his old pal, Peter Burns, in Denver. He even went to Denver to locate her but was unsuccessful. Jimmy spent his own money for the search and mortgaged his house to raise additional funds. He finally gave up, packed her belongings, and left the house. Jimmy hid seven bonds, each worth $1,000, under the carpet and told his stepson about it, but later found out his stepson had sold one bond at Drexel's and gave the money to his girlfriend, whom he later married. Jimmy forced them to refund the money.[272]

Detective Geyer took that information and worked to disprove it, for he knew Jimmy was a liar. But Geyer found out Jimmy's statements were true and refocused his investigation on Alphonso, and his apprentice, Harry Fricke. On March 26, 1895, Detective Geyer met with Harry Fricke and his sister at the house where Johanna was last seen. Fricke said after Johanna disappeared, there was a terrible smell but they used disinfectants to mask it. They had no idea where the smell was coming from. Curiously, after Geyer interviewed Harry Fricke, he had a nervous breakdown and wound up at the same hospital Alphonso's real dad worked at as an attendant.

Detective Geyer traced Johanna's jewelry back to Jimmy's stepson, Alphonso. Jimmy Logue was cooperative. He gave Geyer and Ashbridge information to help them solve the case and swore out a warrant for the arrest of his stepson, who confessed on April 17, 1895.[273]

"On the night of the 22d of February I went back in the kitchen and found Johanna drunk. I feared that if she went back to New York Logue would beat and abuse her. I carried her up stairs and put her to bed with her clothes on, and then tied her feet with a handkerchief and her hands with a clothesline [to prevent her from leaving]. I also wrapped the clothesline around her body. I went down stairs to finish up the night's work, and when I came back I found that Johanna had rolled over on her face. She was dead, having been smothered under the bolster. I forced her room door open and placed the body on the floor."

"I was going to tell about the thing the next day but I was afraid, so I waited until Logue came home. He begged me not to do it and it was Logue that suggested we put the body under the floor. Logue took her watch and jewelry.[274]"

At six o'clock that same night, though, Alphonso made another confession. This time he said Jimmy, had nothing to do with the murder. Johanna accidentally suffocated herself and after he realized she was dead, he used the opportunity to take her jewelry. Alphonso carried her body to the kitchen, pulled up loose boards, then stuffed her underneath and replaced the boards without nailing them down because he thought it would make too much noise.[275]

At the coroner's inquest, several people testified, but the most interesting testimony came from the notorious burglar himself, James "Jimmy" Logue.[276]

"You do solemnly swear," Coroner Dugan said.

"No, I don't," Jimmy Logue said, while he nervously twirled his hat. "I ain't going to testify. I didn't murder my wife and you have kept me in jail for three months and I understand you are going to send me back to the county prison. I'm getting tired of that sort of thing and I won't stand for it."

"Have you counsel?" Mr. Dugan said.

"No, I haven't, and I don't want any," Logue said. "I ain't on trial that I know of."

After some persuasion, Jimmy Logue testified and told of his wife's disappearance and his search for her. His voice was hard to hear in the courtroom.

"Speak louder, Jimmy," Detective Geyer said.

"Here!" Logue said. He turned towards Detective Geyer and waived his arms in anger.

"Don't you call me Jimmy. I've heard that too much. I'm sick of it."

Geyer stayed quiet.

His testimony continued. When asked what he did after his wife disappeared, he said, "I raised the devil." He testified he checked the cellar to see if the ground was disturbed and peered under the joists of the dining room because he was suspicious of his stepson and he knew Johanna was afraid of him.[277]

At the end of Jimmy's testimony, officials gave him a quarter for a witness fee. He carefully looked it over, then spit on it for good luck, and put it into his pocket.[278]

Geyer testified about the investigation and Alphonso's two confessions.

The coroner's jury debated for a moment, then the jury foreman said, "We find that the body found in October 1893, under the kitchen floor at 1250 North Eleventh Street, is that of Johanna Logue, and that Alphonse F. Cutaiar, Jr., is responsible for her death."[279]

Coroner Dugan recalled Jimmy Logue. "I am sorry to say, Mr. Logue, that I will have to commit you to the Central Station as a witness, as you have no permanent abode."

"Who told you that?" Logue said.

"We won't argue the question," Dugan said. Logue left the witness stand mumbling to himself. He told a reporter afterwards, "I'm old and sick and can't stand it. I haven't done anything. I feel sorry for Cutaiar, and I don't want to testify against him. He was like a son to me. I have lost everything since my wife's death, and I'm a wreck. I wouldn't have come back at all and let them halloa murder at me if it hadn't been for my son."[280]

At trial, Alphonso changed his appearance and eerily looked like the murderer, H. H. Holmes. He grew a heavy, dark beard, and his eyes were sharp. The way he looked around, his body movements, attitude, and his hand twirling caused spectators to talk about how much he looked like Holmes.[281]

In District Attorney Graham's opening statement, he said Alphonso's motive was robbery. He brought his bride to the house and passed over Johanna's decaying body often. The stench was so bad it made his wife sick. Neighbors also complained of the smell and health officers were asked to investigate the cause in vain.[282]

The jury deliberated three hours and at one minute past six o'clock, Friday, May 29, 1896, they announced the verdict.[283]

"What is your verdict?" Clerk Henszey said.

Foreman Reiger handed a paper to the clerk.

Judge Yerkes read the contents of the paper. "Gentlemen of the jury, you have found the prisoner at the bar, Alphonse F. Cutaiar, guilty of murder in the first degree."

After trial, Jimmy Logue said, "I don't think the evidence showed that he killed her, but still the family believe that he did. The verdict is satisfactory to me."[284]

Jimmy, who was imprisoned in Moyamensing for eighteen months while awaiting his stepson's trial, walked out of prison a free man with a little over eight hundred dollars in witness fees. However, he had another run in with the law shortly afterwards when his daughter-in-law, Matilda Logue, had him arrested and charged with assault and battery September 11, 1896. She swore that when authorities released Jimmy from prison, he spent his witness fees and was "feeling good." She claimed he hugged and kissed her and attempted further liberties. The Commonwealth felt they had a weak case and intended to abandon it, but counsel for the defendant objected. He asked that the jury be allowed to decide who would pay the costs. When the judge gave the bill to the jury, he instructed them to render a verdict of not guilty. The judge told Jimmy Logan to avoid trouble in the future.[285]

In July 1899, sixty-two-year-old Jimmy Logue, white-haired and decrepit from rheumatism, showed up unexpectedly at Philadelphia detective headquarters at City Hall.

"I have committed my last robbery. I am getting old and want to go some place where I can spend my remaining days away from the sight of those who were companions of mine in crime," Jimmy said.

Jimmy came there penniless and with mercy. He was an old man who didn't want to die a pauper. He begged detectives to make him an inmate at Almshouse so he could live out the rest of his days there. Detectives arranged it and Police Surgeon Andrews took Jimmy to Almshouse in a patrol wagon.

"Oh, but such a treat for the rubber necks," Jimmy said.

James "Jimmy" Logue died of pulmonary edema, three months later.[286]

In an ultimate show of compassion and sympathy, Philadelphia Mayor Ashbridge (the coroner who Logue confided to around midnight in 1895) personally paid to have Jimmy and his wife, Johanna, buried together at St. James Protestant Episcopal Church of Kingsessing at Sixty-ninth and Woodland. Johanna's ashes were encased in a box and placed at the feet of Jimmy. Though she was dead for twenty years, this was the first time her remains received a christian burial. Four employees from the coroner's office and two news men served as pall bearers. Jimmy and his wife, Johanna, were buried six inches away from one of his associates, Martin Laffarty, who Jimmy confessed to cracking safes with.[287]

Alphonso Cutaiar requested a new trial after his conviction, but it was denied. Alphonso was to hang from the gallows. As luck would have it, his sentence was commuted to life in prison following a petition signed by his stepfather, Jimmy Logue, and all of Johanna's relatives.

While Alphonso was in prison in 1905, Alphonso's wife consented for their daughter to marry at the age of seventeen. On the August 9 consent form she wrote, "Mr. Alphonso F. Cutaiar, father of above Ella J. C. Cutaiar, has deserted his family for ten years and . . . has not supported them during that time."[288]

In early 1912, George S. Graham, the district attorney who tried Alphonso, wrote the Board of Pardons a letter in his favor:

"I pressed for murder in the first degree, and the jury convicted the prisoner on that grade of crime. The atrocious circumstances connected with the concalment [sic] of the body helped to give an atmosphere to the case that made everyone at the time accept the verdict as correct . . . When reviewing all the facts and evidence in the case it was impossible for me to exclude the thought that I had not proved first degree murder beyond a doubt."[289]

Governor John K. Tener pardoned Alphonso September 23, 1912, and ordered him released from prison. A 1920 census listed Alphonso as head of household living with his wife, several members of his family, and two boarders, at North 54th Street in Philadelphia's Thirty-fourth Ward. His occupation was listed as Sexton at a local church.[290]

Jimmy Logue.

Fig. 40. James "Jimmy" C. Logue, age 59, notorious burglar and bank robber falsely accused of murdering his wife. Image source: "The Logue Mystery Now Fully Solved," *Philadelphia Inquirer,* April 29, 1895, p. 1.

Fig. 41. Alphonse F. Cutaiar, Jr. Confessed to murdering his aunt, who later became his step-mom, Johanna Logue. Image source: "Murder Will Out Cutaiar," *The Copper Country Evening News*, August 8, 1896, p. 5.

Fig. 42. Alphonse F. Cutaiar, Jr. Cutaiar changed his appearance and stunned everyone by looking like the 'Devil in the White City' H. H. Holmes. Image source: "Fighting for a Life," *Philadelphia Inquirer,* May 28, 1896, p. 4.

Fig. 43. Murder victim, Johanna Logue. Image source: "Fighting for a Life," *Philadelphia Inquirer,* May 28, 1896, p. 4.

Fig. 44. Philadelphia District Attorney George Scott Graham wrote
a letter in favor of commuting Alphonse Cutaiar's death
sentence. Although a jury found Cutaiar guilty of first degree
murder and he was sentenced to death, Graham wrote that after
some reflection in how he prosecuted the case, he felt he did
not prove his case beyond a reasonable doubt. District Attorney
Graham also was the prosecutor in killer H. H. Holmes' case.
Graham was elected to United States Congress as a Republican
and served from March 4, 1913, until his death in 1931.[291]
Image source: "George Scott Graham," *History, Art and
Archives, US House of Representatives*, http://
history.house.gov/Collection/Detail/29017, accessed January
11, 2017.

PART III

Devil in Disguise

CHAPTER 14

Two Enemies

Holmes is greatly given to lying with a sort of florid ornamentation, and all of his stories are decorated with flamboyant draperies, intended by him to strengthen the plausibility of his statements.

-Detective Frank P. Geyer[292]

DETECTIVE FRANK GEYER'S HANDSOME and precise side-part paled in contrast to his bushy eyebrows pointed into an unconnected 'V' at the bridge of his nose. Like Mark Twain, Geyer's overgrown mustache blanketed his unseen mouth. Savvy and driven, Geyer knew what he wanted and wasn't afraid to go after it. This suited him well in his chosen field of law enforcement. A family man with a knack for catching criminals, Geyer's law enforcement career spanned three years short of three decades not counting the two-and-a-half years he resigned from the force in 1881 to pursue a job as a United States postal agent.[293]

Killer H. H. Holmes was also savvy and driven and a man who knew what he wanted and wasn't afraid to go after it. But unlike Geyer, Holmes abandoned family to pursue a life of criminal activities and bigamist ways, which no doubt left emotional scars on loved ones. Holmes sported a similar mustache but was much more timid-looking than Geyer. He weighed in anywhere from 130 pounds at the time of his execution and 150 pounds when a physician examined him in prison—where Geyer was muscular and stout. Holmes was five feet, seven and a half inches tall and Detective Geyer, a six-footer, stood several inches taller than Holmes. H. H. Holmes was a physician and druggist by trade with slate-blue eyes and a dark complexion scattered with scars, marks, and moles. In hindsight, he looked the part of a killer.[294]

The two opposites connected in 1894-96, Geyer, as a world's famous detective, Holmes, as one of America's first serial killers.

Relentless press caught wind of the two savvy and driven enemies after Holmes' arrest in Boston, Massachusetts, and soon, Philadelphia authorities assigned Geyer to investigate the death of Holmes' business partner, Benjamin Pitezel, and to find his three missing children.

CHAPTER 15

Suspicions Intensify

Eight months having elapsed since the children had been heard from, it did not look like a very encouraging task to undertake, and it was the general belief of all interested, that the children would never be found.

-Detective Frank P. Geyer[295]

November 1894 - June 1895

DISTRICT ATTORNEY GEORGE S. GRAHAM requested Detective Geyer attend the trial of a little known, but soon-to-be loathed man charged with conspiracy for swindling a life insurance company in a wild scheme that initially involved a body substitution and fake death. He was best known by one of nineteen-plus aliases—H. H. Holmes. The thin, New Hampshire man, born Herman Webster Mudgett, was a descendent of the first English settlers in Gilmanton. Authorities had apprehended the man in Boston and planned to extradite him to Texas on an outstanding warrant for horse theft, but Holmes begged to go to Philadelphia to stand trial instead for the insurance scam. Texas was notorious for severe horse-steeling penalties. "The Texas people can send Holmes to the penitentiary for twenty years easily enough," Detective Geyer later said.[296]

For the trial Geyer was to observe, officials sent Detective Crawford to Boston to bring H. H. Holmes and his accomplice, Mrs. Carrie A. Pitezel, to Philadelphia November 20, 1894. The two were accused of a $10,000 life insurance scam where Mrs. Pitezel's husband, Benjamin, was to stage his own death using a look-a-like body substitute. Then he would reunite with his family after the policy paid out and Holmes and Pitezel would split the proceeds. Mrs. Pitezel knew about the scam. Ben told her if she found out he was dead, do not believe it because it was a ruse they set up to collect his life insurance. It would have been a good plan too. But they hit a snag when authorities buried the supposed fake body of Benjamin Pitezel in the name of his *alias*, B. F. Perry, at Potter's Field in Philadelphia. To collect on the insurance policy, Mrs. Pitezel was forced to prove the man they buried was her husband, which in reality, should have been the look-a-like substitute. But Mrs. Pitezel was sick so H. H. Holmes persuaded her to send her fifteen-year-old daughter, Alice, instead. All Alice had to do was identify the dead man as her father, whom she believed was in hiding until after the insurance payout.

Holmes and Mrs. Pitezel's attorney, Jeptha Howe, who was also involved in the scam, took Alice to Potter's Field where authorities had exhumed the substitute body. Holmes and Alice identified the body as Benjamin Pitezel and both signed official affidavits.

Despite suspicions, Fidelity Mutual Life Association paid Mrs. Pitezel $9,715.86 on Ben's $10,000 policy, having already advanced H. H. Holmes' travel expenses in order for him to identify the body. For his part in the scam, Attorney Jeptha Howe collected $2,500. This left the remaining amount for Mrs. Pitezel and Holmes to split, but Holmes had another plan. He forged a bogus bank note that showed Benjamin owed him $6,700 for a Fort Worth real estate deal. She had no choice. Mrs. Pitezel paid Holmes and was left with a mere five hundred and some change.

Detective Geyer interviewed Holmes in a cell at City Hall the same day Detective Crawford arrested and brought Holmes and Mrs. Pitezel to Philadelphia.[297]

"He said he had told Benjamin Pitezel how to prepare the substituted body; to place it on the floor with the arm on the breast, put the liquid in the mouth and set fire to it. The liquid had been used for cleaning clothes. He also told him how to force the liquid into the stomach by working the arms," Geyer testified later at Holmes murder trial.

The June 3 trial was not a sensational one and given the circumstances, Holmes' attorneys advised him to plead guilty and face a maximum sentence of only two years in prison. The judge might reduce his sentence as a reward for Holmes' guilty plea. Detective Geyer quietly sat in the courtroom and observed

Holmes' every move, look, and mannerism. What did he do with Mrs. Pitezel's three children that she temporarily let him have custody of? Did he give them to a woman named Minnie Williams, or Hatch, as he claimed when questioned by Graham and his staff about the children's disappearance, or worse, did he kill them? These were questions Detective Geyer would set out to answer.

"I asked him where Pitezel and the children were and he said in South America," Detective Geyer said after he interviewed Holmes, who kept changing his story.[298]

District Attorney Graham had complete confidence in Geyer. With twenty-some years' experience in law enforcement and experience in the intricacies of murder cases, Graham knew if anyone could solve the whereabouts of the missing Pitezel children, it would be Detective Geyer. Graham believed all previous efforts by Fidelity Mutual Life Association to locate Mrs. Pitezel's children during their investigation of the insurance swindle were unskillfully made and he resolved for Detective Geyer to undertake a careful and methodical search for the blunder which a criminal always makes between the inceptions and consummation of his crime.[299]

And so, with funds provided to the City of Philadelphia by Fidelity Mutual Life Association, Detective Frank P. Geyer set out on the evening of June 26, 1895, to investigate what would become the biggest case of his career and one of the most horrific of the century.

Fig. 45. Herman Webster Mudgett *alias* H. H. Holmes. Image source: Frank P. Geyer. *The Holmes-Pitezel case; a history of the greatest crime of the century and of the search for the missing Pitezel children.* Philadelphia, PA: Publishers' Union, 1896.

CHAPTER 16

Sweet Innocence

The deeper we dug, the more horrible the odor became, and when we reached the depth of three feet, we discovered what appeared to be the bone of the forearm of a human being.

-Detective Frank P. Geyer[300]

No. 16 St. Vincent Street, Toronto, Canada, July - August 1895

EIGHT MONTHS PASSED SINCE Mrs. Pitezel heard from Alice, Nellie, and little Howard and it didn't look promising, but Geyer was determined to find the children, dead or alive. He did everything he could to familiarize himself with the case. He carried photographs of the Pitezel family, their travel trunks, and Holmes and his wife Miss Yoke. Together with information from interrogations of Holmes and letters Mrs. Pitezel and her children wrote each other, which were found in Holmes' possession when arrested in Boston, Geyer's first stop was Cincinnati, Ohio. As a professional courtesy, Detective Geyer visited police headquarters in each city and paired with a detective liaison.[301]

Geyer found evidence Holmes and the children were in Cincinnati at one time, but no sign of the children. His next stop was Indianapolis, Indiana. A former Circle House proprietor recognized photos of Holmes and the children and said Holmes told him Howard Pitezel was a bad boy and he planned to put him in an institution or bind him to work with a farmer. The man said each time his son went to the children's room to summon them for meals, he found them crying. Detective Geyer knew he was on the right track. He had a strong feeling little Howard never left Indianapolis alive. Geyer went to Chicago, Illinois next to interview the chambermaid who used to work at Circle House, and she, too, recognized the children. With tears in her eyes, she told Geyer in her native German language the children were alone in the hotel. She saw the children crying and felt bad for them.[302]

While in Chicago, Detective Geyer interviewed Janitor Pat Quinlan at Holmes' Sixty-third and Wallace Street "Castle" in Englewood. There, he had an interesting conversation with the slim man who had light colored, curly hair. Quinlan knew the children well but had not seen them for quite a while and did not know where they were. The interesting part was Quinlan told Geyer if Benjamin Pitezel was dead, H. H. Holmes did it and if the children were missing, Holmes killed them too. Quinlan followed that up by saying that if Holmes were hung for it, he would be glad to spring the trap.[303]

Geyer used the opportunity to ask Quinlan about a man named Edward Hatch, whom Holmes claimed did something with the children. Quinlan told Geyer that Holmes was a dirty, lying scoundrel and the bricklayer he knew as Hatch would do nothing like that. Geyer asked about Minnie Williams, the woman Holmes' at one time claimed also had the children, but other than Quinlan knowing the woman, he didn't provide Geyer with any clues. After a couple more interviews to learn what he could about Minnie Williams and Hatch in the Chicago area, Geyer went to Detroit, Michigan, where Holmes' and the children were spotted.

Detective Geyer found out someone, presumably Holmes, had dug a hole in back of the wall facing cellar steps in a house Holmes rented, but there was no sign of the children or their remains. In another place Holmes rented, a woman recognized the Pitezel girls and Holmes, but she did not see little Howard. Geyer found evidence that the cunning man had the Pitezel children stay in one place, Mrs. Pitezel, Dessie, and her baby in another, and Holmes and third wife in still another place—all within a few blocks from each other.[304]

"It must have taken very careful management to have moved these three separate parties from Detroit to Toronto, without either of the three discovering either of the others, but this great expert in crime did it, and did it successfully," Geyer later said.[305]

Toronto was Geyer's next stop. His old friend, Alfred Cuddy was assigned to liaison with him while there. Geyer and Cuddy searched for evidence Holmes rented hotel rooms and houses in the area. Several people recognized photos of Holmes, Alice, and

Nellie, but no Howard. Geyer got a strong impression the girls were killed somewhere in Toronto. He wrote Philadelphia's superintendent of police:

"It is my impression that Holmes rented a house in Toronto the same as he did in Cincinnati, Ohio, and Detroit, Michigan, and that on the 25th of October he murdered the girls and disposed of their bodies by either burying them in the cellar, or some convenient place, or burning them in the heater."

Geyer and Cuddy interviewed real estate agents and then Geyer met with reporters to give an update on the case, hoping it would jar someone's memory. It worked. He got a tip Holmes rented a remote place on the outskirts of the city in the middle of a field, surrounded by a six foot fence. But it was a false alarm. Though there was a pile of loose dirt under the main building, Geyer and Cuddy took off their coats and crawled into a small hole, but nothing was there. Further investigation found Holmes had never rented the house. Next, Geyer went to Niagara Falls to follow up on leads, where he found Holmes and his wife stayed, but not the children.[306]

Monday, July 15, Geyer again met Detective Cuddy in Toronto, Canada. Cuddy was in a great mood. He received a credible tip.

Mrs. Armbrust opened her St. Vincent Street door and there stood her neighbor, Thomas W. Ryves, and two official-looking men in suits. Ryves introduced Philadelphia Detective Geyer from the United States, and Cuddy, a Toronto, Canada Detective. They were there because Ryves reported Holmes had rented the cottage and he recognized the photos of the two Pitezel girls. Holmes' photo looked familiar but he couldn't say for sure was him. They were also there to follow up on reports of a terrible odor coming from her cellar. The Armbrust's smelled an unbearable stink after they moved into the small cottage, and thinking it might be a water leak, hired Mr. Ryves to fix it. But the smell persisted. Ryves remembered a slender man with two little girls who rented their cottage for a short time before the Armbrust's moved in. The man brought with him a dirty mattress that was so soiled, Ryves didn't think a dog would use it. The man had borrowed Mr. Ryves spade to dig a place in the cellar for potatoes. Ryves told the Armbrust's he would report the smell and the man with the two girls so police would conduct an investigation.[307]

Mrs. Armbrust led detectives to the cellar trap door, hidden underneath an oilcloth in the middle of the kitchen floor. Detective Geyer kneeled down and jimmied the small door open to give a look, but the dirt cellar was pitch-black and the opening was only two by two foot. They needed light to investigate further so Mrs. Armbrust brought detectives a couple kerosene lamps.

The two men, still dressed in professional business suits, descended the narrow steps into the small ten foot by ten foot cellar that was only four and half feet deep.

Geyer and Cuddy crouched down so as not to hit their heads on the low ceiling. With Mr. Ryves spade, the same one H. H. Holmes borrowed, they turned the soil and found a soft spot, so they focused all efforts on that location.[308]

Detectives had a strong feeling Holmes killed the girls and buried them right there. They worked harder, digging and turning over dirt, until at last, they smelled the unmistakable stench of death.

Geyer and Cuddy threw off their coats and continued digging until they reached about three feet in depth and discovered the bone of a forearm. The smell was ghastly—so terrible that once they found the bone, they threw a pile of dirt on top of it to contain the smell while they crawled out of the cellar and planned their next move.[309]

Detective Cuddy contacted his boss, Inspector Stark, to report the discovery and ask for an undertaker to help remove the bodies. Inspector Stark approved of the request and told Cuddy and Geyer to contact the undertaker.

"I suggested to him [the undertaker] to take several pairs of rubber gloves with him, as the bodies were in such a state of putrification, it would be impossible to lift them out of the hole without them," Detective Geyer said.[310]

Undertaker Humphrey had his staff deliver two small coffins to the site while Humphrey and Detectives Geyer and Cuddy worked together to unearth the girls remains.

"Alice was found lying on her side, with her hand to the West. Nellie was found lying on her face, with her head to the South, her plaited hair hanging neatly down her back," Geyer said.[311]

The two girls were stark naked. Eleven-year-old Nellie's limbs rested on top of her sister so they lifted Nellie out first. As careful as Undertaker Humphrey and detectives Geyer and Cuddy were, the state of her decomposed body and the weight of her beautiful long hair caused Nellie's scalp to come completely off her head.[312]

The gruesome sight had to affect Detective Geyer more than anyone could know, as Nellie was only two years older than Geyer's own daughter, Edna. What kind of man would murder sweet, innocent children? Holmes was a coward, a scoundrel, a skeleton of a man without a heart. What motive, other than satisfaction of manipulating and controlling the Pitezel family, would cause Holmes to kill them?

Workers outside the cellar spread a sheet on the ground in which to lay Nellie's remains, then her body was carried to the coffin and placed inside. With sad and somber eyes, the three returned to the putrid-smelling cellar and removed Alice onto another sheet and placed her in the second coffin next to her sister. Together, the sisters were taken to the morgue.[313]

News of the discovery spread like wildfire and citizens and reporters swarmed the St. Vincent Street home.

Detective Geyer slipped away and telegraphed District Attorney Graham and Police Superintendent Linden to notify them of the discovery.

"Thus, it was proved that little children cannot be murdered in this day and generation, beyond the possibility of discovery," Detective Geyer said.[314]

Exhausted, and at the same time, emotional, Geyer returned to his room to write Superintendent Linden and map out a plan for the next day. Much work needed to be done to find little Howard Pitezel.

The next morning, Geyer met with Detective Cuddy and the two set out to find the family that lived in the St. Vincent Street house after Holmes moved out and before the Armbrust's occupied the cottage to see if they remember anything Holmes left behind.

Besides an old bed and mattress, the sixteen-year-old son of the family showed detectives a little wooden toy egg with a snake that sprang out when opened. The boy found it in a leather caba in a closet. To Geyer's surprise, it was listed as one toys Carrie Pitezel sent with the children. This was one piece of the puzzle that helped identify the girls. Another find was after Holmes moved out of the St. Vincent Street house, pieces of clothing and straw were found hanging out of the chimney. One was part of a striped waist, which was grey, and another was a piece of brownish-red woolen garment. There was also a pair of girl's button-boots found in a wood box, along with other pieces of female clothing. All items were thrown in the trash before the new tenant moved in but the description matched what Mrs. Carrie Pitezel provided detectives of clothing worn by the girls.[315]

Whether Holmes removed the girls' clothing before or after he killed them was not known. The fact remains, he tried to destroy their clothing in the chimney because a match was found nearby. Fortunately, the clothing was bound up so tightly, it didn't burn.

Detective Geyer wondered what became of the missing trunk and remembered Mr. Ryves description of a large trunk brought to the St. Vincent Street house while Holmes was there. Maybe Holmes killed little Howard in Detroit, put his body in the trunk, and shipped it to the cottage.

Geyer and Cuddy had several men dig up every inch of the cellar and thoroughly examine the barn and outhouses. But neither Howard or the missing trunk was found.

Meanwhile, Toronto officials prepared to hold an inquest led by Coroner Johnston. On Tuesday morning, July 16, 1895, the coroner summoned jurors to meet at the morgue at half past seven o'clock that evening. The jurors, shocked by the sight of the once pretty Pitezel girls, were overwhelmed by the strong odor of decomposed remains and were on the verge of becoming ill, so Coroner Johnston quickly adjourned the inquest until morning.[316]

Detective Geyer testified the next day.

"On Wednesday evening I attended the inquest and was requested to recite the story of Holmes, and the insurance swindle, and the disappearance and the finding of the children," Detective Geyer said.[317]

He testified for a grueling two-and-a-half hours, after which the coroner called other witnesses, then adjourned the inquest until Thursday morning to await Mrs. Pitezel, who was on her way to Toronto from Chicago, Illinois to identify her girls.

Reporters crowded the Grand Trunk Depot in Toronto and fought for an interview of Mrs. Pitezel when she arrived.

Detective Geyer pushed his way to Mrs. Pitezel and escorted her to a waiting carriage headed for the Rossin House where Geyer stayed. He had arranged to put Mrs. Pitezel in the room across from him to keep an eye on her.

"Oh, Mr. Geyer," Mrs. Pitezel said. "Is it true that you have found Alice and Nellie buried in a cellar?"[318]

"I did all I could to calm her, and told her to prepare for the worst," Detective Geyer said. "I then told her as gently as possible, that I had found the children, but did not describe to her their horrible condition, nor under what circumstances they were discovered."[319]

Despite a protective Geyer threatening to "break the neck of the first reporter who attempted to interview the woman," a determined reporter caught Mrs. Pitezel on her way out of the Rossin House dining room.[320]

"Mrs. Pitezel said she was much exhausted by her trip and trouble and did not care to speak on the subject of her children . . . She had no doubt that her worst fears would be realized and that she would see the dead bodies of her lost children," reported *The Brooklyn Daily Eagle*.[321]

Prior to Detective Geyer and Cuddy bringing Mrs. Carrie Pitezel to the morgue, much care and foresight was made to ensure Mrs. Pitezel would only be shown a little of the remains of her two daughters.

"I told her that it would be absolutely impossible for her to see anything but Alice's teeth and hair, and only the hair belonging to Nellie. This had a paralyzing effect upon her and she almost fainted," Detective Geyer said.[322]

Detectives Geyer and Cuddy brought along brandy and smelling salts as a precaution. Geyer went inside the morgue to see if they were ready for Mrs. Pitezel while Cuddy remained outside with her amongst the large crowd of people hoping to get a glimpse of the traumatized woman.

The coroner's office prepared Alice and Nellie's remains as best as they could. They removed putrid-smelling flesh from Alice's skull and covered the skull with paper that had a hole cut out so Mrs. Pitezel could identify Alice's freshly cleaned teeth without looking at her grotesque face. Staff had washed both children's hair and laid it on the canvas sheet that covered Alice's remains. Only the hair of Nellie was provided for identification. None of her other remains were on display.

They were ready to bring Mrs. Carrie Pitezel inside.

Detective Geyer stood on one side of Mrs. Pitezel and Detective Cuddy stood on the other side. Together, the strong men held the fragile woman by her arms, ready at any moment for a collapse. The two men slowly walked Carrie into the morgue and led her to the canvas-covered remains of Alice.

Mrs. Pitezel took one look at the teeth and identified sweet Alice. She teetered back and forth and became emotional as any mother would. Carrie gathered up her strength and asked where Nellie was but then saw Nellie's long black hair lying on the canvas that covered Alice.

"She could stand it no longer, and the shrieks of that poor forlorn creature are still ringing in my ears," Detective Geyer said. "Tears were trickling down the cheeks of strong men who stood about us."

Detectives Geyer and Cuddy led Mrs Pitezel to a waiting carriage and they returned to the Rossin House, all the while the broken woman screeched out ear-piercing cries.

"The sufferings of the stricken mother were beyond description…[she was] completely overcome with grief and despair, and had one fainting spell after another," Detective Geyer said.

When it all seemed too much to bear, Coroner Johnston made it worse by requesting Mrs. Pitezel attend the inquest later that evening. Geyer wondered if it would be enough time for her to gather her composure but she assured Geyer it would be, and when the time came, for two-and-a-half hours, the poor woman was prodded with all kinds of questions.

"So weak did she become, that at times her voice was

inaudible, and several times we feared she would totally collapse," Detective Geyer said.

"She was returned to the matron's room and was scarcely there, when she became hysterical, and her shrieks for Alice, Nellie and Howard, could have been heard a block away," Geyer said.[323]

Doctors attended Mrs. Pitezel, who was uncontrollably distraught, and after some time, she was returned to the hotel.

The Pitezel girls were buried in Toronto at the St. James' cemetery on July 19, 1895. Toronto authorities graciously paid for the cost of the burial. "The bones of the two children were laid away in one of the prettiest spots in the cemetery and the people in the town have fixed up the graves. Flowers will bloom over the little one's last resting place all the year round," Detective Geyer said.[324]

Geyer and Mrs. Pitezel left Toronto by train July 20. Geyer got off in Detroit and Mrs. Pitezel, accompanied by volunteers from Christian Endeavor Society, continued on to Chicago, Illinois.

In a letter Mrs. Pitezel wrote about Holmes to her attorney, Thomas A. Fahy, soon after, Mrs. Pitezel said, "I see through the mystery now. The wretch intended to kill us all."[325]

Now, only one question remained for Detective Geyer. Where was Howard? Mrs. Pitezel clung to the hope her beloved son was still alive, but Geyer knew in his heart Holmes killed Howard too.

CHAPTER 17

Little Howard

All the toil; all the weary days and weeks of travel,—toil and travel in the hottest months of the year, alternating between faith and hope, and discouragement and despair, all were recompensed in that one moment, when I saw the veil about to lift, and realized that we were soon to learn where the poor little boy had gone with Holmes . . .

-Detective Frank P. Geyer[326]

Irvington Cottage, Indianapolis, August 1895

DETECTIVE GEYER RETURNED TO Detroit to follow up on possible sightings of Howard. He met with Detective Tuttle, and together, they went to a home Holmes rented. Geyer knew he planned to kill the girls there and even dug a hole for them, but because Holmes' friend warned him insurance investigators were on his trail, Holmes left in a hurry and took the girls to Toronto. Maybe he buried Howard's remains before he left.[327]

Detectives thoroughly searched the property but found nothing to show a crime was committed. They read through letters the Pitezel girls wrote while they were with Holmes. One letter proved to be interesting. Alice wrote her grandparents, "Howard is not with us now." Had Holmes already killed little Howard?

Geyer thought long and hard about Holmes' movements and concluded Howard was disposed of *before* Holmes came to Detroit, which led Detective Geyer back to Indianapolis.

On a hot afternoon in July, Geyer arrived in Indianapolis. He met with the local Detective, David Richards, and together they interviewed every real estate agent in the area hoping to find a house that had been rented by Holmes, with little luck.

Everywhere Detective Geyer went, he was congratulated for finding the Pitezel girls, but he wasn't finished yet. More than ever, he had to find little Howard.

Constant news coverage re-printing the photos of the three Pitezel children and killer, H. H. Holmes, sent scores of citizens to meet with Geyer to provide him clues, all of which he investigated.

An *Indianapolis News* reporter caught up with him July 27 and asked him about Hatch.[328]

"He still sticks to it that he gave him in charge of Hatch . . . Find Hatch and you will find the boy, he says."

"Who is Hatch?" the reporter said.

"I wish we could answer that. Hatch was, I believe, mythical. There never was such a person except in the mind of Holmes. I tell you that there was never such a criminal as Holmes. He is shrewd, calculating, long-headed. Say, a man that wants to kill two girls, takes the clothes off them and burns them one place and then buries the bodies in another, so as to prevent identification—he's nobody's fool," Detective Geyer said.

"He is the nicest fellow in the world to talk to, as polite as you please and nervy. He smiles all of the time, and can talk on any subject you choose. There has been an awful lot of rot written about him, but after all there is no doubt that he is the greatest murderer and all-around criminal of the century. He'll be hanged, though. If they don't do it in Toronto or Chicago, or here [Indianapolis], they will do it in Philadelphia. There's no escape for him," Detective Geyer said.[329]

Superintendent Linden was more animated when a reporter asked him to comment on Holmes' attorney, Shoemaker's, claim Hatch is real and, "by-the-by, resembles Holmes in appearance."[330]

"Rot! Absolute rot! Hatch was merely an alias of Holmes. He had as many as a city directory, but he used the name Hatch frequently. If Hatch did the killing, Holmes will hang for it, for Holmes and Hatch are one and the same person," Linden said.[331]

Geyer's forty-second birthday came and went without celebration. Honestly, the best birthday gift Geyer could hope for, was to find Howard Pitezel.

"Days came and passed, but I continued to be as much in the dark as ever, and it began to look as though the bold but clever criminal, had outwitted the detectives, professional and amateur, and that the disappearance of Howard Pitezel would pass into history as an unsolved mystery," a disappointed Geyer said.[332]

Assistant District Attorney Barlow sent Geyer an analysis of three of the children's letters, which showed what Detective Geyer already knew: Howard disappeared either in Indianapolis, or between that city and Detroit.

Geyer returned to Chicago for an interview with police authorities to investigate a report of a child's remains found at Holmes' 63rd Street Castle. But after meeting with Chicago police chief and Inspector Fitzpatrick, Geyer heard enough to determine the remains were not Howard's. It appeared they were the remains of another child Holmes was suspected of murdering, Pearl Conner.

Geyer interviewed Holmes' janitor, Patrick Quinlan, and his wife, who were in the custody of Chicago police, to gain information on the whereabouts of Howard Pitezel and determine if the Quinlan's had knowledge of the death of Benjamin Pitezel. Geyer met Police Chief Badenoch and Inspector Fitzpatrick at Chicago's central police station and Pat Quinlan was brought into Fitzpatrick's office with a stenographer to record his statement. The Chicago *Inter Ocean* reported Patrick Quinlan gave Geyer, Chief Badenoch, and Inspector Fitzpatrick enough information to conclusively prove Holmes committed murder.[333]

Covered in mud and dust, and exhausted emotionally and physically after weeks of non-stop work, Detective Geyer returned to Philadelphia the evening of August 1 to meet with District Attorney Graham and his assistant to provide an update on the investigation and discuss strategies. Afterwards, Geyer was ordered to rest at home.[334]

Mary Geyer and eight-year-old Edna barely got a good look at Frank after his long weeks on the road, when an officer from Fidelity Mutual Life Association showed up at their Sixth Street home. The men had a long conference, during which, the insurance company asked about shadowing Geyer and if he didn't mind, Inspector W. E. Gary would accompany Geyer on his search for Howard Pitezel.

"This was agreeable news to me, because Mr. Gary was not only a pleasant companion, but he was able and skillful in detective work, and possessed a large stock of patience,—an absolutely essential element in such a case as we had in charge," Detective Geyer said.[335]

A reporter from the *Philadelphia Inquirer* interviewed Geyer after the conference. It seemed Geyer's work would never end that night, but that didn't stop sweet Edna from showing daddy how much she missed him. Edna curled up on Geyer's lap and wrapped her tiny little arms around his big shoulders while he talked with the reporter.[336]

"I am convinced," Geyer told the reporter, "that the authorities in Toronto easily have enough evidence to hang Holmes for the murder of the two Pitezel children."

Geyer confirmed he met with Chicago police and Quinlan, but he told the reporter he didn't think Chicago had a clear case against Holmes. When asked, he denied Patrick Quinlan confessed.

Geyer and Inspector Gary left for Chicago Wednesday night, August 7, 1895, and the next day, they met with Inspector Fitzpatrick. The three men went to the Harrison Street station to interview Mr. and Mrs. Quinlan. They wanted to know if Holmes had taken the children to Holmes' Castle in Chicago. Also, did the Quinlan's have information to help detectives find Howard? But the Quinlan's denied any knowledge of little Howard's whereabouts and Detective Geyer was inclined to believe them.[337]

With no helpful information about the whereabouts of Howard, Geyer and Gary left Chicago and traveled to Indiana, Ohio, and Michigan, searching hotels and boarding houses for signs of Holmes and the children, then continued on to Indianapolis.

"I must confess that I returned to Indianapolis in no cheerful frame of mind, and the large stock of hope which I had gathered up in the district attorney's office in the Philadelphia City Hall was fast dwindling away," Detective Geyer said.[338]

Indianapolis authorities were beyond helpful and never wavered once in their support, especially since this was the third time Geyer was in their city in search of the Pitezel children. Local reporters caught wind of the renewal of Geyer's search there and published announcements in the papers, and from that, hundreds of leads poured in. Geyer and Gary investigated all reports of mysterious people who rented houses for a short time and then disappeared. At least nine hundred reports were investigated in all towns in and near Indianapolis except Irvington. Could Holmes have rented a house there?[339]

Geyer wrote a letter to District Attorney Graham in Philadelphia, "By Monday we will have searched every outlying town, except Irvington, and another day will conclude that. After Irvington, I scarcely know where we shall go."[340]

When Geyer and Gary went to real estate offices in the area, they hit pay dirt. Holmes had rented a house there.

"I remember the man very well because I did not like his manner, and I felt that he should have had more respect for my gray hairs," old Mr. Brown said, adjusting his glasses to take a better look at the photograph Geyer showed him.

Geyer and Gary looked at each other and wearily sat down. All the weeks of travel in the hottest months of the year investigating lead after lead, alternating between faith, hope, discouragement, and despair. Finally, of all the cities searched, the last one was where Holmes had rented a house.

"Truth, like the sun, submits to be obscured but like the sun, only for a short time," Detective Geyer said about the veil of truth about to be lifted. Finally, he would learn what happened to Howard Pitezel.[341]

Detective Geyer and Inspector Gary didn't remain sitting for long. Mr. Brown introduced them to Dr. Thompson, the former owner of the house Holmes rented. He recognized Holmes picture and said one of his employees, Elvet Moorman, had seen a little boy with Holmes. Geyer and Gary interviewed Moorman who recognized the photograph of Holmes right away, "Why that is the man who lived in our house, and who had the small boy with him."

Geyer and Gary couldn't get to the one and a half story Irvington cottage fast enough. The empty cottage was in a beautiful grove in a secluded area, about one hundred yards away from other homes. It sat across the street from the Methodist church, some two hundred yards west of the Pennsylvania railroad tracks.[342]

On entering the cottage, Geyer and Gary searched the cellar first but found nothing. The home was divided into two apartments, with one in the rear and one in the front. They searched outside where they found an open lattice piazza attached to the right wing of the house. Geyer looked under the porch there and discovered the broken remains of a large, black trunk. Could it be the children's trunk? Geyer crawled underneath and found the missing trunk. It had a blue piece of calico pasted along the side seam, which was about two inches wide, with a white flower on it. While Geyer was underneath, he noticed loose dirt and used a shovel to dig around for human remains, but could not find any.

Geyer and Gary went back to the hotel to quickly change into comfortable clothes to dig with. While there, reporters caught him off-guard.[343]

"What's that? Well! Why, say, how'd you—where's Gary? Have you seen Gary?" Geyer said, as he called out for Inspector Gary to help him.

"Hi, there, Gary, come here. What do you think of this? Here's the News wanting to know what we've found. Pretty enterprising, isn't it? Well, we didn't want to say just yet what we found. We don't know yet ourselves sufficient to give you a good story. I suppose, though, you've got part of it in type by this time—and, Gary, I guess we can't stop it now, can we?" Geyer said.

Geyer told reporters they found the trunk under the porch, broken up in pieces. When they put it together, it was enough to show it was the trunk that belonged to the Pitezel children.

"After much consideration we decided to begin digging for Howard Pitezel's bones, and we will start in the barn," Geyer said. "We are going to do some digging this afternoon."

Geyer and Gary returned to the cottage and searched the barn which was about fifty yards away. In it, they found a three and a half foot tall coal stove and when Geyer looked on top of it; he found possible blood stains. Had Holmes killed Howard and burned him in the stove? The two searched every soft spot in the dirt. They dug a three-foot deep hole in the southwest corner of the barn where a large soft spot was located.

"There is only one chance in a hundred that we are wrong this time," Geyer said. But after digging for some time, Geyer became frustrated.[344]

"It is no use digging any more in this spot. If there were a body here we could at this depth smell the remains," Detective Geyer announced as reporters watched him dig.[345]

Howard Pitezel's remains had to be there somewhere, Geyer was sure of it. He was close to solving Howard's sudden disappearance and to provide his mother peace in knowing what happened to her son.

Meanwhile, Irvington residents spread the word about the search and several hundred people gathered around the house, seriously hampering their efforts. The sun was setting, and besides, the two were exhausted, so Geyer called it quits at five o'clock. Geyer and Gary needed to rest so they could continue their search the next day.

Three weeks ago, authorities found human remains about a mile from the Irvington cottage. To be sure they weren't Howard Pitezel's remains, Geyer met with the doctor who examined them. Geyer told reporters it couldn't be Howard as the remains were that of a man. "Geyer says it might have been one of Holmes' victims, but could not have been Howard Pitezel," the *Indianapolis News* reported.[346]

Together with Detective Richards, Geyer and Gary went into Indianapolis and met with the agent who rented the cottage to Holmes. They learned Holmes paid one month's rent in advance, and was never seen again. On the way back to the hotel, Geyer stopped at a telegraph office. He knew the pieces he found were from the missing trunk, but wanted to confirm with Mrs. Pitezel. He sent her a telegram:

"Did missing trunk have a strip of blue calico, white figure over seam on the bottom."

She replied:

"Yes, missing trunk had a strip of blue calico white figure on the bottom."

At the telegraph office, Geyer received a call from *Indianapolis Evening News* requesting he come to their office right away. Without delay, Geyer met the editor, who said Dr. Barnhill, the partner of Dr. Thompson, was on his way to their office and Geyer should wait because he had something important to show him. He hoped whatever it was, would help him find Howard.[347]

Dr. Barnhill hurried to the news office as fast as his feet would allow, holding an important package that could break the missing child's case wide open.

Detective Geyer leaned over the editor's desk while Dr. Barnhill opened his package and showed its contents. Inside, was part of a charred human femur bone and skull. Dr. Barnhill, who owned the cottage with Dr. Thompson, explained that after Geyer and Gary left the cottage for the night, three local boys played detective and found remains in the chimney.

"Let's look in here," one boy said then he rammed his hand into the opening in the chimney's flue in the cellar. It was choked up with debris. He pulled his hand out and found pieces of charred bones. The boys were sure it was the remains of Howard Pitezel so they ran at once to Dr. Barnhill's home and he verified their discovery.[348]

Indianapolis Detective Richards and Geyer and Gary planned to conduct a night search of the cottage at 7 o'clock in hopes the large crowd would dissipate. Detective Richards grabbed a lantern and overalls. Together with detectives and reporters, they drove to the cottage only to find the entire neighborhood gathered there. Geyer asked the marshal of police to clear the house as he could hardly move while inside.

"Mr. Marshal, I wish you would get these people out of here. We can not do a thing," Detective Geyer said.[349]

Doctors and members of the press remained in the house, but everyone else was removed. With a hammer and chisel, Geyer took down the lower part of the chimney. He found an old fly screen to serve as a makeshift sieve, and filtered ashes and soot through it.

Sifting through the debris, Geyer found almost a complete set of teeth and a piece of jaw. At the bottom of the chimney was a large chunk of charred mass, which Geyer cut apart and found part of a stomach, liver, and spleen, baked solid and hard. They also found the pelvis and while Dr. Barnhill examined the remains, Geyer and Gary found iron fastenings from the trunk, buttons, a small scarf pin, a crochet needle, and more human remains.

"They were hard, black masses with strips of burned muscle

still visible," *Indianapolis News* reported.

While the detectives and doctors searched the cottage, Inspector Gary went to investigate a report of a child's overcoat. He found a grocer who kept an overcoat for a young man that never came back to get it. There was mud on it and Gary found Sunday school papers in the pockets and a white handkerchief. "The grocer said that early in October, of 1894 a man called at his store and left the coat with him, saying that a boy would call for it the next morning, but the boy never came," Detective Geyer said. The grocer identified the man as H. H. Holmes.[350]

Drs. Thompson and Barnhill talked with detectives about the manner in which they felt H. H. Holmes killed Howard. Geyer was of the opinion that Holmes chopped Howard's body into pieces and burned them. But Thompson and Barnhill said in their own opinion that was not the case. A hypodermic syringe and a strong solution of morphine was found on Holmes when he was arrested. Doctors felt this was the manner he killed his sleeping victims. He would give them an injection of morphine and then smother his victims with chloroform. A large cork and melted glass was found in the debris taken from the chimney. With that, Irvington doctors were under the opinion Holmes gave the boy morphine, and while the boy slept, he used chloroform, then doubled his body up and put it into the stove. He covered it with corn cobs, pieces of the trunk, chunks of wood, and threw the empty chloroform bottle in with the other things. After the body was destroyed and cooled down, they theorized Holmes shoveled the ashes into the stove hole. The stove was in the kitchen and Holmes was not aware that a flue from the stove was located in the cellar, which brought about the discovery of the charred remains.[351]

Geyer, Inspector Gary, and Detective Richards briefed the police superintendent of their findings and each turned in for the night.

Though the outcome for Howard was depressing, for the first time in months, Detective Geyer had a good nights' sleep.

"That night I enjoyed the best night's sleep I had had in two months. I was sure that my work was complete, and as I fell into an easy slumber, I thought that after all, the business of searching for the truth was not the meanest occupation of man. It is the manner in which it is searched for that sometimes makes it ignoble," Detective Geyer said.[352]

People were furious. The most heinous crime ever committed in Indianapolis would likely never be tried there if District Attorney Graham had his way. According to stories local citizens read in newspapers, it appeared Philadelphia gathered enough evidence to try Holmes for Benjamin Pitezel's murder and would soon indict him. If jurors found him guilty, he would hang in Philadelphia.

Regardless of whether H. H. Holmes would be extradited to Indianapolis for little Howard's murder or not, authorities continued the investigation. Among key evidence, Holmes filled several prescriptions and purchased large quantities of chloroform and cocaine from Navin's Drug Store. The clerk discarded the cocaine prescription because Holmes didn't want the bottle labeled, but he did have another prescription on file, which called for bicarbonate of soda and calomel made into No. 12 powders. Detectives recognized Holmes' signature on the prescription.[353]

Officials brought Mrs. Pitezel from her parents home in Galva, Illinois, to Indianapolis to testify before a grand jury. The distraught mother identified Howard's remains, pieces of her children's trunk, a scarf pin, Howard's shoes, and his overcoat given to the grocer by Holmes. She also identified a toy spinning top and tin man that her husband, Benjamin Pitezel, gave Howard before his death. Ben bought it for their son when they went to the Chicago World's Columbian Exposition.

A dentist testified the teeth and portion of the jaw were from a child between eight and eleven and a doctor said portions of a skeleton found were from a child between seven and ten-years-old. The large clump of charred remains found in the chimney contained a liver, stomach and portions of a child's intestines.[354]

Jurors also heard H. H. Holmes brought two cases of surgical instruments into a local business shop near the Irvington house to be sharpened, which may have been the same instruments Holmes used to cut the boy into pieces. With testimony corroborating all

the evidence presented, a true bill was issued—H. H. Holmes
murdered Howard and should Philadelphia fail to indict Holmes
for murder, the Prosecutor would ask Governor Matthews for a
requisition on the Pennsylvania authorities to extradite Holmes.

Mrs. Pitezel remained in the Indianapolis area long enough for
closure. She drove with a friend and Dessie to the Irvington
cottage to see where her little boy died. Emotional and filled with
unthinkable sorrow, Mrs. Pitezel had to see where Howard took his
last breath—where Holmes ripped her son from her. Next, she
went to Pike's store where Howard's coat was left by Holmes. She
also drove to the coroner's office to inquire about Howard's bones.
She asked to see the remains, but Dr. Castor advised against it and
said it would not be wise because the sight of them would only
intensify her agony. He promised, after the trial, he would send the
bones to Galva so she could bury them.[355]

After Detective Geyer testified before the coroner and grand
jury, he returned to Philadelphia to meet with District Attorney
Graham and Assistant District Attorney Barlow, who congratulated
him on the success of his search. But there was so much left to do
to ensure Holmes was convicted.

District Attorney Graham ordered Benjamin Pitezel's body
exhumed in Philadelphia. After H. H. Holmes and Alice Pitezel
identified Benjamin Pitezel's remains in 1894, the body was
returned to its grave. But for reasons unknown, Holmes slipped the
undertaker some money three days later and had Benjamin
Pitezel's body moved to the extreme northeastern part of the
cemetery. Now Benjamin's badly decomposed body would again
be disinterred.

Dr. Henry L. Sidebotham severed Ben's head and then pulled
rotting flesh from his skull, threw the flesh back into the coffin,
and placed the skull in a bag. Sidebotham planned to remove the
rest of the flesh and boil and bleach the skull at the coroner's
office, and then mount it for Mrs. Pitezel's identification.[356]

Benjamin Pitezel did not lay in peace long. His body was
disinterred for the fourth time to sever his leg so Mrs. Pitezel could
identify a scar. Authorities also removed portions of Ben's coat and
trousers.[357]

Geyer spent the next month gathering evidence, tracking down witnesses, and working with the district attorney's office. He made another trip to Indianapolis October 11, 1895, to wrap up his investigation and pick up little Howard's remains and evidence. Geyer brought with him a key H. H. Holmes had in his pocket when arrested in Boston. Holmes insisted he did not rent the cottage and told Detective Geyer witnesses saw a man who looked like Holmes, but it wasn't him. Geyer knew the key would fit the Irvington cottage and it did. The con man, murderer, and liar was going down. Detective Geyer would see to it.[358]

Geyer met Dr. Thompson, Dr. Byram, and several other witnesses to arrange testimony for the upcoming trial. Philadelphia appropriated an additional $300 for a total of $2,500 to bring the witnesses to Philadelphia.[359]

Officials released Howard's remains and other evidence to Geyer, which included Howard's teeth Dr. Byram mounted for ease of identification, pieces of his skull, a shin bone, and a petrified section of his stomach, liver, and spleen, and clothes identified by the family. The district attorney planned to display the grisly remains at trial.[360]

Fig. 46. The Pitezel family killed by H. H. Holmes. Benjamin Pitezel, 28 yrs old, *circa* 1884 (top). Nellie Pitezel, about 6 yrs old, *circa* 1890 (left). Alice, about 10 yrs old, and Howard Pitezel, about 4 yrs old, *circa* 1890 (right). Images source: R. Miller.

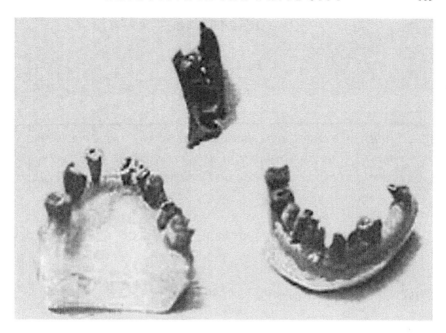

Fig. 47. Little Howard Pitezel's teeth found in the ashes. Image source: Frank P. Geyer. *The Holmes-Pitezel case; a history of the greatest crime of the century and of the search for the missing Pitezel children.* Philadelphia, PA: Publishers' Union, 1896, p. 311.

CHAPTER 18

Just Deserts

Truth is stranger than fiction, and if Mrs. Pitezel's story is true it is the most wonderful exhibition of the power of mind over mind I have ever seen and stranger than any novel I have ever read.

-Judge Arnold, Commonwealth *vs.* Mudgett, *alias* Holmes[361]

Trial, October 28 - November 2, 1895

INSISTENT ON A MURDER trial in Philadelphia and confident of a conviction, District Attorney Graham requested a grand jury review evidence that Holmes murdered Benjamin F. Pitezel. The grand jury convened and only called two witnesses: Detective Frank P. Geyer and L. G. Fouse, president of Fidelity Mutual Life Association. Geyer testified about Benjamin's murder and Fouse told of his private detectives' investigation. The two presented enough evidence to warrant a true bill and H. H. Holmes was indicted for murder. Although Indianapolis already indicted Holmes, District Attorney Graham had decided that if the jury returned a true bill, Holmes would be tried in Philadelphia.[362]

Holmes returned for the bill of indictment and to make a plea. The clerk of the court ordered Holmes to stand, then read the indictment aloud September 23.[363]

"And the grand inquest aforesaid, upon their respective oaths and affirmations aforesaid, do further present that the Said Herman W. Mudgett, alias H. H. Holmes . . . with force and arms, etc., in and upon the body of one Benjamin F. Pitezel, in the peace of God and the said Commonwealth then and there being, feloniously, wilfully, and of his malice aforethought, did make an assault, and then and there feloniously, wilfully, and of his malice aforethought, did give to the said Benjamin F. Pitezel one mortal wound . . . "

"To this Bill of Indictment, how say you, Guilty, or Not Guilty?" the clerk said.

"Not Guilty," Holmes said.

"Pleading Not Guilty, how will you be tried?"

"By God and my country."

"And may God send you a safe deliverance," the clerk said.

Unlike twenty-first century trials where defendants often remain in prison two to four years before facing a jury, depending on the location, Holmes' trial was set to begin Monday, October, 28, 1895, leaving him five weeks from his arraignment to prepare a defense.[364]

Before trial, H. H. Holmes wrote a memoir and diary from Moyamensing Prison hoping to exonerate himself of Benjamin Pitezel's murder and suspicion of others, and by October 16, an advertisement had appeared in the *Philadelphia Inquirer* searching for agents to sell his book.[365]

Without delay, jury selection began October 28, Judge Michael Arnold presiding. Holmes' two attorneys, William A. Shoemaker and Samuel P. Rotan immediately made a motion to continue the case to allow additional time to prepare, especially in light of the Pitezel children discovery, but Judge Arnold denied the request.[366]

"The indictment was found September 12th; the arraignment made September 23d, and this day was fixed for trial. That was equivalent to a continuance, and you have had full and ample notice and time to get ready," Judge Arnold said.

In a highly unusual move, Shoemaker, and Rotan asked to withdraw, declaring they could not defend Holmes without a continuance. But Judge Arnold admonished them and threatened disbarment if Shoemaker and Rotan continued down that path. Reluctantly, they agreed to stay. While jurors were questioned, Holmes interrupted and made a statement:

"May it please the Court, I have no intention to ask Mr. Rotan and Mr. Shoemaker to continue in this case when I can see that it is against their own interests, and, bearing that fact in mind, I ask to discharge them from the case. These gentlemen have stood by me during the last year, and I cannot ask them at this time to stay in the trial of the case, where it is against their interest," Holmes said, then requested a one-day continuance to find another attorney.[367]

Judge Arnold denied his request. "You will have tomorrow for that purpose. The case will not go on today to its full length."[368]

Holmes huddled with his attorneys, then announced that he, alone, wished to question jurors, in which Judge Arnold stated that was his right as a defendant, but he would not dismiss Shoemaker and Rotan. Frustrated, Shoemaker declared he could not stay in good conscious and abruptly left. Rotan, afraid of Judge Arnold's threat of disbarment, remained, but was visibly annoyed.

Holmes examined some of the jurors, then Mr. Rotan interrupted.

"May it please your Honor, there is no use at all for me to stay here. The defendant is going on, and he will not allow me to do anything. I ask leave to withdraw. I will have to do so, when he says that he is not going to let me do anything, and is conducting his case . . . under the circumstances, there being no use in my being here, I shall leave the court room. I am simply doing what I consider my duty." Rotan concluded his statement then left the courtroom and juror examinations continued. At three o'clock, with jurors sworn and seated, District Attorney Graham gave his opening statement. Court adjourned until ten o'clock Tuesday, October 29, 1895.[369]

Holmes barely slept an hour, preferring instead to prepare for trial. Detective Geyer lugged in various bundles and photographs and gave them to Graham. He played a huge role in the Commonwealth's case and spent weeks gathering evidence and helping the district attorney's office get ready for trial.

Right away, Holmes requested jail privileges and discussed trial logistics. He asked to see his third wife, Miss Georgiana Yoke, which District Attorney Graham said she was on standby if needed.

Next, Holmes made an unusual request, at least for 1895. While Detective Geyer sat nearby, H. H. Holmes requested the judge exclude all witnesses from the courtroom until called to testify. But Judge Arnold did not see a reason to exclude them. "It has not been our practice, unless a case developed into a condition requiring it," Judge Arnold said.[370]

"Then it is not my privilege to ask it?" Holmes said.

"No; not as a matter of right," Judge Arnold said.

Holmes' ability to conduct his own defense amazed onlookers, many of whom traveled a hundred miles or more for a chance to observe the famous trial. Prominent judges and lawyers came too. It was quite the spectacle, especially since Holmes was arrogant and defiant and insisted on defending himself in the death penalty case. But Holmes brought up a valid point about the witnesses and everyone knew it. Witnesses could be influenced by listening to others testify.[371]

Judge Arnold and District Attorney Graham gave H. H. Holmes a great deal of leeway and Holmes took full advantage, challenging both of them at every opportunity.

The oldest Pitezel daughter, Jeannette "Dessie" (later called Dessa) was the first witness to testify on Tuesday. Her only job at the moment was to identify a photo of her father, which she did, then Graham made a dramatic point to place the photo in front of Holmes.

Graham called a couple witnesses to verify authenticity of photographs then put Eugene Smith, a patron from B. F. Perry's patent business, on the stand. Mr. Smith described finding B. F. Perry's [Benjamin Pitezel] body at the patent business at 1316 Callowhill Street. When he first found Pitezel, he thought he was shot with a pistol. Eugene Smith summoned police right away and then returned to the house. Graham asked him to describe the scene. The corpse lay with its feet towards the window. There were four small bottles on the mantel, a broken bottle on the floor, and a corncob pipe rested alongside Pitezel with a burned match nearby.

Smith testified Dr. Scott was also present. Graham asked Smith if he ever saw the prisoner before, and Smith said he did. When he first dropped off his patent model, Holmes entered the business dressed in light-colored clothing. He gave a nod to Pitezel, then Pitezel excused himself and followed Holmes upstairs.

He also rode with Holmes to Potter's Field for the exhumation of Benjamin Pitezel's body. Smith recognized him as the man he saw earlier at the patent business. He heard Holmes offer Attorney Jeptha Howe money to cremate the corpse, but Howe told Holmes Mrs. Pitezel would have to approve it first.

"The prisoner and I stood together, while Lawyer Howe was writing, three or four feet from us, and the girl [Alice Pitezel] was there crying. This was before the body began to get examined thoroughly. The prisoner offered $30 to cremate the corpse," Eugene Smith said.

"He offered $30 to have the corpse cremated—burned up?" District Attorney Graham said.

"Yes, sir. He asked Lawyer Howe what about it. Lawyer Howe was very sympathetic, crying with the girl over her father. He turned around and said that he couldn't do nothing until he would see the widow of the dead man," Smith said.[372]

Eugene Smith testified Holmes pulled a lancet out of his pocket and cut pieces off Pitezel's body at the exhumation.

"He pulled out a lance of his own, and went to work and cut these pieces from the body? Did he cut the wart out?" Graham said.

"He turned him on his face out of the box, and cut the wart," Smith said.

"He handled the corpse himself?"

"Yes, sir; he put on doctor's gloves," Smith said.[373]

On cross-examination, Holmes went into a long discussion of the patent business floor plan. Before Holmes got too involved, Graham asked a Bureau of Surveys engineer to verify it, which he did.

Graham recalled Eugene Smith and Holmes made Smith trace every single movement he made inside the patent business. He also questioned Smith about the exhumation at Potter's Field.

"During our journey from the coroner's office to the Potters' Field were you in my company continually?" Holmes said.

"No, sir; I was in Mr. Perry's company, and I was in yours, and I was in the girl's company."

"Did you hold any conversation with me during the time?"

"I wanted to know from you in the cars how these parties came to find out—I asked you first as to what your business was, and you said first you were a patent agent. I said it was strange to me where these parties could telegraph to you so quick and find you when they wanted you, and where. You answered me, cut me short, and I had nothing further to say," Smith said.[374]

Holmes questioned Smith about Dr. Mattern removing his medical gloves and Holmes placing them on his own hands. Graham asked why the gloves were material as he only wished to show that Holmes found the marks of identification to show it was Pitezel's body.

"I object to the blood-thirsty way which the district attorney and this witness are inclined to make it appear that I did rush into that building and mutilate the dead body of my friend," Holmes said.[375]

The judge pointed out that Holmes was the only one drawing that inference. "All the witness says is that Dr. Mattern took off the gloves, and you put them on to point out marks of identification. Nobody has said you did it in a great hurry."

Holmes then questioned Eugene Smith about his turning the body over and removing of the wart. Holmes asked if Smith saw Dr. Mattern help him turn over the body at the exhumation, which he did.

"As far as I can recollect, Dr. Mattern could not identify the body; you were brought there to identify the body; you were to show the marks and tokens by which you would identify the body, and he was trying to examine the body for these marks and tokens that you said were on the corpse. Therefore he looked for the scar on the leg, which he could not find at first, and you brought his attention to it and pulled the skin from the leg, or at least the skin was pulled from the leg, either by you or Dr. Mattern, and the scar was got . . . When I began to catechise you about seeing these marks visible, you said there was a wart on the back of his neck and we will soon see that, and you took hold of the box and you and Dr. Mattern turned the body over. You immediately got the gloves, before he left, put them on, and pulled a lance out of your pocket and gouged this what you call the wart out of the back of his neck. It was placed in paper and handed over to the doctor, with part of the mustache of the man," Smith said.[376]

Holmes requested testimony notes be read back to him, which the judge denied.

"You refuse to grant me the reading of these notes?" Holmes said.

"Yes. You must make your own notes, as I have made mine," Judge Arnold said.[377]

After witnesses testified about drawings of the Callowhill house and the process of developing photographs, Holmes again requested the judge remove witnesses. Holmes and the district attorney argued, and although Holmes sarcastically asked whether it was Graham or the judge that made rulings, Graham agreed to concede as a matter of courtesy because the prisoner had no counsel.

"Mr. Geyer is here, and he may be called as a witness to what you say. Do you want him to go out, too?" Graham said.[378]

"Yes, I want him out," Holmes said. Detective Geyer left the courtroom.

"I want to know about my wife?"[379]

"Which one?" Graham said.

Holmes' face turned red.

"I will answer you as I did yesterday, to one whom you have seen fit to designate as Miss Yoke, thereby casting a slur upon her as well as myself."[380]

"That is what she wants to be designated herself. The man who laid the foundation of the slur is the man who married her with two other wives living," Graham said.[381]

"I shall challenge you to prove that."

"That we shall do," Graham said.

Mayor Warwick and several judges from other counties joined court spectators.[382]

By far, the most important witness testimony of the day was that of Drs. Scott and Mattern, who told of the condition of Benjamin Pitezel's body.

Dr. William J. Scott testified he accompanied police officers to the scene. Officers told him it was a clear case of explosion and a man was burned to death, so he expected to find evidence of that.

The body was composed. He had his right arm over his chest and the left arm at his side. Pitezel's face was severely decayed, which indicated putrefaction and there was considerable stench in the room. Dr. Scott saw a broken bottle and several bottles on shelves containing a red liquid that smelled like benzine, chloroform, and a small amount of ammonia mixture.[383]

The room appeared to be arranged so a draft would carry the stench up the chimney. The smell was not noticeable until you were on the far side of the victim, towards Broad Street.

Pitezel's head had undergone the most decomposition due to the sun. His chin was deep and the head in a downward position, rolled to one side facing right. Pitezel's swollen tongue stuck out of his mouth. Any pressure applied to the stomach or over the chest caused fluid to flow from his mouth, and to raise the head a little caused it to flow rapidly.

His mustache, eyebrow and side of his head and hair was singed as though a flame flashed over it. The right side of his pectoral muscle and the side of his arm were burned, but not underneath.

A filled pipe rested next to his head, turned toward Broad Street. It looked like he had taken a match and made a puff from it.

Dr. Scott testified a broken bottle with shattered glass inside lay beside the pipe. They took particular notice of the pipe as it appeared as if it dropped out of the man's mouth, but his head laid there in such a way it would have been impossible for the pipe to have fallen out that way. If there had been an explosion, like the defendant claimed, glass from the bottle would have scattered all over the room instead of a few pieces inside the bottle.

"It looked as if the bottle had been taken with force and crushed on the floor and broken and the pieces fell inside of it," Dr. Scott said.

Pitezel's shirt, undershirt, pantaloons, underpants, and stockings were in an orderly fashion, except for charring on his right arm and shoulder, burned clear through to the skin.

Dr. Scott said he was present at the postmortem examination of the body, conducted by Dr. Mattern. They looked for signs of agony of death. Though the face was disfigured, the eyes and mouth were not distorted as you would find in agony of death.

They noted the unkept teeth and their peculiar irregularities. The body was muscular and well nourished. He appeared to weigh between 170 and 180 pounds.

Scott testified that when Dr. Mattern opened the skull, they examined the brain carefully, finding it normal with no congestion of any nature. There were no effusions or adhesions on the heart, which was empty, leading them to believe his death was sudden. His lungs were very much congested, both of them in a natural, hydrostatic condition. Blood filled other parts of his lungs.

Pitezel's liver was large and congested, and the same with his spleen. The kidneys were a "pig-back" shape, indicating alcoholism. The stomach was congested, but it was chronic congestion, not acute, like you would expect to find from the fluid in his stomach. It was empty, except for the chloroform.

The lungs had a chloroform odor. Dr. Scott explained that the action of chloroform often stops respiration before it stops the heart. Though they found inflammation, it was tough and thickened, showing it was due to alcoholic effects. Pitezel's bladder was empty, showing his sphincter muscles had been paralyzed. The two sphincters of the bladder and bowels relaxed on the second-story room, not the third-story, as Holmes claimed he found Benjamin Pitezel at before he moved him.

Dr. Scott testified they concluded Pitezel died of chloroform poisoning but not from ingesting it into his stomach. Death was sudden, from inhaling chloroform, not swallowing it. Beyond a doubt, the chloroform found in the stomach was administered *after* death because the stomach did not show acute inflammation as expected if administered while the victim was alive. The empty condition of the heart, and lung congestions, were consistent with chloroform poisoning.

This led Dr. Scott and Dr. Mattern to believe Benjamin Pitezel could not neatly arrange his own clothing, then place himself in a peaceful position if he self-administered chloroform. If a man took chloroform by the mouth to produce death, it would cause spasms and his system would uncontrollably fight the dose and he would vomit. If inhaled, he could go on for a length of time, but after then, would lose consciousness and could not arrange his own clothing and place his hands as they were placed.

Holmes requested a break and again addressed the issue of witnesses.

"I would ask that the Court be adjourned for sufficient time for lunch. I have not eaten anything today, and I feel physically unable to go on with the cross-examination. I dread to refer again to the matter of witnesses, but should witnesses be allowed to converse with each other relative to the case?"[384]

"We cannot lock the witnesses up. We cannot have control over them outside of the court. We have given you a great deal more in the way of privileges and favors than ever has been practiced in the State. I do not know of a case in this State where witnesses have all been excluded, but the district attorney has agreed to it, and, of course, I agreed. We will take a recess until half past two o'clock," Judge Arnold said, denying Holmes request to order witnesses not to discuss the case between themselves.[385]

Dr. Scott's testimony was damaging. On cross-examination, Holmes tried to recover, but instead showed the jury, officials, and spectators he had inside knowledge of what occurred during the murder.

"As a practical man can you state your opinion as to whether, if a quantity of benzine or gasoline had been thrown on the floor and had ignited, and burned this floor, whether it would not discolor it?" Holmes said.[386]

"What time was it ignited? If you poured it on and let it wait, and then ignited it, there would not have been much charring. If ignited immediately, there would have been a slight charring there," Dr. Scott said.

"If any small quantity, half a cupful of benzine or gasoline, had been thrown on that floor, and then immediately, by which I mean within thirty-seconds afterwards, ignited, would it discolor the floor?" Holmes said.

"I should say yes," Dr. Scott said.

"Under these conditions, you would have expected to find the floor discolored?"

"Yes, sir," Dr. Scott said.

Holmes added a scenario of what would have happened if chloroform was thrown on the body.

"As a professional opinion, if large quantities of chloroform had been thrown on this man's face, arm and side, do you think that would have any effect upon discoloring the face, or the parts of the body?" Holmes said.

"It would discolor it in this way. When chloroform is applied externally, it acts, to a certain extent, as a caustic, causing rubification. It would redden the skin, and may produce blisters, but it will not discolor it black, like this face was. It will preserve the flesh, instead of destroying it," Dr. Scott said.

"But it will produce a slight raising of the skin; blisters?" Holmes said.

"Yes, sir," Dr. Scott said.

"Is it not a fact that that is the condition in which this man's face was at this time?"

"No, sir."

"Will you repeat the statement that you made upon the stand in regard to the condition of the face?" Holmes said.

"I think I said his face was swollen. It was dark in color-distorted; what I mean is, swollen—I said it was the same as putrefaction; there were quite a number of bullae under the two skins, between the outer and the inner skin."[387]

Holmes tried to show off his superiority. "State in plain language, so that the jury can understand it, what you mean by bullae?"

Irritated, Dr. Scott said to Holmes, "I told them; watery blisters. It might be water, and it might be air."

"Can you express an opinion as to the difference existing between that watery blister that you speak of as having found upon this man's face, and that which would be produced by chloroform continuously applied to the skin?"

"I never examined very closely into such a condition as that, the effect of chloroform applied to a person either before or right after death."[388]

Dr. Scott testified that even in the discolored condition the body was in, it would be possible to distinguish between blisters and putrefaction. If chloroform were poured on the face, it would preserve putrefaction or retard it; whereas, without chloroform thrown on the face, putrefaction would occur as it did.

Holmes went into the minutia of how they weighed the body;

how they determined the color of the hair; where they took the hair to analyze; and whether it was thin hair and if there was hair on other portions of his face.

Dr. Scott admitted he smelled and tasted a small amount of chloroform from Pitezel's stomach. He said there was a clear (not greenish), sticky mucus smeared all throughout the stomach lining. There was no food, and it did not smell of whiskey.

Next, Coroner's Physician Dr. William K. Mattern testified. He said the external examination found the man had a dark-red mustache and dark hair. The hand across Pitezel's chest was burned, as was his arm on the right side, but not the axilla under arm. His arms where burned in the positions they were found in, making it impossible for Benjamin Pitezel to commit suicide.[389]

Dr. Mattern verified Dr. Scott's testimony. He said there was about one or two ounces of chloroform fluid in the stomach but no irritation as expected if ingested while alive.

He described Benjamin Pitezel's exhumation. They entered the room where the body lay and staff removed the coffin lid. Holmes announced, "That's the body of Pitezel."

Dr. Mattern testified Holmes described all the marks they should look for, and after taking off the true skin—the outer skin—they found a small cicatrix of a wound on the inner side of the right leg, about two-and-a-half inches below the knee. Holmes said there was a wart on the back of the neck, so they turned the body over while it was still inside the box. The true skin peeled off easily, allowing them to find the wart. Dr Mattern said, "I haven't a lancet." Holmes reached inside his pocket and took out a gum lancet. He put on Dr. Mattern's gloves and made a mark around the wart using the lancet. Dr. Mattern, with his ungloved hands, took the wart and set it aside. They also took off two of Pitezel's fingers, one showing a bruise on the forefinger and another showing a bruised nail.

Dr. Mattern testified Alice Pitezel remained outside. After a while, she was brought in to identify her father's teeth.

H. H. Holmes, during cross-examination, questioned Dr. Mattern about Benjamin Pitezel's hair, then requested he read his entire notes of the autopsy.

"The height of the man was about five feet ten and a half; chest measurement, thirty-six inches; small arm below the elbow; fine physique; no deformity of feet. Description of clothing worn; then description of his mouth," Dr. Mattern said.[390]

"It is quite essential that the entire notes be read," Holmes said.[391]

Dr. Mattern then read his notes verbatim to Holmes, going over details of each part of Pitezel's body examined.

Holmes went into a scenario about when Pitezel last drank whiskey.

"If it was possible for you to find traces of chloroform, and if there had been an amount of alcoholic stimulant taken prior; say within an hour or two of his death, would you not have found traces of that as well?" Holmes said.[392]

"Do you mean of the alcohol? In the quantity found there of mucus and so on, there was very little alcohol," Dr. Mattern said.

Holmes asked about drinking and how it relates to the brain, "If this man had been heavily drinking within the past twelve hours, if he had been insensibly drunk at the time of his death, what is termed dead drunk, unconscious, or even considerably under the influence of liquor, would his brain not have shown it? Would you have expected to have found a normal brain?"

"Expect normal brain. Of course, I would find a wet brain, as you would find in drunkards. Where a man is drinking excessively, you find a wet brain," Dr. Mattern said.

Holmes tried to prove Pitezel was drunk, but Dr. Mattern countered and said he was not intoxicated at the time of his death. Pitezel's liver was not such that he would find postmortem for a drunk. Mattern said Pitezel was an alcoholic subject, but, if he was drunk at the time of his death, they would expect to find a wet brain. There was not enough liquor in his stomach that would cause alcoholism or alcoholic poison.

Next, Holmes questioned the doctor about hypodermic injections. This again, showed Holmes had inside knowledge of what may have occurred.

"Did you notice upon the breast of this body, or anywhere in the region of the stomach, any punctures or evidence to denote that hypodermic injections of any kind had been given subsequently or prior to death?" Holmes said.[393]

"The burns would have obliterated that. And there were not any on the other side."

"Do I understand you that there were [*sic*] any burns over the region of the stomach?"

"Not over the stomach; no, sir. It was above the arm, the body lying in this position, from there up to the breast. The collar was not burned," Dr. Mattern said.

"As a medical man, if you were called upon to inject certain liquors or make an injection of any kind—hypodermic injections into the stomach," Holmes said.

"We never do that."

"If it had been necessary for you to do it, that is, directly before death occurred, at the time of death, or within a few hours afterwards, would not some trace be left upon the skin so that you would have noticed it in the careful examination that you made?"

"Do you mean under the skin or back into the stomach?" Dr. Mattern said.

"In looking [at] the flesh overlying the stomach, the external appearance?" Holmes said.

"Under the skin as we use a hypodermic—," Dr. Mattern said.

Holmes discussed the possibility a hypodermic needle injected the chloroform into the stomach.

"Recognizing the fact that chloroform, if there had been a hypodermic injection of chloroform made into the stomach, at the time of death or just a few hours afterwards, in the careful examination of this body that you made, would you not have seen some traces of it?"

"No, sir; not if the needle would go in direct, I would not."

"In your examination of the stomach, of the coatings, the different linings of the stomach as you opened it, was there anything to show that there had been any punctures of any kind?" Holmes said.

"No, sir."

"Either small or large?"

"No, sir."

"Expressing a professional opinion, can you state that chloroform was injected into this man's stomach hypodermically?" Holmes said.

"No, sir; I couldn't say that, because there was no evidence showing puncture of the needle, which would be impossible to see after the decomposition of the body."

If H. H. Holmes claimed Benjamin Pitezel killed himself, why would he ask questions about injections? No needles were in, or near, the body.

Dr. Mattern gave his opinion on how the chloroform got into Benjamin Pitezel's stomach. He said it was placed there *after* death, but before *rigor mortis* had set in. It could have been put there by placing a tube down the oesophagus which was easy, like washing out the stomach in case of poison. The chloroform could not have been swallowed because it would have caused a large quantity of chloroform in the lungs, which he did not find. The lungs were congested with an amount you would find from inhaling chloroform.

Dr. Mattern confirmed that if a man were lying on his back, the greater portion of the chloroform would go into the bronchi, trachea, and lungs. Some chloroform would seep into the stomach, but not as much as the bronchi, trachea, and lungs. In Pitezel's case, no liquid chloroform was in the lungs.

H. H. Holmes seemed intent on pointing out it was himself that found the identifying marks on Benjamin Pitezel's body at the exhumation.

"Did you find any of the marks which had been spoken of?"[394]

"It was far more impossible to find at the time at the Potter's Field on account of the great decomposition that had taken place at the time. You said to me, 'It is on the inner side of the leg, of which I made a little sketch, and at that time I had the glove on, and I pulled off the true skin, which came off very readily, and you said, 'There it is.' And I said, I agreed with it; it was there."

"In making this examination you had looked for the mole, and had failed to find it, had you not, in this building when you were there? You did not find the mole?" Holmes said.

"No. You said there was one on the back of the neck, and there was not."

"And you could not find it?" Holmes persisted.

"No; or it could not be found under the condition that the body was there until we took off the decomposed skin off of that, which will show right here."

Dr. Mattern testified he took hold of the clothing to turn the body over and look for the mole and Dr. Taylor and his assistant turned it over with a spade. Mattern couldn't say for sure if Holmes helped turn the body over.

Holmes attempted to question Dr. Mattern about the gum lancet but District Attorney Graham asked Holmes what the point of the line of questioning was.

"Because I have been charged with going into that building and in ferocious manner mutilating that corpse," Holmes said.

"Nobody said anything about your cutting it. There is no question in the case about that."

"Was there no mention made of my going into this building and mutilating this body or cutting it?"

"No; no pretence [sic] of it."

The news had reported Holmes used his lancet to cut off identifying parts of the body and with each successive report, made it seem as if he pushed everyone aside and furiously cut off his wart. But the Commonwealth was not making an issue about it.

On redirect, District Attorney Graham had Dr. Mattern confirm the cause of death was chloroform poisoning and the effect of chloroform, if swallowed while alive, would have spasmodic contractions, which Mattern verified.

The Commonwealth called Dr. Henry Leffman, an analytical chemist, to testify about the effects of chloroform. He stated the first effects of inhalation of chloroform is excitement and stimulation, which varies a great deal depending on the person administering it. In animals, the effect is usually violent due to fright. In humans, there is often a semi-conscious, involuntary struggle.[395]

Dr. Leffman testified that judging from his own experience, there is a condition of confusion and it would be impossible for anyone to arrange his own body in a perfectly composed condition like that of Benjamin Pitezel's body without the help of someone else.[396]

Chloroform is an irritable substance of a disagreeable sweet character and is difficult to swallow even in small amounts, such as twenty or thirty drops in water. Swallowing chloroform would take considerable effort. It usually provokes vomiting in large doses.

Leffman said if chloroform ran into the mouth in large quantity, it would produce a choking effect, causing the person to move about and disturb the condition. It would not flow quietly without disturbing the individual from a tube placed down into the stomach.

Holmes questioned Leffman on an odd scenario, but Judge Arnold disallowed it.

"There is no allegation here that there was any gallon bottle three-fourths full of chloroform, or any towel on the man's face, or any tube, and really, therefore, it is not necessary to go any further into speculation of what might have been done under some other condition," Judge Arnold said.[397]

"I admit it is wise to leave the further questioning of this witness until after my testimony is given, making him a witness for the defense," Holmes said. And with that, Graham redirected, and it was confirmed chloroform would evaporate almost as rapidly as it would drip down through a tube to a towel and under those circumstances it would not be possible to enter the stomach that way.[398]

Coroner Samuel H. Ashbridge testified next and verified he was present when H. H. Holmes and Alice Pitezel gave him an affidavit verifying the deceased was Benjamin Pitezel.

After Ashbridge's testimony, Holmes addressed the judge.

"I feel that this case will reach an end quicker by having two sessions a day instead of three, on account of my throat condition. It is utterly impossible for me to attend three sessions without breaking down and becoming sick, for I am subject to sick headache, and I have been suffering with it all day. I think two sessions a day, at least for the next few days, will be sufficient."[399]

Judge Arnold denied his request and adjourned until seven o'clock that evening, at which time, Holmes requested attorneys.

"Partly on account of my physical condition, partly because I feel I have been annoyed on the trial unnecessarily by reason of not being expeditious in examining witnesses, and partly because of my counsel being criticised [*sic*], as alleged, for deserting me, I have sent for them in the last half hour, asking them to come here, and if your Honor sees fit to allow them to continue the case, to ask that they will do so. I have asked them to come here and consult with me, and if they are willing to go on, I would like to know if the Court is willing that they shall come in the case," Holmes said.[400]

Judge Arnold allowed his attorney's to return but rejected a continuance. "We must economize our time. It is as much a pain and penalty for me as for you to sit here at this time of night."

The rest of the evening was spent questioning witnesses and neighbors who knew or had seen Benjamin Pitezel as B. F. Perry. Dr. Adella Alcorn testified she rented a room to Holmes and his third wife, Georgiana Yoke, from August 1894 until the day he murdered Pitezel.

On Wednesday, Mr. O. Le Forest Perry with Fidelity Mutual Life Association told about Benjamin Pitezel's life insurance policy. They paid Mrs. Pitezel $9,715.85 on September 24, 1894, and Jeptha D. Howe, as her power of attorney, accepted it. Perry testified there was no suspicion about the payout until the St. Louis police superintendent received a letter of confession from Marion Hedgepeth about the insurance scheme.[401]

District Attorney Graham called additional witnesses from the insurance company and then had Orinton M. Hanscom, Boston deputy superintendent of police, testify. He ordered Holmes placed under arrest for a charge in Forth Worth, Texas. As he recalled, someone in authority from Philadelphia had a coroner's warrant seeking the arrest of Holmes, but Hanscom wasn't satisfied with the document. That's why they wired Texas to see if they had anything on Holmes, which they did, for horse stealing. Hanscom testified Holmes asked to return to Philadelphia to answer the insurance charge instead.

A stenographer verified the authenticity of Holmes' November 22 sworn confession in Boston, then it was read aloud.

In the afternoon, Mrs. Carrie A. Pitezel entered the courtroom, trailed by her daughter, Dessie, and a nurse. Dressed in deep mourning clothing and hat, Mrs. Pitezel stepped onto the stand. She looked as if she would faint at any moment. Large, dark circles surrounded her sad eyes and heavy lines of sorrow were burrowed into her face. Holmes looked up for a moment, then continued taking notes.[402]

District Attorney Graham, as gently as he could, given the circumstances, questioned Mrs. Pitezel, but her replies were so faint that Crier Hart had to lean in to catch her whispers and sobbing answers in order to repeat for the court to hear.

Mrs. Pitezel told of her knowledge of some of Benjamin Pitezel's business dealings. She said after she read a notice in the paper that B. F. Perry was killed by an explosion, Holmes came to her house and told her to use Attorney Jeptha D. Howe to collect the life insurance. Holmes told her Benny was all right and had gone to Puget Sound.

She testified Holmes said he would use $5,000 of the insurance money to pay off a note due from the Texas property and would deed it to her so she could collect rents. He also told her the body wasn't Ben. He said Ben was sick but alive and would come home in a few days. Holmes told her she shouldn't identify the body because she and the baby were sick and also because she might perjure herself, knowing a body was substituted. Instead, Holmes persuaded her to let Alice go with him. He said his cousin, Minnie Williams, would be there to take care of her.

A little later, Holmes told Mrs. Pitezel to let him bring Howard and Nellie to keep Alice company in Indianapolis. "You don't want Alice to be alone, so let me take Howard and Nellie to Alice...," Mrs. Pitezel testified Holmes said. Mrs. Pitezel took Nellie and Howard to the train depot. Attorney Jeptha Howe was there and said the insurance money paid out. Holmes took the children and got on the train.

Mrs. Pitezel saw Holmes again October 2, 1894. They went to Jeptha Howe's office and paid him a fee of $2,500. Holmes took her to the bank so he could 'pay off the note' of Benjamin's. Mrs. Pitezel testified she received $500 of the $10,000 life insurance policy.

She described how Holmes sent her to different locations, all the while saying she would see Ben soon. When Holmes wanted to move Mrs. Pitezel, Dessie, and baby Horton to Toronto, Dessie cried and did not want to go. Holmes said Dessie had to go with her to watch the baby while she signed papers and visited Ben. Mrs. Pitezel explained how she asked Holmes if Dessie could stay with her parents and he said no, it wasn't good for a young person to be with old people.

While they were in Toronto, Mrs. Pitezel and her children went to the store and ran into Holmes. He turned a deathly pale color and told them to wait there and he would be back. She waited, but he never returned so she and Dessie and the baby went back to the hotel.

Holmes moved them again to Winooska Avenue in Burlington, Vermont, but Mrs. Pitezel had enough. She demanded to see Ben. Holmes again told her to wait. Holmes wrote her a letter and said to go to Lowell for the children. At last she would finally see her husband and Alice, Nellie, and Howard. In Holmes' letter he also told her to go down to the cellar and get a bottle of nitro-glycerine dynamite he left underneath the potato bin. Holmes said it was perfectly safe. He said to move it to the attic or at least remove it from where it was and when finished, she could come to Lowell for the children.

Mrs. Pitezel moved the dynamite but didn't carry it up three flights of stairs like he asked her to do. Instead, she put it underneath the basement. She thought if she put it there, the owner wouldn't knock it over like she would have if it was in the attic.

Soon, she received a letter from a man named Mr. White claiming it was from Holmes. The letter told her to come to Boston instead of Lowell. She did so and was arrested, for the letter was a decoy to get Mrs. Pitezel to come to Boston for her arrest.

Mrs. Pitezel testified that after seven months in jail, she was exonerated and discharged without a trial. She did not take part in the insurance scam, but, instead, shielded her husband.

After Mrs. Pitezel's four hour testimony, Graham recalled Dessie Pitezel who verified her mom's testimony for the parts she was a witness to. Holmes at first wanted her mom and her to identify the body, but because she was sick, Holmes suggested

Alice go. Once her mom and her got to Burlington, Holmes took her into the city. On the way back, he asked if her papa had told her about the insurance scheme and she said he had but she didn't believe him. Her papa told her if she heard he was dead, don't believe it.

Holmes said her papa would come to Burlington, but he not dare to go if Dessie was there, so Holmes would have to take her to a hotel or to a friend's house and wait there while papa visited her mamma. Her papa never came, and soon after, they left Burlington.

Dessie was recalled again to identify her father's clothing, which she did.

Graham recalled Mrs. Pitezel regarding the Burlington home and dynamite.

"He went down in the cellar, and I felt impressed that I should go down, and I did so. He requested me to go upstairs; saying I would catch cold. I said I would not, for I was used to going down every day and fixing the fire in the furnace. The windows were out in the basement. He asked me if there was nail and hammer, and I said plenty of them. He requested me to go upstairs and get them, and he would put the windows in. I did so. He put the windows in. There was one place in the cellar that they put hard coal. There were planks, he had removed those planks, and they were standing up on end. He said he wanted to bury a tin box there," Mrs. Pitezel testified.[403]

Attorney Rotan objected and did not see the relevance. Judge Arnold agreed that line of questioning could not continue and adjourned until ten o'clock the next morning.

Thursday's testimony covered the Fort Worth, Texas property, and fake note Holmes gave Mrs. Pitezel. The highlight of the day was one that reporters would talk about for years to come. The first and only time H. H. Holmes became emotional at trial was when his third wife, Miss Georgiana Yoke, testified. When Holmes caught a glimpse of her, his face flushed and tears rolled out of his eyes. He leaned over and talked to his attorneys. Holmes tried to stop her testimony but Judge Arnold denied his request. Holmes asked permission to cross-examine Miss Yoke himself, which Arnold granted.[404]

Miss Yoke gave information about their supposed marriage and discussed some of his business dealings. She talked about how he suddenly wanted to leave Philadelphia on the night of Benjamin's murder while she was sick in bed and how he wanted her to tell the landlady they were going to Harrisburg, when they instead went somewhere else. She testified about going from place to place and to Canada.

During cross-examination, Holmes tried to poke holes in her testimony. He asked about her illness on the night he suddenly wanted to leave Philadelphia. She said she was well enough to sit up in bed and she had packed her own trunk. She clarified that Holmes must have told her they were leaving before he left their place and that's why she had already packed her trunk by the time he got home.

Holmes questioned Miss Yoke about his hurried appearance that day when they left. She answered, "I thought you had been very much hurried and somewhat worried."[405]

Next, Graham called a witness that verified H. H. Holmes rented the house at No. 26 North Winooska Avenue in Burlington for Mrs. Pitezel then he recalled Mrs. Pitezel and Dessie to identify Benjamin Pitezel's tie.

Dessie Pitezel testified again to identify a photo of her little brother, Howard. Graham had Detective Thomas Crawford confirm he brought the prisoner from Boston to Philadelphia and identify two tin boxes that belonged to Holmes and Miss Yoke.

Some excitement in the court occurred in the middle of Detective Frank Geyer's testimony. Graham questioned Geyer about the letters Holmes had that Mrs. Pitezel and the children wrote to each other. They were in one of the tin boxes, labeled "Property of H. H. Holmes." Geyer testified about his interview in Holmes' cell at City Hall, November 20, 1894, where Holmes told him it was a substitute body they found on Callowhill Street that he bought it from a medical student, but he refused to give him the name of the person.[406]

Detective Geyer said he questioned Holmes about the missing children and Holmes said they were in South America. Geyer asked Holmes about his meeting with Benjamin Pitezel before the supposed 'fake' death and Holmes told how Benjamin was to use the substitute body, place it on the floor at the Callowhill house, put one arm across the breast, and poor liquid into the mouth, then set it on fire.

Geyer asked Holmes what the liquid contained, and he said it was known as clothes' cleanser. Holmes told him how Benjamin was to manipulate the body to get the liquid into the stomach.

The next time Detective Geyer saw Holmes was when he walked through the cell area connected to the courts before his trial for conspiracy to cheat and defraud Fidelity Mutual. Holmes spoke to Geyer and said, "Mr. Geyer, the story I told you about that being a substituted body in Callowhill Street was not true."[407]

Geyer asked Holmes if the body was Benjamin F. Pitezel.

"Yes, that was the body of Benjamin F. Pitezel," Holmes said.

Geyer told Holmes if that was the body of Pitezel, then he murdered him.

"No, Mr. Geyer, I did not," Holmes said. "On Sunday morning, September 2d, I left my home on North Eleventh Street about ten o'clock, got on the Tenth Street car and went as far as Callowhill Street. I took a key which I had in my possession, and opened the door, and found Pitezel was not downstairs," Holmes said.

Holmes told Geyer he sat down and read a paper and waited for Pitezel, but he never came. Holmes searched and found him on the third floor. Pitezel was dead on the floor with his arm across his breast and a cloth across his mouth. There was a chair sitting alongside him with a bottle of chloroform on it that had a cork in it. A quill ran through the cork and a gum hose was attached and arranged so the chloroform ran out of the hose and would fall on the cloth. Holmes said he put his head to Pitezel's heart and discovered he was dead. Holmes went downstairs and found a note that told him to look in a bottle in a closet. He found a note in the bottle written in cipher that told him Pitezel was tired of life and had committed suicide and that Holmes should take the body and do with it exactly as he, Pitezel, was to do with the substituted body.

Geyer testified Holmes said he drug Pitezel's body downstairs to the second-story back room, head first, with his feet dragging, and placed Pitezel's body back into the position he found it. Holmes put the bottle of liquid alongside Pitezel's head, breaking it. He lit a pipe and threw the pipe on the floor. Holmes lit matches and threw them down to make it appear as though an explosion had taken place.

After he poured the liquid on Pitezel, he burned it in the same manner he told Pitezel to do with the substituted body.

"Then, Holmes, if that is Pitezel's body, where are the children?" Geyer testified he asked Holmes.[408]

"The children are—Minnie Williams has the children," Holmes said.

"Where are they?"

"Minnie Williams has them in London, England," Holmes said.

Holmes continued, "The last time I saw Howard Pitezel was in Detroit, Michigan, and it was on the Wednesday preceding my departure for Toronto, Canada. Minnie Williams came to Geiss' Hotel and took dinner with me and Howard, and I gave Howard to her to take to Buffalo, New York. After that I went to Toronto, and took the two girls with me, remained there some time, and that morning I took the girls from the hotel and placed them on a train in the Grand Trunk Depot, and went with them to the first station outside Toronto."

"I think it was about five or ten miles, and before leaving Alice I pinned $400 to her dress. Alice and Nellie were to go to Niagara Falls, where they were to be joined by Minnie Williams, who was to take them to Buffalo, where Howard was, and start from Buffalo to New York City, where they were to leave for London, England," Holmes said.

"If you will go to New York City, and make some inquiry there, you will find out at the shipping offices that a woman and two boys and a girl have sailed for London; that I requested Minnie Williams to cut Nellie's hair off, and dress her as a boy, in order to avoid suspicion."

Geyer testified the interview ended and the next time he saw Holmes again was in the county prison a few days prior to June 26,

1895, when he was getting ready to go on his cross-country trip to search for the children.

"Holmes, what became of the children's trunk?" Geyer said.

"Why, when I left Indianapolis to take them to Chicago, I left that trunk in a hotel on West Madison Street, near Ashland Avenue, and I never took it away from there."

Geyer said he interviewed Holmes next at the county prison with Mr. Perry from Fidelity Life. Geyer said he questioned Holmes again about the children and that's when Holmes told Geyer about a man named Hatch. Holmes claimed he gave Howard Pitezel to Hatch, and that's the last time he saw him. He insisted the two girls were in Toronto, Canada.

At this point, Graham stopped Geyer's testimony and proposed to prove Geyer found the children's remains. Judge Arnold removed jurors from the courtroom.

Holmes' attorney Rotan objected, and the court ruled Holmes was on trial for the murder of Benjamin F. Pitezel, not the children. When the case was over, if found not guilty, Holmes' could be extradited to Indiana or Canada and tried for those offenses if necessary, but could not be tried in Philadelphia for them.

Geyer continued his testimony. During cross-examination, defense counsel questioned him about Holmes' statement, specifically about dragging the body from the third-story to the second-story of the Callowhill house.

"I never examined the premises. I only have Holmes' word for it, that he dragged the body downstairs; picked the body up and dragged the feet after him and dragged it down to the second story," Geyer said.[409]

"Feet after?"

"Yes," Geyer said.

"Feet after the body?"

"Yes."

Judge Arnold interjected, "He said he did that?"

"He said he did that; yes, sir."

Mr. Shoemaker asked Geyer if Holmes said he gave Howard to Miss Williams and Geyer testified Holmes said Miss Williams ate dinner with him and little Howard, then he gave Howard to her and she took him to Buffalo, New York.

"I propose to prove that that statement about the children was false; that he did not give them to Miss Williams, did not hand them over to her at Toronto," District Attorney Graham said.

"If you contradict all his statements, you will never get done," Judge Arnold said. And it was true, for Holmes was a habitual liar.[410]

"If that is all, if it is my duty, I will do it if it takes a year. The question is, have not I a right to show whether that statement the prisoner made is not false, that when he made this statement that he gave the children to Miss Williams and sent them to London that it is false?" Graham said. Judge Arnold responded that it was for the jury to settle from the evidence.

Next, Graham called Superintendent Robert J. Linden to discuss another confession Holmes made after his Boston arrest. Linden testified Holmes said Pitezel was alive, and they used a body substitute, then later changed his story to say Pitezel committed suicide.

"He told me different statements here in the cell-room, and I told him I did not believe anything he said," Linden said on cross-examination.[411]

Most of Friday involved testimony of Holmes letters sent to Fidelity Mutual for the exhumation of Benjamin Pitezel's body. District Attorney Graham recalled Mrs. Pitezel to further identify additional items belonging to her husband. On cross-examination Rotan questioned her about Benjamin's possible suicide in which she denied that her husband was suicidal.

Testimony then focused on Holmes' manuscript he wrote in Moyamensing Prison. John King said he was hired to read it and received the manuscript from two different parties, Holmes' attorney, Mr. Shoemaker, and the woman who typed it, Amy Long. District Attorney Graham questioned Mrs. Amy Long and she confirmed she received the handwritten manuscript from Mr. Shoemaker. It was written in pencil. Graham showed Mrs. Long a sample of Holmes' handwriting and she verified it looked very much like it was from the same person who wrote the manuscript she typed.

.m recalled Detective Geyer about Holmes' manuscript. .estified the district attorney's office sent him into Holmes' α cell to search for poison, which he didn't find. Instead, .yer found a handwritten manuscript, along with a letter addressed to Mr. John King regarding publication of the manuscript.

After his trial, Holmes wrote two letters to the publisher, Burke & McFetridge Co., complaining the book differed from his original handwritten manuscript. The only issue he had with the book was the references to his wrongdoings in Grand Rapids, Michigan, which he claimed did not exist in his original writings. The firm didn't pay attention to Holmes' letters because they bought the manuscript and copyright from Holmes' attorney, Mr. Shoemaker, and though Holmes threatened to sue them, they took it with a grain of salt.[412]

"We have no dealings with this man and shall pay no attention to him. We purchased the copyright of this book and its transfer to us is recorded in the office of the librarian of Congress. What Holmes can mean by a prior assignment of the copyright I don't know, unless it is another one of his rascally tricks. However, I have his original copyright and the papers assigning it to me in my safe, so I am not worried very much," Mr. McFetridge said.[413]

Next, District Attorney Graham called a couple witnesses and then recalled a few to clarify earlier testimony, including Detective Geyer, and Dr. Leffman who gave additional information about chloroform and was questioned specifically about *rigor mortis.*

"You say that from about three to six hours after death *rigor mortis* sets in?" Defense counsel Rotan said.[414]

"Yes, sir; it is complete in about from three to six hours," Dr. Leffman said.

"About how long does that last?" Rotan said.

"About twelve hours or rather more; dependent a little on the temperature. The body begins to relax in the course of the next day, twelve or fifteen hours afterwards," Leffman said.

Graham recalled Dr. Mattern to clarify when urinary discharges and excrements take place.

"That would be under the effects while the muscles were relaxed, relaxation in life or before death, or while under an effect, such as while under the effect of an anesthetic, as chloroform or ether," Dr. Mattern said. It occurs immediately before death and not after *rigor mortis* sets in.

District Attorney Graham submitted exhibits in evidence and the Commonwealth then rested their case.

Right away, defense called Miss Georgiana Yoke, whom Rotan defiantly called 'Mrs. Howard,' to question the validity of their marriage but Graham stated that if defense wished to question her, then they must call her as their own witness. Rotan countered that Holmes' life was in peril and they should have the right to show there was a marriage between Holmes and Yoke. Judge Arnold allowed it.

Miss Yoke testified Reverend Wilcox married them in Denver, January 17, 1894. She said at the time she knew the 'Willamette woman' existed [Holmes' second wife], but Miss Yoke did not remember if he ever mentioned he married her.[415]

Graham countered.

"You say you know nothing as to the Willamette marriage. Do you know anything of another marriage prior to this?" Graham said.

"I have heard he was married," Miss Yoke said.

"To Whom?"

"I do not know what her name was, in Gilmington [*sic*], N. H.," Miss Yoke said.

"Have you talked with him about that wife since your marriage?"

"I have."

"When?"

"First in Boston, I believe."

"What excuse did he give to his own family, or explanation, for having married you under these circumstances?" Graham said.

"I object," Defense Attorney Rotan said.

"He told them he married this lady [Miss Yoke] while laboring under a state of mental delusion, that he met her in a hospital, that she attended him when sick; she attended him as his nurse; that he became infatuated with her, and married her while in an unconscious condition," Graham said.

"You may answer the question," Judge Arnold said.

"I was not with him when he visited his people."

Rotan asked if that was admissible if Mrs. Howard [Miss Yoke] was not there.

Graham continued anyway. "Did his sister tell you what had been said?"

"She did."

Rotan objected. He opened a can of worms by calling Miss Yoke to testify about her marriage to Holmes.

Judge Arnold overruled his objection with an exception noted for the defendant.

"Did you not speak to the prisoner about what you had heard from his sister, concerning this story by which he excused himself to his own family for marrying you?" Graham said.

"I did." Miss Yoke testified Holmes' sister said Holmes had been injured in a wreck and taken to a hospital where he remained for a long time. He told his family Miss Yoke was the patroness of the hospital and influenced the physicians to perform an operation saving Holmes' mind and Miss Yoke had married him before she realized who he was.

On cross, Graham got Miss Yoke to admit she knew Holmes married the Gilmanton woman and that the woman was not dead. She knew of that information *before* she married Holmes in Colorado.[416]

Miss Yoke was then questioned about a fake story he told about an uncle in Fort Worth, Texas, and about his aliases.

After Miss Yoke's testimony, defense requested a couple rulings, which Judge Arnold denied and then ordered a recess.

Upon return, Rotan made a shocking announcement. Defense decided *not to* call any witnesses. Rotan said it was because the Court denied a continuance so they could prepare a proper defense, and, in their opinion, the Commonwealth failed to make their case.

Court adjourned until Saturday at ten o'clock.

Attorney William A. Shoemaker called in sick the last day of trial. Defense Attorney Rotan announced it was due to nervous prostration. Rotan said he realized the defendant was allowed two speeches at closing, but he asked for an exception that the district attorney make one speech instead of the right to close after defense. Judge Arnold denied the request. District Attorney Graham stated that if the judge would allow it, he would waive his right to close the case and let defense make the final closing argument. Judge Arnold allowed it.

Rotan asked for an exception to District Attorney Graham's opening address that was done while Holmes was his own attorney because Graham included information about the murders of the Pitezel children. Judge Arnold denied his request because it was not made in a timely manner.

Graham made a two-and-a-half hour closing statement covering all the facts in the case from beginning to end. There were many highlights from Graham's statement, but the one that stood out the most was his discussion of repositioning Benjamin Pitezel's body, as Holmes said he did, to support the suicide theory.

"That he found him there . . . in that third-story room . . . and this man himself—this slight, slim built, thin man, Holmes, took Pitezel, weighing 175 or 180 pounds, who must have been then a stiff, rigid corpse, and dragged him down the stairs from the third-story room to the second-story room, and there placed him in the position of repose in which he was found lying, and he tells you that that condition of repose in which he was found on the second-story floor was precisely the same as that in which he was found on the third-story floor, describing him in precisely the same position down there," Graham said.

"Gentlemen, that body was never on the third-story floor. The relaxation of the involuntary muscles, and the involuntary discharges from the person took place at or immediately before dissolution. These discharges were found on the second-story floor, not on the third-story floor, clearly indicating that death took place where the body was found. This is a very significant fact."

"Dr. Scott is careful to tell you that the shirt and underwear were carefully tucked down into the trousers, with everything in their perfect place, just as a man would fix himself, and just as no one else could do it for him, and anybody who knows anything about the preparation of a corpse for burial, will readily understand why. A corpse is not dressed in clothing, as a rule, but covered, because of the difficulty of dressing the corpse, and a second person not being able to adjust the clothing in nice order all over the person. This man's body showed that he had never been dragged down those stairs," Graham said.

Repeatedly throughout his statement, Graham referred to Detective Geyer, and as reported by numerous news agencies, he gave Geyer and Assistant District Attorney Barlow accolades at the end of his statement.

"I wish to publicly express my personal appreciation for the great work done in unearthing and developing this story, and I desire to thank Detective Frank P. Geyer and Mr. Barlow for their earnest work in [sic] behalf of the Commonwealth."[417]

However, Attorney Rotan objected to those remarks, as reported by *Philadelphia Times,* and it was removed from the court record.

In Rotan's closing argument, he said the Commonwealth did not prove their case beyond a reasonable doubt. Rotan went over facts that proved Pitezel committed suicide, just as Holmes said he did. At the end of his closing statement, Judge Arnold gave jurors their charge.

The jury deliberated for two hours and returned a verdict of guilty in the first degree. As expected, Holmes' attorney immediately requested a new trial, which Judge Arnold said he would hear at another date.

As three judges in the Court of Common Pleas listened to arguments to request a new trial for Holmes, District Attorney Graham and Detective Geyer had a big surprise in store for them.

Holmes' lawyer, William A. Shoemaker, introduced an affidavit of a woman who knew Benjamin F. Pitezel while he lived on Callowhill Street. The woman claimed Pitezel told her he contemplated suicide and was tired of life. Pitezel said he would rather be dead than alive. Shoemaker used the affidavit as grounds for a new trial. He said he worked hard to find the woman, and once he did, she dictated her statement to him in his law office.[418]

Shoemaker pleaded for a few days' delay to secure additional evidence in support of their request for a new trial.

District Attorney Graham promptly stood up and demanded they bring the woman into court so he could cross-examine her.

Rotan countered Graham and said he knew little about the affidavit. He never met the woman and would not permit her to be questioned by the Commonwealth until he spoke with her.

This was the district attorney's opportunity. He announced, "Blanche Hannigan is in court. She has been for some time. I propose to call her."

Shoemaker's face lost all its color and he sank in his chair.

H. H. Holmes fidgeted and asked for a glass of ice water.

"It becomes my duty to say to this court that during the trial of this case word was brought to me that an effort was being made to procure a witness who would testify that Pitezel admitted he intended to commit suicide," Graham said.

Shoemaker attempted to explain himself, but Judge Thayer interrupted and told him to sit. Holmes' hearing was temporarily put on hold and Graham called Detective Geyer to the witness stand.[419]

Geyer testified that while he was at Holmes' recent trial, a court officer handed him a note requesting he meet with private detective John Schwechler, an ex-United States Deputy Marshal. But Geyer was too busy to meet him.

The next day, Mr. Schwechler went to Geyer's home at 2634 North Sixth Street and told him Mr. Shoemaker wanted to find a woman to make a false affidavit. It had to be a woman who would swear in court she knew Benjamin Pitezel, and that he told her he planned to commit suicide.

The next day, Schwechler returned to Geyer's house with the affidavit in question.

Geyer immediately showed it to District Attorney Graham and after Holmes' trial ended, they agreed Geyer would arrange for Police Matron Margaret Rhea to play the role of the woman Shoemaker wanted. Rhea used an *alias,* Blanch Hannigan, and Geyer introduced her to Schwechler.

Graham called Mrs. Margaret Rhea to testify next. She corroborated Geyer's statement and said she and Mr. Schwechler went to Shoemaker's office and Shoemaker had her sign an affidavit he already had typed up.

"Was there anything said about money at the interview?" Graham said.

"I said I would sign for a consideration," Mrs. Rhea said.

"What did he say to you?"

"He said he would see Mr. Holmes. I should call again at 4 o'clock in the afternoon."

Mrs. Rhea testified she went to Shoemaker's office at 4 o'clock and Shoemaker told her he had received no money yet. She went back the following Monday and without her reading the affidavit, or Shoemaker reading it to her, she signed the affidavit and Shoemaker paid her twenty dollars.

Detective John Schwechler also testified and confirmed both witnesses statements. The Court requested he find the stenographer that typed the affidavit, which he did. She testified Mr. Shoemaker dictated the statement to her, while she typed it in Detective Schwechler's presence.

Testimony ended and Judge Thayer directed Mr. Shoemaker to rise. He ordered the disgraced attorney held under a $1,500 bail, to which he stated bail was ready. In the end, instead of being disbarred, William A. Shoemaker was suspended for one year.[420]

The district attorney's shocking revelation detracted from Holmes' proceedings. Mr. Rotan attempted to argue for a new trial on Holmes' behalf. He first asked for a delay due to the circumstances of the unfortunate incident, but it was denied. Rotan continued with his request for a new trial. He took issue with the testimony of Miss Georgiana Yoke and whether she was a competent witness due to the fact, she was Holmes' wife. Judge Arnold spoke and said it was his duty to determine if she was competent and he was satisfied Miss Yoke was not Holmes' wife and thus she was a competent witness.[421]

Rotan also took issue with Graham's theory of Holmes' intent on killing Mrs. Pitezel with dynamite while she was in Burlington. He felt it was not properly deduced from the evidence and should not have been injected into the minds of the jury.

To this, Judge Arnold said, "What did he want the dynamite for? To clean the house with?"[422]

A roar of laughter echoed throughout the courtroom.

Officers called for silence then Graham summarized Holmes' trial to refresh the judges memory. Rotan made rebuttals, then the three judges took the motion under advisement and court adjourned.

On November 30, 1896, Judges Thayer, Willson, and Arnold issued an opinion and denied the motion for a new trial. Judge Arnold pronounced the death sentence. Holmes' case went before the Supreme Court on appeal and in the January term of 1896, all assignments of error were overruled and the judgment affirmed.[423]

Holmes went on a last minute quest for Pennsylvania Governor Daniel H. Hastings to issue a respite just before his execution. He wrote two letters asking for additional time to wrap up his affairs and exonerate himself of additional murders though he had already made his confession of twenty-seven murders thirteen days earlier. Holmes wrote the governor that he was only guilty of the deaths of two women for criminal operations. Governor Hastings received a letter from Mrs. Pitezel's father, R. Canning, in Galva, Illinois, accompanied by a petition signed by about 120 Galva citizens who asked the governor to deny Holmes' request.[424]

After he read Canning's letter and petition, Governor Hastings wasted no time. He wrote across Holmes' letters: "Application for a respite is refused."[425]

As a last ditch effort, Holmes had his attorney give Mrs. Pitezel a letter from him bribing her to ask the Governor for a respite on his behalf. In the May 1 letter, he offered Mrs. Pitezel a house and a lot, free of encumbrances, accompanied by a lease from a tenant paying ten dollars per month, and $2,000 cash, to which she flatly refused.[426]

Considering all the lies and mind games H. H. Holmes played with authorities and the horrific murders he committed, it is a wonder Detective Frank Geyer paid his respects in Holmes' cell on his last day on earth, but he did. Maybe Geyer hoped Holmes would finally tell the truth. Or maybe it was to show Holmes compassion although Holmes showed no compassion to his victims. Whatever his reason, Geyer, the Sheriff, Holmes' legal advisors, Father Dailey, the prison doctor, and a few others crowded into Holmes cell to say their goodbyes.[427]

Detective Geyer closed this chapter in his life and on May 7,

1896, he witnessed the liar himself, once and for all, pay for what he did. Although he wasn't tried for killing the Pitezel children, or anyone else for that matter, Herman Webster Mudgett, *alias* H. H. Holmes' died for Benjamin Pitezel's murder and that was okay with Geyer.

Reporters caught up with Mrs. Pitezel after Holmes' execution. She was glad to hear he received his 'just deserts.'

"Still, that does not bring my husband and my poor little children back to me," Mrs. Pitezel said. Mrs. Pitezel and Dessa drove to Philadelphia's Fairmount Park area to tour some of the places Alice spoke of in letters Holmes confiscated before he murdered her.[428]

After Holmes released his famous confession of twenty-seven murders in the *Philadelphia Inquirer,* April 12, 1896, he sent a letter with seventy-five dollars in travel expenses to Coroner Castor from Indianapolis and asked him to come to the prison in Philadelphia to see him so he could explain little Howard's death. While he waited for Castor, Holmes sent for Detective Geyer, Assistant District Attorney Barlow, and Attorney Thomas Fahy. The three went to Holmes' prison cell for another supposed 'confession.'[429]

First, he restated the fact he did not kill Benjamin Pitezel and instead said Pitezel committed suicide as he claimed all throughout his trial. Old news, old confession. Attorney Barlow reminded him of his admission of killing twenty-seven, including Benjamin Pitezel a few days ago. To that, he said in spite of what he had written, Pitezel committed suicide.

"Now, why don't you tell us the truth? We thought you had sent for us to make a true confession. What is the use of lying about it any longer?" Barlow said.

Holmes then turned to Detective Geyer and spoke of little Howard Pitezel's murder and reasoned he had a look-a-like double, likely referring to the mysterious Hatch he and Attorney Shoemaker mentioned before. Holmes claimed there was a look-a-like double that helped him kill the boy.

"I don't deny I killed the boy," Holmes said. "Now this man was also with me in Toronto and was with me at the time that these little girls were killed."

"You said you were only in the house for fifteen minutes. How could you make the gas?" Holmes was asked. He replied that his look-a-like prepared it for him.

Holmes made so many confessions, authorities were not sure which one was true, if any. And so, Holmes continued lying, even in his last speech on the gallows.[430]

One intriguing piece of information attributed to President Fouse of the Fidelity Mutual Life Association alluded to the true number of how many people Holmes killed. President Fouse told reporters, "Holmes never made a truer statement in his life than when he broke down and told me he had committed enough crimes to hang him twenty times."[431]

The famous spade Mr. Thomas W. Ryves lent to H. H. Holmes to dig a hole for potatoes at the St. Vincent Street cottage in Toronto, and later loaned to Detective Frank P. Geyer to dig up the Pitezel girls, sold to Quaker City Dime Museum for seventy-five dollars. [432]

Michael Arnold.

William A. Shoemaker

Fig. 48. Top left: District Attorney George S. Graham. Top right: Judge Michael Arnold. Bottom left: Defense Attorney Samuel P. Rotan. Bottom right: Defense Attorney William A. Shoemaker. Image sources: Courtesy of Library of Congress [Graham]; Thomas Tileston Baldwin, ed. "An Analysis of the Holmes Case," *The Green Bag*, Vol XIV, 1902, p. 177 [Arnold]; Executive Committee of Founders' Week, 225th Anniversary of the City of Philadelphia. *Official Historical Souvenir and Official Programme.* Philadelphia: unknown publisher, 1908, p. 479 [Rotan]; and "Shoemaker's Fate,"

Philadelphia Inquirer, March 15, 1896, p. 1 [Shoemaker].

Fig. 49. Coroner Samuel H. Ashbridge (left) and Coroner's Physician William K. Mattern (right). Both were assigned to H. H. Holmes case, and both worked on numerous cases with Detective Geyer. After Holmes' trial, Ashbridge went on to become mayor of Philadelphia, April 1899, and remained in office until April 1903. He died at the age of fifty-seven due to Bright's disease and was buried at West Laurel Hill Cemetery. Mattern graduated from the Philadelphia College of Pharmacy in 1874 and then opened a drug store. He studied medicine at Jefferson College and graduated in 1882. Dr. Mattern died from blood poisoning April 1896, which he first contracted in 1893. Blood poisoning was a common illness at the time, as many doctor's, including Dr. Mattern, frequently did not wear gloves because they were too bulky. Dr. William J. Scott, who assisted in Benjamin Pitezel's autopsy, performed Dr. Mattern's autopsy, which revealed his kidneys and liver were completely honey-combed with abscesses, leading to the rupture of an aneurism. Blood poisoning was the original cause of death.[433] Image sources: John Trevor Custis. *Public Schools of Philadelphia; Historical, Biographical, Statistical.* Philadelphia, PA: Burk & McFetridge Company, 1897, p. 563

[Mattern]; and Lincoln Steffens. "Philadelphia: Corrupt and Contented," *McClure's Magazine*, Volume XXI, (1903), p. 261 [Ashbridge].

CHAPTER 19

The Devil in Him

In talking, he has the appearance of candor, becomes pathetic at times when pathos will serve him best, uttering his words with a quaver in his voice, often accompanied by a moistened eye, then turning quickly with a determined and forceful method of speech, as if indignation or resolution had sprung out of tender memories that had touched his heart.

-Detective Frank P. Geyer[434]

HOLMES, A DOCTOR AND pharmacist by trade, was cunning, sly, and articulate, all at the same time. Everything he did was to further his goals, albeit illegal and unethical goals.

Holmes was rather quiet. He had a slouchy gait and preferred to look at the ground when he walked. Holmes reeked of a peculiar odor and his medical school classmates at University of Michigan called him "Smegma," which strangely referred to dead skin cells and fatty oils shed from certain parts of genitalia. One fellow student wrote that Holmes was repulsive in looks, troubled with boils, and did not seem to care for anyone but himself. Another thought Holmes had an odd obsession with death as he took home a dead baby to dissect, and at one time, purchased the foot of a child's cadaver to keep for his own use.[435]

While at the University of Michigan, Holmes' wife, Clara Lovering, lived with him for a short time. Holmes' fellow students noted Clara was subject to epileptic-like convulsions and Holmes would give her large quantities of bromide, which caused her face to break out badly. One student recalled Holmes and Clara did not get along. Another wrote, "Have seen her with blackened eyes as a result of their quarrels."[436]

Dr. Arthur MacDonald, a criminologist from Washington DC, conducted a psychological exam and experimental study of Holmes using a three foot tall device, called a Kymographion. The unusual instrument measured emotional effects of breathing and

speech when exposed to diverse topics. Dr. MacDonald described
Holmes as ambidextrous, which MacDonald opined was common
among criminals. He noted Holmes' left hand was less sensitive to
heat than his right, which was unusual, and he was more acute than
average in his sensibility to pain in his temporal muscle. He also
noted Holmes' palate was higher than most. That, together with his
demeanor, would class him among neurotics according to Dr.
MacDonald.[437]

Holmes wrote, "To-day, I have every attribute of a degenerate
a moral idiot . . . Is it possible that the crimes, instead of being the
result of these abnormal conditions, are, in themselves, the
occasion of degeneracy? . . . within the past few months these
defects have increased with startling rapidity."[438]

Medical doctor Eugene S. Talbot examined Holmes in prison
and observed numerous abnormalities, which caused the doctor to
coin Holmes as a degenerate. He noted Holmes' facial features
were markedly undeveloped, with the right side of the bony cheek
structure, or zygoma, hollowed. On the left side, both his mouth
and arm were lower than the right side, with his arm a pronounced
one and one half inches lower. On the right side, Holmes' ear was
lower than his left. And both of his feet were deformed.[439]

Holmes presented with moderate to severe pectus carinatum, a
chest wall abnormality where the breastbone protrudes outward.
Dr. Talbot diagnosed him with inherited strabismus—Holmes' left
eye was cross-eyed and situated higher on the face than the right
eye.

Dr. Talbot later said, "In twenty years' experience, I have never
observed a more degenerate being from a physical standpoint . . .
Being a medically educated man, he certainly should have been
better acquainted with these malformations, but he had evidently
given this subject little attention…"[440]

Since Holmes' confinement in prison, he lost weight, which
made his deformities more prominent.

"That they had developed as a result of his criminal tendencies
is perfectly absurd," Dr. Talbot said.[441]

These characteristics could have had a major impact on
Holmes' self-image and confidence and may explain why he was
distant and had a tendency to look downward.

Based on Holmes' behavior throughout his short life, he preferred to scheme and take part in undetected criminal activities for his own delight. Mostly, he lied and played intriguing games of deception, without detection, and was a master at it for many years.

Among eighty-five medical school graduates from the University of Michigan, H. H. Holmes came close to not graduating at all because several faculty voted against it. Holmes' fellow student, Dr. J. L. Rose, remembered, "He did not distinguish himself as a student and showed no marks of brilliancy or even acuteness . . . He looked and acted like a clodhopper."[442]

THE KYMOGRAPHION RECORD.

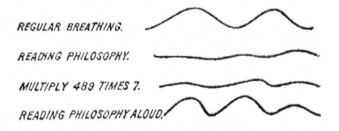

REGULAR BREATHING.

READING PHILOSOPHY.

MULTIPLY 489 TIMES 7.

READING PHILOSOPHY ALOUD.

Fig. 50. Illustration of the Kymographion Dr. Arthur MacDonald
    used on H. H. Holmes. The Kymographion recorded
    movements of the chest as affected by mental and emotional
    states. The higher the waves in the lines the more the subject
    breathes. Image source: Arthur MacDonald. *Man and
    Abnormal Man*. Washington: Government Printing Office,
    1905, pp. 537-541.

PART IV

A Plot, a Riot, and La Grippe

CHAPTER 20

He Must Die

One evening Jim and I were standing on the corner of Eighth and Vine streets, I think, in Philadelphia. A big, broad-shouldered man passed. I heard Jim catch his breath and draw back into the crowd . . . Just as long as he is alive, [Jim said] I am in danger.

-Lizzie DeKalb Confession[443]

Norristown, Pennsylvania, 1896 - 1898

AFTER THE HOLMES TRIAL, Detective Geyer took time to be with family and tend to personal business he neglected. In the midst of new crimes investigated in 1896, District Attorney George S. Graham and Philadelphia Mayor Charles Franklin Warwick gave Geyer permission to write a book and he authored *The Holmes-Pitezel case; a history of the greatest crime of the century and of the search for the missing Pitezel children,* which became an instant bestseller. But that wasn't the end of his great news. The United States Patent Office approved his shutter and door fastener patent application he filed before his search for the Pitezel children. The home security patent featured a series of bolts expert burglars couldn't jimmy. *Philadelphia Inquirer* caught up with him afterwards and lightheartedly wrote, "His associates in the detective bureau naturally look on his work with fear, for they know that when the bolts are put on the market burglars will have to quit the business and detective work will be a lost art." Being a carpenter by trade, Detective Geyer made his own patent models.[444]

Detective Geyer was in high spirits. He received numerous commendations, special recognitions, and consultation offers from all over the country, and now the accomplished detective was a best-selling author and inventor.

But twelve days after one of his book advertisements appeared in the local paper, *Philadelphia Inquirer* featured a lengthy interview with Mr. O. La Forrest Perry of Fidelity Mutual Life Association who claimed Detective Geyer "only tells a little of the story," and Geyer's boss initially declined to investigate H. H. Holmes.[445]

Geyer's book detailed Fidelity Mutual's involvement in the case, so it seemed Mr. Perry was looking for attention. The *Inquirer* article stated that once Perry felt convinced Holmes murdered Benjamin Pitezel, he contacted Philadelphia's superintendent of police, Robert Linden, who "pooh-poohed the idea that there was anything in the story and declined to take up the case."[446]

Fidelity Mutual paid out on the Pitezel life insurance policy, but a few weeks later, they received a written confession from Marion Hedgepeth, the notorious train robber incarcerated with H. H. Holmes in St. Louis. He told of Holmes' plan to defraud the life insurance company of $10,000. Holmes promised Hedgepeth $500 for the name of a dishonest lawyer willing help with his body substitute scheme. Hedgepeth gave him a name, but Holmes never paid. In retaliation, Hedgepeth became a jailhouse informant and wrote out a confession detailing the insurance scheme.

Perry showed Hedgepeth's confession to Police Superintendent Linden, who again declined to take on the case. "Why," he said, in a patronizing manner, "don't you know it is the custom of criminals to try and curry favor with prison officials by exposing crimes, the details of which they concoct? Why, it is absurd to think that a man locked up for a trifling affair should make a confidant of a man serving a long sentence and who could be of no use to him."[447]

Frustrated, Mr. Perry met with District Attorney Graham who told him there wasn't enough evidence for a case. But Perry did not give up. There was another way. Holmes had used the United States mail to send fraudulent letters, so Perry consulted the Postmaster General in Washington DC who suggested he swear out a warrant before Coroner Ashbridge, which he did. Ashbridge, who later became mayor, was the only Philadelphia official interested in the case. He wrote two letters to Superintendent Linden to encourage an investigation but received no response. Seems, the two departments had a strained relationship sometimes unprofessionally documented in the local press. Perry gave the warrant to Boston authorities, but they decided against acting on a coroner's warrant. Philadelphia officials agreed to take charge of the case after H. H. Holmes requested to stand trial for insurance fraud.

Poor sports' efforts of Fidelity Mutual's employees did little to sway potential readers who continued to buy massive amounts of Geyer's popular book.

Geyer brushed off attempts to sideline his successes and investigated numerous high-profile cases that year, like the mysterious death of Annie McGrath, an eighteen-year-old gorgeous brunette, thought to be poisoned or gassed by her boyfriend. Geyer arrested Samuel P. Langdon, Annie's married lover, who was president of the United States Collieries Company. A coroner's jury heard evidence and requested Langdon remain in custody until a grand jury examined the case. But before the grand jury convened, District Attorney Graham surprised everyone and requested the dismissal of Langdon due to failure to determine Annie's cause of death after an autopsy and chemical analysis.[448]

Geyer's biggest case, though, occurred a little over five months after H. H. Holmes' execution. It was the murder of Mrs. Emma Kaiser, and unbeknownst to Geyer there was a surprise revelation awaiting.

AGENTS AND SOLICITORS

10 cents per line each insertion.

THE HOLMES-PITEZEL CASE—A history of the greatest crime of the century. By the world-famous detective, Frank P. Geyer. A true detective story in which the arch criminal planned seven murders and executed four. Published by authority of the District Attorney and Mayor of Philadelphia., Agents make $25.00 a week. Outfit free to agents for 10 cents to pay cost of mailing. P. W. Ziegler & Co., 214 Levant street, Phila.

WANTED—THE "HOLMES-PITEZEL CASE." BY Detective Geyer. A true detective story of thrilling interest. Going like wildfire. Agents coining money. Send for circular or send 10 cents for complete outfit. P. W. ZIEGLER & CO., Philadelphia. .mh14-s&w4t

Our newest book,

"The Holmes-Pitezel Case,"

By Detective Frank P. Geyer (who brought Holmes to justice), gives a very graphic and true account of the most sensational crimes perpetrated in this century. (Including his confession of the crimes). 500 pages of absorbing reading matter.

Price $1.50.

Imperial Publishing House,

224 BANK ST.

Fig. 51. Advertisements for Detective Geyer's Book, The Holmes-Pitezel Case. Image sources: (top) *Philadelphia Inquirer,* March 14, 1896; (middle) "Wanted Agents Holmes-Pitezel Case," *Evening Star*, March 25, 1896; (bottom) "Holmes Will Hang; Our Newest Book, 'The Holmes-Pitezel Case'," *Plain Dealer Cleveland,* April 12, 1896, p. 3.

F. P. GEYER.
SHUTTER OR DOOR FASTENER.

No. 556,141. Patented Mar. 10, 1896.

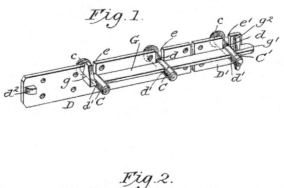

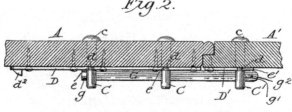

Fig. 52. Frank P. Geyer's Patent, No. 556,141, dated March 10, 1896. Image source: United States Patent Office.

"Look here, boys, Emma Kaiser has no marriage lines. She must have them so no legal question can come up to prevent Charlie from getting the boodle from them insurance folks," Lizzie DeKalb said.[449]

And so, Charles O. Kaiser, Jr., James A. Clemmer and his mistress, Elizabeth 'Lizzie' DeKalb set out to devise a life insurance scam reporters deemed, H. H. Holmes-style. Instead of a body substitution and fake death, Kaiser was to marry Emma, who already used his last name while they lived together, then kill her and split the insurance.

"Toots, wouldn't you like to be married by a minister?" twenty-four-year-old Kaiser asked Emma. Although her friends advised against it, she happily accepted his offer and Reverend Cook performed the ceremony May 11, 1896. Almost immediately, Emma complained to her friends she wished she didn't marry him. He was controlling, abusive, and unbearable when he drank, but she tried to make it work because divorce wasn't a good option. Despite uneasiness on the home front, they bought life insurance for each other and increased the amounts until the coverage was $10,000 each. Emma agreed it was a good investment, but Kaiser had something else on his mind. The couple made wills that named the other as beneficiary with an inclusion that their bodies be cremated in Philadelphia should one or the other die.[450]

Everything was going as planned and soon Kaiser, Clemmer, and Lizzie would be rich. The three decided it would be a good idea to conduct a test run before killing Emma, so Kaiser and Clemmer caught a stray dog in the alley behind Clemmer's Newcomb Street house in Philadelphia and carried it into Clemmer's cellar. They saturated an old cloth with chloroform and covered the dogs' face, but it furiously thrashed about, barking and howling so much that the landlord, Charles Meadowcroft, later testified the commotion greatly annoyed him and he was glad to see them move out. Much to Lizzie's amusement, the men released the anxious dog back into the alley.[451]

Failure did not deter them and they went ahead with their brilliant plan. Clemmer rented a hotel room across from Kaiser and Emma's boarding house and waited. At a predetermined time, Kaiser would chloroform Emma and set the house on fire. Once Clemmer saw smoke and flames, that was his cue, and he would jump into action, run across the street, rescue Kaiser, and leave Emma to die in the fire. Then came Kaiser's grieving husband part. But Clemmer waited and waited. He couldn't see any smoke or fire. Nothing. Maybe Kaiser got the time wrong. Or maybe the chloroform didn't work like in the dog experiment. The next day, Kaiser's excuse for not carrying out their plan was that he could not bring himself to do it.

"You big, blubbering baby," Clemmer said.[452]

The team discussed many plans and if this one was too hard for Kaiser, they could use another method. The three re-grouped. This time fake highwaymen would murder Emma. They staked out the area by making several trips, but when the time came, Kaiser again lost his nerve. They invested too much to give up. Clemmer persuaded Kaiser to take Emma, Lizzie, and a few other girls on a buggy ride to the country where Clemmer would disguise himself and pretend to be a robber. But Emma and some of the girls saw him approach and begged Kaiser to drive away. He whipped up the horse, and they escaped.

Clemmer and Kaiser argued afterward. "Why kill Toots? Why not find another victim?" Kaiser protested. But there was no time to find another victim. Emma's insurance policies were due in a few days and with no money to pay them, let alone the landlord, they had no choice but to act fast.

Frustrated, Clemmer took matters into his own hands and he did not care if his mistress, Lizzie, who became known as the woman in black, died in the process. He hired a vicious horse and buggy and removed the bolts to ensure an 'accident' occurred, then sent Lizzie and Emma on a ride. As soon as they started out, the buggy shafts came loose and dropped to the ground. Several young men caught the horse before he ran away and Lizzie and Emma were unharmed.[453]

Clemmer persisted in convincing Kaiser to kill his wife and Kaiser ceded, promising not to back out this time. They thought up a dozen more murder plots like drowning Emma in the Schuylkill by toppling a boat, or poisoning her. But in the end, they knew which one they had to do, and Charles Kaiser better cooperate or else.

Kaiser met Clemmer and Lizzie at Reading Railway station, October 28, 1896, to finalize details and walk through the timeline. Thirty minutes later, at half past 4 o'clock, Kaiser drove up to his house, where Emma stood at the door.

"Come Toots, let us go for a drive," Kaiser said to his wife.

The couple entered the falling-top buggy, drawn up by a dark horse, the same horse and buggy Lizzie had stolen weeks earlier and sold to Kaiser. As they prepared to leave, Kaiser made a public display of affection in front of watchful neighbors and gave Emma a passionate kiss.[454]

Kaiser and Emma chatted in good humor, enjoying the ride in Norristown, a borough of just under twenty-two thousand people, a few miles northwest of Philadelphia along the Schuylkill River. They turned on Crooked Lane and started up the hill, and as they did, Clemmer and Lizzie passed without saying a word, going the opposite direction. At the bottom of the hill, Clemmer turned the buggy around and gave Lizzie the driving lines. Clemmer jogged up to Kaiser. About halfway up, a bank teller later identified as Benjamin Hughes, walked his bicycle downhill and looked right at Clemmer and Lizzie, an unexpected setback.[455]

Clemmer ignored him and continued.

"Presenting a revolver he put it to Toot's head and demanded her money," Kaiser later testified. Emma burst into tears and surrendered her pocketbook, begging Clemmer not to shoot.[456]

"Toots then took off her watch, which was fastened about her neck, by a chain." As Emma was about to hand it to him, Clemmer shot her in the forehead, above her right eye. "The blood spurted over my back," Kaiser said. In an instant, Emma was dead.[457]

There was no time to waste. "I held up my left arm and Clemmer put a bullet through it, making a flesh wound." Clemmer had originally planned to shoot Kaiser in a corner of his head but Kaiser adamantly objected and insisted on the arm. After Clemmer fired the second shot, he ran to Lizzie and jumped in the vehicle. Kaiser got out of his own buggy, hid his watch beneath a rock by the road to pretend it was stolen, then led the horse along, shouting, "Murder, murder!" at the top of his lungs.

Clemmer grabbed the lines from Lizzie and turned the horse so suddenly, the buggy almost toppled. He snapped the whip and drove as fast as he could, swinging out to avoid a slow-moving team, while Lizzie clung to the seat for fear of falling out. He drove until he found a stream of water and gave the lines to Lizzie. Clemmer removed his overcoat and washed blood from his hands with a handkerchief dipped in water, then took off the bloody cuffs from his overcoat and stuffed them in his pocket to be burned later. Clemmer returned to the buggy, and they went to a hotel to water the horse, then continued driving. At one point, Clemmer stopped the horse and lit a match so he could see if there was any blood inside the buggy, then wiped the lines with a handkerchief.[458]

While Kaiser played up his role as grieving husband, Clemmer and Lizzie went back to Norristown and picked up a little girl named Lulu Cliver, the six-year-old daughter of a servant at the Windsor Hotel, then took her for ride around Norristown as an alibi.[459]

Detective Geyer knew Charlie Kaiser since boyhood and as soon as he read about the murder, it didn't take him long to realize Kaiser was responsible.[460]

"A year and a half ago I came in contact with both Kaiser and Clemmer in a case at May's Landing, N. J., where both men were witnesses. Clemmer then confided to me that Kaiser had proposed to him that he join him in a scheme to insure people and then murder them for the insurance," Geyer said.

"That man Kaiser is the lowest that ever lived. Why, Frank, he wanted me to enter into a scheme with him for marrying women, insuring their lives and then murdering them for the money," Clemmer had told Geyer. At the time, Clemmer was furious at Kaiser for turning states evidence against his friend in the Mays Landing trial.[461]

"When I read of the murder in the *Inquirer* . . . it struck me almost instantly that if Kaiser was the same one we knew he was the murderer." Geyer confided in Superintendent Linden who contacted Norristown authorities. "That is how I happened to be detailed on the case," Geyer said.

Right away, Kaiser's story seemed fake and Norristown authorities suspected his involvement. As soon as they informed him he was under suspicion, Kaiser, a crayon portrait dealer, became hysterical and ripped open his shirt for Officer Gotwals.[462]

"See, my watch is gone. I have no watch," Kaiser said to prove a robber took their belongings. But it was no use. Officers discovered Kaiser's watch hidden under a rock near the crime scene. They also found a .32 caliber pistol covered with blood. What criminal would take the time to stash goods near the crime scene after pistol shots alarmed people in the area?[463]

Footprints from long narrow shoes with a patch on one sole were found at the scene and matched shoes worn by Kaiser.[464]

Detective Geyer arrived in Norristown from Philadelphia and after going over the crime scene, Geyer, Chief William H. Rodenbaugh, and District Attorney Strassberger, put Kaiser on the rack in Rodenbaugh's private office until well past midnight. At one point during questioning, Kaiser got extremely agitated when he saw Clemmer through a window. Clemmer was at City Hall with Lizzie to try and talk to Kaiser.[465]

"Don't let him in. He is the worst enemy I have," Kaiser said.

"That man has been trying to secure counsel for you," Chief Rodenbaugh said, to which Kaiser blushed.[466]

Results of the autopsy proved the bullet could only have been fired by someone from inside the buggy and not on the roadway as Kaiser had claimed. Coroner Kurtz was satisfied the bullet taken from Emma's head came from the discarded bloody pistol found near the scene.[467]

Evidence mounted against Kaiser and it wasn't looking good. Police believed he murdered his wife, and the motive was the insurance money. Their investigation disclosed that Kaiser took out large insurance policies and some were due.

"We have learned that premiums on these policies, or some of them, to the amount of $54 were about to fall due, and that Kaiser would probably have some difficulty in meeting them," Detective Geyer said.[468]

But Kaiser steadfastly maintained his innocence and had not pointed the finger at Clemmer and Lizzie either.

Officials locked Kaiser up in a cell at City Hall after the interrogation to await a coroner's inquest. He woke up in a nervous frenzy the next morning, repeating over and over, "Why don't my father come and get me out." Kaiser paced up and down his cell and, once, when a turnkey walked by, he found Kaiser writhing on the floor in a nervous fit.[469]

The more authorities investigated the case, the more the

evidence pointed to accomplices, specifically James A. Clemmer and Elizabeth K. DeKalb, but just as Geyer and Chief Rodenbaugh were about to bring them in for questioning, Clemmer left his Philadelphia employment and hid from police. He and Lizzie could not be found.[470]

Conshohocken authorities contacted Norristown to let them know about an incident there involving insurance that they now believed was fraudulent. While Clemmer boarded at a home in Conshohocken last summer, he hired a horse and buggy. About nine o'clock that same evening, the horse came back to the stables dragging the buggy with one wheel missing. A search for Clemmer found him lying injured in a gutter. He was examined by a local physician who found that while his injuries were painful, they were not serious and were mostly bruises. While recovering in bed, two people fitting Kaiser and Lizzie's description's requested copies of papers containing the account of the accident to prove a claim for insurance.[471]

Later, Clemmer told a friend the horse did not run away. Instead, he removed the nut from the axle, whipped the horse and let the animal take its course. He then used a coupling pin to beat himself black and blue and then he laid in the gutter.[472]

A pattern emerged showing Kaiser, Clemmer, and Lizzie had a history of undergoing illegal activities together.

Chief Rodenbaugh handcuffed Charles O. Kaiser to himself and brought him into the crowded City Council Chambers for a coroner's inquest November 20, 1896. Kaiser, dressed in a dark cut-away suit, appearing unconcerned, smiled and talked to his attorney's, and his father, and brother, who were all by his side. Numerous witnesses testified, including Detective Geyer, who repeated a statement Kaiser said when he questioned him.[473]

"I did not kill my wife. I know who did, but will not tell you," Kaiser said to Geyer. Chief Rodenbaugh corroborated. Seems, Detective Geyer had Kaiser repeat his statement in front of Rodenbaugh and others.

Kaiser's attorney cross-examined Chief Rodenbaugh and asked if he recalled if Detective Geyer ever told Kaiser, "Charlie, I have got the rope around your neck; you might as well confess." But the Chief denied Geyer ever said that.

Philadelphia ex-Mayor William B. Smith, testified he was the agent for some of the life insurance the Kaiser's obtained for each other in the amount of $10,500. Other witnesses identified both Clemmer and Lizzie as accomplices. The jury returned the following verdict:

"We the jury . . . find, that said Emma P. Kaiser came to her death by a gunshot wound on the 28th day of October . . . and by Charles O. Kaiser, Jr., the said wound being the result of a conspiracy entered into by the said Charles O. Kaiser and others."[474]

Immediately after the verdict, Kaiser was taken before a magistrate to plead to a charge of murder. He waived a preliminary hearing. He was held without bail and ordered to stand trial, set for March 8, 1897. That gave Detective Geyer and others time to locate Clemmer and Lizzie, but to no avail. Kaiser's case went ahead without them and the twelve day trial began as planned.

Court officials parked a buggy, stained with Emma Kaiser's blood, in the court as evidence, the top of which showed a ragged perforation the Commonwealth contended was made from a bullet Kaiser fired through his arm.[475]

Much of what was presented to the coroner's jury was repeated during trial with additional evidence to prove the connection between Kaiser, Clemmer, and Lizzie.

The audience anxiously waited for Geyer's testimony. At 3:45 March 12, the powerful, dark mustached detective took his seat on the witness stand and like a pack of wolves, Kaiser's attorneys requested the judge bar testimony about Clemmer's statement made to Geyer before the murder took place. The judge agreed. Next, defense requested the judge bar testimony about all statements Kaiser made to Geyer without an attorney present, but much to the pleasure of the audience, the judge denied the request.[476]

Geyer began his testimony by describing how he questioned Kaiser.

"Charlie, it was a bad day for you when you met that Jim Clemmer."[477]

"Ah," Kaiser said.

"Yes. You see, the Clemmer association is the one thing that makes people suspect you. Damned if I wouldn't like to help you, Charlie. I wouldn't say much about Clemmer to anybody if I were you, but you can tell me as a friend, Charlie, what you had to do with him, and I can see my way to help you out of the clutch of the country policemen," Geyer said to his old friend to encourage a confession.

Geyer testified that Kaiser rose from his chair, beat his head and cried, "By God, Geyer you are right! I never would have had any trouble if it had not been for him and that Culp." Kaiser signed a confession all right, but it was the fake highwaymen story.[478]

Detective Geyer told of the same off-handed conversational method he used with Clemmer to see if he would admit he knew Kaiser and inadvertently make a statement.

"Why, look here, old man. How goes it? Haven't seen you for an age. You're looking a treat. It's easy to see the world uses you well," Geyer said.

"Oh, yes. I am doing fairly, been very busy," Clemmer said.

"So have I, one of those damned cases up country. They've a chap called Kaiser up there for murder. Decent boy, too; not a bit of harm in him; and those plowboy policemen want to convict him. They can't do it, though. By the way, you know Kaiser, Jim?" Jim knew him and had read the case in newspapers.

Geyer testified he questioned Kaiser again the evening of October 30 at City Hall.

"Then, I charged him with shooting his wife. To this Kaiser replied, 'You're a ——liar.' Later on the prisoner remarked, 'It was a sad, sad day when I met Clemmer, as otherwise I would never have done anything wrong.'" Kaiser then asked to see Detective Geyer alone. Chief Rodenbaugh went out of the room then Kaiser said, "I didn't shoot her, but I know who did; won't say who, but you know who did it." Geyer knew who he meant—James A. Clemmer.[479]

Geyer said he called Rodenbaugh and another officer back into the room and Kaiser repeated what he told Geyer and also said that if Geyer made a round of the pawn shops, he could see who the murderer was.

Later, when Kaiser returned to his cell to await the coroner's inquest, Geyer asked him again who shot his wife. To this the prisoner replied, "It was not Clemmer but you know who it was."

Chief Rodenbaugh testified Kaiser told conflicting stories. He also corroborated Geyer's statements. Rodenbaugh said Kaiser told Geyer in his presence that if he found who had Mrs. Kaiser's watch, he would have the murderer. That was telling because after authorities arrested Clemmer and Lizzie, following Kaiser's trial, they found Emma Kaiser's watch.

Kaiser's attorney, George Bradford Carr, presented a flowery picture of the defendant's life. He and Mrs. Kaiser were a happy couple who like other couples had hopes and ambitions. They were "two souls with but a single thought, two hearts that beat as one." No motive could have broken their bond and their love for each other.[480]

Kaiser testified in his own defense, but that turned out to be a mistake. During cross-examination, he contradicted himself several times and when asked if it was James A. Clemmer who took his pocketbook, he became annoyed and replied smartly, "No, it was not. Do you think I would stand here to be condemned to death if I knew who killed my wife?" Asked why he wanted Clemmer detained on the evening of the 29th when he learned Clemmer was there to obtain a lawyer for him, Kaiser said, "Just to make him prove where he was on the night of the robbery."[481]

District Attorney Jacob A. Strassburger went all out in his closing statement. He reminded the jury of the bloodstained buggy with which Mrs. Kaiser met her death. He went over thirteen points he wished the judge to include in his charge and reminded jurors of evidence presented and the footprints that matched Kaiser's shoes. He then passed around articles taken from the defendant, and said that if he had no right to secure them as he did, then he would resign from his office. The defense had earlier questioned the fact that Geyer and the coroner went thru Kaiser's trunks the day after the crime without a search warrant.[482]

Mr. Carr, in closing, went over inconsistencies. He asked the jury to believe Kaiser's written statement to Detective Geyer about the murder being committed by Highwaymen. "For, if the others are true why didn't they put them in writing and have Kaiser indorse them with his signature?"

The jury deliberated three hours and returned a verdict of

guilty of murder in the first degree at 7:15 on the evening of March 20. Once the bell announced a verdict, no less than 4,000 men, women, and children made a wild dash for the court house, fighting to get inside. The weak were trampled on, and within minutes, 1,800 people crowded into the seats, window sills, and aisles. Kaiser was the coolest of all as jurors prepared to read the verdict. He chewed a quid of tobacco, certain of his acquittal. But it was not to be.[483]

Now that Kaiser was a convicted man, Detectives renewed efforts to search for his accomplices.

Both Clemmer and his mistress, Lizzie, whose mother died when she was young, were under indictment for conspiracy to commit murder and authorities in Philadelphia and Norristown were on the lookout for them.[484]

Chief Rodenbaugh received a tip that Clemmer and Lizzie were in Philadelphia and he asked Captain Miller to assign Geyer to work with him again, which the captain agreed to. But when Chief Rodenbaugh arrived at City Hall, November 9, Captain Miller had already sent Geyer on a trivial errand so he assigned Detective Crawford instead. Rodenbaugh was annoyed but what could he do? The two found Lizzie on a Pennsylvania Railroad train near Broad Street and she was arrested and brought to City Hall where Captain Miller, Rodenbaugh, and Crawford put her on the rack to squeeze a confession out of her. Lizzie DeKalb would not budge. Captain Miller told his boss, the only way to get her to confess was to threaten her with a hearing, which was agreed to. That irritated Norristown. The crime was committed there and she should be brought before a magistrate there instead. But the woman in black was brought before a magistrate in Philadelphia. Press caught wind and covered it in the papers, which Clemmer read, and by the time Chief Rodenbaugh and Crawford went after him, he was gone.[485]

Between the time Clemmer fled after Geyer spoke with him, to when Chief Rodenbaugh and Detective Crawford followed up on the lead in Philadelphia, Clemmer served six months in prison for a petty crime in Conshohocken, which explained why it took over seven months to find him.

After two days in custody, Philadelphia authorities released Lizzie to Chief Rodenbaugh and Norristown was able to hold a hearing of their own. But Lizzie was still not talking. Magistrate Lenhardt heard witness testimony and continued the hearing to December 27, to give police time to find and arrest Clemmer and follow up on leads.

By the end of November, James A. Clemmer was spotted in Newark, New Jersey. District Attorney James A. Strasburger sent instructions for authorities to arrest him and he was decoyed by a fake personal advertisement placed in a New York newspaper purporting to be from Lizzie. Clemmer responded with a letter that fell into the hands of Strasburger and that's how they were able to locate and arrest Clemmer, who denied knowing anything about the Kaiser murder and used an *alias*, Harry E. Youngs. But when police searched him after his arrest, they found a roll of newspaper clippings containing a full account of the murder and the conviction of Kaiser.[486]

While Lizzie was in custody, Clemmer wrote letters to warn her to stay quiet about the murder. But, after she read the recent confession of Mrs. Nack who was described as Lady Macbeth and all the Borgias rolled into one, Lizzie told police, "I am in about the same position as Mrs. Nack, and I don't propose to be caught any more than she was. I was betrayed into your hands by a sneaking lover, who decoyed me from Trenton, and I do not propose to slip my head into a noose to save the head of another lover."[487]

Lizzie became an informant and confessed, proclaiming herself as an unwitting bystander. It was Kaiser and Clemmer that planned and executed the murder. On that fateful day, Clemmer drove slowly behind Kaiser's buggy, stopped, and walked the rest of the way. Clemmer gave a signal that propelled Kaiser into action.

"Kaiser threw his left arm around his wife's neck and forced her to one side of the buggy."

Protecting her lover, Lizzie confessed that Clemmer was afraid to carry out his part of the plan, but Kaiser insisted.

"Shoot, dog, or I'll kill every one of you," Kaiser screamed.

"There was a flash and a crash, and Mrs. Kaiser fell over dead. Her desperate struggles had so scarred the dashboard of the buggy and disarranged the carpet that they carried her from one buggy to the other to avoid suspicion. Clemmer and I rode away together, and Kaiser whipped up and rode home next toT the dead body of his wife. Clemmer and I fled from the town the next day after suspicion fell on Kaiser," the twenty-six-year-old Jacksonville, Florida native confessed.[488]

At fifteen, Lizzie had moved out of her sister's house and went to Pottstown to work as a servant. She took a couple other servant jobs and then moved to Philadelphia, where she became a servant at the home of James A. Clemmer, who was married with five children. She and Clemmer most likely started an affair while she was a household servant, because soon after, they ran off together, moving from one place to another. She said Clemmer wanted to get married in Camden, New Jersey using false names, but Lizzie refused—after all, he was still married. In hindsight, she believed he wanted to marry her, buy life insurance, then kill her like he killed Mrs. Kaiser.[489]

Detective Geyer testified before a grand jury on June 9, 1898, following Clemmer's arrest, but by far the most important witness was Clemmer's lover, Miss Lizzie DeKalb. Dressed in a colored shirt and of course, a black skirt, Lizzie wore a stylish, brown hat. She looked sophisticated, very much unlike the press had previously described her. Clemmer seemed interested as he sat comfortably in a blue serge suit, black derby hat, and striped shirt with a small bowtie, smiling from time-to-time at humorous witnesses testimony. The grand jury indicted Clemmer and set trial for the following Monday, giving Clemmer's attorneys four days to prepare a defense.[490]

Like the trial of Charles Kaiser, Clemmer's trial captivated America. This time both Kaiser and Lizzie testified, as did Clemmer, who emphatically proclaimed his innocence. And so, during the heat of summer, Clemmer's trial did little to disappoint, other than when Lizzie testified—she spoke in such low tones, even people who sat within a few feet of her couldn't hear. Still called 'the woman in black,' her brown eyes flashed defiance at spectators when she spoke. Lizzie shaded her face with her left hand to block Clemmer's eyes from gazing on hers and when that didn't work, she wheeled her chair around to turn away from him. Clemmer smiled as Lizzie told of her illicit love affair with him, serving as a domestic in his house with his wife and five children, and of fleeing the house to be together. She repeated her confession and told of the Kaiser tragedy and how she was a victim too.[491]

On the second day of trial, June 15, defense revealed their cards during Lizzie's five hour cross-examination. Clemmer admitted he and Lizzie were in the buggy that day, but were no where near the Kaiser's buggy.

Again, the Commonwealth displayed the bloodstained, bullet-riddled, rusty buggy in which Mrs. Kaiser met her death. Lizzie recognized it as the one she stole at Gloucester. She testified she obeyed Clemmer because she feared him and swore no promises of immunity were made in exchange for her story. She was later sentenced to only two years in prison for her participation in the crime.[492]

HEADLINE NEWS:

CLEMMER WANTED
TO KILL GEYER

LIZZIE DE KALB WAS TO ASSIST IN
GETTING RID OF THE DETECTIVE

Lizzie shocked the crowded courtroom when recalled to the witness stand the next day. She announced there were two assassination plots hatched by Clemmer.[493]

"After the murder for a few days we went back to the Newcomb Street house in Philadelphia. Clemmer said Geyer knew too much about him. He plotted to lure him to the house and to have me talk with him in the dining room, while he got a blackjack, or sand-bag, or something, and hit him over the head. I told him I wouldn't do it, and that if he brought Geyer in the front way I would go out the back."[494]

Lizzie DeKalb testified she and Clemmer were in Philadelphia when Clemmer spotted Detective Geyer and suddenly ducked into a crowd until he passed.

"One evening Jim and I were standing on the corner at Eighth and Vine Streets, I think, in Philadelphia. A big, broad-shouldered man passed. I heard Jim catch his breath and draw back into the crowd, 'Do you see that fellow?' he whispered. I had seen him. 'Just as long as he is alive, I am in danger. We must think of some way to kill him.'"

Lizzie told of Clemmer's plan to kill the star witness, Benjamin Hughes, who was to testify he saw Clemmer and Lizzie the day of the murder.

"He said he intended to come up and blow his brains out at the same place as we met him on the road just before the murder."

Clemmer told her if they killed Geyer and Benjamin Hughes, police would stop searching for them. But she refused. Geyer, seated among the privileged spectators, gave Lizzie an approving smile—likely grateful for her refusal to help Clemmer kill him, and happy she testified, as it showed just how diabolical Clemmer really was.[495]

For his part in the Clemmer trial, unlike testimony at his own trial, Kaiser admitted to participating in the murder but said Clemmer was the brains behind the plot and Kaiser was afraid of him. Whatever Clemmer told Kaiser to do, he did it. Kaiser also said Lizzie played a much bigger role than she admitted.[496]

Though Clemmer continued to maintain his innocence throughout the trial, a jury found him guilty of murder in the first degree.

Charles Kaiser's appeal was denied, and he was sentenced to hang September 6, 1898.[497]

As crazy as it sounds, the Kaiser's (father and son) each

instituted a lawsuit in the United States Circuit Court of Pennsylvania in 1897 to recover the life insurance money. One was brought by Kaiser's dad, Charles O. Kaiser, Sr., as administrator, to recover two policies of $1,000 and $4,000, and the second was brought by Charles O. Kaiser, Jr., on a joint policy for $5,000 for the lives of himself and his wife, payable to the survivor.

Insurers were sure they would prevail in the two lawsuits because Mrs. Kaiser lied about her age and wrote that she was twenty-three, effectively rendering the applications fraudulent. Her adopted father, George Ruyl, swore before a notary that her real age was twenty-nine years, one month, and ten days at the time of her death. The insurance companies had a valid point and on January 15, 1898, both lawsuits were discontinued by counsel for the plaintiffs. If Mrs. Kaiser had not committed fraud and lied on the applications, her killer and his father most likely would have collected on the life insurance policies, despite Kaiser having been convicted of murder.[498]

Charles O. Kaiser took his own life a few weeks before he was to be hanged. Kaiser stripped naked, except for an undershirt. He took a piece of clock spring, straightened it, and literally stabbed himself to death. Deep cuts were found on each arm, close to his brachial arteries. Near his wrist, there were four more cuts nearly an inch deep, with another deep cut on his left leg. He also stabbed both his feet and his neck. The final step in Kaiser's gory suicide was to hang himself, which he did by tying a bed sheet to a spigot. Sadly, the spring he used was from a clock his parents gave him to keep in his cell. Following his suicide, authorities found it sitting on a small shelf in the corner, hands stopped and pointed to 11:20.[499]

James A. Clemmer's appeal was denied. He filed for a pardon stating six reasons. First, because he was convicted on testimonies of two self-confessed alleged accomplices. Second, because prior to that, he was an upright citizen. Third, because he was the father of five small children, the oldest of whom was thirteen and his execution would be a heavy burden on the innocent children. Fourth, because Lizzie may tell a different story when she gets out of prison. Fifth, because of the infamy and disrepute of Kaiser and Lizzie and uncertainty of the truthfulness of their testimony. And sixth, because he was tried and convicted after Kaiser and all the facts were in newspapers, causing him not to have a fair trial.[500]

Clemmer's pardon was denied, and he was hanged May 18, 1899. A few hours before his execution, Clemmer told the Warden, "For what I have done I hope I have been forgiven, as well by those whom I have wronged as by the God whom I am so soon to meet." Those were the first words Clemmer spoke that could be construed into a confession of guilt.[501]

Elizabeth 'Lizzie' K. DeKalb, the notorious woman in black, pleaded guilty to accessory after the fact, and was sentenced to two years hard labor. It was later reported she sewed clothes in prison, hardly what people envisioned as hard labor. At sentencing, Judge Schwartz admonished Lizzie.[502]

"You have shown no sorrow, no repentance, no fear. You have not one spark of true womanhood," Schwartz said.

Lizzie gave him a stern look as if she would attack him in a rage, but that did not deter him. Judge Schwartz continued. "Lizzie DeKalb, the district attorney has been pleased to allow you to enter merely a plea of guilty as an accessory after the fact. Yet your own confession here, as well as that of Kaiser, prove you to have been guilty to a far greater degree. You certainly were a partner in that awful crime. After the murder you helped a felon to escape and to keep in hiding . . . you have led a bad life, and you have no one to blame but yourself . . . The only reason why your plea has been accepted is on account of your testimony in the case against Clemmer."

Lizzie burst into tears in bitter hatred.

As she was led away, she nastily declared, "I'm sorry that I betrayed poor Jim. If I'd only kept my mouth shut we'd both be free now."

Authorities never tried Lizzie for stealing the horse and buggy because they couldn't find the paperwork for her arrest. After her release, *Philadelphia Inquirer* interviewed Lizzie, who claimed she, too, was a victim. She told the reporter she had planned to move to Trenton, New Jersey, but her attorney advised her to seek a place where she was not known. A cousin reported Lizzie worked as waitress at the same hotel she and Clemmer picked up the little girl to use as an alibi on the day of the Kaiser murder. It was later reported Lizzie fell in love with an escaped criminal named Wilson Hunsberger and the two fled the area and married under assumed names.[503]

Lucky for Detective Geyer and his loving family, Clemmer did not carry out his plot to murder him or anyone else for that matter, at least, that anyone knows of. In 1899, *Reading Times* reported Clemmer's death list, one of which was carried out, and if had not have been caught, it would be a matter of time before he murdered the rest on his list. They were: Mrs. Charles O. Kaiser, Jr., (murdered), Charles O. Kaiser, Jr., Lizzie DeKalb, Benjamin J. Hughes, and Frank P. Geyer.[504]

CHARLES KAISER

MRS. EMMA KAISER

JAMES A. CLEMMER

LIZZIE K. DE KALB

Fig. 53. Top: Charles O. Kaiser, 24, and his wife, Mrs. Emma P.

Kaiser, 29. Detective Geyer knew Charles Kaiser since they were boys.[505] Bottom: James A. Clemmer and his girlfriend, Elizabeth "Lizzie" K. DeKalb, 26, *alias* Bessie Kulp, Elizabeth Moor, Laura Kauffan, and Bertha Lambert.[506] Image sources: "Charles Kaiser Faces a Jury," *Philadelphia Times*, March 9, 1897, p. 5 and "Clemmer's Sin is Expiated," *Philadelphia Times*, May 19, 1899, p. 4.

CHAPTER 21

Regret to Inform You

If an uniformed person should have watched Detective Frank Geyer yesterday as he carefully gathered together a good-sized bundled of odds and ends he would have no doubt wondered what any sensible man would want with such a lot of rubbish. Those familiar with the careers of two famous criminals, H. H. Holmes . . . and Alphonse Cutair [sic] . . . would bear testimony to their value.[507]

-Silent Witnesses' article in the *Philadelphia Inquirer*

Philadelphia, August 1903 - 1907

WHEN MOST PEOPLE THINK of law enforcement, they often assume cohesiveness, camaraderie, and teamwork exist behind the scenes to allow for a seamless execution of their duties, but for Detective Geyer and his fellow officers, it wasn't so easy. Constant changes pitted officers against officers, fighting to stay employed after each election and expected administration terminations, demotions, and updated policies.

Changes took place suddenly, without notice, and most often for political reasons. Officers were fired for not being political enough or for being too political. They were suspended, terminated, or forced to resign for the slightest reasons too, such as not wearing an overcoat, walking or talking with associates or civilians except in the line of police duty, or for carrying an umbrella, all forbidden activities.[508]

Officials implemented inconvenient policies such as forcing all officers to wear winter uniforms until every officer on the force received summer uniforms. While this may seem a minor inconvenience, they took it to the extreme. If 2,451 summer uniforms were ordered, like in 1896, and the tailor fell behind schedule, all officers had to work in blazing hot conditions in heavy winter uniforms until the last one was delivered. And if someone lost or gained weight and needed an alteration, all officers still had to wait.

"When the summer suits are delivered there's always some bow-legged son of a gun up in Kensington whose uniform has to be patched up half-a-dozen times before it fits. That takes a week, and all the rest of us have to swelter. Then a chump in the First ward falls in love and the cut of his clothes has to be changed. That's another week . . . This uniform business makes me tired," an overheated policeman told a reporter.[509]

And here's where the rub came in, detectives did not wear uniforms.

"It's this way. We've got to chase crazy bicyclers day times and fight burglars after dark. Them detectives . . . I saw Frank Geyer and Colonel Almendinger go by here just now in lawn tennis suits. Then there's the harbor police. The breezes blow on them while they drink beer on deck, and they don't know what it is to take a Turkish bath for ten hours a day, with a sergeant coming around to see if you haven't worn too much of the soles off your winter shoes. It ain't a square shake…"[510]

The uniform debacle was an ongoing problem, so much so, officers wrote a poem:[511]

Shine! Shine! Shine!
On our heavy clothes, O sun!
But the vanished sound
Of the Mayor's voice
Will tell us yet, when
He makes the choice,
That Winter's days are done.
-*The Policeman Poet*

All of this took a toll on officers in the nineteenth and early twentieth centuries. Newspapers reported jealousy among officers, back-stabbing, and crazy headlines such as, "Detective War to Be Probed," and "Sleuths War in Philadelphia."

It seemed, officers were against officers, detectives against detectives, departments against departments, and no matter what Detective Geyer did to avoid it, he was sometimes placed in the middle.

In December 1901, Geyer's longtime partner, Detective Thomas G. Crawford got suspended because he had a war of words with a fellow detective while defending Geyer's honor. The two detectives investigated a murder case together, along with a new detective, Jacob S. Welker (later forced to resign). All clues pointed to one suspect but Jacob Welker insisted someone else committed the murder. Welker went behind their backs and convinced the police superintendent. But the district attorney sided with Geyer and Crawford and prosecuted based on that.

The main conflict came about during testimony. Welker ensured an acquittal by telling a jury Detective Geyer had wrung a confession through falsehood. That set Detective Crawford into a frenzy. He was furious and denounced Welker in front of everyone, telling him he was in a conspiracy to clear the prisoner. Words went back and forth between Welker and Crawford and Welker stormed out of the courtroom. The superintendent talked to Welker to get his side of the story but refused to talk to Crawford and instead brought charges against the seasoned detective.[512]

The superintendent, likely annoyed with the district attorney's office who sided with Geyer and Crawford, was hell-bent on getting back at Crawford.

Detective Geyer learned the best way to do his job was to stay clear of politics at work. He watched fellow officers and close friends destroyed by political hatchets. He wanted to do his job and avoid headaches. Unlike fired fellow officers caught in a quandary with no way to support their families, Geyer did his best to stay out of the crosshairs. He only had a few recorded disciplines in his almost three decades as a law enforcement officer, and that, by standards at the time, was an absolute miracle.

In 1891, Geyer ejected a woman from a court hearing. He asked her to leave, but the woman, whose son was in the dock charged with larceny, refused. She claimed Geyer took hold of her wrists and forced her from her chair. As he tried to eject her, she grabbed onto the railing and 'was forcibly torn loose.'[513]

The woman filed a complaint against Geyer and he was

brought before a police court of inquiry, a trial run mostly by police captains. Philadelphia police used the system to investigate officers by trial, resulting in recommendations for mayor approval to terminate, suspend, fine, and reprimand officers. Philadelphia included statistics in a few mayor's reports, one of which listed an astounding 452 cases against police officers tried in a single year. Of those, 414 were found guilty.[514]

Numerous witnesses testified, as did Geyer and a reservist, and there were conflicting statements about who pulled her hands away. The woman had a slight scratch on one hand.

Geyer testified the woman vilified him for arresting her son and intimidated a witness before the hearing. He tried to escort her out of the courtroom but she grabbed onto a rail and refused to comply. He and another officer forcefully ejected her. Geyer said the woman appeared under the influence of liquor. A witness testified he heard the woman swear at Geyer and threaten to get even with him.

The end result was that Geyer received a reprimand. If he had been guilty of excessive force, officials would have fired him on the spot.[515]

Twelve years later when Geyer was at one of his worst moments grieving over his mother's impending death, a heartless supervisor charged him with neglect, a common charge frequently thrown at officers. But the mayor took his efficient service and good record into consideration and decided he was already sufficiently punished.[516] Geyer's beloved mother Camilla died three weeks later and a private funeral was held at his childhood home on Cadwallader.[517]

Detective Geyer came to a point in life where he reevaluated what was important to him. After Camilla's death, his dad moved a half mile away to live with Geyer's sister, Kate, and her husband, Harry Werner, on Orkney. But seventy-seven-year-old Reuben suffered medical setbacks due to spinal sclerosis, a hardening of the spinal cord or vertebrae. Seventeen days before Geyer's fiftieth birthday, the civil war veteran died July 11, 1903.

Whether a coincidence or the press tried to soften his blow, the same day Reuben Geyer's obituary appeared in the *Philadelphia Inquirer*, the paper featured an article about Detective Geyer and Crawford, crediting them with 112 arrests.[518]

The emotional loss had a tremendous impact on Geyer. Concentrating on murder investigations was impossible in his state. He likely remembered the slap in the face he got at the time of his mother's death and took time off from work to recover from his sorrow. Geyer, Mary, and sixteen-year-old Edna left Philadelphia less than a month after Reuben's death for some rest and relaxation.

Time away from work was good for the famous detective. Geyer received a job offer making more money with less stress and the timing could not have been better. With constant political turmoil and uncertainty, it was an easy decision for him. When the family returned from their vacation, Geyer unexpectedly reported to City Hall on Saturday, August 15, 1903, and surprised everyone by announcing, "I regret to sever my connection with the department, but I have decided to accept another position."[519]

Philadelphia Inquirer reported Geyer investigated around 500 murder cases during his long career, many of them noteworthy. Geyer's annual salary was $1,450 in 1903 and upon his retirement, he received approximately $800 a year in pension.[520]

The *Patriot Harrisburg* described Geyer as the best-known of the city's detective force. They stated Geyer had secured a new position as chief detective at Lit Brother's department store, a strong competitor of Wanamaker's. A few days later, a news report surfaced explaining his retirement. Politicians, fellow officers, and local press foreshadowed his resignation because, though he was a man of integrity, he was a no-nonsense guy who refused to take part in politics.[521]

Philadelphia officials let Detective Geyer take artifacts and souvenirs from the H. H. Holmes case and other investigations he conducted over the years. By the time Geyer left the Bureau of Police, evidence in those cases were collecting dust so they had no problem allowing Geyer to take them, especially considering his long service. Detective Geyer's great-granddaughter, Joyce, later remembered one such relic. It was the rope used to hang H. H.

Holmes. Joyce remembered as a child growing up, the rope was
stored in her cedar chest in the attic and they would look at it from
time-to-time. It was said later to have been donated by the family
to the Smithsonian Institution in Washington DC.[522]

Fig. 54. Upon Detective Geyer's retirement from Philadelphia
    Bureau of Police, he worked as a detective for the Lit Brothers
    Store. Image source: Courtesy of Library of Congress.

CHAPTER 22

Police Scandal

I wish it were possible to find some extenuating circumstances for these men, but the language of condemnation is inadequate to describe their offense.

-Judge Kinsey's admonishment statement[523]

April 1908 -1909

GEYER REMAINED CLOSE WITH officials and members of the Bureau of Police after his retirement, taking part in noteworthy events, retirements, and presentations of gold metals and watches throughout the years. He continued to work alongside fellow officers while he investigated cases of his own.[524]

April 1908 brought about a race riot ten minutes from Frank and Mary's home. Three thousand unemployed men answered a job advertisement to build Hammerstein's Opera House, later renamed Metropolitan Opera House. The riot erupted when a large group of Italians showed up to take jobs at a lower rate. "Down with the Italians!" the crowd screamed. "Fire the Italians and employ us!"[525]

Frightened families shuttered windows and bolted their doors, while police officers, reservists, and ambulances lined Broad and Carlisle and Fairmount and Ridge, working to break up the fight. Officers formed a flying wedge and charged into the Italian, African American, and Irish crowd. Angry rioters swung blackjacks and knives and heaved bricks and other objects at each other. Injured men, still swinging fists, were thrown on stretchers and transported to local hospitals. The head of one man was so badly crushed, authorities worried he wouldn't make it, but no reports of any deaths appeared in newspapers. In the midst of the chaos, police arrested just two rioters, Thomas Parson and Edward Connor.

Officials put the riot to rest and began work on the historical Founder's Week event to celebrate the 225th anniversary of the city. Bureau of Police, among others, was to be highlighted during the event, but Philadelphia was about to be thrown into nation-wide headlines.

Officers arrested four disgraced comrades for burglary. Seems they stashed thousands of dollars in valuable goods in one of the officer's home cellars, so much that several patrol wagons were used to haul the goods to the police station. The officers claimed the political system of Philadelphia made them do it because supervisors took one-third of the $1,000 to $1,500 annual salaries for assessments, tickets, and events.

Public Safety Director Clay and Mayor Reyburn denied it.[526]

"I am going to look into it, though, and if it is true, I don't care whether it's organization or not, I'm going to smash it," Mayor Reyburn said. [527]

The officers pleaded guilty to entering without breaking with intent to commit a felony, larceny, receiving stolen goods, and conspiracy.

Judge Kinsey sentenced each officer to seven years in the same prison they helped put criminals in, Eastern Penitentiary.[528]

Judge Kinsey strongly denounced officers in open court, which reverberated in newspapers throughout the country.

"I know of no crime more enormous. They were sworn officers of the law, under oath to guard property during the night hours. They were false to their trust, and by their act they have brought reproach not only upon themselves, but upon the name of the police department and the entire city. I see no reason for mercy in this case. The defendants are guilty of gross treason, and they must meet their punishment."[529]

The City and Bureau of Police felt the pain of dishonor and shame. It was an emotional time for most all of Philadelphia as Judge Kinsey referenced in his admonishment. But the scandal came with a surprise. During the probe into the officer burglaries, officials demanded resignations of seven detectives, including James Tate, Sr., who worked with Geyer on the Hannah Mary Tabbs torso murder case, and at one time was his boss. That wasn't the only surprise in store for Geyer. Officials also forced Detective

Jacob Welker to resign. He was the man responsible for Detective Crawford's suspension and who went against Geyer on the witness stand to ensure the acquittal of a murder suspect.[530]

The same day Judge Kinsey's harsh words appeared in the newspaper, the Geyer's had more pleasant things on their mind. It was Frank and Mary's twenty-third wedding anniversary!

Spring was in the air, Easter around the corner, and there was a wedding to plan. Daddy's little girl was getting married. Sweet Edna blossomed into a beautiful woman with eyes to melt any man's heart. His precious girl who liked to snuggle in his lap, was in love, and in a few days, Frank would have the honor to give his daughter's hand in marriage to Orrie Curtis Strohm.

While Philadelphians readied for sleep on a clear Tuesday evening, proud Detective Geyer and his wife Mary hosted an eight o'clock wedding at their Sixth Street home. About fifty guests attended the small ceremony performed by Rev. Walter G. Haupt, rector of St. Barnabas Protestant Episcopal Church.[531]

"The bride was given away by her father, who for many years was a City Hall detective," the *Bridgeton Evening* reported.[532]

Twenty-one-year-old Edna, beautifully adorned in a white princess wedding gown made of lightweight batiste, captured the air of the night. Edna's maid of honor, Miss Esther Morris of Bridgeton, wore an elegant blue silk pongee gown, that by no means took away from the graceful and exquisite bride. John Oscar Bower took a welcome break from medical studies to honor his friend as his best man. Bower later became an acclaimed physician and Clinical Professor of Surgery at the Temple University School of Medicine and authored numerous papers on acute appendicitis mortality.[533]

After the twilight ceremony and delicious dinner buffet, the newlyweds honeymooned in Orrie's hometown of Newville, Pennsylvania, a small borough in Cumberland County located west of Carlisle.[534]

Orrie, a stenographer at the *Patriot News* in Harrisburg, came from a prominent newspaper family and was the son of John and

Alice Strohm. Orrie's father founded the *Plainfield Times* in Pennsylvania May 1882 and a year later, started a very successful matrimonial paper appropriately called *Cupid's Corner*. He moved the *Plainfield Times* to Newville, Pennsylvania in November 1885 and renamed the paper, *The Newville Times*. John later sold the paper, then accepted a position as manager of the *Shippensburg Chronicle*.[535]

After their honeymoon, the happy couple returned to Philadelphia to their own, smartly furnished home near Frank and Mary at 4123 North Sixth Street.

While Edna and Orrie settled into married life, Geyer opened the Frank P. Geyer Detective Agency and set up his office at 1328 Arch Street, a building with offices for attorneys and other local businesses.[536]

Detective Geyer was a hot commodity and his agency did well. He worked mostly in areas throughout Pennsylvania and New Jersey. Reporters spotted Geyer investigating the 'false moustache' murder case in Norristown, Pennsylvania, and a high-profile murder case in Mays Landing, New Jersey.

Geyer teamed up with District Attorney Charles D. McAvoy and Chief of Police William Rodenbough of Norristown to investigate the 'false moustache' murder case. Four robbers savagely beat and shot a wealthy farmer named George Johnson in his DeKalb Street home. Geyer and Rodenbough found 'false moustaches' on the suspects which led to the arrest of Nick Marengo, Frank Chickereno, John Ballon, and "Grim" Frank Faire. Detective Frank Geyer also helped catch two of their friends, "Fatty" Frank Paruchi and "Yorkey" Antonio Iacovetti and charged them with attempted burglary. The men tried to enter through the second story using an ax and a ladder which they left at the scene when they fled.[537]

The New Jersey case involved a farmer named William H. Strong who was under suspicion for killing his wife. Strong went to a clairvoyant to see if he could find out who killed his wife. And in a round-about way, he sort of confessed to killing his wife. Little did he know the district attorney had sent Detective Geyer and County Detective William Baitzell to hide behind a thin partition.[538]

Based on his confession and other evidence, Mr. Strong was arrested and tried. The clairvoyant testified at his trial she wrote a letter to Strong asking him to come in to see her. After answering questions about his wife and the murder, she said, "Mr. Strong, I have something more to tell you. I have not told you all I know." She repeated what he told her at an earlier reading and he got nervous.[539]

"Finally, I described the man who killed his wife, and he cried, 'That is me!'" the woman testified. She told the jury she quietly said, 'you killed her,' and he broke down and cried.

A jury convicted Strong of second degree murder and a judge sentenced him to thirty years in prison. But the Supreme Court reversed the decision because they didn't believe the clairvoyant's testimony. Also, someone sent anonymous letters while Mr. Strong was in prison claiming responsibility for his wife's death.[540]

Not only was Frank Geyer busy investigating murder cases, but he found time to work on another invention, a Safety-Lock, which promised to prevent burglars from slipping their sticky hands inside pocketbooks and handbags. And in keeping with the safety and security theme, he helped his son-in-law, Orrie, with an alarm invention.[541]

Summer of 1909 brought about a sweet bundle of joy. Frank and Mary became first time grandparents. Adorable Elizabeth Alice Strohm was born in Philadelphia, August 23. Three months later, Mrs. Geyer helped sponsor her baptism at the historic Christ Church on Second Street, known as the Nation's Church where famous revolutionary-era leaders worshipped.[542]

Edna and Orrie blessed the Geyer's with two more grandchildren, Dorothy Edna Strohm, born October 31, 1910, and Frank Wesley Strohm, born May 19, 1915.[543]

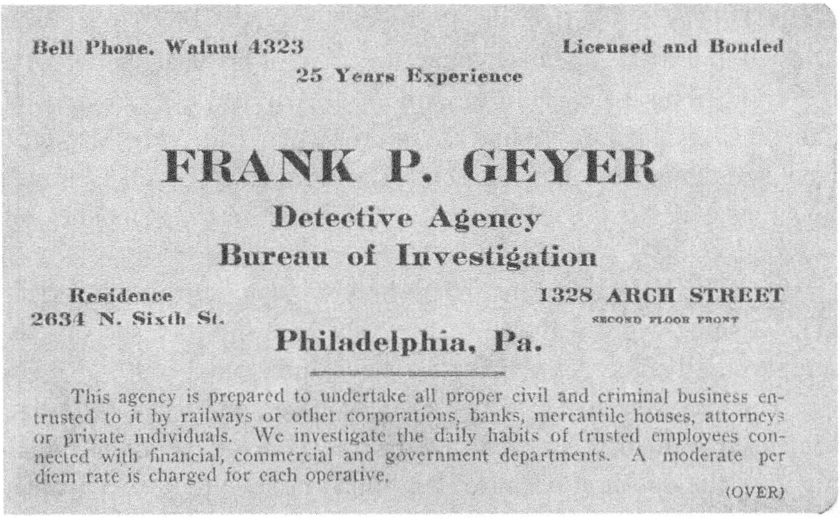

Bell Phone, Walnut 4323   Licensed and Bonded
                        25 Years Experience

FRANK P. GEYER

Detective Agency
Bureau of Investigation

Residence   1328 ARCH STREET
2634 N. Sixth St.   SECOND FLOOR FRONT
                     Philadelphia, Pa.

This agency is prepared to undertake all proper civil and criminal business en-
trusted to it by railways or other corporations, banks, mercantile houses, attorneys
or private individuals. We investigate the daily habits of trusted employees connected with financial, commercial and government departments. A moderate per
diem rate is charged for each operative.

(OVER)

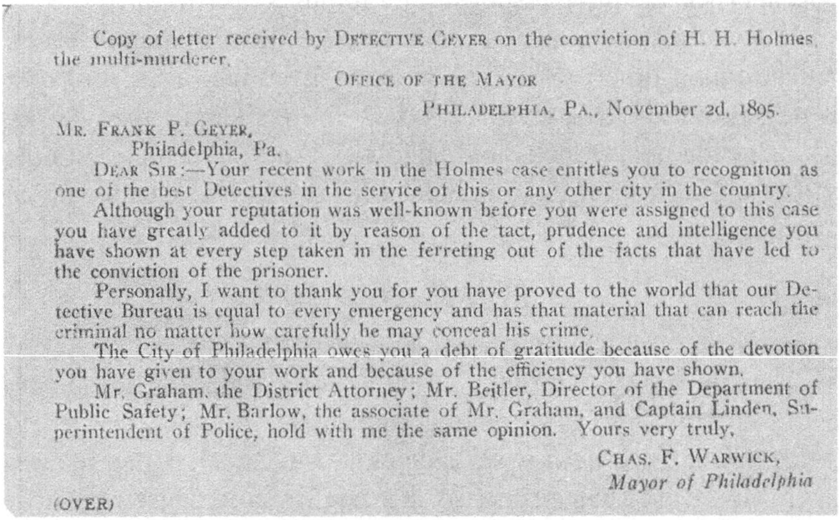

Copy of letter received by DETECTIVE GEYER on the conviction of H. H. Holmes,
the multi-murderer.

OFFICE OF THE MAYOR

PHILADELPHIA, PA., November 2d, 1895.

MR. FRANK P. GEYER,
    Philadelphia, Pa.
    DEAR SIR:—Your recent work in the Holmes case entitles you to recognition as
one of the best Detectives in the service of this or any other city in the country.
    Although your reputation was well-known before you were assigned to this case
you have greatly added to it by reason of the tact, prudence and intelligence you
have shown at every step taken in the ferreting out of the facts that have led to
the conviction of the prisoner.
    Personally, I want to thank you for you have proved to the world that our De-
tective Bureau is equal to every emergency and has that material that can reach the
criminal no matter how carefully he may conceal his crime.
    The City of Philadelphia owes you a debt of gratitude because of the devotion
you have given to your work and because of the efficiency you have shown.
    Mr. Graham, the District Attorney; Mr. Beitler, Director of the Department of
Public Safety; Mr. Barlow, the associate of Mr. Graham, and Captain Linden, Superintendent of Police, hold with me the same opinion. Yours very truly,

                                         CHAS. F. WARWICK,
                                             Mayor of Philadelphia

(OVER)

Fig. 55. Frank P. Geyer Detective Agency business card. Image
    source: Courtesy of Mr. and Mrs. David Elliott and family,
    descendants of Frank Geyer.

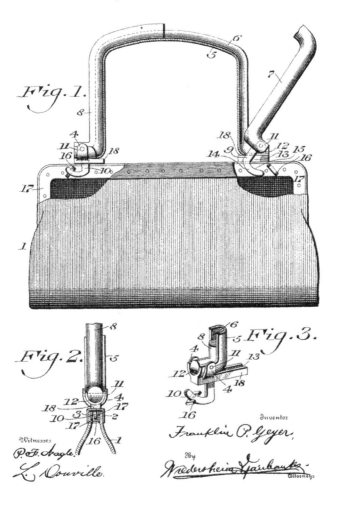

No. 872,619.   PATENTED DEC. 3, 1907.

F. P. GEYER.

SAFETY LOCK FOR POCKET BOOKS AND HAND BAGS.

APPLICATION FILED APR. 24, 1907.

Fig. 56. Frank P. Geyer patent for safety lock, Patent No. 872,619, dated December 3, 1907. Image source: United States Patent Office.

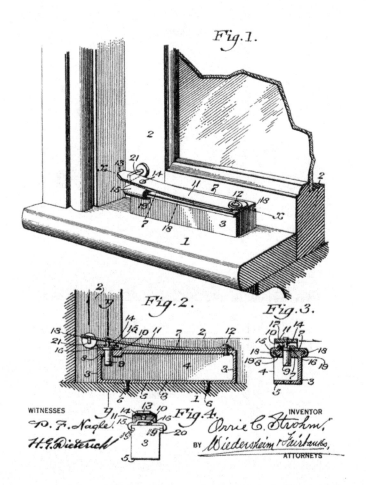

Fig. 57. Orrie C. Strohm patent for alarm, Patent No. 1,206,939, dated December 5, 1916. Image source: United States Patent Office.

CHAPTER 23

La Grippe

Every police station downtown was made an emergency medical office this afternoon through an order issued by Superintendent Mills . . . Lieutenants of police have also been ordered to permit the use of patrol wagons for taking patients to hospitals.[544]

-The *Evening Telegraph*
Re: Philadelphia Bureau of Police

April 1917 to October 1918

DETECTIVE GEYER WAS ABOUT to celebrate his sixty-fourth birthday when President Woodrow Wilson declared a State of War with Germany April 6, 1917. Initially, President Wilson requested volunteers to supplement military troops but soon issued a mandatory draft and Congress passed the Selective Service Act, where all males ages twenty-one to thirty had to register for military service. Congress amended the law in August 1918 to include all men ages eighteen to forty-five. Though Geyer's age was well beyond the upper limit, his son-in-law, Orrie Curtis Strohm, registered at thirty-three.[545]

While United States sent troops to war, bitter racial tensions erupted into an all-out race riot in South Philadelphia. And unbeknownst to a petite, young, professional woman—she was the cause. Never in a million years, would she have known the simple act of buying a house in South Philadelphia would incite one of the worst race riot's in Philadelphia's history in twenty years. The proud new homeowner and municipal court probation officer, Mrs. Adelia Bond, bought a small house at 2036 Ellsworth Street and moved in late July.[546]

"Had I known there was any objection to colored people in the block, I wouldn't have taken the house as a gift. The house was advertical [advertised] in a colored paper. It was offered for sale by a colored agent, and I naturally supposed colored people were welcome. I knew nothing of any objection to me until after I had bought the house. I couldn't get the money back . . . It is true I did try to enter one white woman's house, because the agent told me it was for sale and that she would show it to me. She threatened to beat me with a broom, and I appealed to a policeman. Eventually I bought another house," Mrs. Adelia Bond said later during a hearing.[547]

As Mrs. Bond casually sat on her steps after she moved in, someone hurled a brick through her window. She ran inside, then more bricks followed.

"I didn't know what the mob would do next, and I fired my revolver from my upper window to call the police. A policeman came, but wouldn't try to cope with the mob alone, so he turned in a riot call," Mrs. Bond told a reporter. One of her bullets hit twenty-three-year-old Joseph Kelly in the leg.[548]

The violence expanded to areas surrounding Mrs. Bond's neighborhood. Nearby, Jesse Butler, an African American, made insulting remarks to whites walking past his house. Men gathered around Butler's house and Butler opened fire. Hugh Lavery heard the shots and came outside to investigate. Butler immediately shot Lavery through the heart and he dropped dead.[549]

The riots spread fast. Two frightened teenage girls in another neighborhood screamed after an encounter with two African American's. A half-dozen men ran up to help the girls, and soon the group swelled to twenty or more. They caught the African American's and pounded on them with all their might for no reason other than the two men said disparaging things to the girls.

With local armed forces assistance, the Department of Public Safety activated every officer and reservist to respond to the riot. Officials enacted a sort of martial law. They ordered all saloons in the area closed and posted officers in front. Authorities also cordoned off streets and confiscated hundreds of weapons, then ordered all pawnbrokers in the city to stop selling weapons of any kind until further notice.[550]

On a nearby street, Thomas McVay, stepped off his police patrol wagon, and started towards the angry mob. But Henry Huff was ready for violence. He immediately shot and killed the twenty-four-year-old officer and shot Detective Thomas Myers in his side and thigh. Three United States sailors rushed Huff and held him down until they could summon authorities. Police were so angry when they arrived, they clubbed Huff in the head and face before his arrest.[551]

It was absolute chaos. A huge mob of the slain officers' neighbors and friends showed up at Huff's home on Titan Street, armed with every weapon you could imagine—clubs, axes, knives, bricks, and revolvers. Terrified women and children inside bolted their doors and windows and refused to let the angry mob inside. But that didn't stop them. As they burst the door down, two women and three children escaped out the back door and ran to a neighbors' house.[552]

The crowd burst inside and wrecked the place, throwing a piano out the window. Everything movable was hurled into the street. The revenge-seeking crowd threw oil on mattresses and set the house on fire. They also set fire to the furniture piled in the street. The mob tried to break into another house, but the police showed up and they ran in all directions.[553]

An African American delegation of ministers, headed by Dr. Wright and Rev. J. C. Beckett, and the Knights of Pythias, censured Mayor Smith and sent him a letter about the violence in progress.[554]

"We wish to deplore the fact that your police have not been able to protect our citizens from mob violence," the delegation wrote. "We desire you to understand that we put the whole blame upon your incompetent police force . . . hobnobbing with the mob."[555]

Francis Fischer Kane, the United States Attorney for Eastern Pennsylvania, made a public speech that *Philadelphia Inquirer* reported hit at the cause of the riot. But Kane probably did more to incite hard feelings with his opening statement:

"For a year we have been cognizant of the immense invasion of negroes from the South, who have been lured here by increased wages of war industries." Kane discussed better housing conditions for laborers, but emphasized laborers were . . . "composed largely of negroes."[556]

For the time being, tempers calmed down, and it was a good

thing too, for Philadelphia would soon experience something far worse than a race riot would ever bring.

World War I was coming to an end and the Geyer and Strohm families breathed a sigh of relief because that meant Orrie would not leave Edna and their three children to fight in the war. But the two families were about to be impacted in a major way as Philadelphia and the rest of the world were slammed with a pandemic so catastrophic that it killed more people than World War I.[557]

Spanish influenza (*La Grippe*) hit Philadelphia in September after 200,000 or more Philadelphians and returning soldiers attended the Liberty Loan parade. "The crowd linked arms, sang patriotic songs—breathed on each other—infected each other," a Public Broadcasting Service (PBS) narrator said.[558]

It was the single most devastating epidemic in recorded history. Stanford University reported the pandemic killed somewhere between 20 to 50 million people in the world. In the United States, about 675,000 Americans died. Pennsylvania was one of the hardest hit in the country, almost half of which were from Philadelphia.[559]

Philadelphia officials closed all schools, churches, theaters, and places of amusement for over three weeks starting October 3, 1918. As the situation worsened, police, fire, city administrators, and even garbage men, fell ill. It seemed everyone was affected. The following day, officials closed all liquor establishments, except those filling written prescriptions from known physicians. The city's only morgue, originally designed to hold around thirty-six bodies, was handling more than five hundred—stacking bodies in halls. To ease the pressure on the morgue, officials ordered convicts to dig graves, while government opened five supplemental morgues.[560]

Death carts roamed the city. So many people died, citizens were told to put corpses on their front porches and a truck would pick up the bodies.[561]

Health Director Dr. Wilmer Krusen advised sick people to go

to bed and keep warm. "No two human systems are the same. But while waiting for a physician, go to bed and keep warm," Krusen said.[562]

Officials took additional measures to combat the epidemic. Supervisors ordered officers to enforce the Anti Spitting Law, and all citizens were to give traffic right away to physicians flying green flags. Superintendent Mills even ordered every patrolman with nursing experience to act as emergency nurses and all officer's beds were removed from police stations and placed in local hospitals. In congested areas of Philadelphia, public health assigned physicians to police stations to provide immediate help to the sick. And officers were ordered to take prescriptions to druggists, then deliver them to the patients at their homes. Members of the Bureau of Police volunteered to perform the duties of orderlies, nurses, and to remove bodies from homes and transport them to the morgue in patrol wagons.[563]

People covered their faces with improvised masks made of cloths, but that did very little to prevent people from being affected.

Broad-shouldered, big as a bear, Detective Geyer came down with *La Grippe,* and on October 4, 1918, he shocked beloved Mary, sweet Edna, and his dear family, both real and in law enforcement, and suddenly died.

Hundreds of policeman, detectives, members of the Masons and other groups, and family and friends attended Geyer's honorable funeral, but no one was allowed close enough to view the body due to the influenza epidemic. Geyer was sixty-five.[564]

And so, the determined detective who took down the 'Devil in the White City,' murderers, mutilators, and thugs; the patient man that trekked across the United States and into Canada and Rio de Janeiro; the brave man who risked injury to rescue people from sure death; the tenderhearted, warm teddy bear who bounced his little girl and grandchildren on his knees, and affectionately threw his granddaughter's binky in the water; and the man who never lost his wife and daughter in a fire has died.

Mary Geyer joined Frank on December 19, 1932. Both were buried in a family plot at Hillside Cemetery in Roslyn, Pennsylvania, Section C, Lot 14 and 6.[565]

Fig. 58. A flu victim escorted to the hospital by a Philadelphia police officer, October 1918. Image source: Courtesy of the Special Collections Research Center, Temple University Libraries, Philadelphia, PA. From the George D. McDowell Philadelphia Evening Bulletin Collection.

Fig. 59. Franklin P. Geyer's headstone and large marker located at Hillside Cemetery in Roslyn, Pennsylvania, 2017. Image source: Author.

Fig. 60. James R. Riggins, great-great-grandson of Detective Geyer, stands in front of Geyer's large cemetery plot at

Hillside Cemetery in Roslyn, Pennsylvania, 2017. Detective Geyer's plot spans the entire width of the photo and all the way back to the headstone in between the trees. Hillside Cemetery staff confirmed that although Mary Geyer's name was not added to his headstone at the time of her burial, she joined her husband December 19, 1932. Image source: Courtesy of James R. Riggins, descendent of Detective Frank P. Geyer.

Supplemental Photos

Fig. 61. Family portrait of Frank Geyer, his wife, Mary, and daughter Edna, circa 1887. Image source: Courtesy of Mr. and Mrs. David Elliott and family, descendants of Detective Frank P. Geyer.

Fig. 62. Family portrait of Frank Geyer, his wife, Mary, and daughter Edna, circa 1896. Image source: Courtesy of Mr. and Mrs. David Elliott and family, descendants of Detective Frank P. Geyer.

Fig. 63. Edna Camilla Geyer, circa 1900. Image Source: Courtesy of Mr. and Mrs. David Elliott and family, descendants of Detective Frank P. Geyer.

Nineteenth Section

JOHN WELSH SCHOOL—Anna Lechel. Florence Congdon. Clothilde C. Messick. Alice Mitchell May Barr Schaeffer. Ella Gahle Ferguson, Florence M. Hanson. Lillian M. Hanson. Elsie M. Wrightsen, Elizabeth Peacock. Mabel Ella Jackson. Rose Elizabeth Reyle. Elizabeth Bender. Bessie Gorman. Emma Nollenberger. Ethel May Herms. Jennie Hawkins Edith Mabelle Kolb. Edna Camilla Geyer. Mathilda Selpp, Florence Worman.

Fig. 64. Newspaper announcement of Edna Camilla Geyer graduating from John Welsh School in Philadelphia. Image Source: "Pupils Pass to Higher Studies," *Philadelphia Inquirer*, June 28, 1901.

JOHN WELSH COMBINED GRAMMAR AND SECONDARY SCHOOL,
Fourth and Dauphin Streets.
Nineteenth Section.

Fig. 65. John Welsh School where Edna Camilla Geyer graduated. Image source: Custis, John Trevor. *Public Schools of Philadelphia; Historical, Biographical, Statistical.* Philadelphia, PA: Burk & McFetridge Company, 1897.

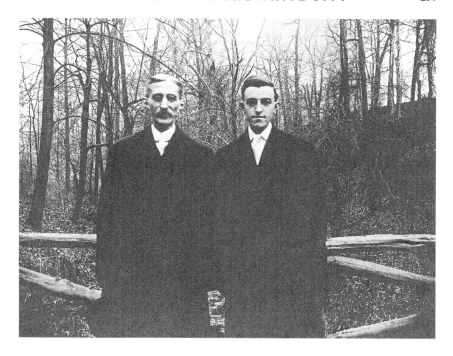

Fig. 66. Frank and Mary Geyer's son-in-law, Orrie Curtis Strohm with his father, John Strohm, circa 1904. Image source: Courtesy of Mr. and Mrs. David Elliott and family, descendants of Detective Frank P. Geyer.

74

BAPTISMS. BAPTISMS.

Full Name	Sex	Parents	Sponsors	Birth Date	Birth Place	Baptism Date	Baptism Place
Wilbur James Barnes		Joseph & Nellie Barnes	Mr & Mrs Edward St Leger	Jan 20th/09	4107 Fairhill	April 18th	Christ Church
Doris Ethel Shephard		Saml T & Muriel E Shephard	The Parents & Miss Ethel Bush	Dec 31st/08	3448 N 6th St	April 25/09	" "
Joseph Stanley Walker		Joseph & Alice Walker	The Parents & Mr Saml [illegible]	Jan 26th/09	3130 Franklin "	"	" "
Eleanor Kennedy Bieber		Daniel H & Emma Bieber	Mrs Gertrude Wolff	July 21st/08	[illegible]	"	" "
Mildred Ashton Keech		James L & Maria Keech	[illegible]	March 20th/09	3603 Marshall St	June 13th/09	" "
Bertha Annie Gerstenlauer		[illegible] & Ada Gerstenlauer	Mr & Mrs John Thomas & Parents	June 13th/09	4055 Fairhill St	July 11th/09	"
Thomas [illegible] Small		Chas & Mary E. Small	[illegible] S. J. [illegible]	May 19/[illegible]	[illegible]	Aug 8/09	" "
Caroline Marie Catharine Jaeger		John & Edna Jaeger	Miss Carrie Jaeger & [illegible]	June 13th/09	3905 N 5th St	Septr 5/09	" "
William Henry Elliott		Henry H & Sarah J Elliott	The Parents & Wm J Elliott	July 1st/09	3447 Mascher St	Sept 12th/09	" "
Bertram Erick Cadwallader	adult	J W & the late [illegible] Cadwallader	In extremis	June 23/88	3646 Marshall "	Septr 21st/09	Home
William John Holl		William & Mary Holl	Frank & John J & Mary A Geyer	Aug 3rd/09	[illegible] N. 7th St	Octr 3rd/09	Christ Church
Mary Esther Morrison		John & Mary Morrison	The Parents & Mrs Mary [illegible]	Septr 20th/09	3850 N 6th St	" "	" "
Elizabeth Alice Strohm		Orrie Curtis & Edna Strohm	" " & Mrs Frank Geyer & Miss Emma Brooks	Augt 23rd/09	4123 N. 6th St	Novr 21st/09	" "
George Alvin Gensbauer		Chas F & Mary A Gensbauer	Miss [illegible] & Mr Chas [illegible]	Jany 8th/09	3439 N 6th St	" "	" "

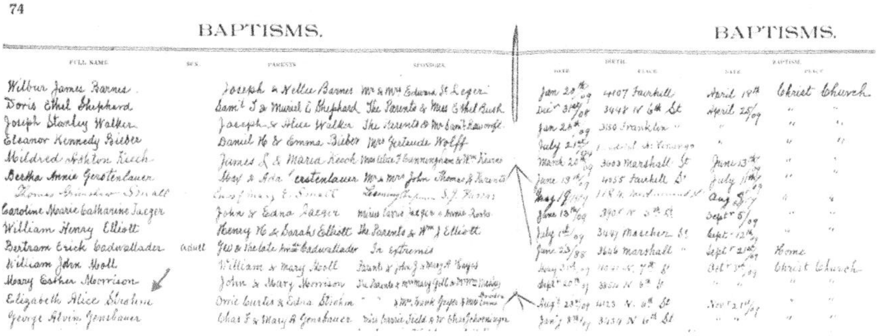

Fig. 67. Mrs. Frank Geyer at the baptism of granddaughter, Elizabeth Alice Strohm, on November 21, 1909. Image source: Christ Church Baptism Record.

Fig. 68. Baby Elizabeth Alice Strohm, born August 23, 1909. Mrs. Mary Geyer helped sponsor the baptism of their granddaughter, Elizabeth Alice on November 21, 1909, at Christ Church, officiated by Rev. John G. Bawn. Image source: Courtesy of Mr. and Mrs. David Elliott and family, descendants of Detective Frank P. Geyer

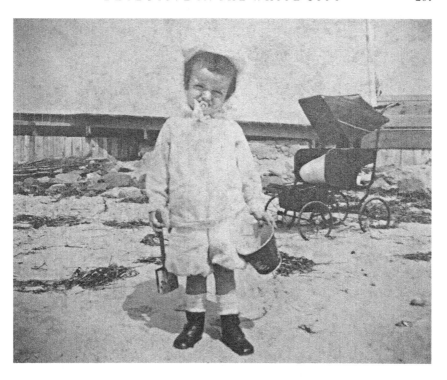

Fig. 69. Elizabeth Alice Strohm, Detective Geyer and Mary's granddaughter, circa 1911. On the day this photo was taken, Detective Geyer lightheartedly weaned Elizabeth off her binky by ceremoniously tossing it in the water. Image source: Courtesy of Mr. and Mrs. David Elliott and family, descendants of Detective Frank P. Geyer.

Fig. 70. Frank Geyer, circa 1913. Image source: Courtesy of Mr. and Mrs. David Elliott and family, descendants of Detective Frank P. Geyer.

Fig. 71. Mary Elizabeth (Rilley, Riley, or O'Riley) Geyer, circa
    1913. Image source: Courtesy of Mr. and Mrs. David Elliott
    and family, descendants of Detective Frank P. Geyer.

Fig. 72. Detective Geyer (center) walks in the Knights Templar
parade in Philadelphia, 1914. Image source: Evening Public
Ledger, Philadelphia, September 19, 1914, p. 4.

Fig. 73. Detective Frank Geyer with his wife Mary, daughter Edna (Geyer) Strohm, son-in-law Orrie Curtis Strohm, and adorable granddaughters Elizabeth and Dorothy, circa 1915. Image source: Courtesy of Mr. and Mrs. David Elliott and family, descendants of Detective Frank P. Geyer.

Fig. 74. Detective Geyer and Mary's grandchildren. Left to Right: Elizabeth, Frank, and Dorothy. Image source: Courtesy of Mr. and Mrs. David Elliott and family, descendants of Detective Frank P. Geyer.

Fig. 75. Edna Camilla (Geyer) Strohm, the daughter that lived. Image source: Courtesy of Mr. and Mrs. David Elliott and family, descendants of Detective Frank P. Geyer.

Fig. 76. Thanksgiving photo of Detective Geyer's family, taken ten
    days before Pearl Harbor, 1941. Left to Right: Edna Camilla
    (Geyer) Strohm, David Elliott, Elizabeth "Betty" (Strohm)
    Elliott, Orrie Curtis Strohm (standing), Frank Strohm, Joyce
    Elliott, Clinton Elliott, Stan Elliott (standing), Joe Elliott,
    brother of Grace (Frank Strohm's wife), mother of Grace
    (Frank Strohm's wife) and Dorothy (Strohm) Elliott. Image
    source: Courtesy of James R. Riggins, descendent of Detective
    Frank P. Geyer.

Fig. 77. This family photo is proof Detective Geyer never lost his wife and daughter in a tragic fire. The photo, taken at the baptism of Mr. and Mrs. James R. Riggins' grandson in 2015, features Frank and Mary Geyer's beautiful great-granddaughter, Joyce (Elliott) Riggins (front row). Joyce is the daughter of Dorothy (Strohm) Elliott and granddaughter of Edna (Geyer) and Orrie Curtis Strohm. Joyce's handsome children (Frank and Mary's great-grandchildren) are shown in the back row (left to right, oldest to youngest): Linda (Riggins) Hernandes, James Riggins, Lisa (Riggins) Atchley, Alan Riggins, and Laurie (Riggins) O'Neil. Image source: Courtesy of James R. Riggins, descendent of Detective Frank P. Geyer.

Fig. 78. Justice of the Peace William Henry Buck (Frank Geyer's cousin, Camilla's nephew). William Buck was a large farmer of Marlborough township in Montgomery County, PA. Born to Charles Buck and Christiana Royer, William Buck's ancestors were from Germany (earlier name was Bock), but have been in Montgomery County for several generations. In April 1871 he took over his father's almost one hundred acre farm near Green Lane station. He was elected justice of the peace of Marlborough Township in 1876.[566] Image source: Samuel T. Wiley. Biographical and Portrait Cyclopedia of Montgomery County, Pennsylvania, Containing Biographical Sketches of Prominent and Representative Citizens of the County, Together

with an Introductory Historical Sketch. Philadelphia, PA: Biographical Publishing Company, 1895. p. 214.

Fig. 79. Rogue's gallery of criminals displayed in the Philadelphia detectives' office. The photos were kept in a large walnut cabinet designed and patented by Police Detective Sergeant

Thomas Adams of New York. Chief of Detectives Francis R. Kelly implemented the cabinet to improve the way the photos were displayed. Image source: Howard O. Sprogle. The Philadelphia Police, Past and Present. Philadelphia, PA: publisher unknown, 1887, p. 275.

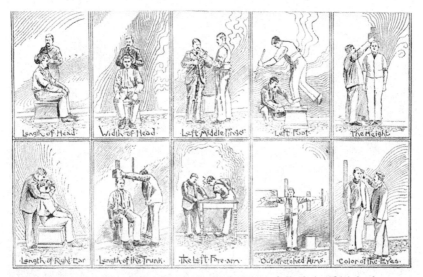

Illustrations for "Alphonse Bertillon's Instructions for taking Descriptions for the Identification of Criminals and Others by the Means of Anthropometric Indications"

Fig. 80. Alphonse Bertillon invented the Bertillon System in 1881 in Paris as a means to identify criminals from the subject's anthropometrical description. The Bertillon System was formally adopted by the Wardens' Association of the United States and Canada at their September 1887 meeting in Toronto. City of Philadelphia adopted the system in 1892. Of particular note, Philadelphia Times reported that a box of one hundred artificial eyes was part of the outfit. The right eye of the subject was matched to one the shapes and the eye color and spots carefully noted. A Bertillon Bureau was established in the United States, with offices in Chicago. In 1892, George M. Porteous was superintendent of the bureau in the US. He trained the Philadelphia Detective Bureau on its use. Bertillon was also the inventor of the Mug Shot.[567] Image source: George Wesley Hale. Police Department. Police and Prison Cyclopaedia. Boston, MA: The W. L. Richardson Company,

1893. p. 753.

LEONA BLAND, ORPHEUM

Fig. 81. Actress, singer, Miss Leona Bland at the Orpheum
Theatre. Police officers wound up in a precarious situation in
1891 when they were sued following an arrest. Detective
Geyer, acting on direction from Chief Wood, went to the Broad
Street station and arrested Miss Leona Bland on a charge of
larceny. Miss Bland said, "The first intimation I had of
anything wrong, was being tapped on the shoulder as I stood in
the station preparing to get my baggage." She claims she was

wrongfully arrested and charged with larceny and taken to the room of Chief Wood who told her she was arrested based on a telegram from New York. She became nervous, burst into tears, and asked to go home, but was refused. She then asked someone to go with her but that was refused too. "Finally, Mr. Geyer and I went to the station and I sent my baggage home." She said at about half past four, they allowed her to go home, but requested her to come back the next day to clear things up with New York.

The next day, she returned and spoke with Chief Wood who said there were no further developments. "Mr. Crawford, another detective, then engaged me in conversation, which he wound up by asking me to become a female detective. This is a sample of what I had to bear from those people," Miss Bland said. She complained she had to return three or four times to clear up the matter and on the last visit, Chief Wood smiled and told her it was all a mistake. Chief Wood gave her a tour of the cell she would have occupied had she been guilty. "He then, in a very paternal manner, escorted me all through the Public Buildings, acting in a most gentlemanly manner," Miss Bland told a reporter. Miss Bland said she suffered greatly from nervous prostration after the incident. She sued the officers for false imprisonment and asked for $1,000 in damages. The case went to trial in 1892. District Attorney Graham represented Chief Wood and Detective Geyer, and they were found not guilty. The two officers were baffled at why she would sue as she came to the station willingly and returned to clear the matter up and afterwards shared anecdotes with the officers while they gave her a tour. Perhaps the actress was looking for publicity.[568] Image source: *Los Angeles Herald*, March 7, 1905.

CHARLES WILFRED MOWBRAY

Fig. 82. Detective Geyer testified against Charles Wilfred Mowbray, an anarchist arrested and charged for inciting a riot. At a rally, Charles Mowbray yelled at the audience, "The police should be blown off the face of the earth, and if I had one of them here on this platform now I could strangle him." Detective Bernstein testified Mowbray continued his rhetoric, telling the audience the American flag would make a good pocket-handkerchief. Mowbray interrupted Bernstein and said, "You mistake my statements. What I intended to imply is that anarchy is not national, but international, and consequently there is no need of a flag. You have my manuscript, read it." Detective Geyer also testified at his his trial. He said, "His words made my blood boil and if there had been any patriotic citizen present apart from the police, who had to stand it, the speaker would have been hurled from a window." At the conclusion of officer testimony, Charles Mowbray was found guilty and sent to Moyamensing Prison, but was released a few months later.[569] Image Source: "Mowbray Talks of Himself," Philadelphia Times, November 22, 1894, p. 6.

PATROL WAGON.

Fig. 83. Philadelphia Police Patrol Wagon circa 1887. Image source: Howard O. Sprogle. The Philadelphia Police, Past and Present. Philadelphia, PA: publisher unknown, 1887.

Fig. 84. Philadelphia police officers stand in front of Marsh's
Saloon, March 15, 1901. The saloon, on South Street, near
Seventh, was the location of an incident where Special Officer
Sullivan responded to in March of 1882. Special Officer
Sullivan removed three boisterous men, Thomas Elliott,
Thomas Bradley, and John McCain and later that evening, the
men attacked Officer Sullivan and savagely beat him in the
head and shoulders. The three men were arrested.[570] Image
source: Courtesy of Philadelphia Archives.

Fig. 85. Philadelphia police guarding car barns as crowds stand by.
Image source: Courtesy of Library of Congress.

Fig. 86. Philadelphia police officers with a police wagon. Image source: Courtesy of the Special Collections Research Center, Temple University Libraries, Philadelphia, PA. From the George D. McDowell Philadelphia Evening Bulletin Collection, April 19, 1905.

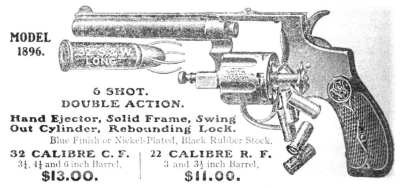

SMITH & WESSON'S LATEST MODELS, 1896 and 1899.

MODEL 1896.

6 SHOT.
DOUBLE ACTION.

Hand Ejector, Solid Frame, Swing Out Cylinder, Rebounding Lock.

Blue Finish or Nickel-Plated, Black Rubber Stock.

32 CALIBRE C. F.	22 CALIBRE R. F.
3¼, 4¼ and 6 inch Barrel,	3 and 3½ inch Barrel,
$13.00.	**$11.00.**

MODEL 1899.—MILITARY AND POLICE REVOLVER.

Double Action, SIX SHOT, with Solid Frame. Swing Out Cylinder and Hand Ejector.

Description.—Lengths of Barrel, 4, 5 and 6½ inches; blue finish or nickel-plate; weight, 1 lb. 14 ozs. Adapted to the following ammunition: Smith & Wesson, 38 Special C. F. Cartridge (extra long); United States Service Cartridge (known as 38 Long Colts); Winchester 32 C. F. Rifle Cartridge.

Fig. 87. 1909 H. H. Kiffe advertisement. According to David Maccar, author of *Best of Guns Digest,* the Smith & Wesson 1896 Model Hand Ejector revolver was taken into service by Philadelphia police. Image sources: Wholesale Price List of Fishing Tackle and Hunting Outfits, H. H. Kiffe; and David Maccar. *Best of Gun Digest: Handguns and Handgun Shooting.* Iola, WI: Gun Digest Books, an imprint of FW Media, Inc., 2015, p. 138.

Fig. 88. Police patrol marches outside Baldwin Locomotive Works. Image source: Courtesy of Library of Congress, 1910.

Fig. 89. Philadelphia police officers keeping the peace outside
Shibe Park for game one of the 1914 World Series,
Philadelphia Athletics vs. Boston Braves. Image source:
Courtesy of Library of Congress.

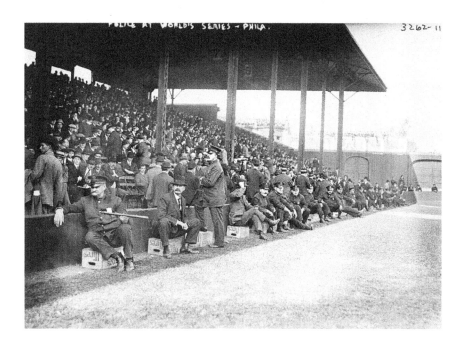

Fig. 90. Philadelphia police officers at game one of the 1914 World
Series at Shibe Park. Image source: Courtesy of Library of
Congress.

Fig. 91. Philadelphia Bureau of Police ride on a motorcycle and a sidecar. Image source: Courtesy of the Special Collections Research Center, Temple University Libraries, Philadelphia, PA. From the George D. McDowell Philadelphia Evening Bulletin Collection, May 26, 1916.

Fig. 92. Philadelphia Police Harbor Patrol, *WMS Stokley*, named after Mayor William S. Stokley. Image source: Courtesy of the Special Collections Research Center, Temple University Libraries, Philadelphia, PA. From the George D. McDowell Philadelphia Evening Bulletin Collection, date unknown.

SEVENTH DISTRICT STATION HOUSE AND PATROL No. 7.

Fig. 93. A new Seventh District station house built in 1894 at the northeast corner of Mintzer and Fairmount Avenue. The 42 x 160 foot lot cost $15,000, and the building, $27,564. Image source: Stuart, Edwin S. *Fourth Annual Message of Edwin S. Stuart, Mayor of the City of Philadelphia, with Annual Reports of the Director of the Department of Public Safety and Chief of the Electrical Bureau for the Year Ending December 31, 1894, Issued by the City of Philadelphia, 1895.* Philadelphia, PA: Dunlap Printing Co., 1895, pp. 6-7.

New Fortieth District Police Station, Twenty-eighth street
below Columbia avenue.

Fig. 94. The new Fortieth District police station at Twenty-eighth
and Oxford Streets was opened October 1, 1913. Image source:
Blankenburg, Rudolph. *Second Annual Message of Rudolph
Blankenburg, Mayor of the City of Philadelphia, with Annual
Reports of the Director of the Department of Public Safety and
Chief of Bureaus Constituting said Department, also
Philadelphia Museums, Free Libraries, Art Jury, Board of
Recreation, and Committee on Comprehensive Plans for the
Year Ending December 31, 1912, Issued by the City of
Philadelphia, 1913, Volume 1.* Philadelphia, PA: Dunlap
Printing Co., 1913, p. 305.

Fig. 95. The new Eighteenth District police and fire building at
    55th and Pine Street. A contract was awarded in 1911 to build
    the combined station with an approximate cost of $100,000 to
    accommodate police, fire, auto-patrol garage and mounted
    police stables.[571] Image source: Courtesy of the Special
    Collections Research Center, Temple University Libraries,
    Philadelphia, PA. From the George D. McDowell Philadelphia
    Evening Bulletin Collection.

Appendix A: Additional Geyer Quotes

Truth, like the sun, submits to be obscured, but like the sun, only for a time.

-Detective Frank P. Geyer
1896 Holmes-Pitezel Book

I was directed to go on, and I determined to do so, hoping that patience and persistent hard work might finally lead me to the light.

-Detective Frank P. Geyer
1896 Holmes-Pitezel Book

...I thought that after all, the business of searching for the truth was not the meanest occupation of man.

-Detective Frank P. Geyer
1896 Holmes-Pitezel Book

We have sufficient evidence to keep Holmes in prison for the remainder of his natural days without charging him for murder. Should he by a technicality escape the conspiracy charge in Philadelphia, twenty warrants on other charges are ready to be served on him.

-Philadelphia Times interview, August 4, 1895

It startles one to realize how such a hideous crime could be committed and detection avoided.

-Detective Frank P. Geyer
1896 Holmes-Pitezel Book and
Philadelphia Inquirer interview, April 12, 1896

It must have taken very careful management to have moved these three separate parties from Detroit to Toronto, without either of the three discovering either of the others, but this great expert in crime did it, and did it successfully.

-Detective Frank P. Geyer
1896 Holmes-Pitezel Book

I never was in such a place before as that cellar in which we found the bodies and it will be a long time before I forget the awful details.

-Philadelphia Inquirer interview, August 4, 1895

Holmes is greatly given to lying with a sort of florid ornamentation, and all of his stories are decorated with flamboyant draperies, intended by him to strengthen the plausibility of his statements.

-Detective Frank P. Geyer
1896 Holmes-Pitezel Book

If they don't hang H. H. Holmes for murder then they ought to stop making hemp.

-Philadelphia Inquirer interview, August 5, 1895
Hemp was used to make paper, ropes, canvas, and fabrics

His words made my blood boil and if there had been any patriotic citizen present apart from the police, who had to stand it, the speaker would have been hurled from a window.

-Philadelphia Times interview, December 30, 1894
Charles Wilfred Mombray hearing

The stench was something awful. We hardly put the spade in the ground before we dug up a human arm.

-Detective Frank P. Geyer

1896 Holmes-Pitezel Book

It was the most awful experience of my life and I have no desire to repeat it.

-*Philadelphia Times* interview, August 4, 1895

Nothing could be more surprising than the apparent ease with which Holmes murdered the two little girls in the very centre of the city of Toronto without arousing the least suspicion of a single person there.

-*Detective Frank P. Geyer*
1896 Holmes-Pitezel Book

Acknowledgements

My interest in writing about Detective Franklin P. Geyer came after the profound sadness I felt while reading Geyer's family died before his assignment to the H. H. Holmes case. I could not imagine the heartache and sorrow he must have felt. At the same time I wondered how he could pick up the pieces after a life-changing tragedy like that, and two short months afterwards work on a complicated cross-country, international murder case. This was a story I knew I had to tell and would not stop until I did.

I would like to give a warm-hearted thank you to Detective Geyer's family, especially to James R. Riggins, who opened his heart to my journey and drove through several states to meet with me and share memories with his family. And a special thank you for being the family liaison and surprise high school rival. A heartfelt thank you to his loving wife and sweet family for their support. And thank you Joyce. You are an amazing woman and I enjoyed reminiscing with you and your son. And thank you to Jeff, David, Ada, and John. I'll never forget your hospitality and for sharing precious memories. I know in my heart, Frank and Mary would be proud of all of you!

At the City of Philadelphia Archives, I am grateful for archivist Virgilia "Jill" Rawnsley, who thoughtfully and patiently answered my questions and provided a wealth of information. And thank you for support staff at the archives who fulfilled what may have seemed like a mountain of written requests, always with a smile, and for providing me gloves to handle fragile documents. Sorry I poked holes in the gloves!

Thank you to the helpful and professional staff who answered many questions and pulled collections and archival documents at the Library of Congress's Manuscript Division in Washington DC.

A warm-hearted thank you to Priya Menzies, Special Assistant to the Director, and especially Bonnie Campbell Lilienfeld, Assistant Director for Curatorial Affairs at the National Museum of American History, Smithsonian Institution. Your helpful search for the donation of H. H. Holmes rope was appreciated.

Thank you to Becky at Hillside Cemetery in Roslyn, Pennsylvania who provided information about the ever elusive

Mary Elizabeth Geyer's burial. My trip to Hillside Cemetery with Detective Geyer's great-great-grandson revealed Geyer's impressive and honorable gravesite, but Mary Geyer was not listed on the headstone. Becky helped solve the mystery of Mary's burial and I am grateful for that. To Paulette Rhone, board president, Friends of Mount Moriah Cemetery in Philadelphia, thank you for your help and also to Jenn O'Donnell.

At the Mark Twain Project, Bancroft Library, University of California, Berkeley, I would especially like to thank Melissa Martin. And thank you to Josue L. Hurtado, Coordinator of Public Services & Outreach, Special Collections Research Center, Temple University Library, Philadelphia.

Librarian Glenys A. Waldman, PhD, at the Masonic Library and Museum of Pennsylvania deserves a special shout out for researching and providing Masonic records for Frank and Reuben dating back to 1868. And thank you to George R. Haynes, ME Secretary, Grand Holy Royal Arch Chapter of Pennsylvania for searching the same. I am thankful for local librarians and staff who provided direction and looked up important records.

A huge heartfelt thanks to my sweet husband for believing in me. Thank you for your love, encouragement, patience, and steaming hot green tea. And thank you for graciously delaying getaways while I worked straight through each week to complete my project. A sweet thank you to my loving mom and dad, sister and family, to my awesome children, beautiful daughter-in-laws, sweet baby dolls, and to everyone who cheered me on.

Many thanks to colleagues and friends in law enforcement, emergency management, and fire and especially to a certain retired highway patrol lieutenant (you know who you are) for your kind words of encouragement and support.

Finally, a special thanks to Gracie and Bella, who squeezed their cute furry heads underneath my busy hands even if they caused a catastrophic typo, for it could always be corrected with a tail wag. And to a sweet Great Dane named Dixi, who showed me the importance of a snuggle break, or two, or three.

-JD

Also by JD CRIGHTON:

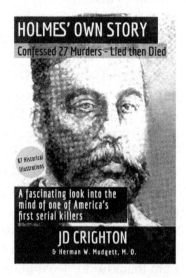

JD on the web:
jdcrighton.com
Twitter: @jdcrighton
Instagram: @jdcrighton
FB: jdcrightonauthor

Email:
jd@jdcrighton.com

Bibliography

Adams, Herbert B., ed. *Johns Hopkins University Studies in Historical and Political Science, Volume V: Municipal Government History and Politics.* Baltimore: Johns Hopkins University, N. Murray, Publication Agent, 1887.

Allinson, Edward P. and Penrose, Boies. *The City Government of Philadelphia.* Baltimore, Maryland: N. Murray, Johns Hopkins University, 1887.

American Criminal Reports, *A Series Designed to Contain the Latest and Most Important Criminal Cases Determined in the Federal and State Courts in the United States, Volume XII: Appeal from Court of Oyer and Terminer, Philadelphia County. William Epps, convicted of murder in the first degree, appeals. Affirmed.* Chicago: Callaghan and Company, 1905.

American Meteorological Society. "Temperature of the Air" and "Precipitation." *Monthly Weather Review,* Volume 14, Number 12. (1886).

Arnold, Hon. Michael. "An Analysis of the Holmes Case." *The Green Bag; An Entertaining Magazine for Lawyers,* Volume XIV, 1902.

Ashbridge, Samuel H., Mayor. *First Annual Message of Samuel H. Ashbridge, Mayor of the City of Philadelphia, Year Ending December 31, 1899.* Philadelphia, PA: Dunlap Printing Company, 1899.

Ashbridge, Samuel H., Mayor. *Third Annual Message of Samuel H. Ashbridge, Mayor of the City of Philadelphia, Year Ending December 31, 1901.* Philadelphia, PA: Dunlap Printing Company, 1902.

Ashbridge, Samuel H., Mayor. *Fourth Annual Message of Samuel H. Ashbridge, Mayor of the City of Philadelphia, Year Ending December 31, 1902.* Philadelphia, PA: Dunlap Printing Company, 1903.

Baltimore Underwriter. "What is Said of Stratagems and Conspiracies to Defraud Life Insurance Companies," and "General Article," *Baltimore Underwriter,* [Sarah Jane Whiteling and Detective Geyer exposed Holmes' Attorney], Volume LV. (1896).

Barclay & Company. *Holmes, The Arch Fiend, or: A Carnival of Crime, the Life, Trial, Confession and Execution of H. H. Holmes, Twenty-seven Lives Sacrificed to this Monstrous Ogre's Insatiable Appetite.*

Cincinnati, OH: Barclay & Co., circa 1896.

Barton, George. The *True Stories of Celebrated Crimes: Adventures of the World's Greatest Detectives*. NY: McKinlay Stone & Mackenzie, 1908.

Bates, Samuel P. *History of Pennsylvania Volunteers, 1861-5, Vol. IV.* Harrisburg, PA: B. Singerly, State Printer, 1870.

Bates, Samuel P. *History of Pennsylvania Volunteers, 1861-5, Vol. V.* Harrisburg, PA: B. Singerly, State Printer. 1871.

Bates, Samuel P. *Martial Deeds of Pennsylvania.* Philadelphia, PA: T. H. Davis & Company, 1875.

Battle, J. H., ed. *History of Bucks County, Pennsylvania.* Philadelphia, PA: A. Warner & Co., Publishers, 1887.

Bean, Theodore W., ed, *History of Montgomery County, Pennsylvania, Volume I.* Philadelphia, PA: Everts & Peck, 1884.

Bell, Clark, Esq., ed, et. al. "Editorial: The Case of Mrs. Whiteling [compares Mrs. Whiteling case to Mrs. Schoop]," *The Medico-Legal Journal*, Vol. VII, (1889).

Billings, Molly. "The Influenza Pandemic of 1918," *Stanford University*, https://virus.stanford.edu/uda/, accessed November 12, 2016.

Birmingham, Ernest P. *The Fourth Estate. No. 358.* New York, January 5, 1901.

Bisel, George T. *The Trial of Herman W. Mudgett, Alias, H. H. Holmes, for the Murder of Benjamin F. Pitezel: In the Court of Oyer and Terminer and General Jail Delivery and Quarter Sessions of the Peace, in and for the City and County of Philadelphia, Commonwealth of Pennsylvania, October 28, 29, 30, 31, and November 1, and 2, 1895.* Philadelphia, PA: George T. Bisel, Law Publisher, Bookseller and Stationer, 1897.

Blankenburg, Rudolph. *First Annual Message of Rudolph Blankenburg, Mayor of the City of Philadelphia, with the Annual Reports of George D. Porter, Director of the Department of Public Safety . . . for the year ending December 31, 1911, Vol 1.* Philadelphia, PA: Dunlap Printing Co., 1912.

Breintnall, Heber R., Adjutant-General. *Report of the Adjutant-General of the State of New Jersey for the Year Ending October 31st, 1906.* Somerville, NJ: The Unionist-Gazette Printing House, 1907.

Bremner, Samuel K., MD. "A Case of Purpura Hemorrhagica, with

Autopsy,"*Archives of Pediatrics,* Volume X, (1893).

Buck, Gurdon, MD, Surgeon to NY Hospital. *An Improved Method of Treating Fractures of the Thigh. Illustrated by Cases and a Drawing.* 1861.

Bureau of Police, City of Philadelphia. *Patrolman's Manual.* Philadelphia, PA: Department of Public Safety, George D. Porter, Director, 1913.

Burr, Samuel J., AM, and S. De Vere Burr, et. al. *Memorial of the International Exhibition: Being a Description.* Hartford, CT: L. Stebbins, 1877.

Childs, George W. Public *Ledger Almanacs for 1870-1897.* Philadelphia, PA: Geo. W. Childs Publisher, 1870-1897.

Childs, Ward. "Crime, Criminals, Law Enforcement and Records (Part IV)," *City of Philadelphia,* http://www.phila.gov/phils/docs/otherinfo/newslet/crime5.htm, accessed March 2, 2016.

The Chronicle. "General Article," [Sarah Jane Whiteling], *The Chronicle.* Volume XLI. (1888).

City of Philadelphia. "Department of Public Safety," *Department of Records,* http://www.phila.gov/phils/docs/inventor/graphics/agencies/A083.htm, accessed May 16, 2016.

The Commissioners for the Erection of the New Public Buildings. The New City Hall Philadelphia Directory of Offices Occupied; or Allotted and in Process of Completion, with Diagrams of Various Floors, and Other Miscellaneous Information Appertaining to the Building. Philadelphia, PA: Printed for the Commissioners, 1890.

Command of Her Majesty. Reports on the Philadelphia International Exhibition of 1876, Vol. 1, presented in both houses of Parliament, 1876.

Commonwealth of Pennsylvania. Journal of the House of Representatives of the Commonwealth of Pennsylvania for the Session Begun at Harrisburg on the Seventh Day of January 1913, Part I. Harrisburg, PA, 1914.

Commonwealth of Pennsylvania, Department of Public Health, Bureau of Vital Statistics Certificate of Death, File No. 143487, Registered No. 26452. Franklin P. Geyer.

Coxe, Robert Davison, of the Philadelphia Bar. *Legal Philadelphia: Comments and Memories.* Philadelphia, PA: William J. Campbell,

1908.

Custis, John Trevor. *Public Schools of Philadelphia; Historical, Biographical, Statistical.* Philadelphia, PA: Burk & McFetridge Company, 1897.

Duke, Captain Thomas Samuel. "Celebrated Criminal Cases of America," *The Police Journal,* Volume IX, No. 5 (1922).

Duke, Thomas Samuel. *Celebrated Criminal Cases of America.* San Francisco, CA: The James H. Barry Company, 1910.

Dyer, Frederick H. *A Compendium of the War of the Rebellion Compiled and Arranged from Official Records of the Federal and Confederate Armies Reports of the Adjutant Generals of the Several States, the Army Registers and Other Reliable Documents and Sources.* Des Moines, IO: The Dyer Publishing Company, 1908.

Executive Committee of Founders' Week, 225th Anniversary of the City of Philadelphia. Official Historical Souvenir and Official Programme. Philadelphia: unknown publisher, 1908.

Fitler, Edwin H. *First Annual Message of Edwin H. Fitler, Mayor of the City of Philadelphia, Volume III.* Philadelphia, PA: Dunlap & Clarke Printers, 1888.

Fitler, Edwin H. *Fourth Annual Message of Edwin H. Fitler, Mayor of the City of Philadelphia, with Annual Report of William S. Stokley, Director of the Department of Public Safety, and Annual Report of the Board of Health for the Year Ending December 31, 1890.* Philadelphia, PA: Dando Printing and Publishing Company, 1891.

Formad, Henry F., BM, MD. *Comparative Studies of Mammalian Blood, with Special Reference to the Microscopical Diagnosis of Blood Stains in Criminal Cases; with Sixteen Illustrations from Photo-Micrographs and Drawings.* Philadelphia, PA: A. L. Hummel, M. D., Publisher, 1888. .

Geyer, Frank. P. *The Holmes-Pitezel case; a history of the greatest crime of the century and of the search for the missing Pitezel children.* Philadelphia, PA: Publishers' Union, 1896.

Gibbs, James M. *History of the First Battalion Pennsylvania Six Months Volunteers and 187th Regiment Pennsylvania Volunteer Infantry.* Central Printing and Publishing House, 1905.

Gibson, Jane M. *Fairmount Waterworks.* Philadelphia: Philadelphia Museum of Art, 1988.

Gould, Robert Freke. *A Library of Freemasonry, Volume 4*. Philadelphia: John C. Yorston, 1906.

Grand Lodge of Pennsylvania. *Sequi-centennial Anniversary of the Initiation of Brother George Washington into the Fraternity of Freemasons, 1902*. J. B. Lippincott Company, 1902. [Frank Geyer selected to represent Frankford Lodge No. 292, Philadelphia].

Franklin, Vincent P. "The Philadelphia Race Riot of 1918," *Pennsylvania Magazine of History and Biography*, Volume 99, (1975).

Hale, George Wesley, Police Department. *Police and Prison Cyclopaedia*. Boston, MA: The W. L. Richardson Company, 1893.

Hatch, Frederick. *Protecting President Lincoln, The Security Effort, The Thwarted Plots and the Disaster at Ford's Theatre*. North Carolina: McFarland & Company, Inc., Publishers, 2011.

Hawley, J. R. *The Assassination and History of the Conspiracy, A complete digest of the whole affair from its inception to its culmination, Sketches of the principal Characters, Reports of the Obsequies, etc, Fully Illustrated*. Cincinnati: J. R. Hawley & Co., 1865.

History of Cumberland and Adams Counties, Pennsylvania. Chicago, Illinois: Warner, Beers & Co., 1886.

Ingram, J. S. *The Centennial Exposition, Described and Illustrated*. Philadelphia, PA: Hubbard Brothers, 1876.

Irving, H. B. "The Mysterious Mr. Holmes." *The National Police Journal*, Volume 4, No. 5. (1919).

Journal of the House of Representatives of the Commonwealth of Pennsylvania for the Session Begun at Harrisburg on the Seventh Day of January, 1913, Part I. Harrisburg, PA: The Telegraph Printing Company, 1914.

Journal of Select Council of the City of Philadelphia, From October 1, 1880 to April 2, 1881. Philadelphia, PA: E. C. Markley & Son Printers, 1881.

Journal of the Select Council of the City of Philadelphia, From October 1, 1885 to April 1, 1886. Philadelphia, PA: Dunlap & Clarke Printers, 1886.

Journal of Select Council of the City of Philadelphia, From April 4, 1887 to September 27, 1887, Volume 1. Philadelphia, PA: Dunlap & Clarke Printers, 1887.

*Journal of Select Council of the City of Philadelphia, From October 6,
    1887 to April 2, 1888.* Philadelphia, PA: Dunlap & Clarke Printers,
    1888.

Jordan, John W. *Encyclopedia of Pennsylvania, Biography.* New York:
    Lewis Historical Publishing Company, 1914.

Kansas City Star. "Caught in the Klondike," [H. H. Holmes], *The Weekly
    Underwriter,* Volume 57, (1897).

"The Keystone Bank Wreck," *The Illustrated American,* Volume VII,
    No. 71, (1891).

Kress, Wilson C. *State Reports Vol. 190 Containing Cases Decided by
    the Supreme Court of Pennsylvania at January and April Terms,
    1899.* Pennsylvania: The Banks Law Publishing Co. 1899.

Kress, William, C., State Reporter. *Pennsylvania State Reports, Supreme
    Court, Volume 174 Containing Cases Adjudged in the Supreme
    Court of Pennsylvania - [Commonwealth v. Herman W. Mudgett,
    alias H. H. Holmes, Appellant.]* New York: Banks & Brothers, Law
    Publishers, 1896.

Larson, Erik. *The Devil in the White City: Murder, Magic, and Madness
    at the Fair that Changed America.* Vintage Books, a Division of
    Random House, Inc.: New York, 2003.

Lewis, John B., MD and Charles C. Bombaugh, AM, MD. *Strategems
    and Conspiracies to Defraud Life Insurance Companies; An
    Authentic Record of Remarkable Cases.* Baltimore, MD: James H.
    McClellan, Publisher, 1896.

Martin, John Bartlow. "The Master of the Murder Castle; A Classic of
    Chicago Crime," *Harper's Magazine,* (1943).

McCabe, James D. *The Illustrated History of the Centennial Exhibition,
    Held in Commemoration of the One Hundredth Anniversary of
    American Independence.* Philadelphia, PA: The National Publishing
    Company, 1876.

McClure's Magazine, [Mayor Samuel H. Ashbridge], Volume XXI,
    (1903).

MacDonald, Arthur. *Man and Abnormal Man, including a Study of
    Children, in Connection with Bills to Establish Laboratories Under
    Federal and State Governments for the Study of the Criminal,
    Pauper, and Defectives Classes.* Washington: Government Printing
    Office, 1905.

McElroy's Philadelphia Directory, 1854-1867. Philadelphia, PA: Edward C. & John Biddle.

Members of the Bar. *Weekly Notes of Cases Argued and Determined in the Supreme Court of Pennsylvania, the County Courts of Philadelphia, and the United States District and Circuit Courts for the Eastern District of Pennsylvania, Volume XX.* Philadelphia, PA: Kay & Brother Law Booksellers, Publishers and Importers, 1888.

Mudgett, Herman W. *Holmes' Own Story.* Philadelphia, PA: Burk & McFetridge co., 1895.

National Archives and Records Administration. Organization Index to Pension Files of Veterans Who Served Between 1861 and 1900. Publication No. T289, Application No. 1079202, Certificate No. 797694 [Reuben K. Geyer Pension].

New York Academy of Medicine. *The Transactions of the New York Academy of Medicine, Vol. II.* New York: Bailliere Brothers, 1863.

Ninetieth Annual Report of the Board of Public Education, First District of Pennsylvania Comprising of the City of Philadelphia for Year Ending December 31, 1908. Philadelphia, PA: Walther Printing House, 1909.

Oldroyd, Osborn H. *The Assassination of Abraham Lincoln, Flight, Pursuit, Capture, and Punishment of the Conspirators.* Washington DC: O. H. Oldroyd, 1901.

Ordinances of the City of Philadelphia From January 1 to December 31, 1886, and the Opinions of the City Solicitor. Philadelphia, PA: Dunlap & Clarke Printers, 1887.

Ordinances of the City of Philadelphia from January 1 to December 31, 1876, and Opinions of the City Solicitor. Philadelphia, PA: Dunlap & Clarke Printing Company, 1877.

Paist, Jos. H. *Manual of City Councils of Philadelphia for 1894-95.* George F. Lasher, Printer and Binder, 1894-95.

Pennsylvania Historical & Museum Commission Death Indices, Franklin P. Geyer, State File No. 143487.

Pennsylvania Historical & Museum Commission, Bureau of Archives and History, Pennsylvania State Archives. Records of Department of Military and Veterans' Affairs, Registers of Pennsylvania Volunteers, 1861-1865 [Reuben K. Geyer, Independent Battery H] www.phmc.state.pa.us/bah/dam/rg/di/r19-65RegisterPaVolunteers/ Independent%20Battery/ind%20battery%20pg%20105.pdf, accessed May 2, 2016.

Pennsylvania Historical & Museum Commission, Bureau of Archives
and History, Pennsylvania State Archives. Records of Department of
Military and Veterans' Affairs, Registers of Pennsylvania
Volunteers, 1861-1865 [Reuben K. Geyer, 204th, Company C]
http://www.phmc.state.pa.us/bah/dam/rg/di/
r19-65RegisterPaVolunteers/r19-65Regt204/
r19-65Regt204%20pg%2010.pdf, accessed May 2, 2016.

Pennsylvania Historical & Museum Commission, Bureau of Archives
and History, Pennsylvania State Archives. Records of Department of
Military and Veterans' Affairs, Registers of Pennsylvania
Volunteers, 1861-1865 [Reuben K. Geyer, 147th, Company E]
http://www.phmc.state.pa.us/bah/dam/rg/di/
r19-65RegisterPaVolunteers/r19-65Regt147/
r19-65Regt147%20pg%2019.pdf, accessed May 2, 2016.

Pennsylvania Historic Church and Town Records, Philadelphia,
[Franklin P. Geyer & Mary Elizabeth Rilley, married March 9,
1885].

Pennypacker, Samuel Whitaker, *Governor of Pennsylvania 1903-1907.
The Autobiography of a Pennsylvanian.* Philadelphia, PA: The John
C. Winston Company, 1918.

Philadelphia City Archives, Death Certificates: Reuben K. Geyer, FHL
microfilm 1,011,832; Bertha Whiteling, FHL microfilm 2,079,096;
John Whiteling, FHL microfilm 2,079,093; Willie Whiteling, FHL
microfilm 2,079,235; James Logue, FHL microfilm 1,787,216.

"Philadelphia History," *Independence Hall Association.* http://
www.ushistory.org/philadelphia, accessed May 2, 2016.

"Philadelphia Property Data, 1647 Cadwallader, Parcel #183145500,"
Data Hub, http://data.philly.com/philly/property/?
formname=parcelDetails&parcel=183145500, accessed April 26,
2016.

Philadelphia Record. *The Record Almanac, 1885, Illustrated.*
Philadelphia, PA: The Philadelphia Record, 1885.

Philadelphia Record. *The Record Almanac, 1890, Illustrated.*
Philadelphia, PA: The Philadelphia Record, 1890.

Public Broadcasting Service (PBS) transcript of American Experience,
"Influenza 1918," 1998.

Ratnaike, R.N., Associate Professor of Medicine, University of Adelaide.

"Acute and Chronic Arsenic Toxicity," *US National Library of Medicine, National Institutes of Health,* (2009).

Roberts, Elwood. *Biographical Annals of Montgomery County Pennsylvania, Illustrated, Volume II.* New York/Chicago: T. S. Benham & Company and The Lewis Publishing Company, 1904.

Reports on the Philadelphia International Exhibition of 1876, Volume I. Presented to both Houses of Parliament by Command of Her Majesty. England: George E. Eyre and William Spottiswoode, Printers to the Queen's Most Excellent Majesty, 1877.

Rowan, Richard W. *The Pinkertons; A Detective Dynasty.* London: Hurst & Blackett, LTD, 1931.

"Samuel Ashbridge letters (Collection 3168)," *Historical Society of Pennsylvania,* http://www2.hsp.org/collections/manuscripts/a/Ashbridge3168.html, accessed February 2, 2015.

"Samuel H. Ashbridge; President McKinley and Mayor Ashbridge of Philadelphia, as himself," *IMDb,* http://www.imdb.com/name/nm0038692/, accessed March 28, 2016.

Schechter, Harold. *Depraved: The Definitive True Story of H. H. Holmes, Whose Grotesque Crimes Shattered Turn-of-the-Century Chicago.* New York, NY: Pocket Books, a division of Simon & Schuster, Inc., 1994.

Schneck, DD, Rev, BS. *The Burning of Chambersburg, Pennsylvania.* Philadelphia, PA: Lindsay & Blakiston, 1864.

Smith, R. A. *Smith's New Guide to Philadelphia.* Philadelphia, PA: G. Delp, 1871.

Smith, R. A. *Philadelphia As It Is, In 1852: Being a Correct Guide to All the Public Buildings; Literary, Scientific, and Benevolent Institutions; and Places of Amusement, With Illustrations.* Philadelphia PA: Lindsay and Blakiston, 1852.

Smith, Thomas B. *Third Annual Message of Thomas B. Smith, Mayor of Philadelphia, Volume I, Containing the Mayor's Message and the Reports of the Departments of Public Safety and Public Health and Charities for the Year Ending December 31, 1918.* Philadelphia, PA: Issued by the City of Philadelphia, 1919.

Smith, William B. *First Annual Message of William B. Smith for the Year of 1884.* Philadelphia, PA: Dunlap and Clarke, Printers, 1885.

Smith, William B. *Second Annual Message of William B. Smith, Mayor of Philadelphia, for the Year 1885.* Philadelphia, PA: Dunlap & Clarke Printers, 1886.

Sprogle, Howard O. *The Philadelphia Police, Past and Present.* Philadelphia, PA: publisher unknown, 1887.

State of Pennsylvania. "District Reports of Cases Decided in all the Judicial Districts of the State of Pennsylvania During the Year 1896," *Legal Intelligencer,* Volume V, (1896).

Stevens, Cyrus Lee, AM, MD, "Honor Roll of Pennsylvania Physicians," *The Pennsylvania Medical Journal,* Volume XLVII, (1917).

Stokley, William S. *Seventh Annual Message of William S. Stokley, Mayor of the City of Philadelphia: with Accompanying Documents, October 16, 1979.* Philadelphia, PA: E. C. Markley & Son Printers, 1879.

Stokley, William S. *Eighth Annual Message of William S. Stokley, Mayor of the City of Philadelphia: with Accompanying Documents, November 4, 1880.* Philadelphia, PA: E. C. Markley & Son Printers, 1880.

Stokley, William S. *Ninth Annual Message of William S. Stokley, Mayor of the City of Philadelphia: with Accompanying Documents, March 31, 1881.* Philadelphia, PA: E. C. Markley & Son Printer, 1881.

Strassburger, Ralph B. *Our Judiciary, Montgomery County's Judiciary, Historical Series Reprinted from Times Herald.* Norristown, PA, 1929.

Swiderski, Richard M. *Calomel in America: Mercurial Panacea, War, Song and Ghosts.* Boca Raton: BrownWalker Press, 2008.

Talbot, Eugene S., MD, DDS. "H. H. Holmes," *Journal of the American Medical Association,* Volume XXVII, (1896).

Taylor, Frank. *Philadelphia in the Civil War 1861-1865.* Philadelphia, PA: Published by the City, 1913.

Thomas, Robert P., MD, "Report of Two Cases of Fracture of the Thigh, *The American Journal of the Medical Sciences,* Volume XLI, (1861).

Thompson, Peter John, PhD. *A Social History of Philadelphia's Taverns, 1683-1800.* Pennsylvania: University of Pennsylvania, 1989.

Tyson, Joseph Howard. *Penn's Luminous City.* Lincoln, NE: iUniverse, 1973.

United States Civil War Soldiers. Index to Compiled Service Records of Volunteer Union Soldiers Who Served in Organizations from the State of Pennsylvania, Record Group 94, Publication No. M554, 1965.

United States Department of Interior. *Office Register of the United States, Containing a List of Officers and Employees in the Civil, Military, and Naval Service, Volume II The Post-Office Department and the Postal Service, July 1, 1883.* Washington: Government Printing Office, 1884.

United States History.org. "The Rise of American Industry: Irish and German Immigration," *US History,* http://www.ushistory.org/us/25f.asp, accessed January 15, 2017.

United States, Pennsylvania Board of Centennial Managers. *Pennsylvania and the Centennial Exposition: Comprising the Preliminary and Final Reports of the Pennsylvania Board of Centennial Managers Made to the Legislature at the Sessions of 1877-8.* Pennsylvania: Gillin & Nagle. 1878.

United States National Library of Medicine, National Institutes of Health. "Dr. (Mary Alice Bennett Biography," *Changing the Face of Medicine,* https://cfmedicine.nlm.nih.gov/physicians/biography_32.html, accessed on February 1, 2017.

United States Patent Office, Shutter or Door Fastener, F. P. Geyer, Patent No. 556,141, March 10, 1896.

United States Patent Office, F. P. Geyer, Safety Lock for Pocket Books and Hand Bags, Patent No. 872,619, December 3, 1907.

United States Patent Office, Orrie C. Strohm, Alarm, Patent No. 1,206,939, December 5, 1916.

University of Pennsylvania Alumni and Faculty of Medicine, ed. *University Medical Magazine,* Volume IV, (1892).

University of Pennsylvania Law Review, ed. "Philadelphia Police Practice and the Law of Arrest," *University of Pennsylvania Law Review,* Volume 100 (1952).

United States World War I Draft Registration Card, NARA M1509, Washington DC: National Archives and Records Administration, 37-7-28, C, serial number 3291, order number 1030 [Orrie Curtis Strohm].

University of Pennsylvania, Wharton School Studies in Politics and Economics. "The Government of Philadelphia: a Study in Municipal

Administration," *University of Pennsylvania, Wharton School Studies in Politics and Economics,* Volume II, (1893).

Vroom, Garret D. W. *Reports of Cases Argued and Determined in the Supreme Court and, at Law, in the Court of Errors and Appeals of the State of New Jersey, Volume LIV.* Newark, NJ: Soney & Sage, 1913.

Walker, Samuel. *A Critical History of Police Reform: The Emergency of Professionalism.* Lexington, MA: D. C. Health, 1977.

Walther, Rudolph J. *Happenings in Ye Olde Philadelphia, 1680-1900.* Philadelphia, PA: Walther Printing House, 1925.

Warwick, Charles F. *Second Annual Message of Charles F. Warwick, Mayor of the City of Philadelphia with Annual Reports of Frank M. Riter, Director of the Department of Public Safety and Chiefs of Bureaus Constituting Said Department for the Year Ending December 31, 1896, Vol. II.* Philadelphia, PA: Dunlap Printing Co., 1897.

Warwick, Charles F. *Third Annual Message of Charles F. Warwick, Mayor of the City of Philadelphia with Annual Reports of Frank M. Riter, Director of the Department of Public Safety and Chiefs of Bureaus Constituting Said Department for the Year Ending December 31, 1897, Vol. II.* Philadelphia, PA: Dunlap Printing Co., 1898.

Warwick, Charles F. *Fourth Annual Message of Charles F. Warwick, Mayor of the City of Philadelphia with Annual Reports of Frank M. Riter, Director of the Department of Public Safety Year Ending December 31, 1898, Vol. II.* Philadelphia, PA: Dunlap Printing Co, 1899.

Watson, John F. *Annals of Philadelphia and Pennsylvania, in the Olden Time; Being a Collection of Memoirs, Anecdotes, and Incidents of the City and Its Inhabitants.* Philadelphia, PA: Edwin S. Stuart, 1887.

Webster, Sidney. *Franklin Pierce and His Administration.* New York: D. Appleton and Company, 1892.

Weekly Notes of Cases Argued and Determined in the Supreme Court of Pennsylvania, the County Courts of Philadelphia, and the United States District and Circuit Courts for the Eastern District of Pennsylvania, Volume XX. Philadelphia, PA: Kay & Brother Law Booksellers, Publishers and Importers, 1888.

Weigley, Russel F., et al. *Philadelphia: A 300 Year History.* New York: W. W. Norton & Company, 1892.

Westcott, Thomas. *The Official Guide Book to Philadelphia: a new handbook for strangers and citizens, with a history of the city, etc.* Philadelphia, PA: Porter and Coates, 1875.

Wilder, Harris Hawthorne, PhD and Wentworth, Bert, Former Police Commissioner of Dover, NH. *Personal Identification: Methods for the Identification of Individuals, Living or Dead.* Boston, MA: Richard G. Badger, The Gorham Press, 1918.

Wiley, Samuel T. *Biographical and Portrait Cyclopedia of Montgomery County, Pennsylvania, Containing Biographical Sketches of Prominent and Representative Citizens of the County, Together with an Introductory Historical Sketch.* Philadelphia, PA: Biographical Publishing Company, 1895.

Young, George H. "Noted Detective Dead." *The National Police Journal,* Volume 3, Number 2, (1918).

United States Census:

1860: Schedule 1, County of Philadelphia, State of Pennsylvlania, June 6, 1860, Line No. 35-39 [Franklin Geyer, 7, living with parents and siblings].

1870: Schedule 1, Cadwallader Street North from Oxford, County of Philadelphia, State of Pennsylvania, November 18, 1870, p. 36, Line No. 35-39 [Frank P. Geyer, 18, living with parents and siblings, 1657 Cadwallader].

1890: Eleventh Census, Special Schedule, Surviving Soldiers, Sailors, and Marines, and Widows, Etc., Supervisor's District No. 1, Enumeration District No. 365, Philadelphia, PA, June 1890, p. 1, From Schedule No. 1, House No. 93, Family No. 101, Line No. 8, 1647 Cadwallader [Reuben K. Geyer, Private, Company E, 147 PA Infantry].

1900: Twelfth Census, Schedule No. 1, Supervisor's District No. 1st PA, Enumeration District No. 400, Sheet No. 56, 19th Ward, Philadelphia, PA, June 6, 1900, Line No. 81-83 [Frank P. Geyer, Detective, living with wife, Mary E. and daughter, Edna C., at 2634 N. Sixth Street].

1900: Twelfth Census, Schedule No. 1, Supervisor's District No. 1st, Enumeration District No. 394, Sheet No. 3, 19th Ward, Philadelphia,

PA, June 2, 1900, Line No. 37-39 [Reuben K. Geyer living with daughter and son-in-law, at 2400 Orkney Street].

1910: Thirteenth Census, Supervisor's District No. 1, Enumeration District No. 326, Sheet No. 8, 19th Ward, Philadelphia, PA, April 23, 1910, Line No. 89-90, [Frank P. Geyer living with wife, Mary E., at 2634 N. 6th Street].

1920: Fourteenth Census, Philadelphia, PA, January 5, 1920, Line No. 88-90, [Mary Geyer, 59, boarder, living with Emma M. Bowden, 47, and Edwin Leary (Bowden brother-in-law, 70, living at 2556 N. 9th].

1930: Fifteenth Census, Cape May County, New Jersey, April 11, 1930, Line No. 85-91, [Mary, 71, head of household, living with Edna Strohm, 43; and Joseph, Elizabeth, Stanley Elliott, boarders; and Dorothy and Frank Strohm, boarders, at 110 Palm, Wildwood].

Newspapers:

Aberdeen Daily News
Alexandria Gazette
Allentown Leader
Altoona Tribune
Ann Arbor Argus
Boston Journal
Bridgetown Evening News
Brooklyn Daily Eagle
Bucks County Gazette
Carlisle Evening News
Central News
Chicago Tribune
Cincinnati Enquirer
Colorado Springs Gazette
Columbian
Conshohocken Recorder
Daily Inter Ocean
Daily National Intelligencer
Daily People
Decatur Daily Republican
Delaware Gazette and State Journal
Elkhart Daily Review
Evening Journal
Evening Leader Wilkes-Barre

Evening Public Ledger
Evening Star
Evening Star Washington DC
Evening Telegraph
Fremont Journal
Harrisburg Daily Independent
Harrisburg Telegraph
Indianapolis Journal
Indianapolis News
Inter Ocean
Kansas City Star
Los Angeles Herald
New Castle Herald
New York Herald
New York Times
New York Tribune
North American
Patriot Harrisburg
Philadelphia Inquirer
Philadelphia Record
Philadelphia Times
Pittsburgh Post-Gazette
Plain Dealer
Reading Times
Rockland County Journal
Salem Register
San Francisco Call
Scranton Republican
Semi-Weekly Messenger
Sentinel
St. Louis Post-Dispatch
Trenton Evening Times
Washington Times
Wheeling Intelligent
Wilkes-Barre Record
Wilkes-Barre Times
Wilkes-Barre News
World Evening Edition

Notes

Prologue: Profound Untruth

1. George T. Bisel. *The Trial of Herman W. Mudgett, Alias, H. H. Holmes, for the Murder of Benjamin F. Pitezel: In the Court of Oyer and Terminer and General Jail Delivery and Quarter Sessions of the Peace, in and for the City and County of Philadelphia, Commonwealth of Pennsylvania, October 28, 29, 30, 31, and November 1, and 2, 1895.* Philadelphia, PA: George T. Bisel, Law Publisher, Bookseller and Stationer, 1897, p. 462.

2. Harold Schechter, *Depraved: The Definitive True Story of H. H. Holmes, Whose Grotesque Crimes Shattered Turn-of-the-Century Chicago.* New York, NY: Pocket Books, a division of Simon & Schuster, Inc., 1994, pp. 247-48. The deaths were unintentionally perpetuated in Erik Larson's wildly popular book, The Devil in the White City. Larson confirmed he sourced the information from Schechter as he also indicated in his notes section. Katherine Ramsland also included the deaths in her two books, *The Devil's Dozen* and *Beating the Devil's Game*, as did Judith Nickels in *A Competent Witness*, though Ms. Nickels' had a tiny bit of wiggle room as she described her book as being a work of speculative fiction, closely based on actual events. Erik Larson. *The Devil in the White City: Murder, Magic, and Madness at the Fair that Changed America.* Vintage Books, a Division of Random House, Inc.: New York, 2003, p. 340. Larson confirmed via email, dated April 17, 2017; Katherine Ramsland, Ph.D. *The Devil's Dozen: 12 Notorious Serial Killers Caught By Cutting-Edge Forensics.* New York: Berkley Books, 2009, pp. 21-22; Katherine Ramsland, Ph.D. *Beating the Devil's Game: A History of Forensic Science and Criminal Investigation.* New York: Berkley Books, 2007, p. 152; and Judith Nickels. *A Competent Witness: Georgiana Yoke and the Trial of H. H. Holmes.* CreateSpace Independent Publishing Platform, 2014, p. 155.

3. Mary's given name: Members of Geyer's descendent's state Mary's maiden name is O'Riley; however, Frank and Mary's marriage record states her last name was Rilley. It would very well be a typo or Mary

could have dropped a few letters from her given name when she moved to Philadelphia. Pennsylvania Marriage Record. Historical Society of Pennsylvania; Philadelphia, Pennsylvania; Collection Name: Historic Pennsylvania Church and Town Records; Reel: p. 643. Mary's job: Author interview with James R. Riggins and Elliott family, descendants of Detective Frank P. Geyer, May 6, 2017, New Jersey. In 1877, Mayor Stokley ordered police officials to conduct a census of taverns and beer-saloons within Philadelphia and 5,455 taverns were counted. John F. Watson. *Annals of Philadelphia and Pennsylvania, in the Olden Time; Being a Collection of Memoirs, Anecdotes, and Incidents of the City and Its Inhabitants.* Philadelphia, PA: Edwin S. Stuart, 1887, p. 367.

Eighteenth Police District Station house location in 1889 (Dauphin Street and Trenton Avenue): Philadelphia Record. *The Philadelphia Record Almanac.* Philadelphia, PA: The Philadelphia Record, 1890, p. 58. New Eighteenth Police District Station house location in 1890 (Fourth and York Streets): Edwin H. Fitler. *Fourth Annual Message of Edwin H. Fitler, Mayor of the City of Philadelphia, with Annual Report of William S. Stokley, Director of the Department of Public Safety, and Annual Report of the Board of Health for the Year Ending December 31, 1890.* Philadelphia, PA: Dando Printing and Publishing Company, 1891, p. 8.

4. US History.org. "The Rise of American Industry: Irish and German Immigration," *US History*, www.ushistory.org/us/25f.asp, accessed January 15, 2017.

5. Founding fathers: Author interview with J. R. Riggins and Elliott family, descendants of Detective Frank P. Geyer, May 6, 2017, New Jersey. General from Revolutionary War: "Detective Geyer's Work," *Indianapolis Journal*, August 28, 1895, p. 2.

6. "Detective Geyer's Work," *Indianapolis Journal*, August 28, 1895, p. 2.

7. Author interview with James R. Riggins and Elliott family, descendants of Detective Frank P. Geyer, May 6, 2017, New Jersey.

8. Methodist Midtown Parish Church Marriage record: Franklin P. Geyer (31) m. Mary Elizabeth Rilley (27) on March 9, 1885. Geyer lived at

1649 (could be 1647) Cadwallader Street in Philadelphia at the time of the marriage. Mary, who was born in Hartford, Connecticut, lived at 2417 Orianna Street, around the corner from her job at the tavern. At the time of their marriage, Geyer was a special officer assigned to Detectives Department, which is likely why his occupation was listed as detective officer on his marriage record. Local press simply shortened his title to 'Detective.' "Weather," *Philadelphia Record*, March 10, 1885, p. 1.

9. Edna Camilla Geyer was born December 27, 1886. Department of Records, Philadelphia City Births, 1886, microfilm 1,289,325; and American Meteorological Society. Monthly Weather Review. December 1886, Volume 14, Number 12, pp. 343-47. Edna graduated from John Welsh School, a combined grammar and secondary school, in 1901 and went on to graduate from the Commercial High School for Girls located on the Southeast corner of Broad and Green Streets. "Pupils Pass to Higher Studies." *Philadelphia Inquirer*, June 28, 1901, p. 9; and "Strohm-Geyer." *Bridgeton Evening News*, April 23, 1908, p. 6. By 1890, the family lived at 2634 North Sixth Street in Philadelphia. During the 1900 census, their Sixth Street home was listed as being free of a mortgage. Twelfth Census of the United States, Schedule No. 1 - Population. Philadelphia, Pennsylvania, Supervisor's District No. 1st PA, Enumeration District No. 400, Sheet No. 6, June 6, 1900. The Census listed Geyer as a detective, age forty-six. Mary was thirty-nine and Edna thirteen. The family lived at 2634 North Sixth Street, Philadelphia; and City of Philadelphia directories 1890-1918.

10. Famous Mason's: Arnold Palmer, Professional Golfer; Brad Paisley, Country Singer; Buzz Aldrin, Astronaut; Shaquille O'Neil, Professional Basketball; Louis Armstrong, Musician; Mark Twain,Writer; Benjamin Franklin, Founding father; Sir Arthur Conan Doyle (Sherlock Holmes Author). Fourteen presidents of the United States: Washington, Monroe, Jackson, Polk, Buchanan, Johnson, Garfield, McKinley, both Roosevelt's, Taft, Harding, Truman, and Ford. "History of the Scottish Rite: Famous Masons," www.scottishritenmj.org, retrieved July 10, 2017; "Past Grand Commander [George S. Graham]," *Patriot,* May 27, 1903, p. 1; and "Little Known Facts," www.32nddegreemasons.org, retrieved July

10, 2017.

11. The 1920 United States Census, Philadelphia, PA, line 90 lists Mary E. Geyer, boarder, living with Emma Bowden and Edwin Leary (Emma's brother-in-law) at 2556 N. 9th Street, Philadelphia. The 1930 United States Census, Cape May, New Jersey, line 85 lists Mary E. Guier (misspell), head of household, living with daughter Edna C. Strum (misspell), and boarders: Joseph Eliott (misspell), Elizabeth Eliott (misspell), Stanley Eliot (misspell), Dorothy Strum (misspell), Frank Strum (misspell) at 110 East Palm Street, Wildwood (Cape May), New Jersey.

Chapter 1 - Franklin Pierce

12. President Franklin Pierce March 4, 1853, inaugural address: "Franklin Pierce," *The American Presidency Project.* www.presidency.ucsb.edu, accessed January 14, 2017.

13. Franklin and Jane suffered the loss of two other sons before Benny, one as an infant and the other at the age of four. Sidney Webster. *Franklin Pierce and His Administration.* New York: D. Appleton and Company, 1892, pp. 30-32.

14. The death of Franklin and Jane's son: "Dreadful Railroad Accident," *Salem Register,* January 10, 1853, p. 2.

15. "The Presidents Progress," *Plain Dealer,* July 14, 1853, p. 2; and "The Presidents Journey to Philadelphia," *Daily National Intelligencer,* July 15, 1853, p. 3.

16. Geyer's date of birth: Though *Police Past and Present* states Geyer was born on July 27, 1853, his death certificate states his date of birth as July 28, 1853. Blacksmith's family: Samuel T. Wiley, ed. *Biographical and Portrait Cyclopedia of Montgomery County, Pennsylvania, Containing Biographical Sketches of Prominent and Representative Citizens of the County, Together with an Introductory Historical Sketch.* Philadelphia, PA: Biographical Publishing Company. 1895, pp. 214-16. Philadelphia population: Russel F. Weigley, et al. *Philadelphia: A 300 Year History.* New York: W. W. Norton & Company, 1892, p. 309. Weigley listed Philadelphia's population at 408,672 in 1850. Named after President Franklin

Pierce: Author interview with J. R. Riggins and Elliott family, descendants of Detective Frank P. Geyer, May 6, 2017, New Jersey.

17. Mark Twain worked at *Pennsylvania Inquirer* located on the corner of Third and Carter's Alley, south of Chestnut.

18. Mark Twain letter about whiskey-swilling: (retrieved from Mark Twain Project, www.marktwainproject.org): "To Orion and Henry Clemens, 26-28 Oct 1853, Philadelphia, PA."

19. Mark Twain letter about working the night shift and complaints about foreigner's in America: (retrieved from Mark Twain Project, www.marktwainproject.org): "To Orion Clemens, 28 November 1853, Philadelphia, PA."

Detective Geyer had a little more in common with Mark Twain other than Twain working two miles from Geyer's home when he was small. Both Geyer and Twain were Freemasons, and besides both of them sporting a walrus-type mustache, they were also inventors. Geyer made two inventions, and Twain, three. Twain also shared something in common with Geyer's wife, Mary, who was born in Hartford, Connecticut. Mark Twain and his family lived in Hartford for many years and he wrote his best-known works there, The Adventurers of Tom Sawyer, The Prince and the Pauper, Adventures of Huckleberry Finn, Life on the Mississippi, A Tramp Abroad, and A Connecticut Yankee in King Arthur's Court. And though Detective Geyer was famous in his own right for his work on high-profile cases, and like Mark Twain, he was an author, albeit an author of a single book that became an instant bestseller, but that would never come close to Mark Twain's status in the writing and literary world. Twain made a huge impact on literature as we know it today. Twain knew he was destined as an author when he penned to his brother, Orion, ". . . it is my strongest suit." Mark Twain House and Museum, Hartford, Connecticut: Mark Twain and his family lived in the gothic-medieval style home. His daughter, Susy, died of spinal meningitis in the home in 1896 and following her death, the family could not live in the house again. The house sold in 1903. Mark Twain, American Writer: "Literary Maturity," Britannica, www.britannica.com/biography/Mark-Twain, April 19, 2017.

20. 1647 Cadwallader Street: Reuben Geyer was listed as living at 1647 Cadwallader Street in 1861 and 1866. In 1874, city records document the transfer of 1647 Cadwallader Street home from Daniel Buck to Reuben K. Geyer. City of Philadelphia Deed of Trust, entered August 18, 1874, Lot No. 166, Plan Book No. 12 N, p. 28; McElroy's Philadelphia Directory, 1854-1867, (Philadelphia, PA: Edward C. & John Biddle); and United States Census, 1870, Cadwallader Street North from Oxford, Schedule 1, Inhabitants in the 57th District, County of Philadelphia, State of Pennsylvania, November 18, 1870, no. 35-39, p. 36.

21. Ancestry notes (alphabetical by given surname):

BUCK, CAMILLA (Frank Geyer's mother): Camilla Buck was born circa 1826 in Sumneytown, PA. She was the daughter of Jacob Buck and Anna Schmeck. Camilla had seven siblings: Charles, Daniel, Henry, Jacob, James, Maria, and Caroline, who died when she was young. Camilla married Reuben K. Geyer on August 22, 1848, at the German Reformed Church in Philadelphia, PA (she was listed as Cornilia Buck on her marriage certificate and Carmilla Buck in the Biographical and Portrait Cyclopedia of Montgomery County. Camilla (Buck) Geyer died November 2, 1893, at the age of sixty-seven. A private funeral was held at the Cadwallader family home at 1647 Cadwallader Street, Philadelphia. Camilla was buried at Laurel Hill Cemetery in Philadelphia, PA. Sources: City of Philadelphia Return of Death, Physician's Certificate no. 9155; and Samuel T. Wiley, ed. *Biographical and Portrait Cyclopedia of Montgomery County, Pennsylvania, Containing Biographical Sketches of Prominent and Representative Citizens of the County, Together with an Introductory Historical Sketch.* Philadelphia, PA: Biographical Publishing Company, 1895, pp. 215-16; Historic Pennsylvania Church and Town Records, reel 166; City of Philadelphia Return of a Death Physician's Certificate no. 9155; "Mortuary Notice," *Philadelphia Inquirer*, November 5, 1893, p. 7; 1850 United States Census, County of Philadelphia, PA, lines 25, 26, 28; 1860 United States Census, County of Philadelphia, PA, lines 35-29; and 1870 United States Census, County of Philadelphia, PA, lines 35-39.

GEYER, ANNA E. (Frank Geyer's sister): Anna Elizabeth Geyer

was born March 27, 1849, in Philadelphia, PA. She was listed on both the 1860 and 1860 Census as Anna. At their son Stanley Reuben's baptism December 4, 1876, she was listed as Annie and continued as Annie off and on for the rest of her life. Anna married Henry H. Favinger August 18, 1875, in Philadelphia, PA. Both Henry and their son, Stanley worked at Frankford Arsenol. Anna E. (Geyer) Favinger died January 3, 1929, in Philadelphia, PA of pneumonia. She was widowed at the time of her death. Her husband died June 13, 1924. Anna and Henry Favinger were buried at Laurel Hill Cemetery in Philadelphia. Sources: Record of Baptisms; County of Philadelphia, Commonwealth of Pennsylvania, Department of Health, Bureau of Vital Statistics, Certificate of Death, File No. 12644, Registered No. 376, listed as Mrs. Annie E. Favinger (mother: Camilla B. Buck, father: Reuben K. Geyer, spouse: Henry H. Favinger); Commonwealth of Pennsylvania, Department of Health, Bureau of Vital Statistics, Certificate of Death, File No. 64646, Registered No. 13480, listed as Henry H. Favinger born February 14, 1849, died June 13, 1924, age 73 (mother: Kathryn Gehman, father: Samuel Favinger, spouse: Annie E. Favinger); Official Register of the United States, 1915, p. 337; 1850 United States Census, County of Philadelphia, PA, lines 25, 26, 28; 1860 United States Census, County of Philadelphia, PA, lines 35-29; and 1870 United States Census, County of Philadelphia, PA, lines 35-39.

GEYER, EDNA CAMILLA (Frank Geyer's daughter): Edna Camilla Geyer was born December 27, 1886, in Philadelphia, PA. She was the only daughter of Franklin Pierce Geyer and Mary Elizabeth Rilley. Edna Geyer married Orrie Curtis Strohm on April 21, 1908, in an evening ceremony held at Frank and Mary's home, 2634 North Sixth Street, Philadelphia. Edna and Orrie had three children, Elizabeth Alice Strohm, Dorothy Edna Strohm and Frank Wesley Strohm. Edna Camilla (Geyer) Strohm died sometime in 1943 and was buried with Orrie, who died ten years after Edna. They are both buried at Cold Spring Presbyterian Cemetery in New Jersey. Sources: Philadelphia, Pennsylvania City Births, Department of Records, 1860-1906, FHL# 1,289,325; 1900 United States Census, County of Philadelphia, PA, Sheet No. 6, line 83 (Edna C. Geyer, born Dec 1886, age 13); Philadelphia Orphan's Court, Marriage

License Index, 1885 to 1916, no. 225717; "Strohm-Geyer," *Bridgetown Evening News*, April 23, 1908, p. 8; and Cold Spring Presbyterian Cemetery, NJ gravestone (Strohm: Edna C. 1886-1943, Orrie C. 1884-1953).

GEYER, FRANKLIN PIERCE: Franklin Pierce Geyer was born July 28, 1853, in Philadelphia, PA. He was the son of Reuben K. Geyer and Camilla Buck. Frank and Mary Elizabeth Rilley married on March 9, 1885, at Methodist Midtown Parish in Philadelphia PA. At the time of their marriage, Frank was thirty-one. His occupation was listed as a detective officer living at 1649 Cadwallader Street, Philadelphia. Frank Geyer died October 4, 1918, at his home in Philadelphia, PA. The cause of death was La Grippe (Spanish Flu or Spanish Influenza). Frank Geyer was buried at Hillside Cemetery in Roslyn, PA. Mary later joined Frank at the time of her death, December 1932 and both are buried in Section C14. Sources: City of Philadelphia, Commonwealth of Pennsylvania, Department of Health, Bureau of vital Statistics, Certificate of Death, File No. 143437, Registered No. 26452 (date of birth stated as July 28, 1853); Howard O. Sprogle. *Philadelphia Police, Past and Present.* Philadelphia, PA: publisher unknown, 1887, pp. 295-96 (date of birth stated as July 27, 1853); Historical Society of Pennsylvania, Philadelphia, Pennsylvania, Collection Name: Historic Pennsylvania Church and Town Records; Reel: 643; City of Philadelphia, Commonwealth of Pennsylvania, Department of Health, Bureau of vital Statistics, Certificate of Death, File No. 143437, Registered No. 26452; "Bury Detective F. P. Geyer," *Philadelphia Inquirer*, October 9, 1918, p. 10; 1860 United States Census, County of Philadelphia, PA, lines 35-29; 1870 United States Census, County of Philadelphia, PA, lines 35-39; 1900 United States Census, Philadelphia County, PA, lines 81-83; and 1910 United States Census, County of Philadelphia, PA, lines 89-90.

GEYER, KATHARINA ELLA (Frank Geyer's sister): Katharina (Kate or Katie) Geyer was born January 20, 1860, in Philadelphia, PA. She was the daughter of Reuben K. Geyer and Camilla Buck. Kate Geyer married Harry Lawrence Werner, a milk dealer, on September 5, 1894, at 2439 North Seventh Street, Philadelphia, PA, which was the residence of the officiating clergyman, Rev. J. F. C.

Fluck. Kate and Harry had a daughter named Esther, October 1895, but she passed away at four months of age and was buried at Laurel Hill Cemetery in Philadelphia, PA. Katharina Ella (Geyer) Werner lived to the age of eighty-one. She died August 21, 1941. At the time of her death, Kate lived at 432 West York Street, Philadelphia, PA. Katharina Ella (Geyer) Werner was buried with her husband, who died a few months before her on February 28, 1941. They were burred at Laurel Hill Cemetery, Philadelphia, PA. Sources: Commonwealth of Pennsylvania, Department of Health, Bureau of Vital Statistics, Certificate of Death, File No. 76847, Registered No. 16736 (Kate Werner, mother: Camilla, father: Reuben Geyer); Baptism, June 12, 1860, Salem-Zion United Church of Christ, baptized as Katharina, mother: Cameilla, father: Ruben Geyer; Philadelphia Orphan's Court, Marriage License Index, 1885 to 1916, file no. 70986; "Marriage (Werner-Geyer)," *Philadelphia Inquirer,* September 9, 1894, p. 7. In the marriage announcement, Kate's name is listed as Miss Katie Ella Geyer; Return of Death in the City of Philadelphia, Physicians Certificate (Esther Werner, 4 months old), No. 16983, date of death: February 16, 1896; 1900 United States Census, Philadelphia County, PA, line 38; 1910 United States Census, Philadelphia County, PA, lines 6-7; 1920 United States Census, Philadelphia County, PA, lines 38-39; 1930 United States Census, Philadelphia County, PA, lines 37-39: Commonwealth of Pennsylvania, Department of Health, Bureau of Vital Statistics, Certificate of Death, File No. 76847, Registered No. 16736 (Kate Werner, mother: Camilla, father: Reuben Geyer).

GEYER, REUBEN K. (Frank Geyer's father): Reuben K. Geyer was born April 27, 1826, in Hazelton, PA. He married Camilla (listed as Cornilia) Buck August 22, 1848, at the German Reformed Church, Philadelphia, PA. Reuben died at the age of seventy-seven July 11, 1903, in Philadelphia. His cause of death was spinal sclerosis. Reuben Geyer is buried at Laurel Hill Cemetery, Philadelphia. Sources: The date of Reuben Geyer's birth was taken from his death certificate, which states Reuben was 77 yrs, 2 mo, 14 days at the time of his death on July 11, 1903. City of Philadelphia Return of a Death, Physician's Certificate no. 1069, Reuben K. Geyer, died July 11, 1903; Historic Pennsylvania Church and Town Records, reel

166; "Mortuary Notice," *Philadelphia Inquirer*, July 12, 1903, 5; and "Mortuary Notice," *Philadelphia Inquirer*, July 14, 1903, 7.

GEYER, WILLIAM HENRY. (Frank Geyer's brother): William Henry. Geyer was born in 1855, approximately two years after Frank Geyer. He died of Purpura Hemorrhagica at the age of nine months on August 19, 1856, in Philadelphia, PA. William Henry Geyer was buried at Odd Fellows Cemetery in Philadelphia, PA on August 23, 1856. Sources: Handwritten certification of death by Dr. Brown; and Pennsylvania, Philadelphia City Death Certificates, Philadelphia City Archives, FHL microfilm 1,976,296.

RILLEY, MARY ELIZABETH (Frank Geyer's wife): Mary Elizabeth Rilley was born July 1860 in Hartford, Connecticut. She was the daughter of unknown parents, both born in Ireland. Mary Elizabeth married Frank Geyer on March 9, 1885, at Methodist Midtown Parish in Philadelphia PA by W. S. Pugh. At the time of their marriage, Mary was twenty-seven and she lived at 2417 Orianna Street, Philadelphia. The Elliott and Riggins families list Mary's given name as O'Riley; however, her marriage record lists Rilley as her given name. There is an 1880 United States Census possibly linked to Mary, where a woman is listed as Mary Riley, age 20, twin, from Hartford Connecticut. Both her parents are from Ireland, which are consistent with later year census' for Frank and Mary. Mary Elizabeth Geyer sometime in December 1932 and was buried in Geyer's plot December 19, 1932, Hillside Cemetery in Rosalyn, PA. Both are buried in Section C14. Sources: Possible 1880 United States Census, Hartford County, Connecticut, lines 36-40; Historical Society of Pennsylvania, Philadelphia, Pennsylvania, Collection Name: Historic Pennsylvania Church and Town Records; Reel: 643; 1900 United States Census, Philadelphia County, PA, lines 81-83; 1910 United States Census, County of Philadelphia, PA, lines 89-90; 1920 United States Census, County of Philadelphia, PA, lines 88-90 (living with Emma Bowden and Emma's brother-in-law, Edwin Leary on North Ninth Street - Emma Bowden was listed as a sponsor with Frank and Mary Geyer for Orrie and Edna's daughters' baptism); 1930 United States Census, Wildwood Crest, lines 85-91 (listed as head of household with adult Elliott and Strohm living with her); and telephone verification, Becky at Hillside Cemetery, July

10, 2017, at 12:05 eastern. Mary's date of death is not listed in cemetery records; however, Mary was buried in Frank Geyer's plot on December 19, 1932. Section C, Lot 14 (C14).

STROHM, DOROTHY EDNA (Frank Geyer's granddaughter): Dorothy Edna Strohm was born October 15, 1910, in Philadelphia, PA. Dorothy married Clinton T. Elliott on unknown date. Dorothy died June 13, 1988 and is buried in New Jersey. Sources: Pennsylvania, Philadelphia City Births, FHL Microfilm 1,289,325; Philadelphia Orphans' Court Marriage License Index 1885-1916, No. 225717, 1908 [Strohm, Orrie C (Geyer)]; United States Social Security Index; United States Social Security Claim; and Cold Spring Presbyterian Cemetery, NJ headstone.

STROHM, ELIZABETH ALICE (Frank Geyer's granddaughter) was born August 23, 1909, in Philadelphia, PA. She married Joseph R. Elliott on unknown date and died in 1997. Elizabeth is buried at Cold Spring Presbyterian Cemetery in New Jersey. Sources: Christ Church Baptism Record, date of birth August 23, 1909, date of baptism November 21, 1909, p. 74; Cold Spring Presbyterian Cemetery, NJ headstone.

STROHM, FRANK WESLEY (Frank Geyer's grandson) was born May 19, 1915, in Philadelphia, PA. He married Grace L. on unknown date. Frank died August 1984 in Cape May, NJ and is buried at Cold Spring Presbyterian Cemetery in New Jersey. Sources: Social Security Death Index; and Cold Spring Presbyterian Cemetery, NJ headstone.

STROHM, ORRIE CURTIS (Frank Geyer's son-in-law) was born November 13, 1884, in Plainfield, PA. He married Edna Geyer April 21, 1908, at the home of Frank and Mary Geyer. Orrie Strohm died at the age of sixty-eight, February 20, 1953 in Cape May, New Jersey and was buried at Cold Spring Presbyterian Cemetery, also in New Jersey. Sources: Commonwealth of Pennsylvania, Department of Health, Bureau of Vital Statistics Certificate of Death, File No. 16468; Philadelphia Orphan's Court, Marriage License Index, 1885 to 1916, no. 225717; "Strohm-Geyer," *Bridgetown Evening News*, April 23, 1908, 8; Commonwealth of Pennsylvania, Department of Health, Bureau of Vital Statistics Certificate of Death, File No.

16468; and Cold Spring Presbyterian Cemetery, NJ headstone (headstone shows year only).

Chapter 2 - American Civil War

22. "The War has Commenced," *Fremont Journal*, April 13, 1861, p. 1.

23. Ibid: "The War has," p. 1.

24. Frank Taylor, *Philadelphia in the Civil War 1861-1865,* Philadelphia, PA: City, 1913, pp. 276-77.

25. Ibid: Taylor, *Philadelphia in*, pp. 267-69.

26. Ibid: Taylor, *Philadelphia in,* pp. 276-77; and Rev. B. S. Schneck, D. D. The Burning of Chambersburg, Pennsylvania. (Philadelphia, PA: Lindsay & Blakiston, 1864), p. 6-12.

27. Ibid: Taylor. *Philadelphia in,* pp. 276-77.

28. Net pay for one year of service was $1,131; two years, $1687; and three years service, $2,145. Nearly all were discharged within a half year; therefore, their compensation equalled a good wage that period of time. Reuben K. Geyer's Civil War information: Roll of Independent Battery H, Captain John J. Nevin. Reuben K. Geyer, private, age 39, mustered into service October 13, 1864 in Philadelphia, Pennsylvania by Captain Lane. Remarks: Transferred to Battery C 204th Regiment P. V. [Pennsylvania Volunteer], January 5, 1865; Samuel P. Bates. *Pennsylvania History of Volunteers, 1861-5, Vol. IV.* Harrisburg, PA: B. Singerly, State Printer, 1870, p. 905; Frank Taylor. *Philadelphia in the Civil War 1861-1865.* Philadelphia, PA: Published by the City, 1913, p. 269; and Eleventh Census of the United States, Special Schedule, Surviving Soldiers, Sailors, and Marines, and Widows. Reuben K. Geyer (line 8), 1647 Cadwallader Street, Private, Company E, 147 PA Infantry, October 13, 1864 to October 15, 1865.

29. Purpura hemorrhagica: Written statement from H. J. Brown, MD, certifying William Henry Geyer, son of R. K. Geyer, aged 9 months, died August 18, 1856 of Purpura Hemorrhagica; and Samuel K. Bremner, MD. "A Case of Purpura Hemorrhagica, with Autopsy,"*Archives of Pediatrics*, Volume X, (1893), p. 513. Bremner

discusses a case of Purpura Hemorrhagica from an autopsy where a
six month old with no previous illness has a gradual onset of
symptoms resulting in death. Purpura hemorrhagica is a bleeding
disorder characterized by a reduction in the number of platelets in
the blood, thus preventing the blood from clotting. Severe
hemorrhagic phenomena occurs with the acute form of hemorrhaic
purpura. Patients develop a purplish or reddish-brown on the skin
caused by the leakage of blood. In extreme cases, it causes bleeding
into the lungs, brain and other vital organs.

30. Frank Taylor. *Philadelphia in the Civil War 1861-1865.* Philadelphia,
    PA: Published by the City, 1913, pp. 298-99.

31. Ibid: Taylor. *Philadelphia in,* pp. 263-64.

32. Philadelphia. Great Central Fair For The U. S. Sanitary Commission.
    Sanitary fair sale. Thomas Birch & son. Auctioneers. Catalogue of
    valuable illustrated German books, needle work, autographs, relics,
    and curiosities, guns, etc. to be sold for the benefit of the Great
    Central fair, on Wednesday morning, Dec. Philadelphia, 1864. Pdf.
    Retrieved from the Library of Congress, www.loc.gov/item/rbpe.
    1580290a/, accessed May 22, 2017.

33. "Battle Unit Details," retrieved from National Park Service at
    www.nps.gov/civilwar, accessed June 16, 2017.

34. Reuben K. Geyer, private, age 39, mustered into service October 13,
    1864 in Philadelphia, Pennsylvania by Captain Lane. Remarks:
    Transferred to Battery C 204th Regiment P. V. [Pennsylvania
    Volunteer], January 5, 1865. It was unknown how long Reuben
    served in that position, but the 204th roster listed Reuben K as age
    thirty-nine, with a note that he transferred to the 147th Regiment,
    Company E on date unknown. Once at the 147th Regiment, with a
    slight of the hand, Reuben Geyer was erroneously listed on the roster
    as age twenty-nine; Samuel P. Bates. *History of Pennsylvania
    Volunteers, 1861-5, Vol. IV.* Harrisburg, PA: B. Singerly, State
    Printer, 1870, p. 556; National Archives and Records Administration.
    Organization Index to Pension Files of Veterans Who Served
    Between 1861 and 1900. Publication No. T289, Application No.
    1079202, Certificate No. 797694; and United States, Eleventh

Census, Special Schedule, Surviving Soldiers, Sailors, and Marines, and Widows, Etc., Supervisor's District No. 1, Enumeration District No. 365, Philadelphia, PA, June 1890, 1, From Schedule No. 1, House No. 93, Family No. 101, Line No. 8, 1647 Cadwallader. Reuben K. Geyer was listed as Private, Company E, 147 PA Infantry, living at 1647 Cadwallader Street.

35. Frank Taylor. *Philadelphia in the Civil War 1861-1865.* Philadelphia, PA: Published by the City, 1913, p. 311.

36. General Robert E. Lee surrendered to General Ulysses S. Grant at the Appomattox on April 9, 1865. Frank Taylor. *Philadelphia in the Civil War 1861-1865.* Philadelphia, PA: Published by the City, 1913, pp. 310-11; and Rudolph J. Walther. *Happenings in Ye Olde Philadelphia, 1680-1900.* Philadelphia, PA: Walther Printing House, 1925, pp. 19-130.

37. Frederick Hatch. *Protecting President Lincoln, The Security Effort, The Thwarted Plots and the Disaster at Ford's Theatre.* North Carolina: McFarland & Company, Inc., Publishers, 2011, pp. 91-117; and William H. Crook (his bodyguard). "Lincoln's Last Day," *Harper's Magazine*, Volume CXV, No. 688 (1907): pp. 519-30. It is uncertain how John Parker was even assigned to guard the president given his record as a police officer. He was brought before the police board numerous times for violations ranging from unbecoming an officer, being drunk on duty, sleeping on streetcars while at work, and visiting a brothel, among other offenses, but never suffered severe consequences or was fired. Instead, Metropolitan police assigned him to the first detail of four officers (working different shifts) to protect the president. In an unusual twist, a letter dated April 3, 1865, (signed by Mrs. Lincoln) requested Parker be assigned to that detail. He may have been kin to Mrs. Lincoln as her maiden name was Parker.

38. Osborn H. Oldroyd. *The Assassination of Abraham Lincoln, Flight, Pursuit, Capture, and Punishment of the Conspirators.* Washington DC: O. H. Oldroyd, 1901, pp. 66-91.

39. Ibid: Oldroyd. *The Assassination*, pp. 66-91.

40. Frank Taylor. *Philadelphia in the Civil War 1861-1865.* Philadelphia,

PA: Published by the City, 1913, pp. 311-12.

41. Osborn H. Oldroyd. *The Assassination of Abraham Lincoln, Flight, Pursuit, Capture, and Punishment of the Conspirators.* Washington DC: O. H. Oldroyd, 1901, pp. 111-12.

42. Ibid: Oldroyd. *The Assassination*, pp. 111-12.

43. J. R. Hawley. *The Assassination and History of the Conspiracy, A complete digest of the whole affair from its inception to its culmination, Sketches of the principal Characters, Reports of the Obsequies, etc, Fully Illustrated.* Cincinnati: J. R. Hawley & Co., 1865, pp. 112-14; Walther, *Happenings in Ye Olde,* 19-130; and Frank Taylor. Philadelphia in the Civil War 1861-1865. Philadelphia, PA: Published by the City, 1913, pp. 311-12.

44. Osborn H. Oldroyd. *The Assassination of Abraham Lincoln, Flight, Pursuit, Capture, and Punishment of the Conspirators.* Washington DC: O. H. Oldroyd, 1901, pp. 98-100.

45. In 1905, James Gibbs wrote that when the 187th Regiment arrived at Camp Cadwallader, they were not permitted to occupy soldier barracks. Instead, they were moved to a corner of the camp near the city's pest house with those who had infectious diseases, without any protection from the cold nights, except for a piece of shelter tent that they carried around with them all summer. Clothing was scant and thin, and nights were cold, but they were not allowed to have a fire to keep warm. Officers requested clothing for the men, but it was a week to ten days before they received them. *Philadelphia Inquirer*, January 23, 1865, (not January 1864 as Gibbs listed on page 8 of his book), reported filthy quarters, miserable diets, embezzlement of soldiers' money, and an utter disregard for the welfare and comfort of the men. James M. Gibbs. *History of the First Battalion Pennsylvania Six Months Volunteers and 187th Regiment Pennsylvania Volunteer Infantry.* Central Printing and Publishing House, 1905, p. 127-28; "City Intelligence: Camp Cadwalader [sic]," *Philadelphia Inquirer,* January 23, 1865, p. 8; and Frank H. Taylor. *Philadelphia in the Civil War* 1861-1865. Philadelphia, PA: Published by the City, 1913, p. 270.

46. Nearly 150 regiments, battalions, independent batteries, cavalry

troops, and detached bodies represented Philadelphia in the Civil War. Large and small employers alike were greatly impacted during the war, including M. W. Baldwin & Company, who manufactured a whopping 456 locomotives. Local merchants, too, were busy. They produced light and heavy artillery, swords and rifles as well as camp equipment, uniforms and blankets. Civil War pension files later listed Reuben K. Geyer as an invalid, meaning he was incapacitated, sick, or disabled. "From Washington," *Massachusetts Spy*, July 14, 1865, p. 4; "City Intelligence," Illustrated New Age, July 19, 1865, p. 2; Frank H. Taylor. *Philadelphia in the Civil War 1861 to 1865.* Philadelphia, PA: Dunlap Printing Company, 1913, p. 14; The Union Army. *A History of Military Affairs in the Loyal States 1861-65- Records of the Regiments in the Union Army-Cyclopedia of Battles— Memoirs of Commanders and Soldiers, Volume I.* Madison, Wisconsin: Federal Publishing Company, 1908, p. 462; Bates. *History of Pennsylvania Volunteers,* p. 556; and National Archives and Records Administration. Organization Index to Pension Files of Veterans Who Served Between 1861 and 1900. Publication No. T289, Application No. 1079202, Certificate No. 797694, December 17, 1891.

Chapter 3 - Centennial Guard

47. The Centennial Guard was organized and managed by Philadelphia Police, who provided their own police officers and detectives, which were attached to the Centennial Guard. Quote from: *Reports on the Philadelphia International Exhibition of 1876, Vol. I,* presented in both houses of Parliament by Command of Her Majesty, p. 1XX.

48. Frank Geyer began his long-standing career in law enforcement as Patrolman, formalized by Mayor William Stokley, May 6, 1876. He was immediately assigned to work in the Centennial Guard for the Centennial Exposition. The police roster at the time included twelve hundred patrolmen, twenty-five turnkeys, twenty-seven lieutenants, four captains, one fire marshal, and one chief of police. Geyer's first appointment to the Philadelphia police force: *Journal of the Select County of the City of Philadelphia, From October 6, 1887 to April 2, 1888.* Philadelphia, PA: Dunlap and Clarke Printers and Binders,

1888, p. 116; Howard O. Sprogle. *Philadelphia Police, Past and Present*. Philadelphia, PA: publisher unknown, 1887, pp. 295-96; and "Holmes' Nemesis to Leave Force," *Philadelphia Inquirer*, August 16, 1903, p. 5.

1876 World's Fair, Philadelphia: The fair had several names. Executive Order of the president of the United States referred to the World's Fair as "International Exhibition" but also recognized its official name, "The International Exhibition of Arts, Manufactures, and Products of the Soil and Mine." It was also simply called, "Centennial Exposition," held in Philadelphia's Fairmount Park, May 10 to November 10 in 1876, it was according to Library of Congress, the first World's Fair held in the United States. "Topics in Chronicling America - Philadelphia's World's Fair (Centennial International Exhibition), 1876, Library of Congress, www.loc.gov/rr/news/topics/worldsPhila.html, accessed March 8, 2017; United States, Pennsylvania Board of Centennial Managers. *Pennsylvania and the Centennial Exposition: Comprising the Preliminary and Final Reports of the Pennsylvania Board of Centennial Managers Made to the Legislature at the Sessions of 1877-8*. Pennsylvania: Gillin & Nagle, 1878, p. 221; and number of exhibitors: J. S. Ingram. *Centennial Exposition Described and Illustrated*. Philadelphia, PA: Hubbard Brothers, 1876, p. 29.

49. United States, Pennsylvania Board of Centennial Managers. *Pennsylvania and the Centennial Exposition: Comprising the Preliminary and Final Reports of the Pennsylvania Board of Centennial Managers Made to the Legislature at the Sessions of 1877-8*. Pennsylvania: Gillin & Nagle, 1878, p. 221. Pennsylvania and the Centennial Exposition: *Comprising the Preliminary and Final Reports of the Pennsylvania Board of Centennial Managers Made to the Legislature at the Sessions of 1877-8*. Pennsylvania: Gillin & Nagle, 1878, pp. 97-99. Ordinance to appoint five hundred men: *Ordinances of the City of Philadelphia from January 1 to December 31, 1876, and Opinions of the City Solicitor.* Philadelphia, PA: Dunlap & Clarke Printing Company, 1877, p. 97.

50. Samuel J. Burr, A.M. and S. De Vere Burr, et. al. *Memorial of the International Exhibition: Being a Description . . .* Hartford, CT: L.

Stebbins, 1877, p. 757.

51. United States, Pennsylvania Board of Centennial Managers. *Pennsylvania and the Centennial Exposition: Comprising the Preliminary and Final Reports of the Pennsylvania Board of Centennial Managers Made to the Legislature at the Sessions of 1877-8.* Pennsylvania: Gillin & Nagle, 1878, p. 98; and Samuel J. Burr, A. M. and S. De Vere Burr, et. al. *Memorial of the International Exhibition: Being a Description . . .* Hartford, CT: L. Stebbins, 1877, pp. 757-59.

52. Centennial Police Station 39, southwest of the Glass Factory and Station 56 1/2, located immediately north of State Avenue and the Hungarian Wine Pavilion were used as sleeping quarters for Centennial Guards, as all Guards employed for the Exposition were required to remain on site at all times, except when provided short-term passes. Station 138, at the Northeast corner of the Main Building, served a dual-purpose, with prisoner cells and barracks for Centennial Guards. The last of the stations, No. 174, was located east of the Hay Press and Agricultural Hall and also provided accommodations for the guards. United States, Pennsylvania Board of Centennial Managers. *Pennsylvania and the Centennial Exposition: Comprising the Preliminary and Final Reports of the Pennsylvania Board of Centennial Managers Made to the Legislature at the Sessions of 1877-8.* Pennsylvania: Gillin & Nagle, 1878, pp. 127-28; and James D. McCabe. *The Illustrated History of the Centennial Exposition Held in Commemoration of the One Hundredth Anniversary of American Independence.* Philadelphia, PA: The National Publishing Company, 1876, p. 620.

53. London Inspector Hagen reported on police and sanitary arrangements to Her Majesty in the Reports on the Philadelphia International Exhibition of 1876 and stated at the end of the hot weather, a week's leave of absence was provided to Centennial Guard staff, two men at a time, in order for them to visit Niagara falls. They were each given free passes by Colonel Scott, the president of the Pennsylvania Railway Company. *Reports on the Philadelphia International Exhibition of 1876, Vol. I, presented in both houses of Parliament by Command of Her Majesty,* p. 1XX;

United States, Pennsylvania Board of Centennial Managers Pennsylvania and the Centennial Exposition: *Comprising the Preliminary and Final Reports of the Pennsylvania Board of Centennial Managers Made to the Legislature at the Sessions of 1877-8.* Pennsylvania: Gillin & Nagle, 1878, p. 98; and "On the Show Grounds," *Philadelphia Times,* July 12, 1876, p. 4.

54. United States, Pennsylvania Board of Centennial Managers. *Pennsylvania and the Centennial Exposition: Comprising the Preliminary and Final Reports of the Pennsylvania Board of Centennial Managers Made to the Legislature at the Sessions of 1877-8.* Pennsylvania: Gillin & Nagle, 1878, p. 203.

55. In a Pennsylvania report made during the 1877-1878 sessions of the Legislature after the close of the Exhibition, the Board of Finance reported just under $478,000 was spent on police expenses for the Exhibition, equivalent to over $10 million in 2015. United States, Pennsylvania Board of Centennial Managers. *Pennsylvania and the Centennial Exposition: Comprising the Preliminary and Final Reports of the Pennsylvania Board of Centennial Managers Made to the Legislature at the Sessions of 1877-8.* Pennsylvania: Gillin & Nagle, 1878, pp. 93, 244.

56. United States, Pennsylvania Board of Centennial Managers. *Pennsylvania and the Centennial Exposition: Comprising the Preliminary and Final Reports of the Pennsylvania Board of Centennial Managers Made to the Legislature at the Sessions of 1877-8.* Pennsylvania: Gillin & Nagle, 1878, pp. 93, 99.

57. Police roll books, City of Philadelphia Archives; Howard O. Sprogle. *Philadelphia Police, Past and Present.* Philadelphia, PA: publisher unknown, 1887, p. 547; William S. Stokley. *Seventh Annual Message of William S. Stokley, Mayor of the City of Philadelphia: with Accompanying Documents, October 16, 1979.* Philadelphia, PA: E. C. Markley & Son Printers, 1879, pp. 842. 847, 861-62; and "Holmes' Nemesis to Leave Force," *Philadelphia Inquirer,* August 16, 1903, p. 5.

58. Samuel J. Burr, A. M. and S. De Vere Burr, et. al. *Memorial of the International Exhibition: Being a Description.* Hartford, CT: L.

Stebbins, 1877, p. 739.

Chapter 4 - Femur and Horses

59. Isaac Hays, M. D., ed. *The American Journal of the Medical Sciences.* Vol. XLI, 1861, p. 97.

60. The police chief reported 40,714 arrests in 1879. Among the arrests, 19,706 were for intoxication, 4,569 for intoxication with disorderly conduct, 2,210 for larceny, and 1,839 for assault and battery. William S. Stokley. *Eighth Annual Message of William S. Stokley, Mayor of the City of Philadelphia: with Accompanying Documents, November 4, 1880.* Philadelphia, PA: E. C. Markley & Son Printers, 1880.pp. vi-vii.

61. "Notes About Town Matters of Interest Briefly Told," *North American,* December 18, 1879, p. 1; and "A Serious Casualty," *Philadelphia Inquirer,* December 18, 1879, p. 1.

62. William S. Stokley. *Ninth Annual Message of William S. Stokley, Mayor of the City of Philadelphia: with Accompanying Documents, March 31, 1881.* Philadelphia, PA: E. C. Markley & Son Printer, 1881, pp. 427-30.

63. City of Philadelphia Archive, police roll book records entry: Geyer, F. P., badge 840, resigned Nov 2nd of '81 to go to work; William S. Stokley. *Ninth Annual Message of William S. Stokley, Mayor of the City of Philadelphia: with Accompanying Documents, March 31, 1881.* Philadelphia, PA: E. C. Markley & Son Printer, 1881, pp. 427-30; "Police Changes," *Philadelphia Inquirer,* November 17, 1881, p. 2; "City News Items," *New York Herald,* March 13, 1882; and "Redmond and Cunningham Convicted of Mail Fraud," *Philadelphia Inquirer,* May 30, 1882, p. 3.

64. City of Philadelphia Archive, police roll book records entry: Geyer, Frank P., badge 887, district 18; and William B. Smith. *The First Annual Message of William B. Smith, Mayor of Philadelphia for the Year 1884.* Philadelphia, PA: Dunlap & Clarke Printers, 1885; Charles F. Warwick. *Second Annual Message of Charles F. Warwick, Mayor of the City of Philadelphia with Annual Reports of Frank M. Riter, Director of the Department of Public Safety and Chiefs of*

Bureaus Constituting Said Department for the Year Ending December 31, 1896, Vol. II. Philadelphia, PA: Dunlap Printing Co., 1897, p. 7; and Howard O. Sprogle. *Philadelphia Police, Past and Present.* Philadelphia, PA: publisher unknown, 1887, pp. 205, 255-62.

65. The Chief of Detectives position was abolished by Councils November 1871, so Lieutenant Francis R. Kelly of the Twenty-Second District was also tasked with a dual role and given the interim title of 'Acting Chief of Detectives' until the position could be reinstated.

66. City of Philadelphia Archive, police roll book records entry: Geyer, Frank P., badge 887, District Eighteen; and William B. Smith. *The First Annual Message of William B. Smith, Mayor of Philadelphia for the Year 1884.* Philadelphia, PA: Dunlap & Clarke Printers, 1885; Charles F. Warwick. *Second Annual Message of Charles F. Warwick, Mayor of the City of Philadelphia with Annual Reports of Frank M. Riter, Director of the Department of Public Safety and Chiefs of Bureaus Constituting Said Department for the Year Ending December 31, 1896, Vol. II.* Philadelphia, PA: Dunlap Printing Co., 1897, p. 7; and Howard O. Sprogle. *Philadelphia Police, Past and Present.* Philadelphia, PA: publisher unknown, 1887, pp. 205, 255-62.

67. University of Pennsylvania, Wharton School Studies in Politics and Economics. The Government of Philadelphia; a Study in Municipal Administration. Philadelphia, PA: Wharton School of Finance and Economy, University of Pennsylvania, 1893, p. 168.

68. Tramps and vagrants at police stations: William S. Stokley. *Annual Message of William S. Stokley, Mayor of the City of Philadelphia: with Accompanying Documents, October 16, 1979.* Philadelphia, PA: E. C. Markley & Son Printers, 1879, p. 848. Dead body at police station: "A Murderers Awful Sequel," *Philadelphia Times*, February 4, 1889, p. 1.

69. Howard O. Sprogle. *Philadelphia Police, Past and Present.* Philadelphia, PA: publisher unknown, 1887, p. 238.

70. Ibid: Sprogle. *Philadelphia Police*, pp. 295-96.

71. The Episcopal Hospital is located at 100 East Lehigh Avenue and extends from the corner of Fourth Street to Leamy, which was later renamed to B Street. Report of the accident was covered in "Courage of a Policeman," *Philadelphia Inquirer*, May 31, 1886, p. 8.

72. Annual mayor's reports, years 1879 to 1903. City of Philadelphia Archives.

73. Annual mayor's reports, years 1879 to 1903. City of Philadelphia Archives.

Chapter 5 - Bullitt

74. S. Davis Page was also appointed to Governor's Commission following the Keystone Bank debacle. Quote for S. Davis Page taken from *Philadelphia Times*, March 24, 1885, p. 1.

75. The Bullitt was named after a member of the House, Mr. W. C. Bullitt. The bill was passed June 1, 1885, and was called the "Act for the Better Government of Cities of the First Class," The Act gave the mayor more power, designating him as chief executive officer, with power vested in him and departments identified as the Departments of Public Safety, Public Works, Receiver of Taxes, City Treasurer, Controller, Law, Education, and Charities and Correction, as well as the Sinking Fund Commission. Philadelphia adopted the Bullitt bill April 1887. The new Department of Public Safety remained intact for sixty-four years until it was abolished by the terms of the Philadelphia City Charter, adopted in 1951. Edward P. Allinson and Boies Penrose. *The City Government of Philadelphia.* Baltimore, Maryland: N. Murray, Johns Hopkins University, 1887, pp. 65-72; "Legends of the Bar: John Christian Bullitt," *Philadelphia Bar, Association*, www.philadelphiabar.org/page/AboutLegends? appNum=4, retrieved January 24, 2016; *Ordinances of the City of Philadelphia From January 1 to December 31, 1886, and the Opinions of the City Solicitor.* Philadelphia, PA: Dunlap & Clarke Printers, 1887, pp. 343-44; City of Philadelphia. "Public Safety, Department of." *Department of Records*, www.phila.gov/phils/docs/ inventor/ graphics/agencies/A083.htm, accessed May 16, 2016.

Mayor William S. Stokley served three terms from 1872 to 1881. Rudolph J. Walther. *Happenings in Ye Olde Philadelphia, 1680-1900,* Philadelphia, PA: Walther Printing House, 1925, pp. 19-130; and Edwin H. Fitler. *First Annual Message of Edwin H. Fitler, Mayor of the City of Philadelphia, Volume III.* Philadelphia, PA: Dunlap & Clarke Printers, 1888, p. 1.

76. Howard O. Sprogle. *Philadelphia Police, Past and Present.* Philadelphia, PA: publisher unknown, 1887, p. 255, pp. 152-53.

77. Members of the Bar. Weekly Notes of Cases Argued and Determined in the Supreme Court of Pennsylvania, the County Courts of Philadelphia, and the United States District and Circuit Courts for the Eastern District of Pennsylvania, Volume XX. Philadelphia, PA: Kay & Brother Law Booksellers, Publishers and Importers, 1888, pp. 315-16; and Herbert B. Adams, ed. *Johns Hopkins University Studies in Historical and Political Science, Volume V: Municipal Government History and Politics.* Baltimore: Johns Hopkins University, N. Murray, Publication Agent, 1887, p. 67.

78. "The Centennial Police; Ex-Mayor Stokley Remembered by the Men Who Served Under Him in 1876," *Philadelphia Times,* May 10, 1896, p. 7.

79. University of Pennsylvania, Wharton School Studies in Politics and Economics. *The Government of Philadelphia; a Study in Municipal Administration, Volume II.* Philadelphia, PA: Wharton School of Finance and Economy, University of Pennsylvania, 1893, p. 159. The Chief of Detectives office became official prior to the Bullitt Bill changes. Francis R. Kelly, Interim Chief of Detectives, was commissioned by Mayor William B. Smith to serve as Chief of Detectives January 1, 1886. Howard O. Sprogle. *Philadelphia Police, Past and Present.* Philadelphia, PA: publisher unknown, 1887, p. 255.

80. *Journal of the Select Council of the City of Philadelphia, From April 4, 1887 to September 27, 1887, Vol. 1.* Philadelphia, PA: Dunlap & Clarke, Printers and Binders, 1887, p. 24; George Barton. *The True Stories of Celebrated Crimes: Adventures of the World's Greatest Detectives.* NY: McKinlay Stone & Mackenzie, 1908, p. 109; "The

Official Ax," *Philadelphia Inquirer,* April 29, 1887, p. 4; and "Banking and Financial Items," *The Banker's Magazine and Statistical Register,* Vol. 43, (1889): p. 286.

81. R. Heber Breintnall, Adjutant-General. *Report of the Adjutant-General of the State of New Jersey for the Year Ending October 31st, 1906.* Somerville, NJ: The Unionist-Gazette Printing House, 1907, p. 149; Howard O. Sprogle. *The Philadelphia Police, Past and Present.* Philadelphia, PA: publisher unknown, 1887, pp. 226-45.

82. The Detective Department of the police force of the City of Philadelphia was first organized October 20, 1859, and reported directly to the mayor. In June 24, 1869, Mayor Fox notified Councils of the reorganization of the Detective Department. Still a department, it was placed under the authority of the chief of police. This at times caused a bit of confusion with the two 'Chief' titles —'Chief of Police 'and 'Chief of Detectives'—one was superior to the other. In 1887, following Philadelphia's adoption of the Bullitt Bill, the Detective Department was re-organized and renamed Detective Bureau. The new Bureau continued to report to the police chief, but police merged into the new Public Safety Department. Thomas Westcott. *The Official Guide Book to Philadelphia: a new handbook for strangers and citizens, with a history of the city, etc.* Philadelphia, PA: Porter and Coates, 1875, pp. 105-14; *Smith's New Guide to Philadelphia,* circa 1870. Philadelphia, PA: G. Delp, 1871, p. 16, 18; and Howard O. Sprogle. *The Philadelphia Police, Past and Present.* Philadelphia, PA: publisher unknown, 1887, pp. 117, 139, 232.

83. The Commissioners for the Erection of the New Public Buildings. *The New City Hall Philadelphia Directory of Offices Occupied; or Allotted and in Process of Completion, with Diagrams of Various Floors, and Other Miscellaneous Information Appertaining to the Building.* Philadelphia, PA: Printed for the Commissioners, 1890, pp. 14-16; "Room Directory," *City of Philadelphia Virtual Tour,* www.phila.gov/virtualch/ body_pages/room_directory.html, accessed May 20, 2017; and "The Municipality," *Philadelphia Inquirer,* May 6, 1887, p. 2.

Chapter 6 - Bizarre Story of a Cat

84. "A Child's Awful Death," *Philadelphia Times*, December 29, 1885, p. 1.

85. "A Dangerous Cat," *Philadelphia Inquirer*, December 28, 1885, p. 2.

86. William B. Smith. *Second Annual Message of William B. Smith, Mayor of Philadelphia, for the Year 1885*. Philadelphia, PA: Dunlap & Clarke Printers, 1886, p. 360; "A Child's Awful Death," *Philadelphia Times,* December 29, 1885, p. 1; and "Stating that a Cat Killed Her Baby," *New York Tribune*, December 29, 1885, p. 1.

87. "The Cat Did Not Kill the Baby," *New York Tribune*, December 30, 1885, p. 1; and "Was it a Murder?" *Philadelphia Inquirer,* December 30, 1885.

88. Ibid: "The Cat Did," p. 1; and "Was it a Murder?" *Philadelphia Inquirer,* December 30, 1885.

89. "Was it a Murder?" *Philadelphia Inquirer*, December 30, 1885.

90. "Annie Gaskins [sic], a Philadelphia Widow, Butchers Her Infant," *St. Louis Post-Dispatch,* December 29, 1885, p. 7

91. "A Child's Awful Death," *Philadelphia Times*, December 29, 1885, p. 1.

92. George W. Childs. *Public Ledger Almanac 1886*. Philadelphia, PA: Geo. W. Childs Publisher, 1886, p. 7; "Dangerous Cat," *Philadelphia Inquirer*, December 28, 1885, p. 2; "Annie Gaskins [Gaskin], a Philadelphia Widow, Butchers Her Infant," *St. Louis Post-Dispatch*, December 29, 1885, p. 7; and "Not Killed by a Cat," *Philadelphia Times*, December 30, 1885, p. 4.

93. "The Cat Did Not Kill the Baby," New York Tribune, December 30, 1885, p. 1; "Not Killed by a Cat," *Philadelphia Times*, December 30, 1885, p. 4; and "Was it a Murder?" Philadelphia Inquirer, December 30, 1885.

94. "Was it a Murder?" *Philadelphia Inquirer*, December 30, 1885. Dr. Henry F. Formad was born in Russia and came to the United States in 1875. In 1881-82 he, along with Professor H. C. Wood,

investigated the contagion of diphtheria, and was commissioned by the government to investigate an epidemic of diphtheria in Michigan that same year. He wrote numerous scholarly papers and opinions and was credited with assisting in the investigation of venom poisoning. He author the book, Comparative Studies of Mammalian Blood, With Special Reference to the Microscopical Diagnosis of Blood Stains in Criminal Cases, a hand-notated copy of which was gifted to the medical library of the University of Michigan by Dr. M. D. Ewell, from Chicago, Illinois. Dr. Formad received the appointment of Demonstrator of Morbid Anatomy and Pathological Histology and Lecturer on Experimental Pathology at the University of Pennsylvania, which he held until his June 5, 1892, death at the age of forty-five years. Sources: University of Pennsylvania Alumni and Faculty of Medicine, ed. University Medical Magazine, Volume IV., (1892), pp. 735-37; and Henry F. Formad, B.M., M.D. *Comparative Studies of Mammalian Blood, with Special Reference to the Microscopical Diagnosis of Blood Stains in Criminal Cases; with Sixteen Illustrations from Photo- Micrographs and Drawings.* Philadelphia, PA: A. L. Hummel, M. D., Publisher, 1888.

95. "Was it a Murder?" *Philadelphia Inquirer*, December 30, 1885.

96. George W. Childs. *Public Ledger Almanac 1886*. Philadelphia, PA: Geo. W. Childs Publisher, p. 7; and "A Good Place to Keep Her," *Elkhart Daily Review*, February 24, 1886, p. 1.

97. Clark Bell, Esq., Ed. *The Medico-Legal Journal*, Volume VI, (1889), pp. 433, 452-53, 535.

98. Ibid: Bell, pp. 433, 452-535.

99. Ibid: Bell, p. 433.

Chapter 7 - A Mighty Gruesome Package

100. "Wilson Confesses," *Philadelphia Inquirer*, February 24, 1887, p. 2.

101. "Dragging the Pond," *Philadelphia Times*, February 19, 1887, p. 1.

102. Silas Hibbs found the headless torso, Thursday, February 17, 1887. "Murder of the Most Foul," *Philadelphia Inquirer*, February 22, 1887, p. 1; and "Following Up a Clew [sic]," *New York Herald*,

February 20, 1887, p. 9.

103. J. H. Battle, ed. *History of Bucks County, Pennsylvania.* Philadelphia, PA: A. Warner & Co., Publishers, 1887, p. 473.

104. "The History of Bensalem," *Bensalem Historical Society*, www.bensalemhistoricalsociciety.com/history.html, accessed July 7, 2017.

105. "Murder of the Most Foul," *Philadelphia Inquirer*, February 22, 1887, p. 1; and "Following Up a Clew [sic]," *New York Herald*, February 20, 1887, p. 9.

106. "From All Parts," *Carlisle Weekly Herald,* February 24, 1887, p. 1; "Mystery Solved," *Philadelphia Inquirer,* February 23, 1887, p. 1; and "The Butchered Corpse," *Delaware Gazette and State Journal,* March 3, 1887, p. 2.

107. "Murdered and Dismembered," *New York Herald,* February 19, 1887, p. 3.

108. "Murder of the Most Foul," *Philadelphia Inquirer,* February 22, 1887, p. 1; "Following Up a Clew [sic]," *New York Herald*, February 20, 1887, p. 9; and "Dragging the Pond," *Philadelphia Times*, February 19, 1887, p. 1.

109. "Following Up a Clew [sic]," *New York Herald*, February 20, 1887, p. 9; and "Gaines Inquest Mrs. Tabbs, Wilson Held," *Philadelphia Inquirer*, March 3, 1887, p. 2.

110. "Following Up a Clew [sic]," *New York Herald*, February 20, 1887, p. 9; and "Murdered and Dismembered," *New York Herald*, February 19, 1887, p. 3; and Charles F. Warwick. *Second Annual Message of Charles F. Warwick, Mayor of the City of Philadelphia with Annual Reports of Frank M. Riter, Director of the Department of Public Safety and Chiefs of Bureaus Constituting Said Department for the Year Ending December 31, 1896, Vol. II.* Philadelphia, PA: Dunlap Printing Co., 1897, p. 73.

111. "A Mad Policeman," *Philadelphia Times*, February 20, 1887, p. 1; and Howard O. Sprogle. *The Philadelphia Police, Past and*

Present. Philadelphia, PA: publisher unknown, 1887, p. 225.

112. John MacIntire was fired from the fire department prior to his employment with police. "A Mad Policeman," *Philadelphia Times*, February 20, 1887, p. 1.

113. "Fired the Whole Armory," *New York Times,* February 20, 1887, p. 10.

114. Ibid: "Fired the," p. 10.

115. Author Howard O. Sprogle wrote that the Sunday Liquor Law went into effect during Mayor Robert T. Conrad's administration [June 13, 1854 to May 13, 1856] and he directed his police officers to enter saloons and drink liquor, in order that they might not lack evidence to maintain the prosecutions. Howard O. Sprogle. *Philadelphia Police, Past and Present.* Philadelphia, PA: publisher unknown, 1887, pp. 103-04. Grand jury report: "Grand Jury Suggestions," *Philadelphia Inquirer,* July 2, 1887, p. 3; "The Grand Jury's Report," *Philadelphia Times*, July 30, 1887, p. 2; and "Sunday Liquor Law," *Philadelphia Inquirer*, July 30, 1887, p. 2.

116. Mrs. Cannon told detectives her name was Mary Tabbs. Mrs. Tabbs most likely was going by her middle name as her signature on her booking photo was Hannah M. Tabbs. See Hannah Mary Tabbs booking photo.

117. "The Woman Found," *Philadelphia Times*, February 22, 1887, p. 1.

118. "A Murder Mystery," *Delaware Gazette and State Journal*, February 24, 1887, p. 3.

119. "Gaines Inquest Mrs. Tabbs, Wilson Held," *Philadelphia Inquirer*, March 3, 1887, p. 2.

120. "The Woman Found," *Philadelphia Times*, February 22, 1887, p. 1.

121. Ibid: "The Woman," p. 1.

122. Ibid: "The Woman," p. 1.

123. Ibid: "The Woman," p. 1.

124. "Murder Confessed," *Philadelphia Times*, February 23, 1887, p. 1.

125. Mrs. Tabbs confession and quotes: "The Mystery Solved," *Philadelphia Inquirer*, February 23, 1887, p. 1; and "Murder Confessed," *Philadelphia Times*, February 23, 1887, p. 1.

126. Ibid: "The Mystery," p. 1; and "Murder," p. 1.

127. Mrs. Tabbs also testified at trial about her black eye, stating she injured it in a fall on the curb stone on Seventeenth Street, above Spruce the day after New Year's, and she had a black eye when she gave items to Hattie Armstrong to take to the pawn shop. Miss Hattie Armstrong testified at trial that when she asked Mrs. Tabbs what was the matter with her eye, she told Miss Armstrong that she had been hanging pictures and standing on a box, and the box having upset, she had struck her eye on a bed post. "A Murder Mystery," *Delaware Gazette and State Journal*, February 24, 1887, p. 3; and "The Gain's Murder," *Philadelphia Inquirer*, June 2, 1887, p. 3.

128. "The Mystery Solved," *Philadelphia Inquirer*, February 23, 1887, p. 1.

129. "A Partial Confession," *Delaware Gazette and State Journal*, March 3, 1887, p. 2; and "Wake Gains Murder," *Philadelphia Inquirer*, February 26, 1887, p. 2.

130. "Telltale Blood Stains," *New York Herald*, February 25, 1887, p. 5.

131. "A Partial Confession," *Delaware Gazette and State Journal*, March 3, 1887, p. 2.

132. "The Mystery Solved," *Philadelphia Inquirer*, February 23, 1887, p. 1.

133. "Gaines Body Disinterred," *Philadelphia Times*, February 24, 1887, p. 1.

134. "Eddington's Gory Enigma," *New York Herald*, February 22, 1887, p. 7; "Mary Tabbs's Confession," *New York Times*, February 23, 1887; "Gains Butchery," *Philadelphia Inquirer*, March 1, 1887, p. 2; and "Murder of the Most Foul," *Philadelphia Inquirer*, February

22, 1887, p. 1.

135. "Gains Butchery," *Philadelphia Inquirer*, March 1, 1887, p. 2.

136. "Gains Inquest," *Philadelphia Inquirer*, March 3, 1887, p. 2.

137. "Ghastly Discovery," *Philadelphia Inquirer,* March 12, 1887, p. 3; and "The Gains [sic] Case, *Philadelphia Inquirer*, March 15, 1887, p. 3.

138. "Wake Gains Murder," *Philadelphia Times,* June 1, 1887, p. 1; and "The Gains Murder," *Philadelphia Inquirer,* June 1, 1887, p. 3.

139. Ibid: "Wake Gains," p. 1; and "The Gains," p. 3.

140. "Dismembered While Living," *New York Herald,* June 2, 1887, p. 1

141. Ibid: "Dismembered," p. 1; "The Gains Murder," *Philadelphia Inquirer,* June 2, 1887, p. 3; and "The Gains Murder Trial," *Philadelphia Times*, June 2, 1887, p. 1.

142. "The Gains Murder," *Philadelphia Inquirer,* June 2, 1887, p. 3.

143. Ibid: "The Gains," p. 1.

144. Information about the trial and quotes: "An Alibi for Wilson," *Philadelphia Inquirer,* June 3, 1887, p. 3.

145. Special Officer Tate testimony: "An Alibi for Wilson," *Philadelphia Inquirer,* June 3, 1887, p. 3.

146. "George Wilson's Alibi," *Philadelphia Times,* June 3, 1887, p. 1.

147. "Dismembered While Living," *New York Herald,* June 2, 1887.

148. "Murderer Wilson Guilty," *Philadelphia Times*, June 5, 1887, p. 1; and "Wilson Condemned," *Philadelphia Times*, June 5, 1887, p. 3.

149. Ibid: "Murderer Wilson," p. 1; and "Wilson," p. 3.

150. Ibid: "Murderer Wilson," p. 1; and "Wilson," p. 3.

151. Philadelphia Record. *The Record Almanac, 1885, Illustrated.* Philadelphia, PA: The Philadelphia Record, 1885, p. 93; and "Wilson Cheats the Gallows," *New York Herald,* July 2, 1887, p.

10.

152. "She Helped to Kill Wakefield Gaines," *New York Tribune*, September 29, 1887, p. 3.

153. "Telltale Blood Stains," *New York Herald,* February 25, 1887, p. 5.

154. "Wilson Condemned," *Philadelphia Inquirer,* June 6, 1887, p. 3; and "Defense of Wilson," *Philadelphia Inquirer,* June 4, 1887, p. 3.

155. *Journal of Select Council of the City of Philadelphia, From April 4, 1887 to September 27, 1887, Volume 1.* (Philadelphia, PA: Dunlap & Clarke Printers, 1887), p. 5; "The Municipality. Mayor Fitler's Administration Gets Under Way," *Philadelphia Inquirer*, April 6, 1887, p. 2.

156. Ibid: *Journal of,* p. 24; "The Official Axe, Ex-Fire Marshal Wood to Supersede Chief of Detectives Kelly," *Philadelphia Inquirer*, April 29, 1887, p. 4.

157. "Guardianship of the Banks. Ex-Chief of Detectives Kelly Makes a Change for the Better," *Philadelphia Inquirer,* May 13, 1887, p. 2. Ex-Chief Kelly testimony at Wilson's trial: "Defense of Wilson," *Philadelphia Inquirer,* June 4, 1887, p. 3.

158. Geyer promoted to Detective on January 7, 1888, formalized by Mayor Fitler at the January 19, 1888 Select Council meeting. *Journal of Select Council of the City of Philadelphia, From October 6, 1887, to April 2, 1888.* (Philadelphia, PA: Dunlap & Clarke Printers, 1888), p. 116.

159. Author's analysis of Geyer's arrests from annual mayor's reports. City of Philadelphia Archives; and Howard O. Sprogle. Philadelphia *Police, Past and Present.* Philadelphia, PA: publisher unknown, 1887, pp. 295-96.

Chapter 8 - Modern Borgia

160. "Her Defense Insanity," *Philadelphia Inquirer,* November 28, 1888, p3.

161. "Monster or Maniac," *New York Herald*, June 16, 1888, p. 2.

162. "Modern Borgia," *Philadelphia Inquirer,* June 14, 1888, p. 2.

163. Ibid: "Modern," p. 2.

164. "Appalling Revelation," *Philadelphia Inquirer*, June 13, 1888, p. 1.

165. "Modern Borgia," *Philadelphia Inquirer,* June 14, 1888, p. 2.

166. R. N. Ratnaike, Associate Professor of Medicine, University of Adelaide. "Acute and Chronic Arsenic Toxicity," *US National Library of Medicine, National Institutes of Health*, (2009).

167. The public bantering between the two City of Philadelphia department staff, Chief of Detectives, Wood, and Coroner Ashbridge was reported in: "Modern Borgia," *Philadelphia Inquirer,* June 14, 1888, p. 2.

168. Mrs. Whiteling's confession: "Appalling Revelation," *Philadelphia Inquirer,* June 13, 1888, p. 1; and "A Terrible Confession," *Alexandria Gazette,* June 13, 1888, p. 1.

169. "The Triple Tragedy," *Philadelphia Inquirer,* June 6, 1888, p. 2.

170. Ibid: "The Triple," p. 2.

171. Ibid: "The Triple," p. 2.

172. "Her Defense Insanity," *Philadelphia Inquirer,* November 28, 1888, p. 3; and "A Woman Executed," *Wheeling Intelligent,* June 26, 1889, p. 1.

173. Ibid: "Her Defense," p. 3; and "A Woman," p. 1.

174. "Mrs. Whiteling's Fate," *Philadelphia Inquirer,* June 26, 1889, p. 1.

175. City of Philadelphia Archives, List of Executions book, 1839-1916; *The Philadelphia Record Almanac.* Philadelphia, PA: The Philadelphia Record, 1890, p. 93; and "Mrs. Whiteling's Fate," *Philadelphia Inquirer,* June 26, 1889, p. 1.

176. "A Woman Executed," *Wheeling Intelligent,* June 26, 1889, p. 1; and "The Brains of Mrs. Whiteling, *Philadelphia Inquirer,* June 26, 1889, p. 2.

177. Ibid: "A Woman," p. 1; "The Brains," p. 2; and relocation of graves:

Chester County Historical Society.

178. John B. Lewis, M. D. and Charles C. Bombaugh, AM, MD. *Strategems and Conspiracies to Defraud Life Insurance Companies; An Authentic Record of Remarkable Cases.* Baltimore, MD: James H. McClellan, Publisher, 1896, pp. 492-93.

179. "Modern Borgia," *Philadelphia Inquirer*, June 14, 1888, p. 2.

180. "The Child Poisoner," *Philadelphia Inquirer,* June 15, 1888, p. 2.

Chapter 9 - White Chapel Row

181. "A Fiends Confession," *Philadelphia Inquirer,* January 1, 1889, p. 1.

182. Ibid: "A Fiends," pp. 1-2.

183. "A Horrible Butchery," *Philadelphia Inquirer,* December 27, 1888, p. 1; "Ghastly Find," *Reading Times,* December 27, 1888, p. 1; and "Murdered and Mutilated," *New York Herald,* December 27, 1888, p. 7.

184. "Ghastly Find," *Harrisburg Daily Independent,* December 27, 1888, p. 1; and "Carved into Pieces," *Evening Leader Wilkes-Barre,* December 27, 1888, p. 1.

185. "A Horrible Butchery," *Philadelphia Inquirer,* December 27, 1888, p. 1.

186. "Ghastly Find," *Harrisburg Daily Independent,* December 27, 1888, p. 1.

187. Ibid: "Ghastly," p. 1; "Carved into Pieces," *Evening Leader Wilkes-Barre,* December 27, 1888, p. 1; and "A Horrible Butchery," *Philadelphia Inquirer,* December 27, 1888, p. 1.

188. "A Horrible Butchery," *Philadelphia Inquirer,* December 27, 1888, p. 1; "Ghastly Find," *Reading Times,* December 27, 1888, p. 1; and "Murdered and Mutilated," *New York Herald,* December 27, 1888, p. 7.

189. "Carved into Pieces," *Evening Leader Wilkes-Barre,* December 27, 1888, p. 1; "A Horrible Butchery," *Philadelphia Inquirer,* ˍ

December 27, 1888, p. 1; and "The Engleside Mystery," *Philadelphia Times,* December 28, 1888, p. 1.

190. Ibid: "Carved," p. 1; and "A Horrible," p. 1.

191. "Ghastly Find," *Harrisburg Daily Independent,* December 27, 1888, p. 1

192. "The Engleside Mystery," *Philadelphia Times,* December 28, 1888, p. 1.

193. "Is it Kruetzman," *Philadelphia Times,* December 30, 1888, p. 2.

194. Newspapers frequently misspelled Jacob's last name. The City of Philadelphia's official Book of Executions and Return of a Death records both spell Jacob's last name 'Schoop.'

195. "Park Mystery Solved," *Philadelphia Inquirer,* December 31, 1888, p. 1; and "Schropp [Schoop] in Prison," *Philadelphia Times,* January 1, 1889, p. 1.

196. "A Fiends Confession," *Philadelphia Inquirer,* January 1, 1889, pp. 1-2.

197. George W. Childs. *Public Ledger 1890 Almanac.* Philadelphia, PA: Collins Printing House, 1890, p. 19; and "Foully Slain for $80," *Daily Inter Ocean,* January 1, 1889, p. 5.

198. "A Fiends Confession," *Philadelphia Inquirer,* January 1, 1889, pp. 1-2.

199. "Schropp [Schoop] in Prison," *Philadelphia Times,* January 1, 1889, p. 1.

200. "A Fiends Confession," *Philadelphia Inquirer,* January 1, 1889, pp. 1-2.

201. "Schropp [Schoop] in Prison," *Philadelphia Times,* January 1, 1889, p. 1.

202. "Susan Schropp's [sic] Story," *Philadelphia Times,* January 3, 1889, p. 1.

203. "A Fiends Confession," *Philadelphia Inquirer,* January 1, 1889, pp.

1-2.

204. "The Murder Rehearsed," *Philadelphia Inquirer,* January 9, 1889, p. 3.

205. "In the First Degree," *Philadelphia Inquirer,* February 22, 1889, p. 2.

206. Clark Bell, Esq., ed, et. al. "Editorial: The Case of Mrs. Whiteling [compares Whiteling to Mrs. Schoop]," *The Medico-Legal Journal,* Volume VII, (1889), pp. 289-90; George W. Childs. *Public Ledger 1890 Almanac.* Philadelphia, PA: Collins Printing House, 1890, p. 19; and "In the First Degree," *Philadelphia Inquirer,* February 22, 1889, p. 2.

207. "The Double Hanging," *Philadelphia Times,* February 21, 1890, p. 3.

Chapter 10 - Send Flowers to My Funeral

208. "A Double Life Tragically Ended," *New York Herald,* February 4, 1889, p. 10.

209. "The Murder Mystery," *Bridgeton Evening News,* February 5, 1889, p. 4.

210. "A Remorseless Villain," *Philadelphia Inquirer,* February 4, 1889, p. 1.

211. Ibid: "A Remorseless," p. 1.

212. "A Double Life Tragically Ended," *New York Herald,* February 4, 1889, p. 10.

213. Ibid: "A Double," p. 10.

214. Ibid: "A Double," p. 10; and "The Murder Mystery," *Bridgeton Evening News,* February 5, 1889, p. 4.

215. The New York Herald reported no gun powder marks on her face and therefore it was concluded that the pistol had been fired from a distance; however, they received information second hand by telegraph for the article. The Philadelphia Inquirer reporter was on site. "A Remorseless Villain," *Philadelphia Inquirer,* February 4,

1889, p. 1; and "A Double Life Tragically Ended," *New York Herald,* February 4, 1889, p. 10.

216. "A Murderers Awful Sequel," *Philadelphia Times,* February 4, 1889, p. 1.

217. "A Remorseless Villain," *Philadelphia Inquirer,* February 4, 1889, p. 1.

218. "A Double Life Tragically Ended," *New York Herald,* February 4, 1889, p. 10.

219. "A Remorseless Villain," *Philadelphia Inquirer,* February 4, 1889, p. 1; and "A Double Life Tragically Ended," *New York Herald,* February 4, 1889, p. 10.

220. "Light on the Tragedies," *Philadelphia Inquirer,* February 6, 1889, p. 2; and "A Remorseless Villain," *Philadelphia Inquirer,* February 4, 1889, p. 1.

221. Ibid: "Light on," p. 2.

222. "A Remorseless Villain," *Philadelphia Inquirer,* February 4, 1889, p. 1.

223. Ibid: "A Remorseless," p. 1.

224. "Light on the Tragedies," *Philadelphia Inquirer,* February 6, 1889, p. 2.

225. Ibid: "Light on," p. 2.

226. "The Curtain Falls," *Philadelphia Inquirer,* February 7, 1889, p. 2; and "Two Funerals in Kensington," *Philadelphia Times,* February 7, 1889, p. 4.

227. "Light on the Tragedies," *Philadelphia Inquirer,* February 6, 1889, p. 2; "The Kensington Tragedy," *Philadelphia Times,* February 5, 1889, p. 1; and "A Murderers Awful Sequel," *Philadelphia Times,* February 4, 1889, p. 1.

228. "Emma Berger's Mind Impaired," *Philadelphia Inquirer,* February 14, 1889, p. 3; and "Married," *Philadelphia Inquirer,* September

21, 1900, p. 14.

229. "Henry Klaus Obituary," *Philadelphia Inquirer,* February 24, 1909,
     p. 15; Return of a Death in the City of Philadelphia, Physician's
     Certificate for Antoinie Klaus, age sixty-four, died on April 26,
     1905, buried at Greenmount Cemeterey, buried from 1637 North
     Second Street, Philadelphia; and Return of a Death in the City of
     Philadelphia, Coroner's Certificate, Anna Klaus, nineteen-years-
     old, date of death February 2, 1889, home address: 1637 North
     Second Street, Philadelphia, cause of death: gunshot wound
     (homicide), signed S. H. Ashbridge, buried at Greenmount.

230. Geyer interview, reporter quote, and quote from Mrs. Kaiser's
     brother: "They Fear Light," *Cincinnati Enquirer,* January 28, 1894,
     p. 17.

231. "Accident Helps a Detective," *Evening Star Washington DC,* March
     12, 1889, p. 8.

232. Ibid: "Accident Helps," p. 8.

Chapter 11 - Secret Search

233. "Geyer's Absence Still a Mystery," *Philadelphia Inquirer,* August
     28, 1892, p. 2.

234. "The Keystone Bank Wreck," *The Illustrated American,* Volume
     VII, No. 71, (1891), pp. 247-50; and "Long Chase for a Culprit,"
     Washington Times, November 13, 1898, p. 5.

235. *Journal of the Common Council of the City of Philadelphia, From
     April 6, 1891 to September 24, 1891, Vol. I.* Philadelphia, PA:
     George F. Lasher, Printer, 1891, p. 143; and "Long Chase for a
     Culprit," *Washington Times,* November 13, 1898, p. 5.

236. "Long Chase for a Culprit," *Washington Times,* November 13,
     1898, p. 5.

237. *Annual Report of the Supervising Surgeon General of the Marine
     Hospital Service of the United States for the Fiscal Year 1898.*
     Washington: Government Printing Office, 1899, p. 581.

238. "Long Chase for a Culprit," *Washington Times,* November 13,

1898, 5.

239. "Geyer's Absence Sill a Mystery," *Philadelphia Inquirer,* August 28, 1892, p. 2.

240. "Long Chase for a Culprit," *Washington Times,* November 13, 1898, p. 5.

241. *Abstract of Sanitary Reports, Vol. VII, No. 3.* Washington, D. C., January 15, 1892, p. 32.; and "All the Dramas of Real Life Eclipsed By the Return of Gideon Marsh," *New York Herald,* November 13, 1898, pp. 1-2.

242. "Long Chase for a Culprit," *Washington Times,* November 13, 1898, p. 5; "Geyer's Absence Sill a Mystery," *Philadelphia Inquirer*, August 28, 1892, p. 2; and "All the Dramas of Real Life Eclipsed By the Return of Gideon Marsh," *New York Herald,* November 13, 1898, pp. 1-2.

243. "Long Chase for a Culprit," *Washington Times,* November 13, 1898, p. 5.

244. Ibid: "Long Chase," p. 5.

245. "Geyer's Absence Sill a Mystery," *Philadelphia Inquirer,* August 28, 1892, p. 2.

246. Ibid: "Geyer's Absence," p. 2.

247. "Long Chase for a Culprit," *Washington Times,* November 13, 1898, p. 5; "All the Dramas of Real Life Eclipsed By the Return of Gideon Marsh," *New York Herald,* November 13, 1898, pp. 1-2; and "Detective Geyer Returns," *Philadelphia Times,* September 16, 1892, p. 5.

248. "A Speech Brings Him Back; Wanamaker Seeks Vindication in a Bank Wrecker's Surrender," *Kansas City Star,* November 11, 1898, p. 5.

249. "All the Dramas of Real Life Eclipsed By the Return of Gideon Marsh," *New York Herald,* November 13, 1898, pp. 1-2.

250. George W. Childs. *Public Ledger 1887 Almanac.* Philadelphia, PA:

Geo. W. Childs Publisher, 1900, p. 41; *Dickerman's United States Treasury Counterfeit Detector and Banker's Merchants Journal,* Volume 20, Number 1, (1903), p. 11; "City Affairs; The Return of Gideon W. Marsh," *City and State; Commonwealth Above Party,* Volume V, Number 19, (1898), p. 1; "All the Dramas of Real Life Eclipsed By the Return of Gideon Marsh," *New York Herald,* November 13, 1898, pp. 1-2; and "A Sentence Commuted; President Exercises Clemency in the Case of Gideon Marsh," *Los Angeles Herald,* December 10, 1902, p. 1.

251. "Gideon W. Marsh Free; President of the Defunct Keystone Bank Leaves Prison," *The Sun,* December 25, 1902, p. 2.

252. "The Keystone Bank Wreck," *The Illustrated American.* Volume VII, No. 71, (1891), pp. 247-50.

Chapter 12 - Etched in Time

253. "Schooley a Suicide," *Philadelphia Times,* May 12, 1892, p. 1.

254. "Tragedy at City Hall," *Philadelphia Inquirer,* May 12, 1892, p. 1; and "Captain Schooley Commits Suicide," *Philadelphia Inquirer,* May 12, 1892, p. 1.

255. The Philadelphia Record Almanac, The Record Publishing Company, 1893; 94; "Captain Schooley Commits Suicide," *Philadelphia Inquirer,* May 12, 1892, p. 1; and "Tragedy at City Hall," *Philadelphia Inquirer,* May 12, 1892, p. 1.

256. Stokley, *William S. Third Annual Message of William S. Stokley, Mayor of the City of Philadelphia, with Accompanying Documents, June 24th, 1875.* Philadelphia, PA: E. C. Markley & Son Printers, 1875, p. 631.

257. Schooley was dismissed by Mayor Smith November 6, 1885, for ignoring gambling within his district. It was officially announced to Philadelphia Select Council via the *Journal of the Select Council of the City of Philadelphia, From October 1, 1885 to April 1, 1886.* Philadelphia, PA: Dunlap & Clarke Printers, 1886, p. 113. November 1885 dismissal: "Police Officers Dismissed," *Philadelphia Inquirer,* November 7, 1885, p. 1. Public Safety Director, ex-Mayor W. S. Stokley, with Mayor Edwin H. Fitler's

approval, re-hired Schooley and appointed him to captain. The appointment was announced to Select Council April 21, 1887, via the *Journal of the Select Council of the City of Philadelphia, From April 4, 1887 to September 27, 1887, Vol. 1.* Philadelphia, PA: Dunlap & Clarke Printers, 1887, p. 11. "Captain Schooley Commits Suicide," *Philadelphia Inquirer,* May 12, 1892, p. 1.

258. "The Schooley-Park Feud," *Philadelphia Inquirer,* November 1, 1889, p. 5.

259. "Political Sluggers," *New York Herald,* October 27, 1889, 1; "Captain Schooley to be Tried," *Philadelphia Inquirer,* November 9, 1889; and "The Schooley-Park Feud," *Philadelphia Inquirer,* November 1, 1889, p. 5.

260. "The Schooley-Park Feud," *Philadelphia Inquirer,* November 1, 1889, p. 5.

261. "Death from the Grip," *Philadelphia Inquirer,* January 3, 1890; and "Captain Schooley Commits Suicide," *Philadelphia Inquirer,* May 12, 1892, p. 1.

262. "A Courageous Officer," *Philadelphia Times*, May 12, 1892, p. 1 and "Linden is Now Superintendent," *Philadelphia Inquirer*, January 3, 1892, p. 6.

263. "Captain Schooley's Death," *Philadelphia Inquirer*, May 13, 1892, p. 1.

264. "A Courageous Officer," *Philadelphia Times*, May 12, 1892, p. 1.

265. "Captain Schooley Buried," *Philadelphia Inquirer*, May 15, 1892, p. 5. William Burns Smith: see Friends of Mount Moriah Cemetery.

Chapter 13 - Where Are You?

266. Commonwealth of Pennsylvania. *Journal of the House of Representatives of the Commonwealth of Pennsylvania for the Session Begun at Harrisburg on the Seventh Day of January 1913, Part I.* Harrisburg, PA, 1914, pp. 312-14.

267. Johanna Logue was last seen February 22, 1879. "The Skeleton that

of Johanna Logue," *Philadelphia Inquirer*, October 18, 1893, p. 1; "Her Skeleton Found after Fourteen Years," October 18, 1893, p. 1; and "Cutaiar is Responsible," *Philadelphia Inquirer*, p. 1.

268. "Her Skeleton Found after Fourteen Years," October 18, 1893, p. 1; "The Logue Mystery Now Fully Solved," *Philadelphia Inquirer*, April 29, 1895, p. 1; and "Another Murder Case," *Philadelphia Inquirer*, May 19, 1896, p. 3.

269. "Old Crime Recalled," *Indianapolis Journal*, April 29, 1895, p. 1; "More Evidence of the Murder," *Philadelphia Inquirer*, p. 2; and "The Logue Mystery Now Fully Solved," Philadelphia Inquirer, April 29, 1895, p. 1.

270. "The Logue Mystery Now Fully Solved," *Philadelphia Inquirer*, April 29, 1895, p. 1.

271. Ibid: "The Logue," p. 1.

272. Ibid: "The Logue," p. 1.

273. Ibid: "The Logue," p. 1.

274. Ibid: "The Logue," p. 1.

275. Ibid: "The Logue," p. 1.

276. "Cutaiar is Responsible," *Philadelphia Inquirer*, May 2, 1895, p. 1 (includes quotes within the paragraphs below).

277. Ibid: "Cutaiar is," p. 1.

278. Ibid: "Cutaiar is," p. 1.

279. Ibid: "Cutaiar is," p. 1.

280. Ibid: "Cutaiar is," p. 1.

281. "Fighting for a Life," *Philadelphia Inquirer*, May 28, 1896, p. 4.

282. Ibid: "Fighting for," p. 4.

283. "Cutaiar is Guilty," *Philadelphia Inquirer*, May 30, 1896, p. 1.

284. Ibid: "Cutaiar is," p. 1.

285. "Jimmy Logue is Free," *Philadelphia Inquirer*, September 12, 1896, p. 3.

286. The Almshouse was renamed Philadelphia General Hospital in 1919. "Ill-Gotten Wealth Has Taken Wings," *Philadelphia Inquirer*, July 20, 1899, p. 1; and Return of Death in the Philadelphia Hospital, Physician's and Undertaker's Certificates, No. 7823, James Logue, October 4, 1899.

287. "Wife at His Feet," *Philadelphia Inquirer*, October 13, 1899, p. 10.

288. Samuel Whitaker Pennypacker, Governor of Pennsylvania 1903-1907. *The Autobiography of a Pennsylvanian.* Philadelphia, PA: The John C. Winston Company, 1918, pp. 330-33; "Doomed to Die, One Fights for Life," *Philadelphia Inquirer,* June 24, 1896, p. 1; and "Cutaiar's Appeal Signed by Logue," *Philadelphia Inquirer*, January 4, 1897, p. 6.

289. "Young Cutaiar Granted Pardon," *Patriot*, December 1903, p. 2; and *Journal of the House of Representatives of the Commonwealth of Pennsylvania for the Session Begun at Harrisburg on the Seventh Day of January, 1913, Part I.* Harrisburg, PA: Press of the Telegraph Printing Company, 1914, pp. 312-14.

290. "One Pardon Approved," *Patriot*, September 24, 1912; Return of Death in the Philadelphia Almshouse and Hospital, Physician's and Undertaker's Certificates, No. 20961, Alphonso Cutaiar, April 2, 1900; United States Census, Thirteenth, 1910, Department of Commerce and Labor Bureau of the Census, Inmate at Eastern State Penitentiary, Line No. 20; and United States Census, Fourteenth, 1920, Department of Commerce, Bureau of the Census, Philadelphia, Pennsylvania, Ward Thirty-four, January 16, 1920, Line No's. 25-32.

291. *District Attorney Graham letter: Journal of the House of Representatives of the Commonwealth of Pennsylvania for the Session Begun at Harrisburg on the Seventh Day of January 1913, Part I.* Harrisburg, PA: The Telegraph Printing Company, 1914, pp. 312-14.

Chapter 14 - Two Enemies

292. Frank P. Geyer. *The Holmes-Pitezel case; a history of the greatest crime of the century and of the search for the missing Pitezel children.* Philadelphia, PA: Publishers' Union, 1896, pp. 53-54.

293. City of Philadelphia Department of Records letter, October 16, 2006; *Philadelphia Inquirer*, May 30, 1882, p. 3.

294. Eugene Talbot, S., MD, DDS. "H. H. Holmes," *Journal of the American Medical Association*, Vol. XXVII, (1896), p. 254.

Chapter 15 - Suspicions Intensify

295. Frank P. Geyer. *The Holmes-Pitezel case; a history of the greatest crime of the century and of the search for the missing Pitezel children.* Philadelphia, PA: Publishers' Union, 1896, pp. 173-74.

296. Ibid: Geyer. *The Holmes-Pitezel,* pp. 143-44; and "The Holmes Case," *Decatur Daily Republican*, August 3, 1895, p. 6.

297. Geyer interview and quotes are from the Evening News trial coverage. "No Delay," *Evening News*, November 1, 1895, p. 25.

298. "No Delay," *Evening News*, November 1, 1895, p. 25.

299. Frank P. Geyer. *The Holmes-Pitezel case; a history of the greatest crime of the century and of the search for the missing Pitezel children.* Philadelphia, PA: Publishers' Union, 1896, p. 161.

Chapter 16 - Sweet Innocence

300. Frank P. Geyer. *The Holmes-Pitezel case; a history of the greatest crime of the century and of the search for the missing Pitezel children.* Philadelphia, PA: Publishers' Union, 1896, p. 231.

301. Ibid: Geyer. *The Holmes-Pitezel*, pp. 173-76.

302. Ibid: Geyer. *The Holmes-Pitezel*, pp. 183-91.

303. Ibid: Geyer. *The Holmes-Pitezel*, pp. 196-97.

304. Ibid: Geyer. *The Holmes-Pitezel*, pp. 198-201.

305. Ibid: Geyer. *The Holmes-Pitezel*, p. 213.

306. Ibid: Geyer. *The Holmes-Pitezel*, pp. 223-28.

307. Ibid: Geyer. *The Holmes-Pitezel*, pp. 231-32; "Holmes Planned Murder," *New York Times*, July 17, 1895, p. 1; and "Murdered the Children," *Philadelphia Inquirer*, July 16, 1895, pp. 1-2.

308. "Detective Geyer Home," *Philadelphia Inquirer*, August 4, 1895, p. 1.

309. Frank P. Geyer. *The Holmes-Pitezel case; a history of the greatest crime of the century and of the search for the missing Pitezel children*. Philadelphia, PA: Publishers' Union, 1896, p. 231.

310. Ibid: Geyer. *The Holmes-Pitezel*, p. 232.

311. Ibid: Geyer. *The Holmes-Pitezel*, pp. 233-48; and "Murdered the Children," *Philadelphia Inquirer*, July 16, 1895, pp. 1-2.

312. Ibid: Geyer. *The Holmes-Pitezel*, p. 233.

313. Ibid: Geyer. *The Holmes-Pitezel*, pp. 233-34.

314. Ibid: Geyer. *The Holmes-Pitezel*, p. 234.

315. Ibid: Geyer. *The Holmes-Pitezel*, pp. 238-41.

316. Ibid: Geyer. *The Holmes-Pitezel*, pp. 241-42.

317. Ibid: Geyer. *The Holmes-Pitezel*, p. 242.

318. Ibid: Geyer. *The Holmes-Pitezel*, p. 243.

319. Ibid: Geyer. *The Holmes-Pitezel*, p. 243.

320. "Pitezel Children Post Mortem," *Buffalo Evening News,* July 19, 1895, p. 1.

321. "Mrs. Pietzel [sic] in Toronto," *The Brooklyn Daily Eagle*, July 19, 1895, p. 12.

322. Geyer quotes (unless otherwise noted) are from: Frank P. Geyer. *The Holmes-Pitezel case; a history of the greatest crime of the century and of the search for the missing Pitezel children.* Philadelphia, PA: Publishers' Union, 1896, pp. 243-52.

323. Ibid: Geyer. *The Holmes-Pitezel,* pp. 243-52.

324. "Detective Geyer Home," *Philadelphia Inquirer*, August 4, 1895, p. 1; and "Pitezel Children are Buried," Chicago Tribune, July 21, 1895, p. 2.

325. "The Holmes Case," *Decatur Daily Republican*, August 3, 1895, p. 6.

Chapter 17 - Little Howard

326. Frank P. Geyer. *The Holmes-Pitezel case; a history of the greatest crime of the century and of the search for the missing Pitezel children.* Philadelphia, PA: Publishers' Union, 1896, p. 287.

327. Ibid: Geyer. *The Holmes-Pitezel*, pp. 256-62.

328. Quotes about Hatch: "Two Letters From Holmes," *Indianapolis News*, July 29, 1895, p. 1.

329. Ibid: "Two Letters," p. 1.

330. "Holmes Has Aid," *Philadelphia Inquirer*, July 18, 1895, p. 3.

331. Ibid: "Holmes Has," p. 3.

332. Frank P. Geyer. *The Holmes-Pitezel case; a history of the greatest crime of the century and of the search for the missing Pitezel children.* Philadelphia, PA: Publishers' Union, 1896, pp. 269-79.

333. "Quinlan Tells All," *Inter Ocean*, August 3, 1895, p. 2.

334. "Detective Geyer Home," *Philadelphia Inquirer,* August 4, 1895, p. 1.

335. Frank P. Geyer. *The Holmes-Pitezel case; a history of the greatest crime of the century and of the search for the missing Pitezel children.* Philadelphia, PA: Publishers' Union, 1896, p. 282.

336. "Detective Geyer Home," *Philadelphia Inquirer*, August 4, 1894, p. 1.

337. Frank P. Geyer. *The Holmes-Pitezel case; a history of the greatest crime of the century and of the search for the missing Pitezel*

children. Philadelphia, PA: Publishers' Union, 1896, p. 283.

338. Ibid: Geyer. *The Holmes-Pitezel*, p. 284.

339. Ibid: Geyer. *The Holmes-Pitezel*, p. 285.

340. Ibid: Geyer. *The Holmes-Pitezel*, p. 285.

341. Ibid: Geyer. *The Holmes-Pitezel*, p. 287.

342. "The Pitezel Trunk," *Indianapolis News*, August 27, 1895, p. 1.

343. Reporters caught Geyer and Geyer's quotes: "Extra! Found in Irvington," *The Indianapolis News*, August 27, 1895, p. 1.

344. "The Pitezel Trunk," *Indianapolis News*, August 27, 1895, p. 1.

345. "Extra! Found in Irvington," *The Indianapolis News*, August 27, 1895, p. 1.

346. Ibid: "Extra! Found," p. 1.

347. Frank P. Geyer. *The Holmes-Pitezel case; a history of the greatest crime of the century and of the search for the missing Pitezel children*. Philadelphia, PA: Publishers' Union, 1896, p. 295.

348. "Pitezel Trunk and Bones," *Indianapolis News*, August 28, 1895, pp. 1-2.

349. Ibid: "Pitezel Trunk," pp. 1-2.

350. Ibid: "Pitezel Trunk," pp. 1-2; and Geyer. The Holmes-Pitezel case, p. 297.

351. Ibid: "Pitezel Trunk," pp. 1-2.

352. Frank P. Geyer. *The Holmes-Pitezel case; a history of the greatest crime of the century and of the search for the missing Pitezel children*. Philadelphia, PA: Publishers' Union, 1896, p. 298.

353. Calomel was sometimes used to keep unruly children in a manageable stupor. If the dosage was increased, it could result in death. Richard M. Swiderski. *Calomel in America: Mercurial Panacea, War, Song and Ghosts*. Boca Raton: Brown Walker Press, 2008, p. 186; "More Holmes Discoveries," *Indianapolis News*,

August 29, 1895, p. 1; and "Two Feet," *Cincinnati Enquirer,* August 30, 1895, p. 1.

354. Frank P. Geyer. *The Holmes-Pitezel case; a history of the greatest crime of the century and of the search for the missing Pitezel children.* Philadelphia, PA: Publishers' Union, 1896, p. 302; and "Foul Deed Laid Bare," *Chicago Tribune,* August 29, 1895, p. 3.

355. "H. H. Holmes Indicted," *The Indianapolis Journal,* September 12, 1895, p. 6; "Mrs. Pitezel at Irvington," *The Indianapolis News,* September 12, 1895, p. 6; Geyer. *The Holmes-Pitezel,* p. 302; and "Slain by Holmes," *The San Francisco Call,* September 12, 1895, p. 1.

356. "More Holmes Discoveries," *Indianapolis News,"* The Indianapolis News, August 29, 1895, p. 1; "Pitezel's Body Taken Up," *Philadelphia Inquirer,* September 1, 1895, p. 9; "Pitezel's Body," *The Wilkes-Barre Record,* September 4, 1895, p. 2; "Pitezel's Body Taken Up," *Philadelphia Inquirer,* pp. 1, 9; and "Pitezel's Bones Disinterred," *Philadelphia Times,* September 1, 1895, p. 1.

357. Potter's Fields: Philadelphia established numerous locations throughout the city, mostly for African Americans and unclaimed bodies. "Pitezel's Body," *The Wilkes-Barre Record,* September 4, 1895, p. 2.

358. "Holmes' Tel Tale Key," *Philadelphia Inquirer,* October 12, 1895, p. 1; and "Revival of the Holmes Case," *The Inter Ocean,* October 12, 1895, p. 1.

359. Cost of witnesses: "Holmes Witnesses Ready," *Philadelphia Inquirer,* October 11, 1895.

360. "Revival of the Holmes Case," *The Inter Ocean,* October 12, 1895, p. 1; and [Geyer quoted about grisly remains, clothing] "Pitezel's Body Taken Up," *Philadelphia Inquirer,* September 1, 1895, p. 9.

Chapter 18 - Just Deserts

361. Detective Geyer, in his 1896 book, summarized Judge Arnold's statement as shown in the chapter quote here. The summarized version was also used by Barclay & Company, *circa* 1896 and

thereafter by subsequent authors. The actual Judge Arnold statement taken from Court of Oyer and Terminer, Charge of Court trial record, dated November 2, 1895 is as follows:

It is this evidence of motive, or rather this suggestion of motive, which makes the testimony of Mrs. Pitezel relevant and important in this case, and I will say that it is such a remarkable story that it proves the truth of the old saying that truth is indeed stranger than fiction; for if the story which she told upon the stand be true, and there seems to be no reason to doubt it, it has shown the most remarkable instance of the power of mind upon mind which I, and perhaps you, have ever witnessed. No novel that was ever written contains a story as thrilling as that which she told here upon the stand concerning the manner in which this man lured her around the country in a deceptive and fruitless hunt after her dead husband. -Honorable Judge Arnold, Charge of Court, Saturday, November 2, 1895. Instructions to jurors: George T. Bisel. *The Trial of Herman W. Mudgett, Alias, H. H. Holmes, for the Murder of Benjamin F. Pitezel: In the Court of Oyer and Terminer and General Jail Delivery and Quarter Sessions of the Peace, in and for the City and County of Philadelphia, Commonwealth of Pennsylvania, October 28, 29, 30, 31, and November 1, and 2, 1895.* Philadelphia, PA: George T. Bisel, Law Publisher, Bookseller and Stationer, 1897, p 530; Frank P. Geyer. *The Holmes-Pitezel case; a history of the greatest crime of the century and of the search for the missing Pitezel children.*Philadelphia, PA: Publishers' Union, 1896, p. 327.

362. "Will be Tried Here for Murder," *Philadelphia Times,* September 13, 1895, p. 2; and "Pitezel's Murder Charged to Holmes," *Philadelphia Inquirer,* September 13, 1895, p. 4.

363. Bisel. *The Trial of Herman W. Mudgett,* pp. 5-8; "Will be Tried Here for Murder," *Philadelphia Times,* September 13, 1895, p. 2; and "Pitezel's Murder Charged to Holmes," *Philadelphia Inquirer,* September 13, 1895, p. 4.

364. Bisel. *The Trial of Herman W. Mudgett,* pp. 5-8; and "Pitezel's Murder Charged to Holmes,"*Philadelphia Inquirer,* September 13, 1895, p. 4.

365. "Agents and Solicitors: Wanted—Live men to sell…," *Philadelphia Inquirer,* October 16, 1895, p. 10.

366. A summary of the trial and witness testimony (unless otherwise noted) were sourced from: Bisel. *The Trial of Herman W. Mudgett,* pp. 5-8; and "Pitezel's Murder Charged to Holmes," *Philadelphia Inquirer,*September 13, 1895.

367. Bisel. *The Trial of Herman W. Mudgett,* p. 12.

368. Bisel. *The Trial of Herman W. Mudgett,* p. 12.

369. Bisel. *The Trial of Herman W. Mudgett,* p. 17.

370. A summary of the trial and witness testimony (unless otherwise noted) were sourced from: Bisel. *The Trial of Herman W. Mudgett.*

371. "Holmes Fights for Life," *Philadelphia Inquirer,* October 30, 1895, p. 1.

372. Ibid: Bisel. *The Trial,* p. 79.

373. Ibid: Bisel. *The Trial,* p. 80.

374. Ibid: Bisel. *The Trial,* p. 100.

375. Ibid: Bisel. *The Trial,* p. 104.

376. Ibid: Bisel. *The Trial,* p. 106.

377. Ibid: Bisel. *The Trial,* p. 108.

378. Ibid: Bisel. *The Trial,* p. 115.

379. "Holmes Fights for Life," *Philadelphia Inquirer,* October 30, 1895, p. 1.

380. George T. Bisel. *The Trial of Herman W. Mudgett, Alias, H. H. Holmes, for the Murder of Benjamin F. Pitezel: In the Court of Oyer and Terminer and General Jail Delivery and Quarter Sessions of the Peace, in and for the City and County of Philadelphia, Commonwealth of Pennsylvania, October 28, 29, 30, 31, and November 1, and 2, 1895.* Philadelphia, PA: George T. Bisel, Law Publisher, Bookseller and Stationer, 1897, p. 114.

381. Ibid: Bisel. *The Trial*, p. 114.

382. "Holmes Fights for Life," *Philadelphia Inquirer*, October 30, 1895, p. 1.

383. A summary of the trial and witness testimony (unless otherwise noted) were sourced from: Bisel. *The Trial of Herman W. Mudgett*, [Dr. William J. Scott testimony, pp. 115-40].

384. George T. Bisel. *The Trial of Herman W. Mudgett, Alias, H. H. Holmes, for the Murder of Benjamin F. Pitezel: In the Court of Oyer and Terminer and General Jail Delivery and Quarter Sessions of the Peace, in and for the City and County of Philadelphia, Commonwealth of Pennsylvania, October 28, 29, 30, 31, and November 1, and 2, 1895.* Philadelphia, PA: George T. Bisel, Law Publisher, Bookseller and Stationer, 1897, p. 124.

385. Ibid: Bisel. *The Trial*, p. 124-25.

386. Ibid: Bisel. *The Trial*, p. 129-30.

387. Ibid: Bisel. *The Trial*, p. 131.

388. Ibid: Bisel. *The Trial*, p. 131.

389. Ibid: Bisel. *The Trial*, pp. 140-65.

390. Ibid: Bisel. *The Trial*, p. 145.

391. Ibid: Bisel. *The Trial*, p. 145.

392. Ibid: Bisel. *The Trial*, pp. 150-51.

393. Ibid: Bisel. *The Trial*, pp. 152-53.

394. Ibid: Bisel. *The Trial*, pp. 162-65.

395. Trial summary and quotes (unless otherwise noted) are sourced from: George T. Bisel. *The Trial of Herman W. Mudgett, Alias, H. H. Holmes, for the Murder of Benjamin F. Pitezel: In the Court of Oyer and Terminer and General Jail Delivery and Quarter Sessions of the Peace, in and for the City and County of Philadelphia, Commonwealth of Pennsylvania, October 28, 29, 30, 31, and November 1, and 2, 1895.* Philadelphia, PA: George T.

Bisel, Law Publisher, Bookseller and Stationer, 1897,   [Dr. Leffman semi-conscious information pp. 166-67].

396. Ibid: Bisel. *The Trial,* pp. 165-73.

397. Ibid: Bisel. *The Trial,* p. 172.

398. Ibid: Bisel. *The Trial,* p. 173.

399. Ibid: Bisel. *The Trial,* p. 176.

400. Ibid: Bisel. *The Trial,* p. 176.

401. Ibid: Bisel. *The Trial,* pp. 5-8; and "Pitezel's Murder Charged to Holmes,"*Philadelphia Inquirer,* September 13, 1895.

402. "Mrs. Pitezel's Story," *Baltimore Sun,* October 31, 1895, p. 2; "Mrs. Pitezel's Sad Story," *Philadelphia Inquirer,*October 31, 1895, p. 1; "Mrs. Pitezel Testifies," *New York Tribune,* October 31, 1895, p. 2; and Mrs. Pitezel's testimony: Bisel. *The Trial of Herman W. Mudgett,* pp. 271-344.

403. George T. Bisel. *The Trial of Herman W. Mudgett, Alias, H. H. Holmes, for the Murder of Benjamin F. Pitezel: In the Court of Oyer and Terminer and General Jail Delivery and Quarter Sessions of the Peace, in and for the City and County of Philadelphia, Commonwealth of Pennsylvania, October 28, 29, 30, 31, and November 1, and 2, 1895.* Philadelphia, PA: George T. Bisel, Law Publisher, Bookseller and Stationer, 1897, p. 344.

404. "Holmes in a Crying Mood," *Philadelphia Times,* November 1, 1895, p. 1; and Miss Yoke initial testimony: Bisel. *The Trial of Herman W. Mudgett,* pp. 353-373.

405. George T. Bisel. *The Trial of Herman W. Mudgett, Alias, H. H. Holmes, for the Murder of Benjamin F. Pitezel: In the Court of Oyer and Terminer and General Jail Delivery and Quarter Sessions of the Peace, in and for the City and County of Philadelphia, Commonwealth of Pennsylvania, October 28, 29, 30, 31, and November 1, and 2, 1895.* Philadelphia, PA: George T. Bisel, Law Publisher, Bookseller and Stationer, 1897, p 370.

406. Ibid: Bisel. *The Trial*, pp. 384-393.

407. Ibid: Bisel. *The Trial*, p. 388.

408. Ibid: Bisel. *The Trial*, pp. 389-91.

409. Ibid: Bisel. *The Trial*, p. 392.

410. Ibid: Bisel. *The Trial*, p. 393.

411. Ibid: Bisel. *The Trial*, p. 395.

412. "Murderer Holmes in a New Role," *Philadelphia Inquirer*, November 10, 1895, p. 2.

413. Ibid: "Murderer Holmes," p. 2.

414. George T. Bisel. *The Trial of Herman W. Mudgett, Alias, H. H. Holmes, for the Murder of Benjamin F. Pitezel: In the Court of Oyer and Terminer and General Jail Delivery and Quarter Sessions of the Peace, in and for the City and County of Philadelphia, Commonwealth of Pennsylvania, October 28, 29, 30, 31, and November 1, and 2, 1895.* Philadelphia, PA: George T. Bisel, Law Publisher, Bookseller and Stationer, 1897, p. 430.

415. Ibid: Bisel. *The Trial*, pp. 433-439.

416. Following Holmes' conviction, his defense team secured his divorce transcript from Cook County, Illinois. Holmes had filed for divorce in 1887 after he married his second wife. He sued Clara A. Mudgett for divorce, citing infidelity with a man named, J. N. Downer at Ann Arbor, Michigan where he went to medical school. His wife lived with him there a short time. The document listed their child, Robert L. Mudgett, then six years old, and asked for legal custody of the boy. Mudgett (Holmes) stated he was married at Action, New Hampshire on July 4, 1878, and lived with his wife until 1883. The case was heard and dismissed due to lack of evidence. "Divorce Transcript Received," *The Inter Ocean*, November 19, 1895, p. 4.

417. "Jury says that Holmes Must Hang," *Philadelphia Times*, November 3, 1895, pp. 1, 8.

418. "Perjury for Holmes," *Philadelphia Times,* November 19, 1895, p. 1.

419. Detective Geyer on the witness stand regarding affidavit: "The Affidavit is False," *Philadelphia Inquirer,* November 19, 1895, p. 1.

420. State of Pennsylvania. *District Reports of Cases Decided in all the Judicial Districts of the State of Pennsylvania During the Year 1896, Vol. V.,* From Vol. 53 of the Legal Intelligencer, 1896, pp. 161-64; and "The Affidavit is False,"*Philadelphia Inquirer,* November 19, 1895, p. 1; "Suspension for W. S. Shoemaker," *Philadelphia Times,* March 15, 1896, p. 6.

421. "The Affidavit is False," *Philadelphia Inquirer,* November 19, 1895, p. 1.

422. Ibid: "The Affidavit," p. 1.

423. Bisel. *The Trial of Herman W. Mudgett, Alias, H. H. Holmes,* pp. 541-602; and "Holmes Must Die," *Boston Journal,* November 30, 1895, p. 1.

424. "Holmes Last Hope is Gone," *Philadelphia Times,* April 30, 1896, p. 10.

425. Ibid: "Holmes Last," p. 10.

426. "In the Shadow of Death," *Philadelphia Inquirer,* May 6, 1896, p. 6.

427. "Holmes Weeps and is Afraid," *Philadelphia Times,* May 7, 1896, p. 1.

428. "Shrewd to the Last," *Trenton Evening Times,* May 8, 1896, p. 4; "Hanged for Many Crimes," *The San Francisco Call,* May 8, 1896, p. 1; "Mrs. Pitezel Talks," *Philadelphia Inquirer,* May 8, 1896, p. 1; and *Austin Weekly Statesman*[Mrs. Pitezel and Dessa], November 7, 1895.

429. Quotes for Holmes' new confession: "Holmes Latest Statements," *Indianapolis News,* April 27, 1896, p. 2; "Holmes is Hopeful," *Philadelphia Inquirer,* p. 3; and "Holmes Last Effort,"

Indianapolis Journal, April 22, 1896, p. 6.

430. Ibid: "Holmes Latest," p. 2; and "Holmes is," p. 3.

431. "Preparing to Try Holmes," *Philadelphia Times,* August 8, 1895, p. 2; and "They Seek His Life," *Chicago Tribune,*August 8, 1895, p. 8.

432. "A Grewsome Relic," *Harrisburg Telegraph,* January 7 1896, p3.

433. Samuel H. Ashbridge: The *Minneapolis Journal* reported about a politician who once worked for former Mayor Ashbridge for three years and said he always insisted that when he ordered you to do something, he expected it done exactly as he wanted. He didn't like it when people took it upon themselves to do it better. A hard lesson learning for the politician after trying to improve on something Ashbridge wanted done, Ashbridge told the following story to emphasize why you should follow instructions exactly:

"There was a young man in love with a rich and beautiful girl. The girl informed him one afternoon that the next day would be her birthday. He said he was glad to hear it. He said he would send her the next morning a bouquet of roses, one rose for each year. So that night he wrote a note to the florist, ordering the immediate delivery of twenty roses to the young lady. But the florist, reading this order, thought he would please the young man by improving on it, and so he said to his clerk: 'Here's an order from Young Smith for twenty roses. Smith is one of my best customers. Throw in ten more for good measure.'" "She Threw Him Over," *The Minneapolis Journal,* May 17, 1906, p. 16.

William K. Mattern: John Trevor Custis. *Public Schools of Philadelphia; Historical, Biographical, Statistical.* Philadelphia, PA: Burk & McFetridge Company, 1897, pp. 563-64.

Chapter 19 - The Devil in Him

434. Frank P. Geyer. *The Holmes-Pitezel case; a history of the greatest crime of the century and of the search for the missing Pitezel children.* Philadelphia, PA: Publishers' Union, 1896, pp. 53-54.

435. Arthur MacDonald. *Man and Abnormal Man, including a Study of*

Children, in Connection with Bills to Establish Laboratories Under Federal and State Governments for the Study of the Criminal, Pauper, and Defective Classes, with Bibliographies. Washington: Government Printing Office, 1905, pp. 537-541.

436. Ibid: MacDonald, *Man and,* pp. 537-541.

437. Ibid: MacDonald, *Man and,* pp. 537-541.

438. Holmes' confession he sold to the newspaper: "Holmes' Confesses 27 Murders," *Philadelphia Inquirer,* April 12, 1896, pp. 1, 8-9, 18.

439. Eugene Talbot, M.D., D.D.S. "H. H. Holmes," *The Journal of the American Medical Association,* Vol. XXVII, (1896), pp. 253-257.

440. Ibid: Talbot, "H. H. Holmes," pp. 253-257.

441. Ibid: Talbot, "H. H. Holmes," pp. 253-257.

442. "The First One Hung," *The Ann Arbor Argus,* Vol. LXII, No 19, (1896).

Chapter 20 - He Must Die

443. "Miss DeKalb's Story of the Conspiracy," *Philadelphia Inquirer,* April 25, 1900, p. 1.

444. Frank P. Geyer. *The Holmes-Pitezel case; a history of the greatest crime of the century and of the search for the missing Pitezel children.* Philadelphia, PA: Publishers' Union, 1896; United States Patent Office, Shutter or Door Fastener, F. P. Geyer, Patent No. 556,141, March 10, 1896; "Caught on the Fly," *Philadelphia Inquirer*, May 13, 1895, p. 6; *Philadelphia Inquirer,* March 14, 1896; "Wanted Agents Holmes-Pitezel Case," *Evening Star,* March 25, 1896; and "Holmes Will Hang; Our Newest Book, 'The Holmes-Pitezel Case'," *Plain Dealer Cleveland,* April 12, 1896, p. 3.

445. "Holmes Great Crimes," *Philadelphia Inquirer,* April 26, 1896, p. 24.

446. Ibid: "Holmes Great," p. 24.

447. Ibid: "Holmes Great," p. 24.

448. "Mysterious Death," *Semi-Weekly Messenger,* April 2, 1896, p. 7; and "Langdon is Free," *Altoona Tribune,* April 10, 1896, p. 1.

449. "The Full Story of the Famous Kaiser Murder," *Philadelphia Times,* June 26, 1898, p. 14.

450. Quote: "The Full Story of the Famous Kaiser Murder," *Philadelphia Times,* June 26, 1898, p. 14.

Charles O. Kaiser and Emma P. Carpenter were married twice. May 11, 1896 marriage: Rev. J. F. C. Cook, of Philadelphia, testified he married Charles O. Kaiser and Emma P. Carpenter on May 11, 1896. "The Coroner's Jury Accuses Kaiser," *Philadelphia Inquirer,* November 21, 1896, p. 1. December 31, 1895 marriage: Application for Marriage, No. 5775, was issued on December 30, 1895 in Blair County for Charles Kaiser (22), Philadelphia, PA. His occupation was listed as artist and Emma P. Carpenter (24), Altoona, PA, her occupation was not listed. Emma's father: Emanuel Carpenter. Charles' father: Charles Kaiser. Marriage No. 5775, Charles Kaiser and Emma P. Carpenter, married in Blair County on December 31, 1895, signed by the clerk of the County. Charles Kaiser married Emma Carpenter prior to their May 11, 1896 marriage described in Rev. Cook's testimony. The author was unable to determine why the couple married December 31, 1895, and again a few months later on May 11, 1896, but perhaps it had something to do with their life insurance policies or it could be that the first marriage was annulled. *Philadelphia Times* reported friends of Emma stated they advised her not to marry Charles. She visited the friends spring of 1896 and in intimate conversations, Emma said they did not get along together and Charles did not treat her well, especially when drinking. She told friends she wished she had never married him and was hoping to be single again soon. "Kaiser Said to Be Weakening," *Philadelphia Times,* October 31, 1896, p. 1.

451. "State News Items; The Prosecution Nearly Closed," *Philadelphia Inquirer,* June 18, 1898, p. 6; and "The Full Story of the Famous Kaiser Murder," *Philadelphia Times,* June 26, 1898, p. 14.

452. "Kaiser Dead in His Cell," *Philadelphia Inquirer,* August 19, 1898.

453. "The Full Story of the Famous Kaiser Murder," *Philadelphia Times,* June 26, 1898, p. 14; "Tomorrow Tells Clemmer's Fate," *Reading Times,* May 1, 1899, p. 1; and "Miss DeKalb's Story of the Conspiracy," *Philadelphia Inquirer,* April 25, 1900, p. 1.

454. Ibid: "The Full," p. 14.

455. "Miss DeKalb's Story of the Conspiracy," *Philadelphia Inquirer,* April 25, 1900, p. 1; and "The Coroner's Jury Accuses Kaiser," *Philadelphia Inquirer,* November 21, 1896, p. 1.

456. Kaiser's quotes about the murder are from his testimony at Clemmer's trial. "Kaiser Dead in His Cell,"*Philadelphia Inquirer,* August 19, 1898.

457. "Lizzie DeKalb's Hearing," *Reading Times,* November 24, 1897, p. 1.

458. "Miss DeKalb's Story of the Conspiracy," *Philadelphia Inquirer,* April 25, 1900, p. 1.

459. "The Full Story of the Famous Kaiser Murder," *Philadelphia Times,* June 26, 1898, p. 14.

460. Knew since boyhood: "Charles O. Kaiser is Now Detained," *Philadelphia Inquirer,* October 30, 1896, pp. 1, 5. Charlie: "The Full Story of the Famous Kaiser Murder," *Philadelphia Times,* June 26, 1898, p. 14.

461. Geyer quotes about Kaiser involvement after reading about the crime: "Geyer on the Verdict," *Philadelphia Inquirer,* March 20, 1897, p. 4.

462. Crayon portraits were popular from mid nineteenth to the early twentieth centuries. To make the portrait, artists enlarged a photograph onto drawing paper with a weak emulsion resulting in a faint image that artists would then trace over with charcoal or pastels. From a few feet away, people often mistook the image as a photograph. "Crayon Portrait, *Aurora Missouri Historical Society, www.auroramohistoricalsociety.wordpress.com/2009/02/23/*

crayon-portrait/, accessed January 6, 2016; and "Kaiser Now Suspected," *Philadelphia Times,* October 30, 1896, p. 1.

463. "Charles O. Kaiser is Now Detained," *Philadelphia Inquirer,* October 30, 1896, pp. 1, 5; and "Kaiser Now Suspected," *Philadelphia Times,* October 30, 1896, p. 1.

464. "Kaiser Locked in a Prison Cell," *Philadelphia Inquirer,* October 31, 1896, pp. 1, 5.

465. In the 19th century, the phrase 'put [insert name here] on the rack' and 'on the rack' was used to describe a police interrogation.

466. "Kaiser Said to Be Weakening," *Philadelphia Times,* October 31, 1896, p. 1; and "Funeral of Mrs. Kaiser,"*Philadelphia Times,* November 2, 1896, p. 1.

467. "Kaiser Locked in a Prison Cell," *Philadelphia Inquirer,* October 31, 1896, pp. 1, 5.

468. Ibid: "Kaiser Locked," pp. 1, 5.

469. Ibid: "Kaiser Locked," pp. 1, 5.

470. "Investigating the Kaiser Case," *Conshohocken Recorder,* November 13, 1896, p. 1.

471. Ibid: "Investigating the," p. 1.

472. Ibid: "Investigating the," p. 1; and "The Coroner's Jury Accuses Kaiser," *Philadelphia Inquirer,* November 11, 1896, p. 1.

473. All quotes from the coroner's inquest: "The Coroner's Jury Accuses Kaiser," *Philadelphia Inquirer,* November 11, 1896, p. 1.

474. Ibid: "The Coroner's," p. 1.

475. "A Carriage Put into Evidence," *Philadelphia Times,* March 11, 1897, p. 6.

476. "Damaging Evidence Against Kaiser," *Philadelphia Inquirer,* March 13, 1897, pp. 1, 5.

477. Geyer and Clemmer quotes: "The Full Story of the Famous Kaiser

Murder," *Philadelphia Times*, June 26, 1898, p. 14.

478. Ibid: "The Full," p. 14.

479. Geyer testimony and quotes continued: "Damaging Evidence Against Kaiser," *Philadelphia Inquirer*, March 13, 1897, pp. 1, 5.

480. "Nearing the End in Kaiser Case," *Philadelphia Inquirer*, March 18, 1897, p. 5; and "Kaiser's Account of the Murder," *Philadelphia Inquirer*, March 17, 1897, p. 1.

481. Ibid: "Nearing the," p. 5; and "Kaiser's," p. 1.

482. Ibid "Nearing the," p. 5.

483. "Kaiser Convicted of the Murder," *Philadelphia Inquirer*, March 20, 1897, pp. 1, 4.

484. "Native of Lehigh," *The Allentown Leader*, December 23, 1897, p. 1.

485. "Another Fugitive Escapes," *Philadelphia Times*, November 11, 1897, p. 1; and "Fair Fugitive Caught," *The Columbian*, November 11, 1897, p. 3.

486. "Clemmer Arrested," *Rockland County Journal*, December 4, 1897, p. 2.

487. "Thorn's Bid for Life," *The World*, November 30, 1897, p. 1.

488. "Confession of Lizzie DeKalb," *Philadelphia Times*, November 11, 1897, p. 1; and "Native of Lehigh," *The Allentown Leader*, December 23, 1897, p. 1.

489. "Native of Lehigh," *The Allentown Leader*, December 23, 1897, p. 1; and "Lizzie DeKalb Faces Clemmer,"*Philadelphia Times*, June 15, 1898, p. 2.

490. "Clemmer Indicted," *Philadelphia Inquirer*, June 19, 1898, p. 14.

491. "Lizzie DeKalb Faces Clemmer," *Philadelphia Times*, June 15, 1898, p. 2; and "Line of Defense is Now Apparent," *Philadelphia Times*, June 16, 1898, p. 5.

492. "Line of Defense is Now Apparent," *Philadelphia Times*, June 16,

1898, p. 5.

493. Headline: "Clemmer Wanted to Kill Geyer," *Philadelphia Times,* June 17, 1898, p. 2.

494. Murder plots and quotes: "Clemmer Wanted to Kill Geyer," *Philadelphia Times,* June 17, 1898, p. 2; and "Miss DeKalb's Story of the Conspiracy," *Philadelphia Inquirer,* April 25, 1900, p. 1.

495. Geyer in the audience: "Clemmer Wanted to Kill Geyer," *Philadelphia Times,* June 17, 1898, p. 2; and "Miss DeKalb's Story of the Conspiracy," *Philadelphia Inquirer,* April 25, 1900, p. 1.

496. "Kaiser Goes on the Stand," *Philadelphia Times,* June 21, 1898, pp. 1-2.

497. Wilson C. Kress, State Reporter. *Pennsylvania State Reports, Vol. 190, Containing Cases Decided by the Supreme Court of Pennsylvania at January and April Terms, 1899* [Commonwealth v. James A. Clemmer, Appellant]. New York: The Banks Law Publishing Company, 1899, pp. 202-222.

498. "May Contest Insurance," *Philadelphia Inquirer,* March 19, 1897, p. 5; *The Weekly Underwriter: An Insurance Newspaper, July 3, 1897 to December 25, 1897, Inclusive.* New York: The Underwriter Printing & Publishing Co., 1897, p. 74; "Kaiser Brings Suit for the Insurance," *Philadelphia Inquirer,* August 8, 1897, p. 11; and "Lost by the Kaiser's," *Pittsburgh Post-Gazette,* January 15, 1898, p. 1.

499. Charles O. Kaiser committed suicide August 18, 1898. "Kaiser Slowly Bled to Death," *Philadelphia Inquirer,*August 20, 1898, p. 2.

500. "For Clemmer's Pardon," *Reading Times,* April 11, 1899, p. 1.

501. "Emma Kaiser Avenged," *Harrisburg Daily Independent,* May 18, 1899, p. 1; and "Clemmer's Sin is Expiated,"*Philadelphia Times,* May 19, 1899, p. 4.

502. Judge Schwartz statements and Lizzie's quotes: "Two Years for

Lizzie KeKalb," *Philadelphia Times,* June 26, 1898, p. 6.

503. "Lizzie DeKalb to Go Free," *Philadelphia Times,* January 16, 1900, p. 2; "Miss DeKalb's Story of the Conspiracy,"*Philadelphia Inquirer,* April 25, 1900, p. 1; "Lizzie DeKalb Gets out of Jail, No Longer Woman in Black," *Philadelphia Times,* April 26, 1900, p. 4; "Local Miscellany (Lizzie in Love w/ Wilson Hunsberger)," *The Bucks County Gazette,*June 14, 1900, p. 3; and "Around the County," *The Central News,* August 16, 1900, p. 1.

504. "Tomorrow Tells Clemmer's Fate," *Reading Times,* May 1, 1899, p. 1.

505. Mrs. Emma P. Kaiser's real age: "May Contest Insurance," *Philadelphia Inquirer,* March 19, 1897, p. 5. Detective Geyer knew Kaiser since boyhood: "Charles O. Kaiser is Now Detained," *Philadelphia Inquirer,* October 30, 1896, p. 5.

506. Lizzie's aliases: "Lizzie DeKalb has a hearing," *The Wilkes-Barre News,* November 24, 1897, p. 1; and "Lizzie DeKalb's Hearing," *Reading Times,* November 24, 1897, p. 1; and "Looks Black for Clemmer," *The Record of Philadelphia Times, (Wilkes-Barre),* December 24, 1897, p. 2.

Chapter 21 - Regret to Inform You

507. "Silent Witnesses that Fed Gallows," *Philadelphia Inquirer,* August 24, 1903, p. 5.

508. Overcoats: Members of the Bar. *Weekly Notes of Cases Argued and Determined in the Supreme Court of Pennsylvania, the County Courts of Philadelphia, and the United States District and Circuit Courts for the Eastern District of Pennsylvania, Volume XX.* Philadelphia, PA: Kay & Brother Law Booksellers, Publishers and Importers, 1888, pp. 315-16; and Herbert B. Adams, ed. *Johns Hopkins University Studies in Historical and Political Science, Volume V: Municipal Government History and Politics.* Baltimore: Johns Hopkins University, N. Murray, Publication Agent, 1887, p. 67. Umbrellas and walking or talking: Bureau of Police, City of Philadelphia. *Patrolman's Manual.* Philadelphia, PA: Department of Public Safety, George D. Porter, Director, 1913, pp. 14, 30.

509. "Still Winter for the Police," *Philadelphia Times,* April 16, 1896, p. 5.

510. Ibid: "Still Winter," p. 5.

511. Ibid: "Still Winter," p. 5.

512. Detective Jacob S. Welker was demoted October 1907 and forced to resign April 1908. "Detective War to Be Probed," *Philadelphia Inquirer,* December 11, 1901, p. 8; "Sleuths War in Philadelphia," *The Pittsburg Press,*December 12, 1901, p. 5; "Detective Crawford has Secret Hearing," *Philadelphia Times,* December 12, 1901, p. 7; "Promoted Men's Careers," *Philadelphia Inquirer,* October 4, 1907, p. 4; and "Seven Philadelphia Detectives Ousted,"*The Scranton Republican,* April 14, 1908, p. 1.

513. "Detective Geyer Accused," *Philadelphia Times,* April 15, 1891; and "Detective Geyer Reprimanded,"*Philadelphia Times,* April 17, 1891, p. 4.

514. Ashbridge, Samuel H., Mayor. *Third Annual Message of Samuel H. Ashbridge, Mayor of the City of Philadelphia, Year Ending December 31, 1901.* Philadelphia, PA: Dunlap Printing Company, 1902, p. 99.

515. "Detective Geyer Accused," *Philadelphia Times,* April 15, 1891; and "Detective Geyer Reprimanded,"*Philadelphia Times,* April 17, 1891, p. 4.

516. "Detective Geyer May Go," *Philadelphia Inquirer,* September 29, 1893, p. 1; and "Geyer was suspended,"*Philadelphia Inquirer,* October 12, 1893.

517. Return of a Death in the City of Philadelphia, Physician's Certificate No 9155, Camilla B. [Buck] Geyer, date of death: November 2, 1893; and "Obituary - Geyer," *Philadelphia Inquirer,* November 3, 1893.

518. "Hand of Police Gripped 65,468," *Philadelphia Inquirer,* July 12, 1903, p. 2; and "Death of Reuben K. Geyer,"*Philadelphia Inquirer,* July 12, 1903, p. 5.

519. "Holmes Nemesis to Leave Force; Detective Frank Geyer Resigns From Department After 27 Years' Service,"*Philadelphia Inquirer*, August 16, 1903, p. 5.

520. Ibid: "Holmes Nemesis," p. 5.

521. Detective Geyer began work at Lit Brothers located on Market Street between 7th and 8th on Sunday, August 16, 1903. "Famous Detective Resigns," *Patriot Harrisburg,* August 17, 1903; and Herbert Welsh, ed. *"City and State Volumes 14-15,* 1903, p. 123.

522. Rope: Author telephone interview with J. R. Riggins and Ms. Joyce (Elliott) Riggins, descendants of Detective Frank P. Geyer, December 18, 2016. Smithsonian: Author telephone interviews and email correspondence with the Smithsonian Institute, April 3, 2017 - November 7, 2017: Smithsonian Institute officials painstakingly went through old archive records, some of which were damaged, to determine if a rope was donated, but as of September 14, 2017, they were unable to find it. Back in the time period the donation was potentially made, H. H. Holmes was all but forgotten. The Institute verified they do have architectural columns from Moyamensing Prison where he was hung. The columns were collected for their architectural significance, not because of the association with H. H. Holmes. Artifacts taken: "Silent Witnesses that Fed Gallows," *Philadelphia Inquirer,* August 24, 1903, p. 5.

Chapter 22 - Police Scandal

523. "Bluecoats Sentenced," *Colorado Springs Gazette,* April 9, 1908, p. 1.

524. "Gold Metal for this Detective," *The Evening Journal,* March 23, 1905, p. 2.

525. "3,000 Seeking Work Engage in a Battle," *Aberdeen Daily News,* April 1, 1908, p. 1; "3,000 Unemployed Fight in Streets," *New Castle Herald,* April 1, 1908, p. 1; and "Workmen in Wild All-Day Riot Besiege Future Opera House Site," *Philadelphia Inquirer,* p. 1.

526. "Bluecoats Sentenced," *Colorado Springs Gazette,* April 9, 1908, p. 1; "Police Burglars," *Daily People,"* April 8, 1908, p. 1;

"Philadelphia's Birthday," *Baltimore American Sun,* April 12, 1908, p. 14; and "Police Burglars," *Daily People,"* April 8, 1908, p. 1.

527. "Police Burglars," *Daily People,"* April 8, 1908, p. 1.

528. "Bluecoats Sentenced," *Colorado Springs Gazette,* April 9, 1908, p. 1

529. Ibid: "Bluecoats," p. 1.

530. "Asked to Resign," *Daily People,* April 14, 1908, p. 4.

531. "Spring Weddings," *The Sentinel,* April 23, 1908, p. 3; "Strohm-Geyer," *Bridgeton Evening News,* April 23, 1908, p. 8; and "Latest from Newville," *Carlisle Evening Herald,* April 24, 1908, p. 4.

532. "Nearby Towns," *Patriot,* April 19, 1908, p. 8; and "Strohm-Geyer," *Bridgeton Evening News,* April 23, 1908, p. 8. Edna and Orrie were married April 21, 1908.

533. "Strohm-Geyer," *Bridgeton Evening News,* April 23, 1908, p. 8; Henry B. Croskey, *Medico-Chirurgical Journal,*Vol. VI, No. 1, January 20, 1905, p. 53; Cyrus Lee Stevens, AM, MD, "Honor Roll of Pennsylvania Physicians," *The Pennsylvania Medical Journal,* Volume XLVII, (1917), p. 319; and *Transaction & Studies of the College of Physicians of Philadelphia, Fourth Series, Volume Z9,* Waverly Press, Inc: Baltimore, MD, 1961, p. 47.

534. "Strohm-Geyer," *Bridgeton Evening News,* April 23, 1908, p. 8.

535. *History of Cumberland and Adams Counties, Pennsylvania,* Chicago, Illinois: Warner, Beers & Co., 1886, pp. 195, 453-54; "The Latest New Enterprises," *The Fourth Estate,* October 19, 1901, p. 14; "East Harrisburg," *Harrisburg Telegraph,* June 6, 1902, p. 3; and "The Newville Times Sold," *Philadelphia Times* [Pennsylvania], March 13, 1886, p. 6. John W. Strohm's book: *"The Life and History of William Denning, who cast the first wrought-iron cannon for the American army at the outbreak of the revolutionary war,"* 1890.

536. Geyer detective agency ad, *Philadelphia Inquirer,* September 13, 1908, p. 3.

537. "Fake Mustaches," *Wilkes-Barre Times,* September 6, 1909, p. 9; and "Fake Moustaches Lead to Arrest on Murder Charges," *Wilkes-Barre Times,* September 6, 1909, p. 9. A Bucks County Statement of Finances showed a $555.65 payment for three bills issued to Frank P. Geyer in 1915 for detective services, an amount worth $12,911 in 2017. "Miscellaneous Bills [Bucks County Statement of Finances, 1915]," *The Central News,* January 26, 1916, p. 7.

538. "Fake Mustaches," *Wilkes-Barre Times,* September 6, 1909, p. 9; and "Strong Murderer Declares Medium,"*Philadelphia Inquirer,* March 29, 1911, p. 16.

539. "Strong Murderer Declares Medium," *Philadelphia Inquirer,* March 29, 1911, p. 16.

540. Garret D. W. Vroom, reporter. *Reports of Cases Argued and Determined in the Supreme Court and, at Law, in the Court of Errors and Appeals of the State of New Jersey, Volume LIV.* Newark, NJ: Soney & Sage, 1913, pp. 177-88; "Negro Once More Writes to Strong," *Trenton Evening Times,* April 3, 1911, p. 2; and "Signs Farmer Strong's Release," *Philadelphia Inquirer,* June 29, 1912, p. 5.

541. United States Patent Office, F. P. Geyer, Safety Lock for Pocket Books and Hand Bags, Patent No. 872,619, December 3, 1907; and United States Patent Office, Orrie C. Strohm, Patent No. 1,206,939, December 5, 1916.

542. Christ Church Baptism Record, Officiating Minister John G. Bawn, PhD, November 21, 1909, pp. 74-75; and The Christ Church Congregation, *"Historic Christ Church,"* June 24, 2016, www.christchurchphila.org/Historic-Christ-Church/73/.

543. Social Security Death Index for Frank Wesley Strohm, August 1984; and Social Security Death Index for Dorothy E. Elliott [Geyer], June 13, 1988.

Chapter 23 - La Grippe

544. "Order Closes Schools, Theatres [sic] and Meeting Places in Grip Fight," *The Evening Telegraph,* October 3, 1918, p. 1.

545. United States World War I Draft Registration Card, NARA M1509, Washington DC: National Archives and Records Administration, 37-7-28, C, serial number 3291, order number 1030 [Orrie Curtis Strohm]. Orrie was thirty-three at the time of his draft registration. His address was listed as 4123 N. 6th Street, Philadelphia, PA and he listed his wife, Edna, as his relative.

546. "Man Shot in Race Riot over Negro Resident," *Philadelphia Inquirer,* July 28, 1918, p. 3; "Mrs. Bond Determined to Occupy Her House," *Philadelphia Inquirer,* July 31, 1918, p. 15;

547. "Mrs. Bond Determined to Occupy Her House," *Philadelphia Inquirer,* July 31, 1918, p. 15.

548. Mrs. Adelia Bond's first name was frequently spelled Adella. "Mrs. Bond Determined to Occupy Her House,"*Philadelphia Inquirer,* July 31, 1918, p. 15.

549. "Riot Victim Died Hero Says Priest," *Evening Public Ledger,* August 1, 1918, p. 2.

550. Vincent P. Franklin. "The Philadelphia Race Riot of 1918," *Pennsylvania Magazine of History and Biography*, Vo. 99, 1975, pp. 336-50; and "Race Riots Grow in Fury as Police Fail to Curb Mobs," *Philadelphia Inquirer,* July 30, 1918, p. 3.

551. "Mrs. Bond Determined to Occupy Her House," *Philadelphia Inquirer,* July 31, 1918, p. 15; "Riot Victim Died Hero Says Priest," *Evening Public Ledger,* August 1, 1918, p. 2; and "Fourth Man Dies Victim of Riots," *Philadelphia Inquirer,* August 1, 1918, p. 6.

552. Vincent P. Franklin. "The Philadelphia Race Riot of 1918," *Pennsylvania Magazine of History and Biography*, Vo. 99, 1975, pp. 336-50; and "Race Riots Grow in Fury as Police Fail to Curb Mobs," *Philadelphia Inquirer,* July 30, 1918, p. 3.

553. Ibid: Franklin, "The Philadelphia, p. 3.

554. Letter quoted in: "Negroes Censure Mayor for Riots," *Evening Public Ledger,* July 30, 1918, p. 1.

555. Ibid: "Negroes Censure," p. 1.

556. "Race Riot Area Dry; Detain Policeman in Shooting Probe," *Philadelphia Inquirer,* July 31, 1918, pp. 1, 15.

557. Molly Billings. "The Influenza Pandemic of 1918," *Stanford University,* www.virus.stanford.edu/uda/, accessed November 12, 2016.

558. Doctors used the term 'La Grippe' on death certificates during this time. Quote from narrator: Public Broadcasting Service (PBS) transcript of American Experience, "Influenza 1918," 1998, p. 7.

559. Molly Billings. "The Influenza Pandemic of 1918," *Stanford University,* www.virus.stanford.edu/uda/, accessed November 12, 2016.

560. "The Great Pandemic, the United States in 1918-1919, Pennsylvania," *United States Department of Health and Human Services.*

561. Public Broadcasting Service (PBS) transcript of American Experience, "Influenza 1918," 1998, p. 15.

562. "Grip Breaks City's Death Rate Record," *The Evening Telegraph,* October 5, 1918, p. 1.

563. Thomas B. Smith. *Third Annual Message of Thomas B. Smith, Mayor of Philadelphia, Volume I, Containing the Mayor's Message and the Reports of the Departments of Public Safety and Public Health and Charities for the Year Ending December 31, 1918.* Philadelphia: Issued by the City of Philadelphia, 1919, pp. 39-40; and "Grip Breaks City's Death Rate Record," *The Evening Telegraph,* October 5, 1918, p. 1.

564. The *National Police Journal* reported Geyer died of heart disease; however, the Commonwealth of Pennsylvania, Department of Health, listed Geyer's primary cause of death as L.a. Grippe

[Spanish Flu], with a duration of twenty-four hours. Angina pectoris was listed as a contributing factor on his death certificate. George H. Young, "Noted Detective Dead." *The National Police Journal: America's Greatest Police Magazine*, Vol. 3, No. 2 (1918): p. 21; and Commonwealth of Pennsylvania, Department of Health, Bureau of Vital Statistics, Certificate of Death File No. 143487, date of death: October 4, 1918, Franklin P. Geyer. The *Inquirer* reported an estate worth $17,500 (equivalent to $283,692 in 2017) was bequeathed by Franklin P. Geyer, a former detective, to his wife and a daughter, Edna C. Strohm. "Bury Detective F. P. Geyer," *Philadelphia Inquirer,*October 9, 1918, p. 10. Geyer's estate information was found in the *Philadelphia Inquirer,* October 12, 1918, p. 10.

565. Author telephone interview with Becky at Hillside Cemetery on July 10, 2017, verified that although Mary Geyer's name was not listed on his headstone at the time, records show she was buried in Detective Geyer's plot (C14) on December 19, 1932. They were unable to provide her date of death as they only tracked the date of burial.

Supplemental Photos

566. Samuel T. Wiley. Biographical and Portrait Cyclopedia of Montgomery County, Pennsylvania, Containing Biographical Sketches of Prominent and Representative Citizens of the County, Together with an Introductory Historical Sketch. Philadelphia, PA: Biographical Publishing Company, 1895, pp. 215-16.

567. Hale, George Wesley, Police Department. *Police and Prison Cyclopaedia.* Boston, MA: The W. L. Richardson Company, 1893, pp. 753-66; and Harris Hawthorne Wilder, Ph.D. and Bert Wentworth, Former Police Commissioner of Dover, NH. *Personal Identification: Methods for the Identification of Individuals, Living or Dead.* Boston, MA: Richard G. Badger, The Gorham Press, 1918, pp. 59-72. *Philadelphia Times* wrote a feature article on the Bertillon System, its background and the City of Philadelphia in "What Criminals Dread," *Philadelphia Times,* July 24, 1892, p. 16.

568. "City Detectives Sued," *Philadelphia Times,* January 15, 1891, p. 1;

and "One of Geyer's Blunders," *Philadelphia Times,* October 11, 1892, p. 2.

569. "Mowbray Talks of Himself," *Philadelphia Times,* November 22, 1894, p. 6.

570. "A Special Officer Badly Beaten," *Philadelphia Times,* March 13, 1882, p. 1.

571. "Contracts Awarded." The Municipal Journal and Engineer, Volume XXXI, 1911, p. 648.

Index

Page numbers in *italics* refer to photos and illustrations.

A
Ackerman, constable, 57
Act for the Better Government, 41, 334
alias, see individual names.
adulterous affair, 72
acute appendicitis mortality paper, 241
African American, 55, 239, 248-49
African American delegation of
   ministers, 249
Albany, New York, 24
Alcorn, Mary, 49-50
Alcorn, Dr. Adella, 183
Alexandria, Virginia, 19
Aldrin, Buzz (astronaut), 313
Almendinger, Colonel (detective, Philadelphia Police), 234
Almshouse, The, 130, 354
Anderson, Major, Fort Sumter, 16-17, *see also* Civil War
Andrews, Mary Jane (Jimmy Logue's first wife), 124
Andrews, Police Surgeon, Philadelphia Police, 130
Ann Arbor, Michigan, 365
Anti Spitting Law, 251
Appomattox, Virginia, 23, 324
American (s)
   against flag and, 275
   consulates and, 109
   died, Spanish flu, 250
   hostile towards Irish and, 2
   legation and, 110
   pride of, 9
   Twain, Mark, comment about hate, 12
   viewed Lincoln's remains, 24
American Civil War, *see* Civil War
ammonia, 173
Anderson, Major, Fort Sumter, 16-17, *see also* Civil War
Andrews, Police Sergeant, Philadelphia Police, 130
Arch Street, 1328 Philadelphia (Geyer's detective office), 242
Argentine Republic, 110-11
Armbrust, Mrs. (rented home that Pitezel girls were found in), 145-47
   terrible odor in cellar, 145

Armstrong, Hattie (torso murder case), 341
    trial testimony and, 69
Armstrong, Louis (musician), 313
army, 19, *see also* Civil War
Arnold, Judge Michael, Philadelphia (Holmes trial), 166-67, 172, 186,
        194, 196, 198, *202*
    allowed, Holmes, attorney requests
        attorneys, return to case, 183
        Holmes, question Yoke, 187
        right to close, exception Commonwealth only one, 195
        Rotan, question Yoke as their witness, 193
    denials, Holmes, attorney requests
        attorney withdrawal, 168
        continuance request, 183
        exception, opening statement, 195
        odd scenario, Holmes' told, 182
        remove witnesses, 169
        right to close, exception Commonwealth only one, 195
        stop Miss Yoke testimony 187
        two sessions instead of three, 182
        witnesses conversing, 175
    if contradict Holmes' statements, never get done, 191
    joke, dynamite and, 198
    judgment affirmed by Supreme Court and, 199
    ruling for Geyer to testify, Pitezel children deaths, 190
    truth stranger than fiction quote and, 166, 361
    see also Holmes, H. H.
arrest of
    Ballon, John, 242
    Bland, Leona, 273
    Bradley, Thomas, 277
    Callahan, Ellen, *39*
    Chickereno, Frank, 242
    Clemmer, James A., 223, 225
    Connor, Edward, 239
    Constable Ackerman, 57
    Cutaiar, Alphonso, Jr., 126
    DeKalb, Elizabeth "Lizzie," 223-24, 230
    disgraced officers, 240
    Elliott, Thomas, 277
    Faire, Frank "Grim," 242
    Hepting, Albert, 35
    H. H. Holmes, 138, 140, 143, 160, 163, 183, 191
    Huff, Henry, 248

Iacovetti, Antonio "Yorkey," 242
Langdon, Samuel P., 212
Logue, James "Jimmy," 129
Marengo, Nick, 242
McAvoy, James (*alias* Reardon), 35
McCain, John, 277
McCracken, Annie, 34, *38*
Mowbray, Charles Wilfred, 275
Parson, Thomas, 239
Paruchi, Frank "Fatty," 242
Pitezel, Mrs. Carrie, 185
Schoop, Jacob, 93
Schoop, Mrs. 93, 96
Strong, William H., 243
Tabbs, Hannah Mary, 60
thieves and, 73
Whiteling, Sarah Jane, 78
Wilson, George, 64
see also individual names listed above
arsenic, 72, 77, 81, 89, *see also* poison
    symptoms of, 77-79
Ashbridge, Samuel H., Philadelphia, 66, *203*
    characteristics of, 367
    coroner work of, 66, 72, 77-78, 81, 82, 96, 125-26, 182, 211-12, 350
    deputy coroner work of, 49
    Logue at home of, 125
    mayor work of, 130
    roses, story of, 367-68
    shows compassion to Logue, pays for burial, 130
    trial testimony, Holmes' case, 182
Atchley, Lisa (Geyer's great-great-granddaughter, surname Riggins), *269*
attempted murder, 72, 74
attorney, *see* individual names
autopsy, 84, 177, 203, 212, 219, 323

B
Badenoch, Police Chief, Chicago, 154
bail, 50, 198, 221
Bahia, South America, 111
Bailey, Mary C. (Mrs. Tabb's neighbor), 70
Bainbridge Street, Philadelphia, 69
Bainbridge Street Wharf, 72
Baitzell, County Detective William, New Jersey, 242

Baldwin Locomotive Works, Philadelphia, *280*

Ballon, John (Johnson murder case), 242

Bank of Chambersburg, Pennsylvania, *18*

Bank of North America, 113

bank scandal, 107, 111-13

Bardsley, John, Philadelphia, 113, *116*
    loaned public money, collected interest and, 113
    nickname, "Honest" Bardsley, 113
    pardon of, 113
    pleaded guilty and, 113
    received discounted notes and, 113
    sentencing of, 113

Barksdale, General (Gettysburg), 20

Barlow, Assistant District Attorney, Mr., (Holmes' case), 154, 162, 196,
    200, *see also* Holmes, H. H.

Barnhill, Dr., Indianapolis, 158-60
    charred bones package to Geyer and, 159

basement, 186
    Burlington, Vermont and, 185
    dynamite in, 185
    see also Holmes, H. H.

baton, 28, 56

Beale, Lieutenant, Philadelphia Police, 94

Beauregard, Brigadier General P. G. T., 16-17
    letter to Walker and, 16-17
    see also Civil War

Beaver, Governor James A., Pennsylvania, 84

Beck, former district attorney, Pennsylvania, 113

Beckett, Rev. J. C. (delegation of ministers), 249

Behrens, House Sergeant, Philadelphia Police, Eighth District, 118

Beitler, Public Safety Director, Philadelphia, 125

Belknap, Myrta Z., (Holmes' second wife), *see* Holmes, H. H.: wives

Bell, Alexander Graham (inventor), 28

Bennett, Dr. Mary "Alice," Norristown, PA, 51, *52*, 83-84
    first woman superintendent, 52
    testified at Annie Gaskin's hearing, 51

Bennett, Walter, Philadelphia, (with boys who found body), 91

Bensalem Township, Pennsylvania, 54

benzine, 173, 175

Berks Street, Philadelphia, 98

Bernstein, Detective, Philadelphia Police, *275*

Bertillon, Alphonse, inventor, *272*
    Bertillon System and, *272*
    mug shot and, *272*

Bertillon Bureau, United States, *272*
Bertillon System of Criminal Identification, *272*
  one hundred artificial eyes and, *272*
bicarbonate of soda, 161
bill of indictment, 113, 166-67, 224
blackjack, 57, 228, 239
blackjack brush, 91
blacksmith, 11
Bland, Leona (actress), *273, 274*
  arrest of, *273*
  lawsuit against Geyer, Chief Wood and, *274*
blisters, 176
Bristol, Pennsylvania, 54, 60
Board of Pardons, 124, 130
boarder (s), 6, 131, 307, 313
body, 55, 62-64, 66, 84, 91-92, 101, 103-04, 118, 121, 127-30, 140, 147,
      169, 171-74, 179-80, 189, 195-96, 226
  at police station, 35, 100
  dismembered and, 54, 69-70, 94, 96, 159-60
  exhumation of, 162, 170, 177, 180-81
  postmortem exam of, 173, 178
Boenning, Dr. Henry C., Philadelphia (conducted autopsy of Whiteling),
      84
bond, 107-08, 126
Bond, Mrs. Adelia, Philadelphia (unwitting cause of race riot), 247
  fired a revolver and, 248
  hearing of, 248
  house of, 247
  municipal court probation officer work of, 247
  name variations of, 380
  shot man in leg and, 248
  statement of, 248
Booth, John Wilkes, 23, 25
  assassinated President and, 23
  death of, 24
  Deringer pistol of, *26*
  holed up in barn and, 23-24
Boston Braves, *280-81*
Boston, Massachusetts, 111, 187, 193, 212
  Holmes, H. H., arrest in, 138-39, 143, 163, 191
  Pitezel, Mrs. Carrie, arrest in, 183
Bower, John Oscar (Orrie Strohm best man), 241
  author of medical papers of, 241
  physician, clinical professor or surgery work of, 241

Bowden, Emma (Mary Geyer boarded with, after Geyer's death), 307,
    313, 321-22
  sponsor, baptism, Elizabeth Strohm (Geyer's granddaughter), 321
Bradley, Thomas, Philadelphia, *277*
Brazil, South America, 111-12
Bridgeport, Pennsylvania, 63
Bridgeton Evening, 241, 312
Broad Street, Philadelphia, 23, 27, 47, 56, 60, 63, 173, 224, 273, 312
Brooklyn, New York, 109
Brooklyn Daily Eagle, 149
Brown, Captain, Philadelphia Police, 118, 120
Brown, H. J., MD, Philadelphia, 323
Brown, Attorney Mr., Philadelphia (Wilson trial, torso case), 70
Brown, Mr., Irvington, Indianapolis, 156
Brown, Sarah Jane, 75, *see also* Whiteling, Sarah Jane
Buchanan, President James, 313
Buenos Ayres, Argentine Republic, 110
Buck, Camilla (Geyer's mom), *see* Geyer, Camilla
Buck, Caroline (Geyer's aunt), 316
Buck, Charles (Geyer's uncle), 270, 316
Buck, Daniel (Geyer's uncle), 316
Buck, Dr. Gurdon, New York, (inventor), 37
Buck, Henry, (Geyer's uncle), 316
Buck, Jacob (Geyer's grandpa), 316
Buck, James (Geyer's uncle), 316
Buck, Maria (Geyer's aunt), 316
Buck, William Henry (Geyer's cousin), *270*
Bucks County, 54, 55, 62, 65, 69, 379
Bucks extension traction, *37*
Buffalo, New York, 24, 189-90
buggy, 63, 216-20, 223, 225-27, 230
  in courtroom, 221, 227
  see also carriage
bullae, 176
Bullitt Bill, 41-42, 46-47, 333-36
  departments authorized by, 334
Bullitt, W. C (member of House Committee), 333-34
Bull Run battlefield, 22, *see also* Civil War
Bureau of Detectives, *see* police, Philadelphia
Bureau of Police, *see* police, Philadelphia
Bureau of Surveys engineer, Philadelphia, 170
burglar (s), 127, *131,* 234, 240, 242
buried, *see* individual names
Burke and McFetridge Company (publisher, Holmes' memoir), 192

Burlington, New Jersey, 54
Burlington, Vermont, 185-87, 198
burn (ed, ing), 18-19, 145, 148, 153, 157, 160, 169-70
Burns, John, as house robber, 33
Burns, Peter (Logue murder case), 126
Butler, Jesse, Philadelphia (race riot, murdered Hugh Lavery), 248
Butler, Judge, Philadelphia (Gideon Marsh trial), 112
Byram, Dr., Irvington, Indianapolis, 163

C
Cadwallader, General John (American Revolutionary War), 54
Cadwallader Street, Philadelphia, 12, *13*, 80, 82, 307
Cadwallader Street, 1212, Philadelphia (victim murdered, dismembered; street nicknamed White Chapel Row), 90, 93-94
Cadwallader Street, 1219, Philadelphia (Whiteling trial witness), 82
Cadwallader Street, 1227, Philadelphia (Whiteling murder), 75
Cadwallader Street, 1647, Philadelphia (Geyer childhood home), 12, *13*, 236, 307, 312, 315-16, 323-24
Cadwallader Street, 1649, Philadelphia, 318
Callahan, Ellen, Philadelphia, as thief, *39*
Callowhill Bridge, Philadelphia, 64
Callowhill Street, No. 1316, Philadelphia (Benjamin Pitezel Patent business), 169, 172, 187, 188, 190, 196
calomel, 161
    used, unruly children and, 359
Camden, New Jersey, 226
Camp Cadwallader, Philadelphia, 27, 326, *see also* Civil War
Canada, 143, 145, 187, 189-90, 251, *272*
Canning, Mr. R. (Mrs. Pitezel's dad)
    petition to Governor to deny Holmes' respite and, 199
    see also Holmes, H. H.
Cannon, Jennie Mrs. (torso murder case), 59, 340
Cape May, New Jersey, 4, 308, 313, 322
Cape Verde Islands, 111
Carlisle Street, Philadelphia, 239
carpenter, 11, 29, 53, 124, 210
Carpenter, Emma P., *see* Kaiser, Emma
Carpenter, Officer, Philadelphia Police, 58
Carpenter Street, Philadelphia, 121
Carr, George Bradford (Kaiser's attorney), 223
carriage, 9, 27, 36, 92-94, 149-50, *see also* buggy
Castor, Coroner, Irvington, Indianapolis, 162, 200
castle, *see* Holmes' Castle
Catalonia ship, (Liverpool to Boston), 111

Centennial Exposition, Philadelphia, 28-29, *32*, 327-331
    Anniversary, twentieth, 42
    Commission of, 30
    diseases at, 30
    guards of, *see* police, Philadelphia: Centennial guard
    number of exhibitions and, 28
    Philadelphia appropriation and, 30
    twentieth anniversary of, 42
Centennial Guard, Philadelphia, *see* Police, Philadelphia: Centennial
    Guard
Central National Bank, 113
Central Station (Police Headquarters), 34-35, 64, 94, 101, 124, 128
    see also, police, Philadelphia
Chambersburg, Pennsylvania, 17-19
    burning and, 18
    homeless and, 18
    ransom demand and, 18
    ruins and, 18
    see also Civil War
charred human remains, 159-61
Centennial Guard, *see* police, Philadelphia: Centennial Guard
Chestnut Hill, Philadelphia, 21
Chestnut Street, Philadelphia, 23, 43, 65, 314
Chicago, Illinois, 24, 143-44, 149, 151, 153-55, 190, 272
Chicago World's Columbian Exposition, 161
Chickereno, Frank (Johnson murder case), 242
clairvoyant testimony, 242-43
chlorate of lime, 109
chloroform, 160, 173, 175-76, 178-79, 193
    doctor tastes from stomach, 177
    effects of, 181-82
    Holmes, H. H. and
        confession to Geyer about, 188
        prescription and, 161
        what if scenarios, trial questions and, 175-76, 178-79, 188
    Pitezel, Benjamin and, 174, 180-81
    practice on stray dog and, 215
chloronet of zinc, 109
cholera morbus, 50
Christian Endeavor Society, 151
Christian Street, Philadelphia, *31*
Cincinnati, Ohio, 143, 145
Circle House, 143
City Council Chambers, Norristown, PA, 220

City Hall, Philadelphia, 43, *45-46,* 47, 61, 64-66, 118, 120-21
  criminals locked up in, 65
  floor plan of, *46*
  Geyer, Frank at, 35-36, 41, 73
  National Historic Landmark and, 120
  sixth floor of, 120
  suicide in, 120
Civil War, 16, 19, 44
  Appomattox, Virginia and, 23
  Beauregard, P.G.T., Brigadier General and, 16-17
  Bull Run battlefield, 22
  Camp Cadwallader and, 27
  celebrations of, 22-23
  Chambersburg, PA and, 17-18
  confederate soldiers of, 16-17, 23
  Fort Sumter, 16
  fundraiser for, 20
  Grant, General Ulysses S., accept surrender of Lee, 23
  hospitals of, 20, *21,*
  Independent Battery "H" Light Artillery, 19
  Lee, General Robert E., surrender, 23
  Lincoln, President Abraham and, 16, 19
  Navy Shipyard and, 20
  187th Regiment, 322
  147th Regiment, Company E, 22, 27, 320,
  Philadelphia and, 19-23, 326
  16th New York Calvary, 25
  substitutes, 17
  204th Regiment, Battery C, 5th Heavy Artillery and, 22
  uniforms of, 17
  Union League Battery and, 23
  union soldiers of, 16-17
  Union Volunteer Refreshment Saloon and Volunteer Hospital, *22*
  United States Sanitary Commission's Great Central Fair and, 20
  Walker, L. P., Secretary of War, 16-17
  see also Geyer, Reuben K.
Clay, Public Safety Director, Philadelphia, 240
Clemens, Samuel L., *see* Twain, Mark
Clemmer, James, A., 214-20, 222-23, 226, *231*
  alias Harry E. Youngs, 225
  appeal of, 229
  arrest of, 225
  attempt kill Lizzie DeKalb, 216
  chloroform, practice on dog, 215

confession of, 230
death list of, 231
decoyed, advertisement and, 225
execution of, 230
grand jury indictment of, 226
indictment of, 224
insurance scam, buggy accident and 220
murder plots, kill Kaiser wife:
    chloroform, 215
    drowning, 216
    fake highwaymen, 216
    set fire to house, 215
pardon reasons and, 229-30
plot to kill Geyer and, 227-28
plot to kill Hughes and, 228
statement to Geyer and, 218
trial of, 226-28
verdict and, 228
witnesses identification of, 221
clerk of the court, Philadelphia, 129, 166-67
Cleveland, Ohio, 24
Cliver, Lulu, as Clemmer's alibi, 218
coffin, 103, 146-47, 162, 177
cocaine, 161
Cole, Thomas J., Philadelphia, hanged, 97
Cold Spring Presbyterian Cemetery, New Jersey, 317, 321-22
Colonel Mann's Ice Pond, Eddington, PA, 53
    handle with care package, 53
    torso found at, 53
Columbia Avenue, Philadelphia, 80, 91, 100,
Columbus, Ohio, 24
Commercial High School for Girls, Philadelphia, 312
Committee of One Hundred, Philadelphia, 119
conductor, 55-56, 59-60, 63, 101, 106
confederates, *see* Civil War
confession of
    Clemmer, James A., 225, 230
    Cutaiar, Alphonso, Jr., 127-28
    DeKalb, Elizabeth "Lizzie," 210, 227
    Hedgepeth, Marion, 183, 211
    Holmes, H. H., 140, 191, 199-201
    Nack, Mrs., 225
    Schoop, Jacob, 90, 96
    Strong, William H., 242

Tabbs, Hannah Mary, 61-64, 69-70
Wilson, George, 53
Whiteling, Sarah Jane, 78-81
    see also individual names listed above
Connor, Edward (arrested, race riot), 239
Conrad, Mayor Robert T., Philadelphia, 340
    directed officers to drink to enforce Sunday Liquor Law, 340
Conshohocken, PA, 220, 225
Consolidated National Bank, 113
Cook County, Illinois, 365
Cook, Reverend J. F. C., Philadelphia, 215, 369-70
Corbett, Sergeant Thomas "Boston," *25*
    caused a ruckus and, 25
    disobeyed orders and, 25
    insane asylum in, 25
    killed John Wilkes Booth and, 24
    peddling and, 25
    pistol of, 25
Corliss Steam Engine, 28
Cornwalls station, Pennsylvania, 56, 63
coroner, *see* individual names
coroner's inquest, 35, 49-50, 54, 65-66, 69, 82, 96, 120, 127, 148-50,
    166, 219, 220, 222
corpse, 169-71, 181, 195-96, 250
Court of Common Pleas, 196
Couch, General, 17, *see also* Civil War
Crawford, Detective Thomas, 56, 59, 61, 64-65, 72, 77-78, 92-93, 107,
    109-111, 124-25, 139-40, 187, 224, 237, 274
    as execution juror, 84
    defends Geyer, 235
    discipline of, 235, 241
criminologist, 205
Crooked Lane, Norristown, Pennsylvania, 217
Cuddy, Detective Alfred, Toronto, Canada, 144-50
Cumberland County, Pennsylvania, 241
Cumberland Valley, Pennsylvania, 17
Cunningham, Robert (mail fraud), 34
Cutaiar, Alphonso, Jr., (murdered Johanna Logue), 124-25, 128, 130,
    132, 133
    commutation request and, 124, 135
    confessions of, 126-27
    coroner's inquest and, 127
    first degree murder and, 129
    looked like H. H. Holmes, 128-29

petition from family to commute sentence, 130

real dad of, 126

sentence of, 130

stolen bond and, 126

stolen jewelry and, 126-27

trial of, 129

verdict, trial of, 129

Cutaiar, Ella J. C. (Alphonso Cutaiar's daughter), 130

D

Dailey, Father (H. H. Holmes, Jacob Schoop's priest at hanging), 97, 199

Daniel Buck and Brother Lumber Yard, 12

Darby, Miss, as teacher, Philadelphia, 80

Dauphin Street, Philadelphia, 30

death warrant, 84

Declaration of Independence, 28

Detectives Department, *see* Police, Philadelphia

degenerate, 206, *see also* Holmes, H. H.: degenerate

DeKalb, Elizabeth "Lizzie" (Kaiser murder), 210, 214-21, 224, 226, 229, *231*

admonishment of, 230

aliases of, 231

arrested, 223-24

as Clemmer household servant, 226

as waitress, 230

avoid Clemmer at trial and 227

clothing of, 226

confession of, 210, 225-26

elope, escaped criminal and, 231

indictment of, 224

informant, Clemmer trial and, 226

mistress, Clemmer, and, 226

nickname, "Woman in Black," 216, 230

plot to kill Geyer and, 227-28

response to admonishment, 230

testimony of, 226-28

trial of, 230

signature of, 210

stole horse and buggy and, 217, 230

DeKalb Street, Norristown, PA, 242

Delaware River, 9, 12, 54

Denver, Colorado, 126, 193

Dercum, Francis Xavier, Philadelphia physician, 84

Department of Public Safety, *see* Police, Philadelphia

detective, *see* Police, Philadelphia; and individual names
detective liaison, 143
Detroit, Michigan, 144-45, 148, 151-52, 154, 189, 288
disinterred, 162,
dismembered torso, 53, 65, 66, *see also* Gains, Wakefield; Tabbs,
    Hannah Mary; and Wilson, George
District Attorney, *see* individual names
Donal, Clerk, Philadelphia court, 66
Downer, J. N., (Holmes accused wife, Clara, of cheating with), 368
Doyle, Sir Arthur Conan (Sherlock Holmes author), 313
draft, military, 247
Drexel's, Philadelphia, 126
drugstore, 79, 161, 203
drunk, drunkenness, 29, 33, 57-58, 99-100, 126, 178, 325
Dugan, Coroner, Philadelphia, 120, 127-28
Duke of Cambridge, 20
Dunks Ferry, Philadelphia, 54
dynamite, 185-86, 198

E
Eastern State Penitentiary, Philadelphia, 72, 112-13, 124, 240
Eckstcin, Officer, Philadelphia Police, 105-06
Eddington Flag Station, Pennsylvania, 53
Eddington, Pennsylvania, 54-56, 59-60, 63, 65-66
Eddington Schoolhouse, Pennsylvania, 54
Eddington's constable, *see* Jackson, Frederick
Eighth Street, Philadelphia, 210, 228
Eleventh Street, Philadelphia, 188
Eleventh Street, 1250 North, Philadelphia (Johanna Logue murder), 124,
    128
Elliott, Clinton T, (married Dorothy Strohm) *13, 268*, 321
Elliott, David, *268*
Elliott, Dorothy, *see* Strohm, Dorothy
Elliott, Elizabeth, *see* Strohm, Elizabeth
Elliott, Joseph R. (married Elizabeth Strohm), *13,* 321
Elliott, Joyce (Geyer great-granddaughter, married name Riggins),
    268-69
Elliott, Stanley, *268*
Elliott, Thomas, Philadelphia, *277*
Ellsworth Street, 2036 (race riot inciting event) Philadelphia, 247
Englewood, Illinois, 144
Episcopal Hospital, Philadelphia, 33-34, *36,* 37, 56, 103, 333
estate of
    Frank Geyer, 382

Captain Joseph Schooley, 121
Ewell, Dr., Chicago, Illinois, 338
executed, Philadelphia
    Clemmer, James A., 229-30
    Cole, Thomas J., 97
    Holmes, H. H., 137, 199-200, 212
    Schoop, Jacob, 97
    Whiteling, Sarah Jane, 84, *88*
    see also individual names listed above
exhumation, 77, 170-71, 177, 180, 191
explosion, 118, 172-73, 184, 189
extradite, 139, 161-62, 190

F
Fahy, Thomas A. (Mrs. Pitezel's attorney), 151, 200
Faire, Frank "Grim," (Johnson murder case), 242
Fairmount Avenue, Philadelphia, 239, *284*
Fairmount Park, Philadelphia, 90, 200, 328
fake death, 139, 188, 214
Fania, Louisa (Annie Klaus friend), 98, 101
Favinger, Henry H. (Geyer's brother-in-law), 316
    burial of, 317
    death of, 316
    marriage of, 316
    worked, Frankford Arsenal, 316
Favinger, Stanley Reuben (Geyer's nephew), 316
    worked, Frankford Arsenal, 316
Ferguson, Lieutenant, Philadelphia Police, 48
Fidelity Mutual Life Association, 141, 154, 188, 191
    Fouse, L. G., President of, 166, 201
    Gary, Mr. and, 2, 154-60
    Perry, O. Le Forest and, 183, 190, 211, 212
    Pitezel insurance payout, 140, 183
Fifty-fifth Street, Philadelphia, *286*
fire, 1, 3, 27, 104, 120, 140, 186, 188, 215, 249, 251, 269, 326
First Judicial Court of Common Pleas, 47
First National Bank, 113
Fitler, Mayor Edwin H., Philadelphia, 46, 72-73, 119-20, 344, 352
Fitzpatrick, Inspector, Chicago, 154-55
flu pandemic, *see* Spanish Flu
Fluck, Rev. J. F. C., Pennsylvania, 319
Ford, President Gerald, 313
Ford's Theatre, 23
forgery, 140

Formad, Coroner's Physician Dr. Henry F., Philadelphia, 50, 66, 71, 84
    appointed Demonstrator of Morbid Anatomy and, 337
    blood poisoning and, 50
    book of, 337
    cholera morbus death, 50
    investigated diphtheria and, 337-38
    investigated venom poisoning, 338
    scholarly papers and, 338
foreign-born inhabitants, 108
Fort Sumter, Charleston Bay, 16-17
Fort Worth, Texas, 140, 183, 186, 194
Founder's Week, Philadelphia, 240
Founding Fathers of America, 2, 311
Fourth Street, Philadelphia, 1, 311, 333
Fouse, Levi G. (Fidelity Mutual President), 166, 201
Frankford Arsenal, Philadelphia, 316
Frankford Lodge No. 292, Philadelphia, 297
Franklin, Benjamin (Founding Father), 4, 313
Franklin, Superintendent Benjamin (Pinkerton, detective agency), 107
fraud, 34, 73, 188, 211-12, 220, 229
Francis, Lieutenant, Philadelphia Police, 65
freemason, *see* Mason
Fricke, Harry (Cutaiar's apprentice), 126
Friend, Mrs. Mary Ann (Logue neighbor), 125
Fuller, Rev., New York, 9-10
funeral, 9, 79, 98
    Geyer's relative, 33
    Geyer, Camilla (Buck), 236, 316
    Geyer, Franklin P., 251
    Kayser, Otto, 103-04
    Klaus, Annie, 103-04
    Schooley, Captain Joseph, 121
    White House, Lincoln, 24

G
Gahan, William (Joanna Logue's brother), 124
Gains, Wakefield (torso murder victim), 71-72
    attacked by Tabbs and, 59
    characteristics, description of, 59
    dismembered and, 62, 64-65, 69-70
    exhumation of, 65
    how murdered and, 61, 66, 69
    identification of, 59, 66
    missing and, 59, 64

gallows, 130, 201
Galva, Illinois, 161-62, 199
Garfield, President James A., 313
Gary, W. E. Inspector (Fidelity Mutual), 2, 154-60
Gaskin, Annie (murdered baby Joseph), 48, 52, 83
 characteristics of, 50-51
 claim of cat attack, 49-50
 committed to Norristown and, 51
 inquest and, 50
 release of, 51
 trial of, 50-51
Gaskin, Joseph (10 week old murder victim), 48-51
Geiss' Hotel, 189
George Bille's drugstore, Philadelphia, 79
German shoe dealer, Philadelphia, 98
German nationality, 92
Germany, 29, 95, 247, 270
German Reformed Church, Philadelphia, 316, 320
German steamship *Martha,* 109, 118
Gettysburg, battle of, rebel killed, 20
Geyer, Anna E. (Geyer's sister, married Favinger), 12
 birth of, *13,* 316
 burial of, 316-17
 death, cause, 316
 death of, *13,* 316
 marriage of, *13,* 316
 son of, 316
Geyer, Camilla (Geyer's mother, given name Buck), 317-18
 birth of, *13,* 315
 buried at, 237, 316
 death of, *13,* 236, 316, 376
 funeral of, 236, 316
 marriage of, *13,* 316
 sickness of, 236
Geyer, Edna Camilla (Geyer's daughter, married Strohm), 3-4, 154,
  237, 251, *255-58, 265, 267-68,* 313, 321, 380, 382
 birth of, 3, *13,* 312, 317
 burial of, 317-18
 children of, *13,* 243, 250
  see also Strohm, Elizabeth, Dorothy, and Frank
 childhood of, 90, 100, 109, 154-55, 237, *255-58*
 curled up, daddy's lap and, 155
 death of, *13,* 317
 erroneous fire and, 3, 6, 251, 310

graduation announcement of, 258
high school graduate and, 312
marriage of, *13,* 241-42, 317, 322, 378
not Esther and, 1, 3-4
Geyer, Franklin Pierce, *7, 255-56, 262, 265.*
able seaman and, 109
accident of, 33-34
alias Frank P. Roberts, 109-10
ancestry of, 4, *13,* 311, 315-22, *see also* individual surnames, e.g.
    Buck, Elliott, Geyer, Riggins, Strohm
anniversary of, 109, 241
annual salary of, 237
as execution juror, 84
birthday of, 17, 27-28, 110, 153, 236, 247
birth of, 11, *13,* 314, 318
bond, South America trip, 108
Book, authored by, *The Holmes-Pitezel case; a history of the greatest*
  crime of the century and of the search for the missing Pitezel
  children, 4, 7, 210
burial of, 251, 318
business card of, *244*
carpenter skills of, 29, 210
cases of, *see* individual names
centennial guard, position, 28-30, 327
characteristics and description of, 1-4, 29-30, 104, 137, 221, 237, 251
child of, 3-4, *13, see also* Geyer, Edna Camilla
childhood and adolescence of, 11-13, 16-23, 27
compared to boxer John L. Sullivan, 104
death, cause of, 251, 318
death of, *13,* 251, 318
detective agency of, 4, 242, *244*
detective promotion of, 46, 73
discipline of, 235-36
dual role of, 34-35, 45-46
election officer, position of, 34
estate of, 382
fire falsehood, Geyer's family killed and, 1, 3-4, 251
fractured femur of, 34, 37
founding fathers and, 4, 311-12
gave murderer cigar and, 94
general, Revolutionary War and, 2
grandchildren, great-grandchildren, great-great-grandchildren of, 3,
    13, 237, 243, 251, *253, 259-60, 261, 265-66, 268-69,* 290, 311,
    314, 318

Knights Templar parade, *264*
La Grippe and, 251, *see also* Spanish Flu
life insurance, South America trip, 108
Lit Brothers department store work of, 237, *238,* 377
marriage of, 3, *5, 13,* 317-18, *see also* Geyer, Mary Elizabeth
mason and, 4, 251, 314
named after President Franklin Pierce and, 11, 314
nicknames of, 3, 11, 56, 104-106, 137
patents of, 4, 210, *214, 245,* 383
patrolman, position, 28, 30, 34, 327
pension of, 237
plot to kill and, 227-28, 231
promoted to detective and, 45, 73, 338
promoted to special officer and, 30
quotes of, 153, 287-89
reported to Coroner Ashbridge, 125
resignation of, 34, 137, 237, 327
        foreshadowed and, 237
retirement of, 237-39
revolver and, 104
saved woman from fiend, 105-106
saved people and, 36
secret search, 107-117
souvenirs from murder cases, 237
        H. H. Holmes' rope, 237-38
special officer, position, 33-35, 45, 48-49, 56, 59, 69, 73, 312
statistics of, 73-74, 237
testimony of, cases of
        Clemmer, James A., 226
        Cutaiar, Alphonso, 128
        Gaskin, Annie, 50
        Holmes, H. H., 140, 148-49, 166, 187-92
        Kaiser, Charles O. Jr., 220-23
        Mowbray, Charles Wilfred, Geyer "blood boil" statement, 275
        police court of inquiry, 236
        Shoemaker, William A. (Holmes' attorney), 197
translation, German and, 93, 95-96
United States postal agent, position, 34
uniform and, 28
vacation and, 4, 6, 237
vacation home of, 4, *6*
see also Police, Philadelphia
Geyer, Katharina "Kate" Ella (Geyer's sister, married Werner), 12, *13,*
        19, 236

baptism of, 319
birth of, *13,* 318
burial of, 319
daughter of, 319
death of, *13,* 318
marriage of, *13,* 236, 318
Geyer, Mary Elizabeth (Geyer's wife, given name Rilley), 1-6, *13,* 108,
    237, 239, 241-43, 251, *255-56, 263, 265,* 307, 315, 317-18,
    320-22
    birth of, *13,* 314, 320
    birthday of, 110
    burial of, 251, 254, 321, 382
    child of, 3-4, *13, see also* Geyer, Edna Camilla
    death of, *13,* 320, 382
    erroneous fire, and, 1, 3-4, 251, 310
    grandchildren, great-grandchildren, great-great-grandchildren of, 3,
        13, 237, 243, 251, *253, 259, 260, 261, 265, 266, 269*
    marriage of, 3, *5, 13,* 312, 318
    not Martha, 1, 4
    occupation of, 1-2, 312
    possible census linked to, 321
    statement about Geyer's unexpected absence and, 107-111
    variations, given name of, 311, 320
    see also Geyer, Franklin P.
Geyer, Reuben K. (father), *13,* 17, 237, 315-20
    Civil War and, 19-20
        147th Regiment, 22, 27, 324
        204th Regiment, Battery C, 22, 322, 324
        Independent Battery "H" Light Artillery, 19, 322
        invalid and, 327
        mustered in, 19, 323-24
        mustered out, 27
        net pay, 322
        pension, 326-27
        private, 323
        provost guard duty and, 19
        see also Civil War
    birth of, *13,* 319
    burial of, 320
    carpenter business and, 11
    death, cause of, 319
    death of, *13,* 236, 320
    marriage of, *13,* 316, 319, *see also* Geyer, Camilla
    sickness of, 236

spinal sclerosis and, 236
Geyer, William Henry (Geyer's brother), 12
    birth of, *13,* 320
    burial of, 320
    death, cause of, 320, 323
    death of, *13,* 320
Gilbert, Charlie (Whiteling murder case), 80
Gilbert, Elizabeth (Whiteling murder case), 82
Gillan, Annie, Philadelphia, 49
Gillingham Street, Philadelphia, 94
Gilmanton, New Hampshire, 139, 194
Gloucester, Pennsylvania, 227
Gotwals, Officer, Norristown, 218
Graham, District Attorney George S., Philadelphia, 6, 68-69, 71,
        129-30, *135, 202,* 210, 212, 274, 313
    Holmes, H. H. case, 139, 141, 147, 154, 156, 161-62, 166, 169-72,
        181-87, 190-95, 198-99
        closing speech, 195-96
        opening statement, 168
    letter to Board of Pardons in favor of Cutaiar, 121, 130-31
    Shoemaker, William A. (Holmes' attorney), 196-98
    quote of, 1
    request commutation and, 124
grand jury, 58, 83, 161-62, 166, 212, 226
Grand Rapids, Michigan, 192
Grand Trunk Depot, Toronto, 149, 189
Grant, General Ulysses S., 23
    accepted surrender of Lee, 324
    see also Civil War
Greenmount Cemetery, Philadelphia, 104, 349
Groom, Evan J. (coroner's physician), 54-55

H
Hagen, Inspector (London Metropolitan Police), 28, 329
Hammerstein's Opera House, Philadelphia, 239
    race riot at, 239
Hancock Street, Philadelphia, 80
Hanscom, Deputy Superintendent Orinton M., Boston, 183
handcuffed, 220, *see also* nippers
hanged, 153, 200, 229-30
Hare, Judge (torso murder case judge), 71-72
Harding, President Warren G., 313
Harrisburg, Pennsylvania, 24, 187, 241
Harrison Street [police] station, Chicago, Illinois, 155

Hart, Crier, Philadelphia court, 184
Hartford, Connecticut, 5, 312, 315, 320
      Twain, Mark and, 314-15
Hastings, Governor Daniel H., Pennsylvania, 199
hatchet, 69
Hatch, Edward (Holmes' *alias,* alter ego*)*, 141, 144, 153, 190, 200
      see also Holmes, H. H.
Hatch, Frederick (one of President Lincoln's guards), 23
Haupt, Rev. Walter G. (Edna Geyer, Orrie Strohm marriage), 241
Hedgepeth, Marion (Holmes' case, notorious bank robber), 183
      as informant, 211
hemp, 288
Henry, Mayor Alexander, Philadelphia, 119
Henry Deringer Firearms Factory, Philadelphia, 26
Henry, Special Officer, Philadelphia 78, 93-94, 96
Hepting, Albert, Philadelphia (assault/larceny), 35
Herald, David (John Wilkes Booth's partner), 23
Hernandes, Linda (Geyer's great-great-granddaughter, given name
      Riggins), *269*
Herwood, George, Philadelphia (with boys who found body), 91
Hibbs, Silas (Tabbs and Wilson murder trial, found torso), 53
Hillside Cemetery, Roslyn, Pennsylvania, 251, *253,* 254, 290-91, 318,
      320-21, 382
Hoffman, Levi, Philadelphia (friend of murdered Annie Klaus), 98
Holmes' Castle, 144, 154-55, *see also* Holmes, H. H.
Holmes, H. H. *142*
      abnormalities of, 206
      arrest of, 138-40, 143, 160, 163, 183, 191
      as 'Devil in the White City,' 1, 3, 133, 251
      attempted murder, dynamite and, 198
      bicarbonate of soda and, 161
      bigamist and, 137
      bill of indictment and, 166-67
      birth name of, 139
      bogus bank note and, 140
      boils and, 205
      borrowed spade and, 146, 201
      bribes Mrs. Pitezel, for respite and, 199
      cadaver
            baby and, 205
            foot of child and, 205
      castle, 144, 154-55
      characteristics and description of, 137, 139, 145, 147, 163, 206-07
      child of, divorce and, 359

chloroform and, 160, 173-74, 188
 questions at trial by, 175, 178-79
 purchased large quantities by, 161
 see also chloroform
claims of,
 little Howard, bad boy, 143
 pinned $400 to dress, 189
 requested Nellie's hair cut like boy, 189
cocaine and, 161
confessions of, 140, 191, 199-201
conviction of, 196
death of, 199-200
deformed feet of, 206
degenerate and, 206
descendent of, first English settlers, New Hampshire, 139
divorce transcript of, 366
doctor examination of, 205-06
dug hole in cellar and, 144, 146
exhumation of Pitezel, Potter's Field
 gloves, used doctors' and, 172
 turned Pitezel over and, 172
 used lance and, 172
 removed wart, mustache and, 172
execution of, 200
failed to pay Hedgepeth, Marion, 211
grand jury and, 166
home, north Eleventh Street and, 188
in cell at City Hall, 140
insurance scam of, 139-40, 183, 185-86, 211
key to Irvington cottage and, 163
Kymographion and, 205, *208*
lance, from pocket and, 170-71, 177, 181, 187
letters from Pitezel's and, 143, 152, 154, 200
look-a-like body substitute and, 139
medical exam of, 205-06
medical school and, 207, 365-66
memoir of, 167, 192
moved Pitezel downstairs and, 174, 188-90, 195
Mudgett, Herman Webster, given name of, 139
paid undertaker, move Pitezel and, 162
pectus carinatum (pigeon chest) of, 206
peculiar odor of, 205
pleaded guilty at insurance fraud trial of, 140
prescriptions and, 161

prison diary of, 167
psychological exam of, 205-06
Quinlan, Patrick (Holmes' janitor), *see* Quinlan, Patrick
requests Governor, respite and, 199
strabismus of, 206
surgical instruments and, 161
trial of, murder, *see also* Arnold, Judge Michael
    complains of slur and, 172
    complains of sickness and, 182
    inside knowledge, how Pitezel murdered and, 175, 178
    irritated of claims he mutilated corpse, 181
    new trial request and, 198-99
    represents himself at murder trial and, 168-183
    request judge order notes read back to, 172
    request to remove Geyer from court, 172
    request two sessions per day, not three, 182
    request witnesses be excluded until testimony, 169
    verdict and, 196
    witnesses, no conversing with each other, 175
University of Michigan, Ann Arbor, and, 205, 207
warrant for horse theft and, 139
wives of,
    Holmes, Myrta Z. (second wife, Willamette marriage, given name
        Belknap), 193,
    Mudgett, Clara A. (legal wife, given name Lovering), 205, 368
        as Gilmanton woman, 194
        black eye of, 205
        bromide treatment and, 205
        epileptic convulsions of, 205
    Yoke, Georgiana (third wife, assumed given name following
            Holmes' arrest), 143, 168, 172, 183, 186-87, 193, 198
        admits, she knew Holmes' married first wife, 194
        crazy story, Holmes' told, 194
        married Holmes and, 193
Hope Street, Philadelphia, 98, 100
horse (s), 36, 90, 93-94, 216-18, 220
    theft of, 139, 183, 230
Hotel Frietas, Rio de Janiero, 110
Howe, Jeptha (Pitezel attorney), 140, 170, 183-84
Huff, Henry, Philadelphia (murderer, race riot)
    held by sailors, 249
    killed Officer McVay, 248
    mob retaliation, at home of, 249
Hughes, Benjamin (witness, Kaiser case), 217, 228, 231

human remains, 93, 157-58, 160

I

Iacovetti, Antonio "Yorkey" (burglar), 242
identification marks, Pitezel, *see* Pitezel, Benjamin
immigrated, 2
imprisonment, 113, 129, 274, see also arrest
Independent Battery "H" Light Artillery, 19, 323
    see also Civil War
Independence Hall, Philadelphia, 9, 22, 24
Indian rupee, 110
Indianapolis News reported, 153, 158, 160
Indianapolis, Indiana, 24, 143, 153-56, 159, 161-63, 166, 184, 190, 200
inflammation, 76, 174
influenza, 120, 250-51, see *also* Spanish Flu
inmate, 130, 357
inner skin, 176
inquest, 35, 49-50, 54, 65-66, 69, 82, 96, 120, 127, 148-50, 166, 219, 220, 222
inspection general of Health of Ports, Rio de Janeiro, 109
insurance, 75, 79-81, 84, 108, 120, 139-41, 148, 152, 154, 183-86, 211-12, 216, 218-21, 226, 229, 370
International Centennial Exposition, *see* Centennial Exposition, Philadelphia
Inter Ocean reported, 154, 156, 158, 160-161
Ireland, 2, 320
Irish, 1-3, 239
Irish American, 104
Italian, 55, 92, 239
Irvington cottage, Indianapolis, 152, 156, 158, 162-63, *see also* Holmes, H. H.
Islington Lane, Philadelphia, 27

J

Jackson, Constable Frederick, Eddington, PA, 54
Jackson, President Andrew, 313
Jacksonville, Florida, 226
Jack the Ripper
    anonymous letters and, 93
    next victim a lawyer and, 93
jail, 66, 127, 168, 185, 211
Jefferson Medical College, Philadelphia, 55
Jenkintown, Pennsylvania, 61
John L. Stevens (steamship), 9

John Hancock Insurance Company, 79
Johnson, George (murder victim), 242
Johnson, President Lyndon B., 313
Johnston, Coroner, Toronto, Canada, 148, 150
John Welsh School, Philadelphia, *258,* 312
jury, 51, 58, 66, 68, 71, 81-84, 96, 128-30, 135, 161-62, 166-67, 175-76, 191, 196, 198, 212, 221, 223, 226, 228, 235, 243, *see also* Grand jury

K
Kaiser, Charles "Charlie" O., Jr., 214-17, *231*
    as crayon portrait dealer, 218
    bullet through arm of, 221
    bought stolen horse and buggy and, 217
    chloroform test on dog and, 215
    confession of, 222-23, 228
    coroner's inquest and, 220
    handcuffed to Chief Rodenbaugh, 220
    knew Geyer as a boy and, 218
    lawsuit of, 229
    life insurance of, 215, 219, 221, 229
    marriage of, 215
    murder plots to kill wife Emma
        chloroform, 215
        drowning in Schuylkill, 216
        fake highwaymen, 216
        poisoning, 216
        remove bolts on buggy, 216
        set fire to boarding house, 215
    nervous fit of, 219
    ripped open shirt and, 218
    statement to Geyer and, 220, 222-23
    suicide of, 229
    testimony at Clemmer trial, 228
    trial of, 221
    verdict and sentence of, 224
    will of, 215
Kaiser, Charles O., Sr., lawsuit, 229
Kaiser, Mrs. Emma "Toots" (murder victim), 212-13, *231*
    autopsy of, 219
    description of killing of, 217
    given name, Carpenter and, 372
    life insurance of, 215
    marriage of, 215
    real age of, 229

will of, 215
Kane, Francis Fischer (United States Attorney, Eastern PA), 249
Kansas City Star, 111
Kansas House of Representatives, 25
Kayser, Mrs. (Otto's wife), 102
    children and, 102
    hospitalization of, 103
    throat slashed and, 102
    would like to see the devil, statement of, 98
Kayser, Otto (killed Annie Klaus), 99, 103, *106*
    alias Tom Lynn, 101-102
    admitted to killing and, 99
    attempted murder of wife, 102
    as conductor, 101, 106
    death expression of, 103-104
    description of, 101
    drunk and, 99
    fired and, 101
    funeral of, 103
    murder of Annie Klaus and, 102
    suicide of, 102
    waves .32 caliber Defender and, 99
Kelly, Francis R., Philadelphia Police, *43,* 56, 59-61, 272, 332
    bank guardianship position and, 73
    chief of detectives position and, 35, 43, 55, 59-61, 335
    fire brigade chief position and, 43
    interim, chief of detectives position and, 335
    secret service agent position and, 43, 73
    offer of demotion of, 73
    removal as chief of detectives and, 73
    resigned and, 73
    testimonials of, 73
Kelly, Joseph, Philadelphia (race riot, shot by Adelia Bond), 248
Kenny, Thomas, Philadelphia (with boys who found body), 91
Kenney, Special Officer, Philadelphia Police, 78
Kensington Avenue, Philadelphia, 33
Kensington Avenue, 2738, Philadelphia, (Otto Kayser, suicide at), 102
Kensington, Pennsylvania, 234
Keystone National Bank, Philadelphia, 107, 111, 113-16, 333
Kiel, Captain Ahren (*Martha* steamship), 110
King, John (Holmes' trial), 191-02
Kinsey, Judge, Philadelphia, 239-41
    statement, against disgraced police officers, 240
Klaus, Annie (murder victim), 35, 98, 102, 104, *106*

body at police station, 35
   funeral of, 103
   gun powder on face, 349
   identification of, 100-101
Klaus, Antoinie (or Antone, Annie Klaus' mother), 101, 350
Klaus, Henry (Annie Klaus' father), 101, 349
Knight of Pythias (delegation of ministers), 249
Knox, Attorney General, 113
Krusen, Health Director Dr. Wilmer, Philadelphia, 250-51
Kurtz, Coroner Milton R., Norristown, Pennsylvania, 219
Kurtz, Detective E. D., Philadelphia Police, 73
Kymographion (instrument used on Holmes), 205, *208*
   see also Holmes, H. H.

L
Laffarty, Martin as safe cracker, 130
La Grippe, 250-51, *see also* Spanish Flu
Lamon, Superintendent John, Philadelphia Police, 73, 120
lancet, 170, 177, 181, *see also* Holmes, H. H.
Lane, Captain (Union Army), 324, *see also* Civil War
Langdon, Samuel P., Philadelphia (Annie McGrath case), 212
Langford, Mr. (Marsh case), 110
Lare, Mrs. (Kayser's mother-in-law), 99
Larson, Eric, 310
laudanum, 95
Laurel Hill Cemetery, Philadelphia, 203, 316-17, 319-20
Lavery, Hugh, Philadelphia (race riot murder victim), 248
law enforcement, characteristics of, 233
   see also Police, Philadelphia
Lawrence, William H. (secretary of American legation), 110
Lee, General Robert E, 23
   surrendered, 325
   see also Civil War
Leffman, Dr. Henry, analytical chemist, Philadelphia (Holmes' trial),
      77-78, 192
   chloroform effects on
      animals and, 181
      humans and, 181-82
      see also Holmes, H. H.
Levy, Nathan, as highway robber, 33
Liberty Bell, 24
Liberty Loan parade, Philadelphia, 250
Liberty Torch, *32*
Lincoln, President Abraham, 16, 20, 25, 27, 325

assassination of, 23
call for volunteer soldiers and, 19
footman and, 23
funeral of, 24
hearse of, *26*
wife of, 325
Linden, Superintendent Robert J., Philadelphia Police, 107-08, 147, 191, 212, 218
pooh-poohed Holmes investigation and, 211
quote, absolute rot, 153
Liverpool, England, 111
Logue, James "Jimmy" (career criminal), *131*
accused, attempting liberties with relative, 129
alias, coroner imposed, 125
bigamy and, 124
burial of, 130
characteristics of, 125, 129
coroner's inquest and, 127
hid bonds under carpet and, 126
interesting testimony of, 127-28
kept in jail as witness and, 127
legal wife of, 124
married Johanna, courthouse dock, 124
requests to go to Almshouse for last days, 129-30
showed up unannounced at coroner's house and, 125
signed petition to commute Alphonso's sentence, 130
stepson, Alphonso Cutaiar, 125
witness fees and, 128-29
Logue, Johanna, Philadelphia (Jimmy's wife, murdered), 126-29, *134*
body found of, 124
burial of, 130
identification of, 124
marriage of, 124
Logue, Matilda (Jimmy's daughter-in-law), 129
accused Jimmy of attempting liberties, 129
London, England, 28, 189, 191, 330
Lovering, Clara (Holmes' wife, Mrs. Mudgett), 205, 365-66
as Gilmanton woman, 194
black eye of, 205
bromide treatment and, 205
epileptic convulsions of, 205
see also Holmes, H. H.
Lowell, Massachusetts, 185
lumber mill, 11

Lyman, Benton T., *see* Pitezel, Benjamin: *alias* Lyman, Benton
Lyons, Lieutenant Edward, Philadelphia Police, 57-58

M

MacDonald, Dr. Arthur, Criminologist, Washington DC (Holmes case), 205-06, 208
MacIntire, Officer John, Philadelphia Police
    blackjack assault and, 57
    drunkenness of, 57
    firing of, 58
    suspension of, 56
    threat, kill lieutenant and, 56
    workplace shooting and, 56-58
Magg, John, Philadelphia farmer, 90
magistrate, 66, 221, 224-25
malaria, 30
manuscript of Holmes, H. H., 191-02, 275, 290
Marengo, Nick (Johnson murder case), 242
Marine Hospital Service, 108
Marsh, Gideon Wells, Philadelphia (ex-bank president), 107-10, *114,* 121
    fined and, 112
    fugitive and, 107
    pardon of, 113
    sentence of, 112
Marsh's Saloon (South Street, Philadelphia), *277*
Martha steamship, 109
Martin, Dr. (Cadwallader St, Philadelphia), 80
Mason, Officer, Philadelphia Police, 48-49
Masons, 4, 251
    famous and, 313-14
    presidents and, 313-14
Mattern, Dr. William K., Coroner's Physician, Philadelphia (Holmes' trial), *203*
    at exhumation, 177, 180
    chloroform in stomach, 180
    Pitezel not intoxicated, 178
    removal, Pitezel's fingers, 177
    trial testimony, 177-181
    ungloved hands, 177
    see also Holmes, H. H.
Matthews, Governor Claude, Indiana, 162
Matthews, Undertaker, Philadelphia, 66
Matthias and Lee's chair-caning, 71

mayor, Philadelphia, *see* individual names

Mays Landing, New Jersey, 218, 242

McAvoy, Charles D., District Attorney Norristown, 242

McAvoy, James, Philadelphia (*alias* Reardon), 35

McCabe, Frank, Philadelphia (with boys who found body), 91

McCain, John, Philadelphia, *277*

McCausland, Brigadier General John, 18, see also Civil War

McCracken, Annie, Philadelphia (larceny), 34, *38*

McCuen's Saloon, Philadelphia, 119

McFetridge, Mr. (Holmes' book publisher), 192

McGrath, Annie, Philadelphia (mysterious death), 212

McKibben, Special Officer, Philadelphia Police, 100

McKinley, President William, 313

McVay, Officer Thomas, Philadelphia Police (murdered in race riot), 248

    mob retaliation of, 249

Meadowcroft, Charles, (Kaiser murder case), 215

Mechanics Cemetery, Philadelphia, 77

Media, Pennsylvania, 62

Methodist Midtown Parish, Philadelphia, 312, 318, 320

Metropolitan Opera House, 239.

    see also Hammerstein's Opera House

Metropolitan Police, London, 28, 325

Michigan, 144-45, 155, 189, 192, 338

Miller, Peter, Philadelphia Police

    captain work of, 56, 224

    detective work of, 56, 59

Mills, Dr. Charles K (Whiteling murder case, expert witness), 75, 83

Mills, Superintendent, Philadelphia Police, 247, 251

Mintzer Street, Philadelphia, *284*

missing children, *see* Pitezel, Alice; Pitezel Howard; and Pitezel, Nellie

mixed-race relationship, 72

Modern Borgia poisoner, 75-88, *see also* Whiteling, Sarah Jane

Monroe, President James, 313

Montevideo, South America, 111

Moon, Reuben O. (Holmes' attorney), 84

Moorehouse, Lot (found murder victim Annie Klaus), 98

Moorman, Elvet, Indianapolis, 156

moral degenerate, *see* degenerate and Holmes, H. H.: degenerate

morgue, 93-94, 147-50, 250-51

morphine, 160

Morris, Esther, Bridgeton, PA (Edna bridesmaid), 241

motive, 80, 92, 102, 129, 147, 219, 223, 361

Mount Moriah, Historic Cemetery, Philadelphia, 121, *123,* 291

Mowbray, Charles Wilfred (anarchist), *275*
     American flag as handkerchief, *275*
     Geyer, blood boil, hurl out window statement, *275*
     police, blown off earth, *275*
Mower General Hospital, Philadelphia, 20, *21*
Moyamensing Prison, Philadelphia, 65, 84, 97, 129, 167, 191, 276, 377
Mudgett, Clara (Holmes' only legal wife, given name Lovering), 205,
          368
     as Gilmanton woman, 194
     black eye of, 205
     bromide treatment and, 205
     epileptic convulsions of, 205
     see also Holmes, H. H.
Mudgett, Herman W., *see* Holmes, H. H.
Mudgett, Robert Lovering (Holmes' son), 366
Murray, John Detective, Philadelphia Police, 73
mutilated victim, 53-54, 92, 94
M. W. Baldwin and Company, Philadelphia, 326

N
Nace, Officer, Philadelphia Police, 99-100
Nack, Mrs., 225
National Historic Landmark, 121
Navin's Drug Store, Indianapolis, 161
Navy Yard, Philadelphia, 9, 20
Newark, New Jersey, 225
Newcomb Street, Philadelphia, 215, 227
New Jersey, 4, 6, 12, 54, 225-26, 230, 242, 309, 311-12, 314, 318
Newville, Pennsylvania, 241-42
New York, 9, 11-12, 126, 189, 225, 272, 274
New York City, New York, 24, 189
New York Herald, 72
New York Times, 122
Niagara Falls, 30, 145, 189, 330
nippers, 33, 65, *see also* handcuffs
nitro-glycerine, 185
No. 12 powders, 161
Norristown Asylum, 25, 51-52, 96
     see also Bennett, Dr. Mary "Alice"
Norristown City Hall, Council Chambers, 220
Norristown, Pennsylvania, 51, 210, 217-20, 224-25, 242
notary public, 229
No. 210 car of Second and Third Street line, 101

O

odor, 66, 143, 145, 148, 174, 205

Odd Fellows' Cemetery, 27, 320

Old Town, Philadelphia, 24

O'Neil, Laurie (Geyer's great-great-granddaughter, given name
     Riggins), *269*

O'Neil, Shaquille (pro basketball), 313

Orkney Street, Philadelphia, 236

Orkney Street, 2400, Philadelphia, 307

Orianna Street, 2417 Philadelphia, 312, 320

Our American Cousin play, 23

Oxford Street, Philadelphia, 12, *285,* 307, 315

P

Page, S. Davis (Chairman, Joint Committee Bullitt Bill), 41
     appointed Governor's Commission and, 333

Paisley, Brad (country singer), 313

Palm Road, 110 East, Wildwood Crest, New Jersey, *6*

Palmer, Arnold (pro golfer), 313

Palmer, Mrs. (Annie Klaus case), 98

pandemic, 250, *see also* Spanish Flu

Park, Common Councilman James P., Second Ward, Philadelphia
     bar fight with Schooley, 119
     fire damage to business and, 120
     Mount Moriah Cemetery and, 121
     see also Schooley, Captain Joseph

Parker, John Frederick (Lincoln guard), 23
     police officer issues of, 325
     possible relative of Mrs Lincoln, 325

Parson, Thomas, Philadelphia (arrested, race riot), 239

Paruchi, Frank "Fatty" as burglar, 242

patent, 169-71, 210, 214, 245-46, 272, 305, 369, 379

Patriot Harrisburg, 237

Patriot News, 241

patrol wagon, Philadelphia Police, 91, 96, 100, 130, 240, 247-48, *276*

pectus carinatum (pigeon chest), 206

Penn National Bank, 113

Pennsylvania Governor, letter of forceful admonishment, 19

Pennsylvania Railroad, 53, 55, 156, 224

Pernambuco, South America, 111

Perry, B. F. (*alias* of Benjamin Pitezel), *see* Pitezel, Benjamin: *alias*
     Perry, B. F.

Perry, Ophir Le Forrest (Fidelity Mutual), 183, 190
     complains about Geyer and Philadelphia Police, 211-12

postmaster general and, 211
swear out warrant and, 212
pest hole of the earth, 110
phenic acid, 109
Philadelphia Athletics, *280-81*
Philadelphia General Hospital, 354
renamed, from Almshouse, 354
Philadelphia, Pennsylvania, 2, 4-5, 9-12, *13,* 17, 19-20, *21-22,* 23-24, *26,*
    27-30, *31,* 33, 36-39, 41, 43-44, *45,*48, 53, 55-56, 59-61, 63, 65,
    67-68, 72, *74,* 75, 84, 88, 91, 93, 95-96, 104, 107-09, 111-13, *114,*
    116, 118-21, 124, 126, 129-31, *135,* 138-41, 145, 153-56, 161-63,
    167, 183, 187, 190, 200, *202-03,* 210-12, 215, 220-21, 224-28,
    233-34, 236-37, *238,* 240-43, 247, 250-51, *252, 258, 264, 271-*72,
    276-78, 279, *281-86,* 290-91, 309-21, 323-31, 338-39
Centennial Exposition in, 28, 328, *see also* Centennial Exposition,
    Philadelphia
City Charter of, 334
City Hall, 35-36, 43, *45-47,* 61, 64-66, 73, 118, 120-21, 125, 129,
    140, 155, 187, 219, 222, 224, 237, 241
Civil War and, 19-23, 326
Department of Public Safety, 41, 248, 334, *see also* Police,
    Philadelphia
departments against departments in, 234
first execution of a woman in, 84, 88
forceful admonishment of, 19
mourning, black cloths of, 24
race riot, Hammerstein's Opera House, 239
225th Anniversary of, 240
vagrants housed in, 35
World's Fair in, 28, 328
Philadelphia Inquirer, 11, 65, 73, 78, 109, 155, 167, 200, 210-11, 230,
    233, 237, 249, 287-88
Philadelphia Memorial Park, 84
Philadelphia Times, 35, 120, 196, 273, 287-89
Pierce, Benjamin "Benny" (President Pierce's son)
tragic death of, 9-10, *15,* 313
Pierce, Jane (President Pierce's wife), 9-10, *15*
loss, two other sons and, 313
Pierce, President Franklin, 9
as President-elect, 10
loss, two other sons and, 313
speech of, 10
Pike's Store, Irvington, Indianapolis 162
Pine Street, Philadelphia, *286*

Pinkerton, detective agency, 107
pistol (s), 25, *26,* 29, 57-58, 100, 102-03, 219
    shot, 24, 98, 118, 169
Pitezel, Alice (murdered by H. H. Holmes), 144, 149, 152, *164,* 184-85,
        189, 200
    at Potter's Field, 140
    burial of, 151
    coffins and, 146
    condition of body, 147
    crying and, 143, 170
    discovered body of, 146-47
    identification of
        mother and, 150
        papa's teeth and, 162, 177
    inquest of, 148-50
    signed affidavit and, 140, 182
    see also Holmes, H. H.
Pitezel, Benjamin F (murdered by H. H. Holmes), 138-39, 144, 154, 161,
        164, 166-67, 171-74, 177, 182, 187, 190, 196-97, 200, 211
    alias B. F. Perry and, 140, 169-70, 183-84
    cause of death of, 174, 181
    exhumation of, 162, 170, 191
    head severed and, 162
    how chloroform, in stomach of, 180, 188
    identification marks of, 171, 180
    position found in, 173, 181, 195
    postmortem exam of, 173-74, 203
    see also Holmes, H. H.
Pitezel, Jeanette 'Dessie and Dessa,' 144, 162, 184-85
    testimony of, 169, 185-87
    see also Holmes, H. H.
Pitezel, Horton (baby), 144, 185
Pitezel, Howard (murdered by H. H. Holmes), 143-45, 147-48, 151-58,
        160, 162, *164,* 184-85, 187, 189-90, 200
    clothing of, 160-61
    crying and, 143
    remains of, 146, 159-61, 163
    teeth of, 159, 161, *165*
    toys of, 161
    see also Holmes, H. H.
Pitezel, Mrs. Carrie Alice, , 139-41, 143-44, 158, 161, 166, 170, 187,
        191, 199, 200, 361
    arrest of, 139, 185
    attempted murder of, 185-86, 198-99

closure, death, tour of Irvington, 162
distraught and, 149-51
Geyer threatened reporters for, 149
helped by, Christian Endeavor Society, 151
identification of children, 149-50
inquest, testimony of, 150-51
insurance settlement and, 140, 183-84
jail and, 185
ran into Holmes at store and, 185
refuses Holmes' bribe and, 199
trial testimony of, 184-87, 191
see also Holmes, H. H.
Pitezel, Nellie (murdered by H. H. Holmes), 143, 145, 149, 151, *164,*
    184-85, 189
burial of, 151
clothing found of, 148
coffins and, 146
crying and, 143
inquest of, 148
remains of, 146-47, 149-50
see also Holmes, H. H.
pleurisy, 76
poem, police uniforms, Philadelphia Police, 234
poison (ed), 72, 79-84, 87, 174, 178, 180-81, 192, 212, 216
see also arsenic
Police, Philadelphia, 1, 28-29, *31,* 41, 47, 49, 55, 57-58, 61, 64, 76, 90,
    93, 95, 99, 102, 105, 118-21, 169, 172, 220, 247-249, 273-74,
    277-78, 280-83, 288, 311, 339
arrest statistics, 33, 331, 344
badge, detectives and, *74*
board of inquiry of, 119
boat, *Samuel G. King,* 64
boat, *WMS Stokley,* 283
drinking alcohol and, 58, 234
Bureau of, 42, 72-73, 237-39, 240, 247, 251, *282*
Bureau of, Detectives, 43, 336
    badge of, *74*
Centennial Guard, 28-29, 327, 329-30.
    deaths of, 30
    lost children and, 29
    police expenses and, 330
    police stations of, 29, 329
    time off and, 329-30
    unusual lost items and, 29

see also Centennial Exposition, Philadelphia

Central Station, 34, 66

chief, *see* individual names

court of inquiry of, 236

detective war and, 234

Department of, 3, 29, 33, 42, 56, 73, 76, 107, 109-11, 212, 235, 237, 240,

Department, the Detective, 43, 310, 331

    chief of, nuances and, 336

    first organized, 336

    reorganization of, 336

    reported to, 336

Department of Public Safety and, 41, 248, 329, 331

Detectives, Chief of, 335

disgraced officers of, 240

    pleaded guilty and, 240

    sentence of, 240

Districts of,

    dead bodies kept at, 35, 100

    Eighteenth (18th) and, 30, 100, *286*

        estimated cost, *286*

        location, 311

        statistics, 30

    Eighth (8th) and, 118

    Fifth (5th) and, 60

    Fortieth (40th) and, *285*

    Seventh (7th) and, *284*

        cost of, *284*

    Twentieth (20th) and, 118

    Twenty-fourth (24th) and, 99

    Twenty-second (22nd) and, 328

    Twenty-third (23rd) and, 56, 91-92

    vagrants housed at, 35

Divisions of

    First (1st), 119

    Third (3rd), 30

evoke uneasiness in people and, 105

guard, car barns and, *278*

Harbor Patrol, *WMS Stokley, 283*

headquarters of, 105

jealousy among, 234

lieutenant, *see* individual names

motorcycle with sidecar and, *282*

officer (s) and, 3, 28-30, *31,* 33-35, 41-42, 44, 48-49, 56-60, 65-66,

69-71, 73, 78, 90-94, 96, 99-103, 105, 121, 125, 172, 197-98,
233-37, 239, 240, 248-49, 251, *252,* 273-75, *277,* 278, *280-81,*
327, 340
     see also individual names
patrol box and, 100
patrol marching and, *280*
patrol wagon and, 91, 96, 100, 130, 240, 247-48, 251, *276, 278-79*
pension fund of, 121
policies of
     drinking from saloon to saloon, 58
     must buy revolver, last minute notice, 56-57
     no politics for officers, 34
     no umbrellas while on duty, 233
     no walking and talking while on duty, 233
     wear uniforms until all are issued, 233-34
Policeman Poet, 234
political hatchets and, 235
public rift between departments and, 75, 78-79
Public Safety, Department of, 41, 334
     date abolished, 334
Public Safety Director
     security deposit, city required, 41
     salary of, 41
     see also individual names
revolver of, *279*
Rogues' Gallery Book
     Tabbs, Hannah Mary, arrest photo and, *67*
     Wilson, George H., arrest photo and, *68*
Rogues' gallery of criminals, *271*
roster of, 327
scandal and admonishment of officers of, 239-40
superintendent, *see* individual names
Spanish Flu, *252*
     as emergency nurses, 251
     doctors, physicians at police stations, 251
     ordered to assist and, 250
     police beds to hospitals, 251
     patrol wagons, bodies, and, 251
     see also Spanish Flu (not this sub-category under police)
statistics of, 30, 33, 74, 237, 331, 344
superintendent, *see* individual names
suicide and, 3, 118, 120-21
take part of salary of, 240
terminations of, 240

turmoil of, 72, 234-35
uniforms of, 233-34
    poem about, 234
World Series, Shibe Park, and *280-81*
workplace shooting and, 56-58
Polk, President James K., 313
Pomeroy, Mrs. Emma (Whiteling trial), 82-83
Pooley, E. F., Philadelphia, 112
Port Royal, Virginia, 23
Porteous, George M., Superintendent, United States Bertillon Bureau,
    272
Portugal, Spain, 111
postmortem examination, 173, 178
post office, 34
Potter's Field, Philadelphia, 65, 140, 170, 180, 360
Pottstown, Pennsylvania, 226
Powers, Coroner Thomas J., Philadelphia, 50, 77
prescriptions, 161, 250-51
prison, *see* Moyamensing Prison; and Eastern Penitentiary
Public Broadcasting Service (PBS) narrator statement, 250
Puget Sound, Washington, 184
Pugh, Rev. W. S., Philadelphia, 3, 320
purpura hemorrhagica, 19, 320, 323
putrefaction, 173, 176

Q
Quaker City Dime Museum, Philadelphia, 201
Quinlan, Patrick, 154-55
    description of, 144
    if Holmes' hung, would spring trap, 144
    Holmes' dirty lying scoundrel, 144
    see also Holmes, H. H.
Quirk, Captain, Philadelphia Police, 101

R
race riot, Philadelphia, 239-40, 247-50
    Adelia Bond and, *see* Adelia Bond
    fire the Italians and, 239
    officer murdered and, 248
    pawnbrokers ordered, stop selling weapons, 248
    saloons ordered closed and, 248
    weapons confiscated and, 248
Rathbone, Major Henry (Lincoln's guest), 23
Reading Railway station, 216

Reading Times, 231
real estate, 121, 140
 agents, 145,152
 offices, 156
Redmond, James, B. (mail fraud), 34
Reed, John R., (Wanamaker attorney), 107
Reed, Judge, Quarter Sessions, Philadelphia, 58
Regiment, 147th, Company E, *see* Civil War
Regiment, 204th, Battery C, 5th Heavy Artillery, *see* Civil War
Reservoir Hotel, Philadelphia, 90
Reuben Cohen's Pawn Shop, Philadelphia (Seventeenth and Bainbridge),
 69
Revolutionary War, 2, 54
reward, 108, 125, 140
Reyburn, Mayor John E., Philadelphia, 240
Rhea, Police Matron Margaret, Philadelphia (Holmes' case, false
 affidavit), 197-98
 alias, Blanche Hannigan, 197
Richards, Detective David, Indianapolis, 152, 158-60
Richards Street, 1642, Philadelphia (Gains, Wakefield killed at), 53, 61
Richardson, Annie (Tabbs niece, torso case), 59-60
Riggins, Alan (Geyer's great-great-grandson), *269*
Riggins, James R. (Geyer's great-great-grandson), *253, 269*
Riggins, Joyce (Geyer's great-granddaughter, given name Elliott),
 268-69
Rilley, Mary (Geyer's wife), *see* Geyer, Mary Elizabeth
Rio de Janeiro, 108-11, *117*, 118, 251
Rodenbaugh, Chief William H. (Norristown, PA), 219-20, 222-25
Rogers, Patrolman, Philadelphia Police, Eighth District
 suicide of, 118
Rogues' Gallery Book
 Tabbs, Hannah Mary, arrest photo and, *67*
 Wilson, George H., arrest photo and, *68*
Rogues' gallery of criminals, *271*
Roosevelt, President Franklin D., 313
Roosevelt, President Theodore, 113, 313
Rose, Dr. J. L. (Holmes' fellow student), 207
Rossin House, Toronto, Canada, 149-50
Roslyn, Pennsylvania, 251, 253-54, 290, 318
Roslyn, Washington, 118
 forty-five minors die, 118
Rotan, Samuel P., Philadelphia (Holmes' attorney), 168, 186, 190-94,
 196, 197-99, *202*
 asks for exception, one speech, 195

closing argument of, 196
judge threatens disbarment and, 167
rests case, no witnesses, 194
quits case and, 168
see also Holmes, H. H.
Rough on Rats poison, 81, *88*
Ruyl, George (Emma Kaiser adopted father), 229
Ryves, Thomas W., Irvington, Indianapolis (identified Pitezel girls)
fix water leak and, 145
identified Pitezel photos, 145
spade loaned to Holmes and Geyer, 146
see also Holmes, H. H.

S
Salem-Zion United Church of Christ, 319
Samuel G. King police boat, Philadelphia, 64
Santos, South America, 110
Satterlee General Hospital, Philadelphia, 20
secret service, 43, 73
Schilling, Anton, Philadelphia (murder victim), 93, 95
dismembered and, 94
evidence found and, 93
identification of, 93
Schmeck, Anna (Geyer's grandmother, married Buck), 315
Schooley, Captain Joseph M., Philadelphia Police, 118, *122*
as acting superintendent, 120
board of inquiry, 119-20
burial of, 121, *123*
chewed thumb in bar fight with Councilman Park, 119
description of, 118
estate of, 121
feelings about suicide, 119
fired then rehired and, 119
funeral of, 121
illness of, 120
intimidating voters, 119
inquest of, 120
invalid wife of, 120
investigation of, 119
rumors of firing and, 120
suicide of, 118
wife, donation to police, 121
Schoop, Jacob, Philadelphia (killed Schilling), 93, 95-96
cancer-stricken wife of, 94

confession of, 94
  dismembered victim, 94
  execution of, 97
  smoked cigar from Geyer, 94
  trial and sentence of, 96
Schoop, Susan (Jacob's daughter), 95
  statement to Geyer, 95
Schoop, wife and stepmother
  arrest and, 95-96
  cancer and, 96
  found insane and, 96
  Norristown Hospital and, 96
Schwartz, Judge, 230
  admonishment of Lizzie, 230
Schwechler, Detective John (fake affidavit issue), 197, 98
Schuylkill River, 64, 216-17
  dredging for body parts, 65, 70
  head found in, 72
Scott, Lieutenant, Philadelphia Police, 100-03
Scott, Dr. William J., Philadelphia (Holmes' trial), 169, 172
  condition of body, 172-73
  testimony of 172-77
  tasted and smelled stomach contents, 177
Selective Service Act, 247
  amended, 247
Shibe Park, Philadelphia, *280-81*
Shoemaker, William A. (Holmes' attorney), 167-68, 190-92, *202*
  arrested, false affidavit and, 198
  bail of, 198
  claim Hatch looks like Holmes and, 153, 200
  false affidavit and, 196-98
  judge threatens disbarment and, 167
  nervous prostration and, 194
  quits Holmes' case and, 168
  request new Holmes' trial, 196-97
  sickness, last day, trial, 194
  suspended one year and, 198
  see also Holmes, H. H.
shooting, 56, 58, 222
Sidebotham, Dr. Henry L., Philadelphia, 162
Silbert, Coroner William S, Buck's County, PA, 54-55, 69
16th New York Calvary, 25
Sixth Street, North 2634, Philadelphia (Geyer's home with Mary and
  Edna), *5*, 197, 307, 312-13, 317

Sixth Street, North 4123, Philadelphia (Orrie Strohm and Edna Geyer
      first home), 242, 380
Sixty-third Street, Chicago, IL (Holmes Castle), 154
skeleton, skeletal, 124, 147, 161
Slough, General John P., 19, *see also* Civil War
Smith and Wesson 1896 Model Hand Ejector advertisement, *279*
Smith, Dr. George, Philadelphia (Whiteling murder case), 76-80
Smith, Eugene, Philadelphia (witness, Holmes' trial), 169, 172
      at Pitezel's exhumation and, 170
      catechise Holmes and, 171
      conversation, Holmes and 171
      described murder scene and, 169
      discovered Pitezel's body and, 169
      identification of Holmes and, 169
      witnessed
            Lawyer Howe cry, 170
            don gloves, Holmes, 170
            handle corpse, Holmes,170
            Holmes' removal, pieces of body, 170
      see also Holmes, H. H.
Smith, Magistrate, Philadelphia, 66
Smith, Mayor William Burns, Philadelphia, 119
      as insurance agent, 221
      burial of, 121
      censured by delegation of ministers and, 249
      fired Captain Schooley and, 121, 352
      Mount Moriah Cemetery and, 121
Smith's Brewery, Philadelphia, 65
Smithsonian Institution, Washington DC, 238, 290, 377
Snyder's Woods, Philadelphia, 91
South America, 107-09, 141, 188
spade, 146, 181, 201, 288, *see also* Holmes, H. H.
Spanish Flu (Philadelphia area), 250, 318, 382
      Anti Spitting Law and, 251
      bodies and, 250
      closures and, 250
      death carts and, 250
      health director statement and, 250-51
      improvised masks, 251
      inciting event and, 250
      makeshift morgues and, 250
      physicians, green flags, 251
      physicians to police stations, 251
      police as emergency nurses, 251

police beds to hospitals and, 251
police ordered to assist and, 250
police patrol wagons and, 251
statistics of, 250
Spanish influenza, 250, 318, *see also* Spanish Flu
spinal meningitis, 315
spinal sclerosis, 236, 320
Springfield, Illinois, 24
Stanford University, flu pandemic stats, 250
St. Barnabas Protestant Episcopal Church, 241
St. Thomas, West Indies, 109
St. Vincent Street, No. 16, Toronto, Canada (Pitezel's girls murdered at),
    143, 147-48, 201
St. Vincent, West Indies, 111
Star Saloon, 23
State Lunatic Hospital, Norristown, 51, *see also* Norristown Asylum
stenographer, 119, 154, 183, 198, 241
Stewart, General James, Jr., Philadelphia Police, *44*
    gave staff short notice, must by their own guns, 56
Stokley, Mayor William S., Philadelphia, 28, 311, 327
    "Martinet," 41
    as public safety director, 41, 73, 119-20
    boat, *WMS Stokley,* named after and, *283*
    term, served as Mayor, 334
    terminated officers and, 42, 73
Strong, William H. (murder suspect), 242
    conviction of, 243
    supreme court ruling and, 243
Stuart, Mayor Edwin S., Philadelphia, 107-08
St. James' cemetery, Toronto, Canada, 151
St. James Protestant Episcopal Church of Kingsessing, 130
St. Louis, Missouri, 183, 211
strabismus, 206
Strassburger, Jacob A. (District Attorney, Kaiser trial), 223
Strohm, Alice (Orrie's mom), 242
Strohm, Dorothy Edna (Geyer's granddaughter, married Clinton T.
    Elliott), 243, *265-66,* 269, 313, 317
    birth of, 321
    burial of, 321
    death of, 321, 380
    marriage of, 321
Strohm, Edna. *See* Geyer, Edna
Strohm, Elizabeth Alice (Geyer's granddaughter, married Joseph Elliott),
    243, *259-61, 265-66, 268,* 313

baptism of, 243, *259,* 321-22
birth of, 321
burial of, 321
death of, 321
marriage of, *13,* 318
Strohm, Frank Wesley (Geyer's grandson), 243, *265, 268*
birth of, 322
burial of, 322
death of, 322, 380
marriage of, 322
Strohm, Grace (Frank W. Strohm's wife), *268*
Strohm, John (Orrie Strohm's dad), 241-42, *259*
founder of
Cupid Corner, 242
Plainfield Times, 242
manager, *Shippensburg Chronicle,* 242
Strohm, Orrie Curtis (Geyer's son-in-law), *259, 265, 268,* 269
birth of, 322
burial of, 322
children of, *13,* 243, 250
see also Strohm, Elizabeth, Dorothy, and Frank
death of, 322
hometown of, 241
marriage of, 241, 317, 322, 378, 389
occupation of, 241
patent of, 243, *246,* 305, 379-380
registered, draft, 247, 250
Sullivan, John L. (boxer, first heavyweight champion), 104
Sullivan, Special Officer, Philadelphia Police, *277*
Sumneytown, Pennsylvania, 315
Sunday Liquor Law, Philadelphia, 58
superintendent, *see* individual names
Supreme Court, 42, 199, 243
surgeon general, 108
surgical instruments, 161
Swain, Frank, Philadelphia (conductor, torso murder case), 55-56, 59-60

T
Tabbs, Hannah Mary (torso murder case), 3, 59-60, *67,* 69, 71, 240
accessory to murder and, 66, 72
arrest of, 60
attacked Wakefield Gains and, 59
black eye and, 64, 70, 341
characteristics of, 63-64, 66, 70

confession of, 61-64
identified by witnesses and, 65
inquest and, 66
name variation of, 340
poisoned Wakefield Gains and, 72
sentence of, 72
testimony of, at George Wilson trial, 69-70
threaten to kill Wakefield Gains and, 59
threw torso in pond and, 63, 66
trial of, 72
violent outbursts of, 72
Taft, President William Howard, 313, 392
Talbot, Dr. Eugene S. (Holmes' doctor in prison), 206
Tate, James Sr., Philadelphia Police
detective promotion and, 73
forced resignation of, 240
special officer work, 56, 59-60, 64-65, 70, 72
tavern (s), 1-2, 311-12
telegram, 16, 93, 158, 274
Temple University School of Medicine, 241
testimony, *see* individual names
Texas, 139, 184
Thayer, Judge, Philadelphia, 197-99
Third Street Road, Philadelphia, 101
Third Street, north, 943, Philadelphia (Whiteling witness), 82
Thirty-third Street, Philadelphia, 91
.32 caliber Defender, 99
.32 caliber pistol, 219
Thompson, Dr., Irvington, Indianapolis, 156, 158-60, 163
Thompson Street, Philadelphia, 80
Titan Street, Philadelphia (race riot), 249
tomcat, vicious, 48-49
Toronto, Canada, 144-45, 148-49, 151-53, 155, 185, 189-91, 201, 272,
288-89
torso, 3, 53-56, 58-60, 63, 65-66, 69, 73-74, 92-93, 240
Tothams Creek, 66
train crash, 9-10
Travis, Edward (found murder victim Annie Klaus), 98-100
Trenton Avenue, Philadelphia, 30
Trenton, New Jersey, 225, 230
trial, *see* individual names
Truman, President Harry S., 313
trunk,
as a body and, 55, 70, 92

travel, to hold belongings and, 143, 148, 157-61, 187, 190, 223
Turkish bath, 234
Tuttle, Detective, Detroit, 152
Twain, Mark (writer, given name Clemens, Samuel L.), *14,* 137
    books of, 315
    complaint of foreigners and, 12, 314
    daughter, Susy, 315
    freemason and, 4, 313
    house and museum, 315
    letters to Orian and, 11-12
    likes Phila and, 11
    substitute typesetter and, 11
    whiskey-swilling, 11, 314
    worked at, *Pennsylvania Inquirer,* 11, 314
    worked two miles from Geyer, 314
Twenty-eighth Street, Philadelphia, *285*
typhoid fever, 30

U
Union League Battery, 23, *see* Civil War
union soldiers, 17-18, *see* Civil War
uniform, 17, 28, 56, 233-34, 327
United American Mechanic's Cemetery, 84
United States Circuit Court of Pennsylvania, 229
United States Congress, 247
    amended Selective Service Act, 247
    passed Selective Service Act, 247
United States Post Office, 34
United States Sailors (held murderer, race riot), 249
Union Volunteer Refreshment Saloon, Philadelphia, *22, see also* Civil
    War
Union Volunteer Hospital, Philadelphia, *22, see also* Civil War
United States Collieries Company, 212
United States Patent Office, 210
United States Sanitary Commission's Great Central Fair, 20
University of Michigan, 205, 207, 338
University of Pennsylvania, 338

V
variola (smallpox), 30
Vine Street, Philadelphia, 210, 228
Virginia, 18, 23
viscera, 77

W

Wagner, Louis, Philadelphia, (director of Public Works), 47, 73

wagon (horse-drawn), 90, 94, *see also* patrol wagon

Walker, LeRoy P. (Confederate States Secretary), 16-17
   see also Civil War

Wanamaker, John, Philadelphia, 107, 108, 112, *115*
   as postmaster general, 107, 111
   received discounts from Keystone Bank, 107
   statements to Marsh in papers and, 111-12

Wanamaker's store, Philadelphia, 43, 237

Wanamaker, William H., Philadelphia, 107-08, 110
   bond for Gideon Marsh, 107

Wardens' Association of the United States and Canada, *272*

wart, 170-71, 177, 181

Warwick, Mayor Charles Franklin, Philadelphia, 172, 210

Washington DC, 27, 43, 205, 211, 238, 290

Washington, President George, 313

Weaver, Officer, Philadelphia Police, 90

Welker, Detective Jacob S., Philadelphia Police, 235
   conspiracy to clear prisoner, 235
   forced resignation of, 241
   testified against Geyer, 235
   verbal argument, Crawford and, 235

Werner, Esther (Geyer's niece), 319
   death of, 319

Werner, Harry Lawrence (Geyer's brother-in-law), 236
   burial of, 319
   death of, 319
   marriage of, 318-9
   milk dealer, worked as, 319

West Point, New York, 17

Western National Bank, 113

White Chapel Row (Cadwallader Street), 90

White House funeral, 22

Whiteling, Bertha "Birdie" (murder victim), 75, *87*
   burial of, 84
   death of, 76-77
   exhumation of, 77
   theft and, 80

Whiteling, John (murder victim), 76, *87*
   death of, 76-77
   exhumation of, 77

Whiteling, Sarah Jane (murdered her family), 3, 52, 76-77, *86,* 90
   arrest of, 78

as Brown, Sarah Jane, 75
characteristics of, 75, 77, 82
confessions of, 78-82
coroner's inquest and, 82-83
devil must have possessed her and, 81
dropped child on stove and, 83
eggnog and, 81
execution of, 84, *88*
grand jury indictment and, 83
insanity defense and, 83
insurance proceeds and, 79
last meal and, 84
poison candy to kids and, 82
reprieves of, 84
sanctimonious memoriam's on wall and, 84-86
trial of, 83-84
Whiteling, William "Willie" (murder victim), *87*
death of, 76-77
exhumation of, 77
Wilcox, Rev., Denver, Colorado, 193
Wildwood, New Jersey, 4, 6, 313, 321
Williams, Minnie R., 141, 144, 184, 189, 190-91
see also Holmes, H. H.
Willson, Judge (Philadelphia), 199
Wilmette, Illinois, 193
Wilmington, Pennsylvania, 95
Wilson, George (torso murder case, murderer), 3, 61-64, *68,* 69
arrest of, 64
break away from custody and, 65
chewed tobacco given by detective, 66
confession of, 53, 64
coroner's inquest, 66
given beer and cigars by police, 70
plea of, 71-72
sentence of, 72
threw head and limbs in river, 64
trial of, 68-71, 73
new trial and, 71
see also, Tabbs, Hannah Mary
Wilson, President Woodrow, 247
declares State of War, Germany, 247
mandatory draft, 247
Winooska Avenue, 26 North, Burlington, Vermont, 185, 187
WMS Stokley, Philadelphia harbor patrol, *283, see also* Police,

Philadelphia
Wood, Chief of Detectives Charles, W., Philadelphia Police (ex-fire marshal), 43, 73, 78-79, 92-93, 96, 120, 273-74
Wood, Professor H. C., 337
    investigated diphtheria and, 337
Woodland Avenue, Philadelphia, 130
World's Fair, 42, 328-330, *see also* Chicago, Illinois, World Columbian Exposition and Centennial Exposition, Philadelphia
World Series, 1914, Shibe Park, *280-81*
World War I, 250
wounded soldiers fundraiser, 20
Wright, Dr. (delegation of ministers), 249

Y
yellow fever, 108-09
    bodies in street and, 110
    cease labor in hot hours and, 110
    death statistics of, 108
    hoist signal of medical visit, 110
    see also, Geyer, Franklin P.: secret search
Yoke, Georgiana (Holmes third wife, assumed given name following Holmes' arrest), 143, 168, 172, 183, 186-87, 193, 198
    admits, she knew Holmes' married first wife, 194
    crazy story, Holmes' told, 194
    married Holmes and, 193
    see also Holmes, H. H.
York Street, Philadelphia, 4, 311
York Street, 142 West, Philadelphia, 48
York Street, 432 West, Philadelphia, 319

Made in the USA
Monee, IL
02 December 2019